# SIT DOWN BE COUNTED

*The Cultural Evolution of a Television Station*

**LELIA DOOLAN
JACK DOWLING
and
BOB QUINN**

*No one is saved and no one is totally lost*

MERLEAU-PONTY

Legal and Publisher information

Copyrights © Lelia Doolan, Jack Dowling, 1969

Count Me Out © Bob Quinn, 1969
Droch-Bholadh Sa Tigh Againn © Eoghan Harris 1969

First published Wellington Press 1969
Republished by Data Ocean Limited 2019

This book is typeset with a setting of 11.5 on 17.5 point Minion Pro

# SIT DOWN AND BE COUNTED

*The Cultural Evolution of a Television Station*

# CONTENTS

*Introduction*   vii
*Authors' Preface (1969)*   xi
*Unscientific Assessment*   xvii

## 01. A CAUTIONARY TALE
The Cultural Evolution of a Television Station   2

## 02. COUNT ME OUT
The Cultural Evolution of a Television Producer   262

## 03. COMMUNICATIONS AND THE COMMUNITY
Technology and Neutrality   282

## 04. THE MEDIUM IS THE MATTER
Culture and Communications   306

## 05. DROCH-BHOLADH SA TIGH AGAINN
RTÉ Agus an Ghaeilge   352

## 06. TWO NOTIONS OF AUTHORITY
Power and Service   364

## 07. THE SWEET RACKET
Advertising and the 'Mass'   382

## 08. THE (DIS)ORGANISATION...MAN
The Structures of RTE   410

## 09. ACTS TO GRIND
The Broadcasting Authority Acts, 1960-77   428

## 10. WHAT CAN WE DO?
Proposals for Unmasking the 'Mass'   450

*Appendix I*   460

*Appendix II*   462

*Appendix III*   466

*Index*   510

# INTRODUCTION
*By Raymond Williams*

*Free communications begin with* the freedom of professional communicators. Their direct interest in doing their work in their own way can be easily dismissed as a sectional demand or even as personal selfishness. But it is undoubtedly the case that on their freedom the quality of a whole culture comes to depend. Of course, it is true that this freedom is, at its best, a varied response to the needs and interests of a whole society. But communications can only discover and meet these needs and interests by the free exploration of a body of people who can follow their ideas and their inquiries wherever they lead. Resistance to this will come often from particular individuals and groups in the society, who object to an idea or a style being broadcast in that way. Professional communicators need always to be ready to answer that kind of objection, in an open, equal and public way: taking responsibility for those things for which indeed they are directly responsible.

Out of that open, equal and public argument, only good can come. But the more characteristic and much more difficult situation is that in which an intermediate authority exercises direct control over the communicators. Such an authority does not make programmes, in any creative way, nor is it, though it often claims that it is, the public. In many different kinds of society, this intermediate authority comes to preoccupy all the waking hours (and often the should-be-sleeping hours) of the professional men and women who are trying to get the difficult work done. And this is, again, far more than a sectional worry: people's natural disturbance when there is a clash of wills and purposes. For in the end the only effective guarantee of the creative freedom of communications, on which the truth and the growth of a whole society can depend, is the day-to-day freedom of the people who have actually to get the work done.

In recent years, there have been several important cases in which professional communicators have clashed with different kinds of intermediate authority. In the West, for political reasons, we have heard most about the events of Prague, where the renewal of freedom in communications—that astonishing surge of open inquiry and open argument—was the leading wave of the attempted renewal of the structure and spirit of the whole society. That brave effort was beaten back, at least for a time. And it is a sign of the extraordinary importance of communications in modem society that this factor in its general remaking attracted the most bitter and most implacable hostility from the external and finally invading controllers. The events of Prague are now almost unbearably poignant, in their courage and their final irony. But their lesson is not lost, in Prague and elsewhere. This is what freedom sounds like, in any man's ears, and we are not so naive as to suppose that it always wins at the first attempt.

For consider also the almost contemporary events in Paris, where in the attempted renewal of the society, by students and workers, the

INTRODUCTION

well-trained radio and television service suddenly found its full voice and began speaking as it needed to speak and not as in expediency it had found convenient and manageable. With the failure of the general renewal, a serious revenge was taken on the professionals involved. Many of them were dismissed, and, as in the case of Prague, too few of their colleagues elsewhere showed the necessary solidarity and support. But that was not the end of the story. For the voices had been real voices, and the whole reality of the situation continued to develop. Though slower than was needed or hoped, some of the changes they spoke for are beginning to come through.

This will be the case also, I believe, in the recent difficulties in Dublin, from which this present book springs. In a crowded few days there, this spring, I saw the unmistakable signs of an extraordinary creative vitality—of the kind we can properly expect from an Irish culture—and, less happily, some of the signs of that familiar tension between producers and an intermediate authority. I do not know the events from within, but I am sure of this: that the voices I heard there, speaking of their own land and of its renewal, are at once Irish and international, in the most authentic senses. Deeply responsible to their own people, rather than to an Irish sector of the international market; painfully aware of the pressures and conflicts of real growth and change; they spoke in Irish accents of Irish problems which were to me, from across the sea, structurally very close to the problems of culture and society, the internal but general problems of communications, throughout Europe and North America.

I was then distressed when I heard of the further events which this book records, but I am glad they are being recorded, and publicly discussed, instead of disappearing into an internal row. The issues presented here—the issues underlying the events—are of importance to everyone, in and beyond Ireland. I wish the book the sustained attention and response which it so clearly deserves.

Raymond Williams
Jesus College,
Cambridge,
September 1969

# AUTHORS' PREFACE (1969)

**W**e *have written this* book as a continuation of the work we tried to do within the national television station during the past few years. We had become convinced that radio, television and the press are essentially dialogue-forms, at least as important to the health of the community as the Arts. Being daily and experimentally aware that there is a constant temptation to reduce dialogue to monologue, we have opposed the persons, institutions and modes of thought that tend to sterilise or silence the dialogue. We tried to use the station's structures to keep this dialogue developing. We failed.

We had used our personal influence, the organs of Trade Union action and The Radio, Television and Film Guild of Ireland to try to bring our colleagues and superiors to a realisation that a healthy polarity of temperament and interests within the station itself is essential to the carrying out of its function. The poles of tension remain present: those who regard the maintenance of organisation as the matter of primary concern and those who regard the work to be done as of primary concern. We realise that each is convinced that his thought includes everything that is valuable in the point of view of the other.

It has been said that what separated us from RTE Management was only a matter of emphasis. We disagree. It has been our deepest conviction that it is a difference of kind, in attitude to the broadcasting function. This book is an attempt to make clear that there are diametrically opposed views of culture within the station and that these reflect, in little, the crisis in process outside it.

The immediate incident that occasioned our personal action last May was the setting up of an outmoded structure of organisation and authority, imposed upon the television Programmes Division because it was known to be without substance or life. It failed its first challenge, Bob Quinn's accusations. It had to be brought, we believed, to an active realisation of its own futility. To our colleagues and Management this was a matter of opinion. To us it was self-evident from their inability to do anything but discuss Quinn's walk-out, our resignations and the staff's disquiet, in camera. The national press was discussing it publicly.

Our views and actions, we now realise, suffered one major defect: we depended too exclusively on the conscience of our own kind—the Producers. We had failed adequately to make common cause with the floor staffs, supportive staffs and public through a sense of what was 'proper' to our responsibilities as management personnel. The struggle for free dialogue will not be won by the Producers. This is not to denigrate them.

As H. C. Rumke, late Professor of Psychiatry at Utrecht University, wrote in 1967, an essential part of any creative protest is respect for the psychological forces which resist it. Where these are anxious for the preservation of the values entrusted to them, their resistance is healthy and brings the protestors and those on whose behalf they protest to a deeper awareness of the issues. Resistance to protest may have one of two origins, he wrote, or a mixture of both: security in the values of the status quo, and repressed guilt about passively suffering the evils

## AUTHORS' PREFACE (1969)

protested against. Neither of these is unhealthy unless the resistance to the protest takes on a querulous character. 'Then', he wrote, 'we are in the pathological domain'.

Protest itself, we suggest, is as worthy of the attention of the community (as part of its own consciousness) as scepticism about its motivations.

What is not often realised, however, is that a pathological querulousness in the protestant may be the only mode of protest open to him. In a society organised by powerful forces made available to conservatism by techniques of organisation and persuasion, the alternatives to violence are, increasingly, eccentricity or withdrawal. According to Professor Rümke, gaiety and playfulness are the means available to keep protest healthy and sane.

We have been assisted in our attempts to retain this sanity by the loyalty, affection and material help of our families, friends and colleagues.

We are particularly indebted to Raymond Williams, not only for his gracious Introduction to this book but also for his defence of our position in public in Great Britain and for the stimulation and excitement of his seminars in Dublin in April. His work in this field has been an inspiration to broadcasters. His friendship has had a special value for us.

Without the help of Conn O'Donovan, S.J., Jack Kelly, S.J., Philip McShane, S.J., Dr. Aidan O'Hara, Justin Keating, T.D.,

Dermot Doolan and the Executive of Irish Actors' Equity, and Eoghan Harris this book could not have been written.

The advice and help of Michael Barry, Eamonn Andrews, Philip Pettit and Brendan McGann have been invaluable. In addition, Brendan McGann, as a psychologist, wrote the analysis of the creative person contained in Appendix I.

Mr. Maurice Gorham and Dr. Leon Ó Broin gave us their valuable time and experience on points that had been obscure to us. Mr. Gorham also gave us free access to, and use of, his splendid Forty Years of Irish Broadcasting.

Professor James Halloran, Alf Mac Lochlainn, Austin Flannery, o.p., Ciaran Mac An Aili, Seamus Heavey, John Brady, S.J., Ronald Lindsay and Breandán Ó hEithir placed their learning at our disposal on special difficulties. We are especially grateful to Patrick McEntee for his close and conscientious scrutiny of the text. Patrick Dillon-Malone and Fred Littman allowed us to use, in part, material written by them on audience assessment.

We are grateful to Mr. Vincent Browne for valuable facilities and encouragement; to Una Claffey, Diane Lonergan, John Dowling and Rosita Sweetman for their painstaking research, and to Micheal Ó hUanachain, Oliver Donohoe and Deirdre Dowling who worked ceaselessly on the preparation of the text.

Our friends Aileen Orpen, Sean Mac Réamoinn, Colin Bird, Eric Spain, Donal O'Hare, Nora O'Hare, Doreen Gillen, Ann Harris, Charlie Doherty, Betty Dowling, Lil Doolan, Denis Ryan, Siobhán McKenna, Alacoque Kinane, Niall Kinane, Patrick McLarnon, Fionnuala O'Shannon, Agnes Cogan, Tish and Tony Barry, Anne Gallagher, Eugene Field, Tom Kelly, Ted Crowley, John Cadden, Joan Birthistle, Joan Collins, Paddy Gallagher, Dónall Farmer and Cian Ó hEigeartaigh all contributed their skills, generosity and special knowledge.

The support and encouragement of an tAthair Connla Ó Dubhshlaine, S.J., and the Galway members of Conradh na Gaeilge; of Maolsheachlainn Ó Caollaí, Uachtarán Chonradh na Gaeilge; Col. Eoghan Ó Néill, Uachtarin Chomhdháil Náisiunta na Gaeilge; Éamon Ó Muiri and Micheál Breathnach are deeply appreciated. Mary and John O'Shea of the Everyman Theatre in Cork; William Peacock, Kate O'Callaghan, Ann Clune and members of the Limerick branch of Tuairim, and Liam Maguire all helped to develop the thought which went into the making of the book.

Jim Doolan read several chapters and made many searching comments.

Patrick Lynch read the whole book in manuscript and suggested many improvements of expression.

Of course, none of those above is responsible for any expression of opinion contained in these following pages.

We must also make it clear that we have written this book as television programme people. If this has necessarily created an imbalance in the general picture of the activities of the station we apologise and can only plead, like Dr. Johnson, that the cause was pure ignorance.

One special note requires comment. In order to avoid misunderstanding in the text, we have used capitals throughout for Producers, Directors and Production Assistants. We could think of no other way in which this could be avoided without adding confusion to the ambiguity inherent in these words.

On the assumption that readers would want to know what kind of persons wrote this book, we have included a view of Jack Dowling and Lelia Doolan, entitled 'Unscientific Assessment'. Modesty and our publisher required that this should be contributed by an onlooker. Bob Quinn's persona emerges in the chapter 'Count Me Out'.

A last word of thanks to Radio Telefís Éireann. Without it, this book would not have been necessary—and our experience would have been much the poorer.

LELIA DOOLAN
JACK DOWLING
BOB QUINN
Dublin, September 1969.

# UNSCIENTIFIC ASSESSMENT

Jack Dowling and Lelia Doolan were, in a sense, more prepared to deal with Management than most others in the station; they knew Michael Garvey in his new role, as probably no others had the opportunity to do—Lelia personally and Jack through his experience of Michael Garvey's handling of the Home Truths affair. Lelia Doolan, while Producer of *7 Days*, had seen at first hand the interests which were always ready to intervene between the broadcaster and the community. Jack Dowling had seen these same interests coldly and deliberately grope for the nerve of *Home Truths* and neatly crush it. Both had observed how Management in RTE had not only 'thrown the switch' in order to bring about a decent obscurity but had heard them praise the resulting darkness as a proper concession to the people from whom the station drew its main revenues.

For over a year they had compared notes, attempting to work out a philosophy of communications.

The *7 Days* episode interrupted this work and put them unexpectedly into positions of actual leadership with experienced Trade Unionists, Jim Plunkett Kelly and Aindreas Ó Gallchóir.

They were singularly ill-equipped for the task.

In dealing with his colleagues, Jack Dowling had what is called a personality problem.

Physically, he looked like Jehovah in tweeds. Intellectually, he matched his looks. Even for his friends, his company could be trying. Morning coffee with a philosophical logic-chopper who never stopped working at his craft could be a disturbing experience. For sensitive artists it could be, and often was, maddening. He seemed unaware that his army training gave his most casual remarks an awful tone of finality. As a military historian he found it normal to conduct Trade Union struggles in terms of logistics, estimates of the courses open to opponents, strategy and tactics. The process seemed tedious and unintelligible to those who had formerly made do with courage and an Irish huzzah.

He considered the slide-rule the best instrument for working out a Production-Assistant's wage-claim—how un-Irish! Yet his ancestors had fought at Clontarf, another had stood with Wolfe Tone at his trial, another relative had been executed as an Invincible.

Simple people found him kind; intelligent people found him stimulating. Clever people found him intolerable and even brutal in his knack of revealing them to themselves. Few understood that he never thought it a really friendly thing to accept an illogicality or allow a sentiment to pass for a concept.

He had enemies and he was tactless in dealing with them.

Some engineers resented the fact that his training in computers and factory systems helped him to identify their esoteric language for what it was: a language of non-think. Administrators had the intentions of their euphemisms revealed by an inexorable logic. It was poor consolation to them that the technique of analysis belonged to St. Thomas Aquinas. The *status quo* meant nothing to him. He never expected to mean anything to its defenders. He was never disappointed. Among them were some Producers.

Those preoccupied with power believed that he was authoritarian. Some thought his accent West-British; West Britons felt that he was a troublemaker. Status-seekers said he was a snob; snobs saw him as waging the class-war. Some, suspecting that he told the truth, concluded that he was a charlatan.

His friends endured his lectures and his homilies. They knew that he was honest but, since he was subtle, few ever knew what he was at. He seldom explained. He was witty and given to an amused irony that was often taken for sarcasm. That he had fought Blue-Shirts at ButtBridge, standing beside Tom Barry until Barry had been knocked unconscious, few knew. They wouldn't have been surprised—Chloe Gibson once said that he was a kind of John the Baptist! He would, likely, stand as fast by an enemy as a friend if any principle was involved—but make his life hell afterwards.

Lelia Doolan provoked similar hostilities and loyalties. She had, however, more friends than enemies. She still has.

She came to RTE from the affectionate, bitchy and intellectually lazy world of theatre. RTE has many people with these qualities and for a time she indulged them. Her detractors said she was ambitious and ruthless. They were right. She was ambitious for her work. She was ruthless in her intention to be professionally competent, and to push the incompetent to a realisation of their real needs. Her close friends knew that her angular personality, boyish approach, and forthright language masked a shyness. Gunnar Rugheimer said that she swore like a boiler-stoker! She could use her tongue like a rasp and it often offended. These poses never quite hid an embarrassing generosity. When not working, she suffered fools gladly. This was a failing.

Gamin, intelligent, female, she revolutionised the production methods of *The Riordans* and re-orientated the treatment of Public Affairs. She worried, gnawed, scratched, pushed, cajoled, comforted and studied a disparate collection of individualists into the team that became *7 Days*. She had the energy of a whippet. Reared in Drama, she had been for a time a journalist, a waitress, a singer of Irish ballads, a school teacher and a student of Brecht at a German University.

In certain areas, she had a disconcertingly detailed learning— or enormous tracts of ignorance. She was, equally disconcertingly, unashamed of these. Confronted now, as Producer of *7 Days* by the raw stuff of politics, she realised that this was no longer dramatic fiction but dramatic fact. She began to read, and reflect on society, to experience the paradox of the dirt and the selflessness of politics and, most of all, to appreciate its tremendous importance in the cultural development, and destruction, of human beings. She was an extraordinary mixture of middle-class niceness, bohemian mannerism and rural Irish boisterousness.

She once startled a sedate gathering of Producers and Executives by characterising the views of the incumbent Director-General as fascist.

She had style. She also had a disarming humour and unstudied sophistication—a very complicated yet balanced character.

Television became an obsession. She drove her colleagues and associates half demented. This was somewhat mitigated by a wacky and self-mocking badinage.

Her enemies, who had knowingly remarked that George Colley's sister-in-law would 'see the Party right', were temporarily shocked when her programmes on Vietnam and broadcasting freedom attacked the Establishment. Then, seeing she was in earnest, they waited eagerly for the appearance of that ancient Irish spectacle— an intelligent woman making a fool of herself. She seemed determined to satisfy them.

Her friends, who had seen in her promotion another Irish spectacle—buying off the rebel—were at first incredulous and then shocked to hear her criticisms continue, launched now from more commanding heights. Baffled by her intransigence, refusing to believe that common-sense was no longer, for her, an adequate philosophy, both friends and enemies sought different explanations: she was over-worked or, like Dowling's other friends, she was having her thinking done for her.

Only the little group who knew Dowling and herself well, realised that an original mind, long preoccupied with drama, had turned to the understanding of real life, with all that characteristic energy and concentration which she gave to everything she does, and which she shares with Jack Dowling. This book, for example, was written in two months.

These then, were the persons who had begun separate battles. Now, realising that they were engaged in a common campaign, they came together with Jim Plunkett Kelly, Aindreas Ó Gallchóir, Paddy Gallagher, Eoghan Harris, Rita Foran and her Production-Assistants and many others, to see the struggle to a close. Throughout that period alliances would form around them, fluctuatingly friendly and hostile. At first the station, like a fat, rich man at a health clinic, was indulgent of their therapeutic attentions; winced at their testing and probing, their constant efforts to turn its head to the fresh air.

As they crusaded around the corridors, the dignified watched them with unease and the self-interested with apprehension feeling, like the gombeen men in Brinsley McNamara's *Clanking of Chains*, that all this drilling and training by the Volunteers could only lead to trouble!

They were right. Those who cared for the truth decided to put their old prejudices behind them. With Kelly and Ó Gallchóir they were like four rocks in a gale—immovable. Having made the decision, it was soon discovered that Jack Dowling's academic dissertations and

Lelia Doolan's single-minded intensity were products of a concern for human values. These had, perforce, been turned to the problems of countering a system which they believed was essentially anti-human. They were very human indeed.

# 1

## A CAUTIONARY TALE
## THE CULTURAL EVOLUTION OF A TELEVISION STATION

## CHAPTER 1: A CAUTIONARY TALE

*In the mid-1880s, the youthful, red-bearded George Bernard Shaw and his friend, William Archer, decided to collaborate on a play....*

*... Six weeks later, Shaw startled Archer by saying: 'Look here, I've knocked off the first act of that play of ours and haven't come to the plot yet. In fact, I've forgotten the plot. You might tell me the story again.'...*

*... Three days later, Shaw again visited Archer.*

*I've written three pages of the second act and have used up all your plot,' Shaw said in a matter-of-fact manner. 'Can you let me have some more to go on with?'*

—MYRICKLAND

*In the beginning was the Act.*
—GOETHE

Irish *television went on* the air for the first time on the last, cold, night of December 1961.

At Donnybrook, the celebrities picked their way through pools of mud to reach the half-completed studio building. In O'Connell Street, outside-broadcast cameras panned across the crowds near the Gresham Hotel. Inside the hotel, 'a tremendous party'[1] was in progress under the observing eyes of another pair of cameras.

The festivities in O'Connell Street were 'live' and punctuated an evening's transmission of otherwise largely recorded material. The station opened with the Anthem at seven o'clock.

The traditional national proprieties were observed.

---

1   Forty Years of Irish Broadcasting, Maurice Gotham, 1967

President Éamon De Valera inaugurated the service. The Taoiseach, Sean Lemass, and the Minister, Michael Hilliard, 'also spoke'. The Archbishop of Dublin, Most Rev. Dr McQuaid, gave Benediction. The artists added their *imprimatur*: Siobhán McKenna and Micheál Mac Liammóir.

The show was on.

Jimmy O'Dea, Maureen Potter, Mary O'Hara, Dermot O'Brien's Céilí Band gave a cead mile failte. The Newsroom contributed film of major events throughout the country. The three women continuity announcers led a tour to 'Meet the People'. Every so often the 300,000 audience at 35,000 sets were whisked back to the Gresham to see the spree.

To mark the occasion, there were no advertisements.

Among those who must have watched with special interest were Eamonn Andrews, Chairman of the Authority, Edward Roth, Jnr., Director-General, and Michael Barry, Controller of Programmes.

It was half past midnight before the little white dot shimmied from the screen. As the floor manager, Charlie Roberts, counted down the last few seconds to the New Year on the floor of the Gresham ballroom, the newspapers were preparing to tell a bemused and bedazzled television audience what they thought of the night's doings.

They liked it, was the consensus—and they'd wait and see.

A group in the Irish Club in London telephoned three times during the night for reports on how things were going.

Passengers on late night flights out of Dublin were questioned by Irish exiles on arrival in Britain: how had the whole thing gone?

As television Producers, performers, writers, technical crews, engineers, administrators and salesmen readied themselves for the next night and the next week and the next month of filling the screen five hours a night with information, education and entertainment; as

## CHAPTER 1: A CAUTIONARY TALE

advertisers, religious interests, cultural groups, political parties, purveyors of 'canned' programmes prepared their wares for the hard sell or the soft sell; as cinema owners, theatre owners, sound broadcasters, churches, political parties, pundits and cultural groups revised their warnings on the dangers of The Box; as the neighbours returned to their own houses chatting away about 'what your man said' and about 'how your woman looked', the nation sat back to gaze at the circus that had arrived in its front room.

If the people liked it, the critics had their doubts. There was talk of a square-eyed population in the next generation. One critic complained petulantly:

> "The people most to be pitied last night were Sean Bracken's Loch Gamhna Céilí Band. They were launched onto the screen and abandoned …"

Another asserted that there was, after the first night, little to distinguish Irish television from the standard pattern of commercial television.

But the nation was in no mood for Jeremiahs. The 'mass' medium, the new technological toy, the goggle box, the great communicator had come to dance with us in Ireland. A pretty dance it was to be.

\* \* \*

That night in December had been preceded by more than forty years of statements and counter-statements; questions and reports, advice, appointments, debates, decisions and action.

\* \* \*

The only exhaustive history of broadcasting in Ireland is Maurice Gorham's invaluable *Forty Years of Irish Broadcasting*.

Unlike his book, this chapter is not intended as a history of Irish television. Its intention is, rather, to tell the story of the station's policy vicissitudes so far as the present writers saw them in their experience or research. It is, necessarily, selective. We are programme people, not historians.

It is more than forty-three years since the word 'images' in relation to broadcasting cropped up in an Act of the new Irish Parliament and since the first Irish television picture was seen in Co. Down.

The word occurs in the Wireless Telegraphy Act, 1926, in connection with the setting up of the National Sound Broadcasting Service, Dublin2RN.

The first television picture was transmitted in the previous year by a curate, the Rev. Luke Donnellan, from his house in Dromintee near Newry to a shed four miles away. The picture was a fellow-curate's eye, peering into the tube-like contraption.

James Logie Baird, the Scottish television inventor, is said to have visited Dromintee to compare notes with Father Donnellan. They, in fact, never succeeded in meeting. Baird himself lectured on television in Dublin on 8th February 1927 at the Theatre Royal. Little official note was taken of what he said, but one Dublin journalist thoughtfully found a practical application for the remarkable invention:

> A piquant point arises in the case of bookmakers now that their calling is legalised. Intending punters can be present at a certain hall where the racecourse would be shown and betting only conducted on those horses present at the post. What a relief to those who are continually backing the nonstarters!

## CHAPTER 1: A CAUTIONARY TALE

The Irish Independent wrote in consternation:

> The practical influence of television in everyday life excites the imagination. Will it kill man? No longer will it be necessary to reconnoitre an enemy's position as of old. A general has only to tune in to a certain station where he will see hostile assemblies at work and hear decisions meant to be secret. We tremble when we visualize the effect of television on our daily life. Will privacy be non-existent? Perhaps the growth of modern science is too rapid to be beneficial and further inventions may be needed to counteract it.

It was twenty years later, in 1947, that Mr. Paddy Little, Fianna Fáil Minister for Posts and Telegraphs told Radio Éireann's Advisory Committee that the possibilities for Irish television would be borne in mind in the designing of a new Broadcasting House, on the grounds of Ardmore on the Stillorgan Road. Radio would be first to move there from its cramped quarters in Henry Street.

Twenty-two years later, the first sod was cut for the radio building.

Statements on, and interest in, television began to increase from the early fifties.

In 1952 Mr. Erskine Childers expressed the fear that television might well destroy the art of conversation in Ireland. Mr. Childers (Paddy Little's successor as Minister) told the Dáil in 1953 that the Government had no immediate plans to start a television service. In that year programmes were being received in Ireland both from Wales and from the new BBC transmitter in Belfast. In the same year Erskine Childers gave radio a measure of independence by setting up Comhairle

Radio Éireann, a group of five advisers.[2] He employed a professional in communications, Mr. Maurice Gorham, as Director of Broadcasting.

Between them, Gorham and the Comhairle ran the policies and programming of Radio Éireann for the next seven years. The Comhairle's non-statutory status kept them dependent on each successive Minister's views on broadcasting. The staff of Radio Éireann remained Civil Servants.

In 1953, also, a committee was set up by Leon Ó Broin, Departmental Secretary, comprising T. J. Monaghan, Maurice Gorham and himself. Its purpose was to investigate and report on the implications (financial, technical and programming) of an Irish television service.

They submitted two reports—both, as the fortunes of General Elections determined, to the Minister for Posts and Telegraphs of an Inter-Party Government (1954-57), Mr. Michael Keyes. They recommended a service publicly owned and managed.

References to the possibility of television for Ireland continued to be made in the Dáil.

Mr. Childers expressed the view that when television did come it should be absolutely first-class and involve itself in the development and preservation of our national culture. Some apprehension was beginning to be felt at this time at the increasing availability of British television programmes, and a consequent conditioning of our people to the British view of life.

It was not to Dáil Éireann but to a meeting of the Wireless Dealers Association in Dublin, in October 1956, that Michael Keyes declared the Government's intention that television, when it did come, would

---

2   Its members were: Pádraic Mac Con Midhe, Patrick Lynch, Seán Ó Suilleabháin, Theodore W. Moody, Charles J. Brennan.

be publicly owned and managed, as had been recommended by Leon Ó Broin's committee.

Into this atmosphere of expressed intention, the statement of Mr. Neil Blaney, Keyes's successor, fell a year later.

An Irish television service was to be largely commercial in character, depending on its revenue from advertisers. He went on: 'the Government are prepared to consider proposals from private interests' who would provide and operate studios, transmitters and capital 'in consideration of a licence to operate commercial programmes for a term of years'. 'The television system,' the statement said, 'will become State property and will be under the control of a television authority to be set up.'

Public reaction was like the curate's egg—good in parts.

The Irish Times on 8th November said: 'Our Irish television, in a sentence, is likely to compare with the great majority of sponsored "sound" programmes from Radio Luxembourg—and for that matter from Radio Éireann. Who the lucky commissionaire may be is still unknown and does not matter; he will be at the mercy of his advertisers and will transmit the type of programme that his advertisers wish.'

The Irish Independent did not agree.

In a leading article on 9th November 1957 it regarded the Minister's attitude as 'thoroughly sound': 'Television is a luxury service and those who enjoy it will have to do so without grant or subsidy'.

Again: 'The national finances are such that it is out of the question to introduce any scheme that will involve a charge on the revenue'.

Culturally, there was little awareness at that time, in either the official, political or popular mind, that committing a television service to commercial enterprises might compromise the national identity. There were, however, some thoughtful and experienced men who had grave misgivings; Mr. Maurice Gorham, Leon Ó Broin, Dr. Roger McHugh, etc. Mr. Gorham even expressed doubts about the advisability of embarking on television at all in our circumstances. The Comhairle of Radio Éireann shared these misgivings.

Mr. Blaney had a short innings as Minister and was succeeded by Mr. Seán Ormonde early in December. Three months after his appointment he set up the twenty-man Television Commission which was to report the following year on proposals for a service in Ireland.

The Commission came into being in March 1958. It represented most business, religious, Irish language and political institutions in the country.

The Commission had no practising broadcasters, journalists or artists among its members. The only practising theatre man was the Earl of Longford, and he resigned from the Commission six months after it began its sittings, on the grounds that it was useless.

The course of its deliberations was surprising.

\* \* \*

*Now to the banquet we press;*
*Now for the eggs and the ham;*
*Now for the mustard and cress,*
*Now for the strawberry jam!*
—SIR WILLIAM S. GILBERT

Some of the sittings appear to have been colourful; some even amusing. The proposers, nine in all, came mainly from Britain and America. Promises were prolific and of astounding generosity. At one stage, the scene took on the air of an early Evelyn Waugh novel. Tycoons arrived with documented portfolios; a dazed Irish artist came from the Aran Islands; Monsignori from the Vatican in full regalia stood in discreet ecclesiastical patience, waiting to be called. They were part of the retinue of the most exotic of the proposers, a man whose nationality was never satisfactorily established. On a polite enquiry from an official as to what their purpose was, they modestly admitted that they didn't know.

One applicant made the astonishing promise to a stunned Commission that he would, as a bonus, on receipt of the television franchise, provide the State with a commercial medium-wave radio station which would cover the North American Continent! In reply to a question from an incredulous member of the broadcasting service as to how he proposed to reach the North American Continent on medium wave, he replied grandly and mysteriously that he knew of a band on which it could be done but he wasn't going to tell.

It would be impossible to convey credibly the picture of intrigue and reconnoitring that went on in Dublin during those months.

One clear fact emerged: whatever the Irish authorities wanted they could have, for nothing—except, of course, the grant of the franchise. As we write, this whole episode takes on an extraordinary plausibility if one accepts The Sunday Times account (3rd August 1969) of the promises made by those bidding for the commercial franchise of the new ITA companies in 1967.

The Commission met weekly for more than thirteen months and submitted an Interim Report nine months after it had begun. The report was never published. The final Report was published on 8th May 1959, containing a Minority Report.

Neither of these is wholly intelligible, since each presupposes that the reader will have access to a Supplementary Report. In fact, nobody among the Irish public has access to it. It was never published. Nobody knows why, or, at least, nobody who knows will tell. We enquired of the Secretary of the Department of Posts and Telegraphs, Dr. Leon Ó Broin, now retired. He refused in the public interest (sic) to discuss the contents of what he said were 'secret State papers'. What an intriguing document this Supplementary Report must be.

The most important framework to which the Commission's hands were tied was its basic term of reference. This required that it proceed 'on the basis that no charge shall fall on the exchequer either on capital or on current account, and that effective control of televised programmes must be exercisable by an Irish public authority to be established as a television authority'.

> *And thus the native hue of*
> *resolution*
> *Is sicklied o'er with the pale*
> *cast of thought*
> *And enterprises of great pith*
> *and moment*
> *With this regard their currents*
> *turn awry*
> *And lose the name of action.*
> —SHAKESPEAR

It had been required to examine the technical practicability of establishing a television service; to recommend arrangements for its ownership by the State; examine proposals already received by the Government from commercial firms; indicate the powers and duties of the television authority and its constitution. In particular, it had been obliged to specify the special arrangements that should be made

(a) to provide for the use of the Irish language and for the adequate reflection of the national outlook and culture, and

(b) to govern the presentation of information and news in the television service.

Further, it was enjoined to look into the desirable relationship between the television service and the sound broadcasting service and any other relevant matters to which 'the Commission deems it advisable to draw attention*.

The Commission referred on a number of occasions to the financing term of reference. One revealing quotation from their report runs:

> if the necessary capital was available television should, if possible, be provided on the basis of a public service[3]. A television service on ... [this basis] ... is, however, not possible within the terms of reference of the Commission.

What was possible was a television service which would be set up as a profit-making enterprise, under a governing authority exercising on behalf of the State the duty to maintain and direct it. The programming was to become the responsibility of the selected proposer, financed mainly by revenue from advertisements. The selected proposer was to be represented on the authority. This was the main recommendation.

Briefly, the Commission's other recommendations were: the establishment of a television service based on private profit; further consideration be given to a changeover to a public service system when circumstances should favour it; control of the commercial organisation operating the service; the authority, with a chairman, should comprise nine members; a method of appointing the members of the authority

---

3   The term 'public service' broadcasting is current among professional broadcasters in the rather special sense of a television or radio service financed wholly from public funds by way of licence fees, grants and/or subsidies. Its alternative is some form of commercial financing by trading profit, like the sale of advertising-time.

should be the responsibility of the Taoiseach, possibly after consultation with the leaders of the Opposition.

It also recommended impartiality in the treatment of news and information. It suggested that broadcasting should occur for a minimum of twenty-one hours per week in the early period with a possible rise to a maximum of fifty hours after a suitable interval.

\* \* \*

Obviously, no member of the Commission had the remotest notion of the resources needed to provide fifty hours of transmission.

It stated that, perforce, the amount of Irish material would at the beginning be small but this could grow as the television service itself expanded. The Commission was satisfied that 'Ireland would certainly be the poorer if it did not have this material available as part of the total programme fare\*. It was convinced that 'as a nation it cannot accept the flow of other nations' culture without running the grave risk of a cultural osmosis that could dilute and finally eliminate its own national characteristics\*.

For radio, the Commission's recommendation was that it be controlled 'for some years to come' by a separate but independent body which would give it equal standing with the television service.

\* \* \*

On 29th June 1959 Mervyn Wall wrote, on behalf of the Arts Council, an open letter to the Television Commission. It was a thoughtful and valuable contribution to the debate and proposed that no system whatsoever of commercial television should receive the sanction and support of an Irish Government. Among other things it said:

> in commercial television not only does self-interest, of its nature, over-ride cultural values for the sake of appealing to mass audiences but, in doing so, produces a proportionate and progressive vulgarisation of public taste as a whole;

and

> the establishment of commercial television here, far from diminishing the influence of television from elsewhere—not to speak of eliminating it—will, on the contrary, by increasing the habit of televiewing among the public, make this influence more and more widespread.

It was also argued that any really effective control of the objectionable features of commercial television had been proved by experience to be impracticable.

Fears of the influence of commercialism run right through the Majority Report of the Commission. They are explicit in the Minority Report. This had suggested a non-commercial television station, financed from funds raised by international commercial sound broadcasting, like Radio Luxembourg. This suggestion, which had been put forward some years before, had been turned down by the Government. The contradictory implications are, however, clear both in the Commission's Report and in the public debate which followed: broadcasting must pay its way and the standards of national culture must be preserved and improved.

Broadcasting has been sitting on the horns of this dilemma ever since.

\* \* \*

On 8th August 1959 Mr. Michael Hilliard, the new Fianna Fáil Minister for Posts and Telegraphs, announced yet another approach. The essence of this departure on the part of the Government was given at a concert by the RE String Quartet in Cork. It involved not only the setting up of a public authority for television, but the transfer of Radio Éireann's functions to it.

The statement was a bombshell to the commercial interests and the public alike.

The Minister seemed to cut the ground from under the Television Commission, reverse its terms of reference, reject the public-service concept of the Minority Report, turn down the offers of the commercial proposers, retain Government control by appointing an 'independent' authority, promote the national cultural aims by a service required to run its finances as if it were a private enterprise dependent on advertisers.

\* \* \*

> 'I know what you're thinking about,' said Tweedledum; 'but it isn't so, no how!'
>
> 'Contrariwise,' continued Tweedledee, 'if it was so, it might be; and if it were not so, it would be; but as it isn't, it ain't. That's logic.'
>
> 'I was thinking,*' said Alice very politely, 'which is the best way out of this wood: it's getting so dark!'

\* \* \*

As the Minister was to say in the Dáil on the Broadcasting Estimate, May 1960:

> Private interests with considerable experience in this field were satisfied that they could make a profit without any assistance from licence revenue. If they could do so, I do not see why a public authority, supported to a very substantial extent by licence revenue, cannot do likewise.

So, the State was proposing to enter into competition with private enterprise, the British commercial networks, the Irish and British newspapers and magazines, the display advertisers. Apart from maintaining itself, broadcasting was, in Mr. Hilliard's words, to make a profit. He was right. It did.

*  *  *

Perhaps a review of the proposals put before the Government by foreign and domestic enterprises may have helped it to make up its mind. We understand that a novel and modest proposal put forward by Gael-Linn was set aside. The Government's plan was designed to have the best of both worlds—profitability and public utility.

As Mr. Gorham said on hearing the news. 'Not Gaelic merely, but free as well'.

Mr. Gorham tendered his resignation as Director of Broadcasting on 24th August 1959. On the 27th of that month, Mr. Eamonn Andrews called on the Minister for Posts and Telegraphs. Two weeks later Mr. Andrews was announced as chairman of an advisory committee which was to be set up to steer financial, technical and programming affairs until the Bill should be drafted and the new Authority chosen and established.

The other members of the committee were Mr. E. B. McManus, a businessman and Fianna Fáil party member, Commander George

Crosbie, a newspaper proprietor from Cork, reputed to support Fine Gael, and Mr. P. P. Wilkinson, a solicitor from Naas, allegedly Labour. Both McManus and Crosbie had been members of the Television Commission.

Eamonn Andrews' post was part-time. He had refused the position of Director-General. He wished to continue his BBC commitments. He intended to keep in close contact with the BBC in planning the development of the Irish project.

The committee met daily during the Summer. Land bought for RE in 1947 at Ardmorehad later been exchanged with University College, Dublin, for a site on the opposite side of the road, at Montrose. Plans for studio blocks at this site had been entrusted to Mr. Raymond McGrath, architect for the Board of Works, by the Commission.

The Bill was now drafted and was simultaneously debated in both chambers of the Oireachtas.

\* \* \*

> *Mr. Speaker, I smell a rat;*
> *I see him forming in the air and darkening*
> *the skies; but I'll nip him in the bud.*
> —IRISH HOUSE OF COMMONS, 1780

\* \* \*

The sections which came under most intense fire in both Houses were those which remain a matter of public controversy up to the present. These, mainly, are the method of selecting the members of the Authority; the possible pitfalls over the business interests of its members; the rights of the Minister to interfere either by way of suppression or by way of requirement to broadcast particular matters; the section dealing with impartiality and the exemption for political party broadcasts; the sections enabling the Authority to sell advertising time, and those instructing it to keep in mind, always, the national aims and promotion of the Irish language.

The Bill was debated in the Senate first—a measure which caused many Senators to express their gratification with almost maidenly pleasure. The proceedings in the Senate had something of the quality of a minuet in their exquisite formality; those in the Dáil resembled more closely the sweaty 'tackiness' of the Siege of Ennis. Both debates were lively and stimulating; the Senate being particularly well-informed. The debate in the Dáil was marvellously colourful and unhindered by any knowledge of the facts. It was, however, strong on matters of opinion.

The four-man Committee with its Chairman, Eamonn Andrews, had become designate members of the new Authority. In the absence of other nominations for the Authority, much of the debate revolved around the compromising nature of those business interests of members which might be in conflict with their public duties.

Noel Browne put forward an amendment that any member of the Authority should divest himself of his interests or resign. Dr. Browne also had much to say on the matter of the conflicts and contradictions of a national service which was also a commercial enterprise. He believed that monies to subsidise such an enterprise should be public money in order that the lower paid would benefit and those whose incomes warranted increased taxation should bear the brunt.

Patrick McGilligan, among others, was not in favour of the method of appointment of the new Authority. It was suggested in both Houses that appointments should be made by an independent body, or after consultation with the Opposition leaders.

The Minister, Michael Hilliard, demurred.

He was sure apprehensions on a conflict of interests were ill-founded. In discussions between the Taoiseach, himself and Eamonn Andrews, when first interviewed, Andrews had made it clear to them that in the event of any conflict of interests he would resign.

The setting up of a public body to run television should, the Minister felt, prevent commercial interests from dictating the policies of the new venture. The Government, he informed the House, had come to this view after reading the Commission's recommendations and taking into account other factors, including 'the improvement in the capital position'. In spite of the need for the service to pay its way, he did not see that 'its policy should be dominated by the profit motive'.

This was in diametrical opposition to his feeling expressed during the debate on the Estimate in May of the same year, 1960.

Senator George O'Brien addressed himself to the question of advertising and the function of advertising in television: 'I think it important to emphasise that advertising is not all bad, that it is really a form of conveying information'. Senator O'Brien could hardly have foreseen the claims which advertisements were to make, but the ring of confidence already surrounded his prognosis.

He continued: 'Advertising has a definite commercial value in that it makes competition more keen. The more successful products tend to supplant the less successful ... [and] ... the public is getting the article cheaper because it is advertised. ... There is no doubt that advertising plays its part in maintaining competition in the modem world'.

Senator Ó Maoláin welcomed the Bill. He said: 'This is a good Bill; its provisions show that we have grown up'.

There was debate on the section in which the Minister may direct the Authority in writing to allocate broadcasting time for any announcement on behalf of a Minister of State in connection with the functions of that Minister. It came in for criticism in both Houses. This section was in fact somewhat curiously amended in the Act itself. The insertion 'by or on behalf of any Minister of State in connection with the functions of that Minister' replaced 'by or in connection with the functions of any Minister of State'.

Senator O'Quigley, adverting to what he regarded as preferential treatment given to Government spokesmen and party members on radio, said that he was 'scandalised at the audacity of people in public employment using Radio Éireann for party political purposes'. He continued on the section about impartiality saying that no amount of statutory regulation could legally secure the need for impartiality 'because, in the last analysis you must depend on the integrity of the people who are in charge of that service'.

Senator Sheehy Skeffington referred also to the section on impartiality: 'Occasionally in the news you get a kind of thing that should never happen, that a Minister's reply to a question or some kind of criticism is given by itself, without any reference at all to the criticism. This is clearly not impartial and should never happen.' He, too, went on to refer to Section 31, which gives the Minister a complete and absolute veto, without appeal, on any particular matter that is to be broadcast.

Mr. Michael Hilliard, the Minister responsible, continued to maintain throughout the debates that the power vested in him to require the Authority 'to refrain from broadcasting' was a proper one in view of the responsibility which the Government had for the maintenance and policies of the service, particularly under circumstances of national emergency.

The question of priorities in the nation's economic progress was referred to by Deputy Oliver Flanagan: 'I wonder if the Government have really sought an answer to one question, namely, whether in present economic circumstances expenditure on a television service is necessary'. He went on, in his inimitable way: 'If the proposed television service is to be anything like RE then I ask the Minister to drop the matter because RE is not alone disgusting but it provides probably the most useless broadcasting service that any broadcasting authority in the world puts on the air.'

All through the debate much play was made of the 'power of television' and the kind of uses to which it would be put—from the educational and highbrow, to song and dance of a national character, to Senator Quinlan's view that farmers could be told when to sow early grass.

In many of the contributions there was much of that innocent hopefulness that accompanies total professional ignorance, yet is the main ethical strength of the democratic theory of law. There was a sense that the Bill was potentially a good one, provided that the Authority should be a body of cultured and courageous men, chosen with care and, also, providing that the sections dealing with the powers of the Minister to interfere were redrafted. This reflected no doubt in the mind of either House about the personal integrity of the Minister.

The Bill passed into law on 6th April 1960 and the Authority members were nominated one month later.

The nine names were: Eamonn Andrews, Chairman; Ernest Blythe, then of the Abbey Theatre and a former Minister for Finance; Fintan Kennedy, General Secretary of the Irish Transport and General Workers' Union and a member of the National Executive of the Irish Congress of Trade Unions; Charles J. Brennan, Chairman of Brennan Insurances Ltd., who had been the Chairman of the old Comhairle Radio Éireann; Dr. T. W. Moody, Senior Lecturer and Professor of Modem History at Trinity College Dublin, also from the old Comhairle; Aine Ni Cheannain, Gaelic teacher and writer; James Fanning, Editor of the Midland Tribune and a founder of the Birr Little Theatre Group; E. B.

McManus and Commander George Crosbie, who had been members of the advisory committee.

The members of the Authority were paid £500 a year and the Chairman was paid £1,000. All nine remained in office for the maximum term of five years permitted under the Act. Four of them were then replaced when the new temporary Authority was set up in 1965 for a term of one year. Fintan Kennedy, Theo Moody and James Fanning remained members of the Authority to the time of our resignations.

\* \* \*

> *Erect thy tabernacle here,*
> *The new Jerusalem send down,*
> *Thyself amidst thy saints appear,*
> *And seat us on thy dazzling throne.*
> —HYMN

A week after the new Authority took up office, it advertised for its first Director-General. The advertisement stated that essential qualifications would include experience of administration and organisation in television, preferably with knowledge of programming and production. Sound broadcasting and commercial experience would also be desirable.

\* \* \*

In the middle of June the plans which Mr. Raymond McGrath had prepared for the design of the studio building at Montrose were abandoned in favour of Mr. Michael Scott's, an eminent Dublin architect, who was engaged by the Authority to prepare designs for the building of television studios at Montrose.

\* \* \*

In November 1960 the Authority actually appointed its first Director-General for a period of two years. He was Mr. Edward Roth, an American. He had been a consultant in management with the National Broadcasting Corporation of America and had set up broadcasting stations in Peru and Mexico.

The Sunday Independent commented on 13th November. 'Roth is to be paid £7,500 per annum. Surely he will be the highest paid official in Government or semi-Government service in Ireland. Are we to take it that the Government puts a higher value on television than on anything else?

'Members of the Government who have to work hard and for many hours, day and night, are not paid half that amount.

'Funny world, isn't it?'

Yes, it's a scream—Juno's peacock.

Mr. Roth gave a press conference in Dublin in the middle of November and was the subject of a number of press interviews and comments around that time. He intended, he said, that as far as possible Irish personnel would be recruited; it would be the experts in the television service—the programme makers—who would determine the type of service and programmes. He would have as many Irish-originated programmes as possible—about thirty to sixty per cent Irish material in the beginning.

Roth was optimistic about the influence of commercials, although he saw that it would require strong direction to prevent the servicing of public needs being reduced in favour of sheer entertainment programmes.

He saw the Authority as responsible for the selection and production of normal programmes and the sponsors as being restricted to buying time for their advertisements. He did, however, see that the willingness of people to spend money was always conditioned by the returns they expected.

On the extent of programming in Irish he said that this would depend on the demand from viewers.

Asked about the sort of programmes he would expect to buy from abroad he said: 'Say for children, the *Bugs Bunny* cartoons. Then a mystery on the lines of Perry Mason. A comedy show like *Father Knows Best* or the *Life of Reilly*. A Western—I love Westerns—for relaxation. Say, one like *Gunsmoke*.'

Asked whether the station would have to follow the policy of the Government in order that the service should have an Irish outlook he said he didn't think so. Juno's peacock said nothing.

The listenership of Radio Éireann at the time of the take-over was 493,000 providing an income from licence fees and advertisements of some £530,000 a year. Sound radio was running at a loss. The Authority's initial capital was advanced by the Government.

Work was begun on the site at Montrose early in 1961. Temporary offices had been taken in Clarendon Street and in Chatham Street. The Authority and its chief executives made their headquarters there.

The new Authority took over a staff of just under four hundred with eleven sound studios in Henry Street, two in Cork; the Phoenix Hall and Portobello, which were used for musical transmissions mainly. They also took possession of the transmitters, sites, offices and equipment at Dublin, Cork and Athlone. Under the Act they were a corporate body legally able to hold and dispose of property; able to sue and be sued.

Irish television was in business.

*  *  *

In March, Mr. Niall Sheridan, Advertisement Sales Manager of Irish television told a meeting of the Irish Press Club in Dublin that if all went well, broadcasting should start before the end of the year.

The advertising rate was struck. A caption in The Irish Times read: 'Advertising on television at £93 a minute'.

By the end of March the first appointments of production staff began, appointments in the engineering and administration areas being well advanced.

At the end of April it was announced that a five-month course of training for production trainees would begin in June in the Marian College in Ballsbridge. Courses were conducted for every kind of production staff.

In the public mind the planning was over. The assembly began. In a sense it was, for many, the return of the Wild Geese. Every Irishman with a usable skill working abroad seemed to be on his way home.

The public shared something of this excitement. Newspapers ran features and photos with learned explanations of electronic mysteries. Enthusiasms were geared to prodigies. Prodigies gave free rein to enthusiasms, miracles and muddles. Some sane and experienced foreign experts assessed the situation coldly and declared it to be impossible. Others caught the atmosphere and waded in.

Gardeners became vision-mixers. A Coca-Cola bottlewasher became a sound operator. A motor car salesman became a cameraman. A ship's wireless operator became an electronic telecine engineer. Insurance salesmen became interviewers. A hotchpotch became a team—of a kind: 'The Irish have a genius for ad hoc organisation' as Mr. De Valera once pointed out during the Emergency and as Miss Bernadette Devlin has confirmed in Derry.

The impossible is more difficult in Ireland than the improbable —but it takes a shorter time.

CHAPTER 1: A CAUTIONARY TALE

During the late spring and early summer of 1961 appointments of Heads of Programme Departments began.

Here there was, perhaps, more to build upon. There was a tradition of theatre from which to draw. There were people with radio production and administration experience. There was an excellent body of Public Affairs and Sports journalists.

The basis of a News Division already existed in radio and its expansion was under way.

Traditions for the organisation of these activities were already native and workable.

* * *

By July, vision equipment for Kippure was beginning to arrive at the Pye factory at Dundrum. Three weeks later test signals were received in Galway, Limerick and Tipperary.

* * *

At the beginning of August Richard Butterworth's design for the St. Brigid's Cross, which was, in developing form, to be the station symbol for the next nine years, was seen by the public for the first time, in the newspapers.[4]

By the middle of August new rates for licence fees had been announced. The combined television and sound licence was to cost £4. The single radio licence was to go up from seventeen and sixpence to £1.

---

[4] The design published on 9th December 1969, in which the cross of St. Brigid is retained by the ingenious device of incorporating one of its arms into the 'R' of the station's initials, is a fit subject for the vitriolic pen of Myles na gCopaleen. It is so incredibly vulgar that one wonders if it is not thought to be some kind of error or joke. It is no joke.

While signing contracts for the building of transmitters at Mount Leinster, Mullaghanish, Maghera and Truskmore, Mr. Roth, on 19th August 1961, stated that Irish television would show a profit in two years. The staff of the new television service was reported at 140 persons.

All the senior appointments had now been made, except that of Controller of Programmes for television. This was, surely, the key position under that of the Director-General, yet it was said that it had not been possible to find a suitable Controller up to that time. It might have been regarded as advisable and necessary by any broadcasting organisation that as the making and transmitting of programmes was its main reason for existing, the man most essential for the formulation and proper orientation of the organisation was a television controller. Apparently, this was not considered of vital importance.

On 30th August the appointment of Mr. Michael Barry as Controller of Programmes (Television) was announced.

Michael Barry had an established reputation, both in theatre and television in Britain and America. He was a writer who, at the time of his appointment, was Head of Drama at BBC television. He was seconded to Irish television for a three-year period and his duties, which began at the end of September, included day-to-day responsibility for establishing a programme schedule.

A man of quiet courage and energy, he was too sensitive and modest to shine. He had considerable organisational ability and a fund of persistent enthusiasm but little stomach for intrigue, backstairs politics and infighting. His military background, perhaps, gave him an instinctive loyalty to his subordinates and a certain stubborn determination to shield them from criticism by interposing his person between them and his own superiors.

The organisation which Mr. Barry found upon arrival was a mixture of broadcasting organisation ideas from Britain and America with local adaptations. Administrative and Management sections looked after personnel, services and finance; there was an Engineering section which looked after maintenance, development and electricians, telecine (the nerve centre for recordings and transmissions), film, video-tape recording, television operations (including cameramen, lighting-men and sound-men) for studios and for outside broadcasts. There was already a News Division which was not regarded, BBC fashion, as having any direct relationship to the Programmes Division of radio or television.

Finally, the Programmes Division itself was organised on mainly BBC lines—that is, with Departments for particular sections of programme-interest, each with its own Head and group of Producers, Production Assistants, Scriptwriters, Researchers, and so on. It must have been all quite familiar to Mr. Barry and all something of a *fait accompli*.

The brave, new, Irish experiment, entering into the 'new' field of television wound up with an organisation that could be interchanged with that of any other broadcasting organisation, anywhere in the world[5].

With something less than three months to go before the first night, the prospects must have seemed daunting. There were about a dozen half-trained, untrained and fully-trained Producers; semi-trained and experienced technical staffs.

---

5   Professor James Halloran, Director, Centre for Mass Communication, Leicester University, made, when a University Lecturer in Sociology there, tentative approaches to the new service soon after it was set up. He pointed out that there was a unique opportunity of setting up a phased research programme to study the effects of television on an English-speaking urban community (he suggested Cork) which had not hitherto been exposed to it, by conducting 'before-and-after' research. His object was to gain empirical evidence of television programming effects. As television transmissions went on, they could be progressively studied and the data analysed and used. This would have provided the Authority with a scientific base upon which to build a programme policy. Professor Halloran has made two further approaches which have been received affably. Nothing has been done but talk. A member of RTE's programme staff, Michael Morris, had attempted to do work of a similar kind in his spare time but failed to get sufficient support. His project had to be dropped.

In a matter of days after his arrival, the new Controller was handed two Authority decisions: (1) to provide forty-two hours of programmes a week; (2) to open the station before the end of 1961—'even on the last day'.

Michael Barry asked the Director-General to make it quite clear to the Authority that in the circumstances he could not promise more than the News and perhaps one half-hour programme of home origin by the end of the year.

He soon saw, however, that disappointment of public anticipation would bring about a situation of outrage and anger. So, he concluded: 'We would have to take our coats off and do a great deal better than that. Financially we were going to programme at an average of £214 an hour. At that time the BBC were programming in the order of £2,500 an hour: therefore, to obtain programmes, we would have to rely on simple things, ensuring that they had a quality of their own sort, and this is what we set out to do.

'What happened was that we stuck our necks out and began to record programmes in the Marian College Hall. The first programme to be recorded was with Frank O'Connor, I believe. Then we rented the studio which the Strand Electric people were preparing in Abbey Street. They hastily made this available to us, so we set-to and recorded programmes back-to-back from morning to evening, sometimes three to four programmes a day, for the first six months.'

In the first week in December 1961, four weeks before the opening of the service, the first issue of the Authority's official Journal appeared. In an interview the Controller referred to the amount of advertising and said that he expected it would be about ten per cent—or six minutes in any clock hour. The Minister was prepared to allow up to seven and a half minutes in a clock hour.

In the next issue, on 8th December, there was an interview with the Director-General. He insisted that in the early stages of Irish television we would have to rely heavily on the purchase of American filmed programmes. The reason for this was quite simple and evident. There was virtually no other source. We would buy only what was necessary (that is, 75 per cent of the programme material) and it would be of the 'best available quality'. Irish programmes were being created which, he believed, would make a lasting contribution to the growth and development of Irish culture. The Irish people must appreciate that this was a major effort and might very well take years to develop. Later he explained:

'So, our problem is, we've got to please the people by giving them what they want, and we've got to please the advertisers by giving them big audiences and we must conscientiously obey the law of actual practice.'

The peacock died.

We went on the air on the last day of December, as required.

*  *  *

> *A vast automaton, composed of various mechanical and intellectual organs, acting in uninterrupted concert for the production of a common object, all of them being subordinated to a self-regulating force.*
> —DR. ANDREW URE, 1835

During the first year of its life, the service transmitted close on eighteen hours per week of home-produced material (about four hours less than it is currently producing, and with approximately one-third the present number of Producer-Directors).

In January 1962 the number of licence-holders was 35,766. By February it had almost doubled. A year later it had reached a figure of 150,000.

In April 1962 the staff moved out to Montrose from the offices in the city.

Among the early television projects realised in Public Affairs was *Broadsheet*, with John O'Donoghue, Ronnie Walsh and P. P. O'Reilly; there was *Let's Draw* in Children's Programmes, which is still running; *Beirt Eile*, a programme of traditional music and dance; *The Late Late Show*, *Pick-of-the-Post*, sports coverage and reports both on G.A.A. and foreign games. There were fashion, cookery and magazine programmes. Besides all this, fourteen drama productions were done up to March of the following year.

The new service was obviously affecting the public. There appeared to be constant debate at every level about the quality, temperament or personality of those who appeared in front of the cameras. The tone of the debate was acrimonious in the Irish fashion, and almost all of it had to do with the home-produced programmes. The nation had its usual love-hate relationship with anything that deeply concerned it. Why not with television?

One happy and angry man rang up and said he would throw his television set out the window if Verona Mullen appeared again on the Late Late Show, were not for the fact that he didn't want to miss the show on the following week!

\* \* \*

# CHAPTER 1: A CAUTIONARY TALE

Up to this, the new television service and the public had effected a marriage of sorts. Life is a temporary expedient. Now the honeymoon was over. The domestic scene in TE was dominated by housekeeping and kitchen chores. The Programmes Division held a weekly meeting for discussion of programme ideas. It was chaired by the Controller and discussed and criticised programmes already screened; it debated future proposals.

The dialogue between the station and the public became, perhaps, a trifle shrill. The pressures of work within the station, the widespread inexperience, the disappointments about the 'abundance of Irish talent', all began to be sorely felt by Producers. Public relations were neither sufficiently extended, intense nor sustained. The main source of disappointment is, perhaps, best expressed by the Controller's ambition for the station— 'not just to get a station on the air but to get an Irish voice on the air, making Irish programmes with Irish people about Irish things.'

We have a self-satisfied confidence in ourselves as talkers. If this ability existed, the electronic camera could pick up little of it. Enthusiastic recommendations of talented persons and characters from all over the country were, for the most part, eagerly followed up and tried. They were almost uniformly disappointing. The pool of talent in a population of under three millions was pathetically small in terms of the broadcasting philosophy of 'professionalism'[6] which our competitive relationship with the British networks forced upon us.

It was soon discovered, too, that the frontiers of debate were tightly constricted. Subjects that could be freely discussed in a pub

---

6   Professionalism is ambiguously used in television. We can only make our own view clear. Real television is professionally produced to allow the nation to talk to itself. 'Professional' television aspires to produce 'professional' talkers to talk at amateurs. See chapters on Culture and 'Count Me Out'.

were regarded as shocking or unsuitable on the screen. The Producers quickly learned that the nation had little stomach for satire, irony or criticism of revered institutions or personalities. It had two standards. In private anything could be said and often was. In public—on television particularly—wit flagged, ideas evaporated, humour became pawky and gauche. The new Irish, apparently, were determined to be terribly, terribly respectable. They were, to a depressing extent, terribly, terribly dull.

The mechanics of production in studio seemed to intimidate those amateur participants who are the lifeblood of professionally produced television. It proved virtually impossible to convey to most people that accepted television techniques just didn't allow adequate development of points in the sense people were used to in conversation.

The conflicting demands for programmes of different kinds made it impossible to please everybody, which was normal, and difficult to please anybody, which was irritating.

To the Producer, the daily grind was a mad scramble for new talent that seemed like Hamlet's father: "Tis here! 'Tis here! 'Tis gone!' The public that could participate had no notion of the split-second timing that television requires, nor, indeed, of the need of punctuality. Understandably, the production staff became disillusioned about the entertainment value of 'talking heads'; in fact these are the finest entertainment in the world—if there is anything in them. The public became disillusioned with a technique so cold, remote and foreign to their still largely rural temperament.

An audition that resulted in a rejection often ended in a feud. Accusations of favouritism, nepotism, 'pull', prejudice and bolshevism were frequent.

Sacred cows were being continually insulted, people said, by arrogant, overpaid and overbearing upstarts out in Donnybrook.

Programme makers were not free from pressures during this period: never having enough time, never enough money, or perhaps, enough expertise—they were, on occasion, subject to external and direct influences from public institutions or personalities. These were not taken very seriously, yet a Dublin newspaper has referred to this time as one in which 'unwholesome touting and lobbying' was widely thought to be practised. Our people can always be depended upon to expect skulduggery, except when it is actually happening. We then become terribly, terribly judicious and fair-minded.

\* \* \*

Of course, there were members of the Authority who were regarded as being partisan Fianna Fáil members. There was a certain member of the Authority (now deceased) who was regarded as a Fianna Fáil 'hatchet man'. He, on at least one occasion, exerted pressure to have staff members who had 'overstepped' the bounds of impartiality, sacked or suspended.

The first major policy decision that Michael Barry had to try to implement in 1962 was to provide adequate budgets for better programmes with little hope of increasing the amount of total money available. Secondarily, he had to try to relieve the inhuman pressure of work upon an already exhausted staff. His plan was simple: to cut back heavily on Summer production and transmission of home-originated material.

The cost of foreign material was working out at about £20 per hour in a projected average of £214 per hour for home-made programming.

He stepped up the transmission of imported material massively for the summer of 1962. He sought sources other than the U.S. and Britain for film and began to plan and stockpile home productions for the Autumn programmes. Such a major policy decision had the concurrence of his superior and the Authority.

The public outcry was immediate. They didn't like it and said so. Criticism began to pour in day after day.

Mr. Barry was of Irish descent but of English nationality. He was genuinely concerned about the Irishness of the station, perhaps to the point of exaggeration. This counted for nothing with public institutions or personalities. He was socially isolated and as soon as the criticisms reached crescendo, he became aware that Mr. Roth, also a foreigner, was being subjected to similar criticisms and pressures.

The two men gradually withdrew confidence from one another in a mutually protective attempt to disguise these public antagonisms, each from the other. Roth passed the criticisms of the Authority to Barry, without added personal comment. Barry tried to hold the buck for his staff at his own desk.

Behind all of this, there were three factors: the first, that the almost superhuman performances of the opening year's work had led the public to expect an output that couldn't be maintained because the public were fundamentally ignorant of the size of the task. They had been conditioned to measure everything against the criterion of the British networks which had more than twelve times our resources of men, money and talent. Secondly, apart from Eamonn Andrews, the Authority knew nothing of the professional consequences of the decisions they passed down for implementation. Thirdly, the Government, the Authority and the public required, without realising the fact, basically incompatible things.

None of these need have brought about a crisis, if Roth, Barry and their senior executives had had the professional solidarity to withstand them and at the same time make their difficulties intelligible to the

Authority and the public. They could not do this and the station's public relations resources were inadequate to the task.

Unable to stand together, they fell separately.

Four months after the opening night of the television service Mr. Ernie Byrne, the Executive Producer, resigned because of 'differences over policy between myself and the television chiefs.' This was not surprising; they had not agreed among themselves.

Relations between the Authority and their senior executives were already strained. Mr. Barry offered his resignation in September and commented:

> 'When the Authority were criticising individual programmes and individuals in programmes, I made the point that on such occasions I should be present at their meetings because I was not prepared to receive notes from other persons about criticism of individuals, which I would then have to discuss with them. Yet I myself was unable to face these criticisms at source.'

Mr. Roth retired at the end of 1962.

Upon leaving RTE Mr. Roth, in interviews with the Press, remarked on the impossibility of the station's ever being able to improve the quality of programmes under the terms of the Act:

> 'We are keenly aware of ... [the shortcomings and weak spots of the service.] ... One of the ironies of that situation was that no member of the Authority was claiming, nor was any member of the station, that we had a first-class service at that stage; much of the criticisms seemed to suggest that we believed we had' (our italics).

On future prospects:

> 'The dilemma of Irish television is that it combines two objectives; one, to establish and maintain a service which will further national culture and aims and have regard to the prestige of the nation, and, secondly, that the service must be a paying commercial enterprise.[7]'

\* \* \*

Studio 1 had become operational in May 1962 and Studio 2 in September of the same year. Productions, therefore, at the studios in Abbey Street had ended in the last days of May.

An office had been acquired in London. This was to house the London Sales staff for advertising promotion and was acquired in October 1962 at Oxford Circus.

Home produced programmes, from April to June 1962, occupied nineteen hours a week—fifteen hours a week in the three summer months, and eighteen hours a week from October to March[8]. This output, including News and News Feature programmes, made up about 45 per cent of the total transmission output. The balance, of course, was imported or foreign material.

The demand for home produced programmes was, as we have said, insatiable.

The Authority's first Annual Report declared: 'The Authority would wish to have been in a position to meet this demand more fully but

---

[7] Gorham, Forty Years of Irish Broadcasting.

[8] Cf. Radio Éireann Annual Report 1962-63.

could not do so because of the expansion in staff, equipment and facilities that this would have entailed'.

From April 1962 to March 1963 the total transmission output had been 2,200 hours; of this, 990 hours were home produced.

On a selected day in 1963 Ireland was found to be broadcasting a greater number of hours than any of the following: Denmark, Sweden, Belgium, Holland and Austria. This was being done for a licence fee substantially less than those countries. Income from advertising on television was £700,000 and over £122,000 for radio in the first full year of operation. This £822,000 was the direct product of staff sweat and anxiety. Due to Mr. Barry's unpopular skill it was possible to raise the average budget per programme hour to about £400. This figure may be misleading if one is not clear that it included the cost of imported programmes running, as we saw, between £18 and £20 per hour—cheaper even than Hong Kong television!

\* \* \*

The post of Director-General to fill the vacancy left by Mr. Roth was not advertised but the search began in autumn 1962. That for the new Programme Controller was advertised in November. Mr. Kevin McCourt was appointed Director-General the following month.

The new Director-General arrived on 1st January 1963—one year after the opening of the television service.

A Kerryman, his career had been in the business field—as successor to Erskine Childers as Secretary to the Federation of Irish Manufacturers; later as a founder member of the Industrial Development Authority and as a Director of Carrolls, the cigarette manufacturers. Immediately before his appointment to Telefís Éireann he had been vice-president in charge of international operations in a firm based in The Hague. He had had no previous experience in radio or television.

Again, there were public questions about his salary, about his expenses and the provision of a house for him by the Authority. It was stated in the Dáil by the Minister for Posts and Telegraphs that Mr. McCourt's salary was to be £5,500 per annum with an official motor car and a contribution to insurance for superannuation. Free housing, it transpired, was not being provided for the Director-General. He was to have a house at an economical rent, and the rent was fixed at £500 per annum.

There was little understanding that the kind of experienced executive needed for a growing enterprise of this character simply could not be engaged at the Irish 'rate for the job'. In fact, we can say authoritatively that Mr. McCourt accepted the appointment at a scale of remuneration that involved a considerable personal loss.

There were, we believe, more than 300 applications received for the post of Programme Controller to replace Michael Barry. Gunnar Rugheimer was appointed to the job in March 1963 and took up office shortly afterwards.

* * *

> '... impartiality is fundamental to the concept of a national service; a complementary duty, which must equally be recognized, is to bring issues of controversy and debate before the public'.

The Authority tried to clarify:

> '... it is of the greatest importance that all necessary steps be taken to ensure that conflicting interests and viewpoints shall be fairly represented[9].'

\* \* \*

Ominously this was the broadcasting situation into which Kevin McCourt and Gunnar Rugheimer stepped early in 1963. These two men were to work in tandem for the next three and a half years—a period of pressure, advance and continuing contradictions.

> *Man is a political animal.*
> —ARISTOTLE

Gunnar Rugheimer had come from television broadcasting in Canada where he had worked since 1947 as a Producer and later as Programme Director of the CBC English language television network. Subsequently he moved to the Music Corporation of America's London office. He had visited Ireland in connection with sales of television programmes, which our station was negotiating with MCA.

The two men made an interesting contrast of temperament and style. Kevin McCourt was fastidious and dapper, gifted in organisational ability, a Daniel in money matters, and, according to those who knew him well, a man of charm, humour and imagination—and something of a dreamer. If he had an Achilles heel, it was a certain sensitivity which may have laid him open, in his role as a representative of broadcasting, to the thin winds of Dublin society's backbiting gossip.

---

9   Annual Report 1962-63

He was an experienced and shrewd business administrator. When he was able to maintain the necessary stolid detachment, he was a good judge of people and their capabilities. Like many men whose experience was derived from the competitive field of commerce, the subtle bonds of *esprit de corps* and corporate loyalty to dependent subordinates, whom he did not personally know, were not instinctive to him. This is not to say that Mr. McCourt was by nature a disloyal superior but, rather, that a conflict of loyalties was resolved for him within a framework of priorities. These were determined for him by consideration of the greatest good of the greatest number and not by any instinct to protect those for whose dissident judgments he was responsible. This was to have unfortunate consequences for him in the years which followed.

Gunnar Rugheimer, his Controller of Programmes, was of a different piece altogether. A large man—physically and mentally —he was a political animal; forthright, vigorous and inventive. His deepest interest was in Current Affairs, News and topical events, which he regarded as the nerve centre of a broadcasting service. He was a strong man who enjoyed and was used to all the demands on stamina and nervous energy which the daily slog of television makes. He required the same commitment from others and could be merciless when he regarded their performance as falling below standard. If he had an Achilles heel, this was it. His decisiveness, in a society that abhors it, built up for him a reputation for ruthlessness. As a foreigner, he knew his time was limited. Dealing largely with an untried production staff, he saw his task as one of testing each of his subordinates to find their breaking-point. He encouraged strength where he found it. He rammed vagueness and indecision against the wall. He made many enemies, but he also made good friends. His personality pervaded not only the station but its whole output.

The first years of the McCourt-Rugheimer partnership produced many changes, both in organisational terms and in the tone and volume of programmes.

\* \* \*

The Kennedy visit had been announced just about the time of the new Controller's arrival. This left very little time for preparation. The coverage, if it was to do justice to what the nation expected, would be a major event. In these circumstances, Michael Barry agreed to remain temporarily as Controller of the normal run of programmes, while Gunnar Rugheimer ran the Kennedy operation.

The station had only one Outside Broadcast Unit and with this, and some additions, it could field six television cameras. Estimates of what could be done by these available resources were either conservative to the point of futility or imaginative to the point of impracticability. Rugheimer decided that more equipment was necessary. He just went and got it, with the co operation of the BBC.

The visit was finally covered by thirty cameras, at least three times as many sound inputs and a large research, script and commentating team—as well as a number of film camera-units working both for the News Division and for the Programmes Division.

This was probably the first large foreign sales/exchange effort on the part of Irish television. Stations in America, Britain and the Continent wanted coverage of the visit and shipments of video-tape and film went twice and three times daily from Dublin and Shannon.

Plans were co-ordinated by Rugheimer himself, Jack White, Head of Public Affairs, Padraig Ó Raghallaigh, Head of Presentation, Pearse Kelly, Head of News, and, on the engineering side, Phil Parker and Tom Hardiman who was in charge of the Outside Broadcast operations. The enterprise must have given the new Controller a sharp insight into the workings of his organisation and into the mettle of his production staffs.

Co-operation between the Programmes and the News Divisions was perhaps closer during Rugheimer's time than before or after.

* * *

The Head of News, Pearse Kelly, had been a professional newspaper man in Dublin as Editor of the Evening Herald. He was now responsible for the work of a large number of journalists on both the radio and television news services. The Newsroom is always a sensitive pressure point in a broadcasting service, and it was Mr. Kelly's business to face the consequences when Ministers and politicians of all parties rang up to protest, which they frequently did. This may have made him, understandably, nervous of his own staff. A lack of candid communication between them and their chief may have led to a recalcitrance on their part. The suggestion was made at the time to bring the News Division under the responsibility of the Programme Controller. This did not materialise.

The News Division had its internal professional and Trade Union difficulties which resulted in a strike in March which lasted for six weeks. This industrial action was not supported throughout the house; this led to further strains. Mr. Jack White resigned his membership of the National Union of Journalists—a socially representative act in a sense that couldn't have been foreseen. It was, we suggest, the first tiny fissure which later widened into a distinction between management and workers more proper to private than to public enterprise. It also had the unfortunate result of leaving him unprotected in an area where the equivocal position of Public Affairs programmes, of which he was Head, was determined by the ambiguities of the Act and the ambivalent constitution of the Authority.

Mr. Kelly's position was equally, if not more, difficult.

The avoidance of personal unpleasantness, failure on all sides to meet problems face-on, and a damping down of the situation by pragmatic solutions of particular problems undoubtedly had much to do with the sense of unease and bad morale which existed in the News Division and continues to this day.

The professional traditions of the News staff derived from the procedures of newspaper offices in Dublin and the Provinces. They were not always readily adaptable, we understand, to the conditions of television newsrooms. The background and intellectual training and formation was literary rather than visual and the structures of control and responsibility often had different requirements in the two media. They carried into television one asset of enormous advantage which the Irish public do not always sufficiently appreciate: a high professional integrity. There had never been a 'gutter' press in Ireland and the whole bias towards sensationalism, so characteristic of certain levels of reporting in Britain and the US was totally foreign to the radio and television News staff.

McCourt and Rugheimer now had to face the strategy of steering an Autumn programme schedule through the Board. They had to overcome difficulties of re-organisation which this output was going to need. McCourt's attitude at that time was: 'Look, I know about money and organisation. I'll look after that. You know about programming; you tell me what's needed and we'll get it between us.' There was now a triumvirate: Eamonn Andrews, McCourt and Rugheimer. They had a common attitude to broadcasting.

The financial situation looked healthy enough. Income from television advertising was almost twice as much as income from television licences, a relationship which has remained more or less until the present. There was an increase in the licence fees, from £4 to £5 for a combined television and sound licence and from 20/- to 25/- for a sound licence only, in Autumn 1963. This created an income expectancy for the coming year that was quite comfortable, bearing in mind the continuing rise in advertisers' interest.

By September 1963 some changes had already been made in the structures of organisation. There were now seven divisions. Administration, including Services and Finance, headed by John Irvine; Personnel, headed by Hugh Duffy; Phil Parker had been made Director of Engineering with John O'Keeffe as his deputy and George Waters as his assistant; Sales and Promotion, managed by John Talbot; News Division (radio and television) was headed by Pearse Kelly; Radio Programmes, with Roibeard Ó Faracháin as Controller; and Television Programmes controlled by Gunnar Rugheimer.

In the Television Programmes Division, Jack White was promoted to Assistant Programme Controller. He still retained responsibility for Current Affairs. Pádraig Ó Raghallaigh had moved up from Presentation to be the second Assistant Controller. A programming group consisting of Rugheimer, White, Kelly and Ó Raghallaigh came into being and produced its first plan for an Autumn programme schedule to carry the station through 1963-64.

> *When we speak of 'the necessity for the protection of the Irish nation' we mean it not as a protest against imitating what is best in the English people, for that would be absurd, but rather to show the folly of neglecting what is Irish.*
> —DOUGLAS HYDE

The idea was to create a programme service which was to give a closer, more accurate and up-to-date reflection of Irish life. Rugheimer saw TE as a national electronic newspaper, in which the topics of the day would be given prime treatment. Features, sports interests, entertainment interests, business interests would be satisfied as well. Its bias was frankly informative, even educational, in as entertaining a fashion as possible. It was hoped that this would bring about a closer identification of the station with a diversity of audiences and their needs and, at the same time, reduce the dependence of the service on imported film. The vast bulk of this imported material was still coming from America, due to copyright and language difficulties. There was considerable unease, among programme-makers and Authority alike, about its indifferent quality and its outlook on life.

The new policy was, by reducing the amount of foreign entertainment films, to increase the possibilities for making a more critical selection of the films which unavoidably would still have to be bought. At the same time, it was intended to make greater use of Eurovision for programmes with a non-American bias. The strange fact was (and remains) that the Government, the Authority and the Irish public were unconvinced that these imports were necessary at all. But they would not agree to cutting down transmission hours.

There was simply no public realisation of what a gluttonous medium television is. It devours talent, energy, money and ideas nightly for 365 nights a year—perennially. No production system anywhere in the world can meet television's mindless and voracious needs. The sad thing is that the 'needs' are created by this view of the medium.

The intention of the new schedule was to diminish this appetite by providing special-interest programme nights.

Its main features were to be liveliness and informality. It would run five nights a week, Monday to Friday inclusive, from 6 p.m. to 11 p.m. Children's programmes which were transmitted before six o'clock did not fall under the scheme; nor did Sports programmes, nor News. These would, however, co-operate closely at the planning stage in order to obtain the fullest integration.

Newscasts were to be more frequent and shorter and would be transmitted at rigidly set times. The remainder of the evening would be filled as fluidly as possible; not fixed to half-hour or one-hour 'slots'.

> *Sunday was dedicated to the*
> *mystery of the Holy Trinity,*
> *Monday to the Holy Ghost,*
> *Tuesday to the Guardian Angels,*
> *Wednesday to Saint Joseph,*
> *Thursday to the Most Blessed Sacrament of the Altar,*
> *Friday to the Suffering Jesus,*
> *Saturday to the Blessed Virgin Mary.*
> —JAMES JOYCE

Each night would have its own special character, with a host to give it a personality and develop its theme:

> **Monday** would have a rural flavour. Programmes of information and technical instruction to farmers; provincial news-reels; reviews of the provincial press; programmes featuring the activities of rural organisations and the social aspect of country life would get special treatment.

***Tuesdays*** would have a leaning towards the sciences, the arts (including drama and nature study); serious music and, maybe, good jazz.

***Wednesday*** would impress an accent on young people's interests and needs. Programming would be fairly light-hearted, with pop music and dancing, though not ignoring the interests of serious young people. It would include student debates, advice on careers and so on.

***Thursday*** the general theme was to be current affairs, politics, comment, foreign affairs, features, documentaries, political interviews and discussions.

***Friday***, family night, covering the special interests of women; housekeeping affairs, Monica Sheridan's cookery, consumer information, fashion spots—a family series or serial.

***Saturday*** and ***Sunday***: On these nights the magazine format would be dropped and there would be a leaning to entertainment programmes, such as feature films, to start early. This was to be made possible by moving the News back to eight o'clock. There was also an idea to run a dance in Studio 1, with a top band and dancers from clubs around the country in order to get, as one memorandum of the time noted, 'the ordinary people involved with us and our "Crystal Palace", seeing it as theirs too'.

It was hoped to get as much 'live' Sport as possible on Saturday afternoons and again on Sundays. On Sunday night News would be earlier, again at eight o'clock, in order to allow the night's programming to be built around two main entertainment features, possibly a quiz and a ballad-singing contest.

Rigid programme departments, already in existence, were to be 'softened up', except for Drama, Children's and Sports Departments. Producer-Directors would emerge in new groups with project-teams of Production Assistants. Interviewers, Scriptwriters, Researchers. Three such groups, each with an Editor in charge and an Executive working Producer, were planned.

Team One was to be responsible for *Monday* and *Friday* nights. It had P. P. O'Reilly as Editor, Edith Cusack as Assistant Editor and Michael Johnston as Executive Producer.

Team Two was to be responsible for *Tuesday* and *Thursday* nights. It had Pat Kearney as Editor and Denis O'Grady as Executive Producer.

Team Three was to have responsibility for *Wednesday, Saturday,* and *Sunday* nights. For this team James Plunkett Kelly was Editor and Burt Budin was Executive Producer.

The Drama Group was headed by Jim FitzGerald and was a permanent group, with Bill McCrow as a permanent designer.

Maev Conway was Head of Children's programmes. It remained an entity also.

An Outside Broadcast group was formed.

The ramifications of the new programming ideas were viewed in many quarters with apprehension and alarm. More office accommodation would obviously be needed. Great demands would be made on the administrative section, on the typing pool, on the section responsible for contracting artists, on car parks.

Rugheimer had discovered, shortly after taking up his duties, that the studio capacities and machine-loading were underemployed. His new plan was determined to use them to their limits.

This profoundly affected the engineering personnel who rose to the occasion manfully and gained an increase in their staff establishment to cope with the new load.

The scheme came to be known as 'vertical' planning and went into operation in the Autumn. It had, of course, undergone a number of changes and refinements in the course of implementation.

> *Victory lies with him who can get there firstest with the mostest.*
> —GENERAL FORRESTER

The first and obvious thing to be said about this plan is that it was a good idea.

The second thing to be said is that the Irish tendency to mock at anything with which it is not familiar, may have led, both inside and outside the station, to a slow but inexorable return to the *status quo ante*.

Third, the plan perhaps required too many factors to mesh at the same time. It was one thing to gather together a bunch of people to storm the Bastille. It was another to ask them to storm it 365 nights of a year and then begin all over again. A team of crack professionals might have done it, if they had been able to form themselves into ad hoc groups and be masters of their own resources. The difficulty with any large organisation (and Telefís Éireann was getting larger every day) is that it tends to preserve its life as *an organisation* at the expense of the very work which it is organised to do.

Eventually the needs for orderliness in the scheduling of engineering and technical crews, in the arranging of the work of administrators and secretaries, in the placing of time bought by advertisers, all tended to smother the very thing for which the plan itself had been set up.

It is possible, too, that the youth and inexperience of our personnel, 'long' on enthusiasm and dedication, 'short' on training and expertise, may have foundered on a plan of such imaginative scope and vision.

Our tendency to revert to the tried and familiar was irresistible.

Rugheimer's energy and clarity were not enough; he needed an enormous 'back-up' of enthusiastic and skilled staff who shared his view. They were not ready, and they never did share it, wholly.

All this was not to say that the plan was not a success. It was by no means a failure. It might well have grown into an organic thing had it been given a chance to start in a smaller way, and at a slower pace. For all that, it kept the public interested to the point where another 70,000 households wanted to see what was going on, and bought television licences and sets in order to find out.

* * *

Overall planning was run by the Programmes Planning Board, which now included the Head of Sport, Michael O'Hehir. Its composition was intended to ensure that attention would be given to all facets of the country's life and interests. It was to guide the overall planning of the service and to ensure balance on matters of opinion and sparkle in matters of interest; to stimulate the Producers and to review their suggestions and ideas. More important, besides looking after broad planning, the board was to keep the actual daily output under constant review.

Gunnar Rugheimer and Jack White involved themselves closely with Producers in an attempt to stimulate and develop them in the exercise of their own maturing programme judgments. This was seen by some as dictatorship, by others as participation. The Controller had, himself, a Producer's mind. Many of the programme ideas during the next months and years came from his office. Those Producers who were not intimidated by him were given responsibility. They were allowed to exercise it. Those who were intimidated by his energy and very un-Irish frankness of expression retired into an uneasy and, at times, defiant isolation. The general body of Producers carried on reasonably with their work, in the belief that 'the show must go on'.

\* \* \*

There were other new appointments and changes in the team system as it got under way. The teams became known as groups. Group A looked after weekend programming, including religion and entertainment, and was headed by Tom McGrath as Executive Producer. Group B, into which most of the Public Affairs and documentary programmes fitted, was headed by Michael Johnston.

Group C, with Denis O'Grady as Executive Producer, looked after family programmes, such as Home for Tea; young peoples' programmes; and eventually some religious programmes. The system of supervising Editors melted after the first months into thin air. P. P. O'Reilly moved on secondment to the 'Buy Irish' Campaign. Edith Cusack left to get married. Pat Kearney returned to production on agricultural programmes. James Plunkett Kelly became Executive Producer in charge of Special Projects.

\* \* \*

The expanding activities of the station required new personnel with special knowledge, experience and skills.

The appointment of Father Romuald Dodd was the first to be announced in November 1963.

Another important appointment on the religious programmes staff came in the middle of January 1964 when the Rev. Fergus Day became religious adviser for Protestant programmes.

In January 1964 a new Head of Drama was appointed. Chloe Gibson had been a distinguished Producer with the station in the early days, left, and had returned from London as a Drama Producer. She now replaced Jim FitzGerald who had resigned as Department Head some weeks previously.

Liam Ó Murchú, a higher executive officer in the Department of Health, and a prize-winning playwright in Irish, was appointed as Editor of Irish programmes early in 1964. He wrote the first Irish teaching programme for television—*Labhair Gaeilge Linn*— and co-operated with its first Producer, Michael Garvey, in its screen realisation. Later in the year Ó Murchú is quoted in The Irish Times as saying that the programme was 'designed to unfreeze the knowledge of Irish learnt in schools—we'll be using some very attractive actresses'. They did use some very attractive performers; it did 'unfreeze' some Irish learnt in schools.

The first agricultural adviser, Patrick Jennings, was appointed in March of 1964.

\* \* \*

*There are two kinds of attention, spontaneous and voluntary.*
*In spontaneous attention the object and the immediate motive of attention coincide, while in voluntary attention the object and the motive are distinct. We fix our attention on a difficult book, not because the book itself interests us, but because it will help us to acquire*

*knowledge which we desire for another motive.*
—J. F. DONCEEL

'The land of saints and scholars' has had a curious attitude to scholarship—and religion.

We have, as a people, a profound devotion to both—profound, indeed, to the point of passionate and partisan commitment.

It may seem like a cheap paradox to say that our attachment is one of loyalty rather than a labouring pursuit of the virtue of either.

There is nothing that we need more than education—sacred and profane. There is nothing we resist more violently than straightforward instruction in either.

On the other hand, there were and are changes of attitude clearly detectable to the broadcaster. Particularly among the lower income groups there was what W. B. Yeats called a 'self-improving' streak. This, of course, varied from disinterested curiosity to a straight-on-the-line determination to get on. The business of broadcasters is to be aware of and use these attitudes helpfully.

Television certainly and radio probably can be used in either of two specifically different ways:

> As 'closed circuit' information media;
> As an emergent art-form seeking its specific idiom.

We think that each is necessary in itself and each is essential to a national broadcasting service.[10]

The closed circuit use of television is its employment as an information medium in the same way as it might be used in a store or a hospital.

---

10   See chapter on Culture

It simply conveys information to limitless numbers of people. It has the same value as a telescope with the addition of sound. It brings the object closer than the unaided human eye can do. It is not the characteristic use of television, but it is important because it can be used on a national scale. Gunnar Rugheimer with Kevin McCourt's backing determined to use it in this role in two sectors: schools' education and agriculture.

In January 1964 Telefís Éireann announced its first plans for direct educational broadcasting on 'closed circuit' television used on this national scale. At a press conference to announce the proposed *Telefís Scoile* series, Mr. McCourt expressed the view that educational programmes should be made in Ireland for Irish teachers and Irish students and said that the success of the project depended on the teachers.

Investigations had been made among other broadcasting services and it was discovered that two possible attitudes had emerged. One was to provide an audio-visual *aid* to conventional school teaching. The other view was straightforwardly a teaching role. Both of these possibilities were what we have described as 'closed circuit' uses of the medium. In most countries television was regarded as an ancillary aid to education except in Italy where illiteracy is a special problem.

Plans were drawn up and approved by the Authority which merely stated as a first principle that Telefís Éireann would not get into the field of supportive enrichment but would try to do a job of direct teaching. The Minister for Education, Dr. Patrick Hillery, welcomed the plan, which at that stage was to transmit two forty-five minute programmes weekly, from January 1964. The yearly cost was to be £17,000 to the station.

The areas proposed were Physics and Chemistry, in parallel with the Intermediate Syllabus 'A' Schools Course.

There were two important reasons for going into these areas of education: television techniques could be used to prime advantage and there were shortages and weaknesses of teaching strength in just these subjects in the schools.

The Minister for Posts and Telegraphs decided that the Authority could only undertake schools broadcasting if it was financed from sources outside the Authority's own revenue, in other words, by the Department of Education. This held up the announcement of the plans and gravely embarrassed McCourt and the Authority who felt that Dr. Hillery might well see them as playing a double game: exciting his interest to the point of public commitment and then sending him the bill! McCourt believed the Department of Posts and Telegraphs to be wrong, not merely from the broadcasting point of view, but also because at that time the revenue situation in TE was good. It was felt that this cultural venture would take some of the taint off the commercial character of the station's activities.

However, the round was lost to the Civil Servants; the Department of Education footed the bill, and has been paying it ever since. This was to prove a mixed blessing. Many broadcasters regarded it as detrimental to the service. The Department of Education's calling the tune was now inevitable. So it turned out to be.

The vexed question of commercial advertising was evidently in the mind of the Authority at this time. Its compliance in plans to open up the schedule to more home-originated material gives some evidence that it was aware of its predicament. Perhaps, too, it had been affected by a tart reminder from Professor Moody in which, it was alleged, he had complained to his fellow-members that the mixture of the programme schedule had been conveyed to them by means of a promotional letter from the Sales Division to advertisers. These gentlemen's ears were very red.

This was reinforced by the fact that, it was reported, the Government was casting long looks at our output of 'cowboys and soapsuds'. This was felt to be due largely to the advertisers' requirements, who, because 'spots' were so expensive, wanted to make sure that their advertisements would go out before, during or after a 'pop' programme.

Why, asked The Irish Times, not have a radio station financed by revenue from the State? The Government, it went on, should not have direct control over RE.

Another report of the same time, November 1963, stated that the general impression in broadcasting circles, meaning, presumably, the Authority, was that opposition to more direct control from Government should be strong; however, it should not be explicit 'but diplomatic'.

In the Dáil on 23rd November 1963 the Minister, Mr. Michael Hilliard, referred to Government concern that programmes were not representing Irish culture fully. His listeners were reminded of the aims of the service—on the one hand to further national cultural aims, and on the other to remain a self-supporting commercial enterprise.

He had expressed similar views, on his own part, to people who, he knew, shared his concern for the quality of the service and the need that it be distinguishable from any other station. He, like Mr. Childers, was always listened to with respect by friends and opponents when he spoke about his feelings for the Irishness of broadcasting affairs. It was difficult to agree with either in his expressed view; it was impossible not to acknowledge the real depth of their concern.

Mr. Hilliard went on to say that it was with considerable misgivings that the Government had granted the Authority its present 'independence'. The Government might have to 'reconsider' its implications.

\* \* \*

*How do Jacobs get the figs
into a fig roll?
Who cares, Habibi, they're
gorgeous.*
—OVERHEARD

The Jacobs' Awards for outstanding television achievements had been instituted. These awards were given by a firm of Dublin biscuit manufacturers. The first was held in December of 1963. Ria Mooney, the celebrated Abbey actress and producer, refused to accept such an award as best actress. Jimmy O'Dea turned down his award on the plea that he had won too many! James Plunkett Kelly refused a nomination for an award on the grounds that as a writer he had never entered into any competition and the selection of nominees in different categories could place the artists in an invidious position.

*Angers that are like noisy
clouds have set our hearts
abeat.*
—W. B. YEATS

By the beginning of 1964 a new booster station had been opened in Cork, in order to improve reception in the Munster area. By the end of the year twelve other satellite transmitters had been brought into operation with the same end in view.

The contradictory aims of the service were now being raised insistently in public. Irish Actors' Equity complained of the underemployment of Irish actors, the range of Irish-made material, the meanness in setting fees by the two services.

A Dublin man, Proinsias Ó Mianáin, on 24th March 1964 was reported in the Dublin newspapers as having been jailed for refusing to pay his television licence, in protest against the Authority's attitude towards Irish language and culture on Telefís Éireann.

250 students marched from the Mansion House to protest about the poor standards of programmes and handed in a letter to the Director-General. Comhaltas Ceoltóiri Éireann called for more native music on RE.

Paddy Belton of Fine Gael asked that there should be a ban on British-produced commercials.

Bishop Michael Browne of Galway criticised Telefís Éireann for its attitudes towards Catholic missionary activities in African countries.

Mr. Dónall Ó Móráin, then Chairman of Gael-Linn, complained about nearly everything.

The Authority 'piped not one note'.

Gunnar Rugheimer denied giving in to political pressures. He was asked to comment on a remark in Dáil Éireann by Labour Deputy Jack McQuillan, referring to Mr. Eddie McManus: 'if Eddie says no, it's curtains for the show'. Rugheimer replied: 'We are completely independent'. We were. He was supported by Jack White and Pearse Kelly in this statement.

Kevin McCourt, at student debates and speaking to various institutions, defended 'canned' programmes and said that BBC also used them—*The Flintstones* and *Paladin* were, he said, as well known around the world as they were in Ireland.

The public was appreciative. It was critical. It was vociferous. The station was not apologetic or ashamed. It gave back as good as it got.

\* \* \*

## CHAPTER 1: A CAUTIONARY TALE

It cost the average viewer 3/4d per hour to watch television or listen to radio. In July 1964 a television surplus of income over expenditure was announced. Telefís Éireann was in credit to the tune of £258,000 and radio was afloat with £14,000 to spare.

In a leader in *The Irish Times*, a few days later, it was remarked:

> 'while progress has been made, the inanity of some of the interviewing on TE is beyond belief ... TE has failed, we think, to get down properly to the recruitment and training of its own staff'

\* \* \*

There were new programmes that Autumn of 1964 which now seem part of the national landscape: *Newsbeat*, a news-magazine programme running five nights a week; a serial about a farming family—*The Riordans*; the Irish language refresher course mentioned earlier—*Lubhair Gaeilge Linn*; *On the Land*, for the farming community. Ireland for the first time entered the Eurovision Song Contest in which Dickie Rock was to sing us into fourth place at Luxembourg the following year. There were some special projects; one, an hour-long programme on Éamon De Valera—and a visual autobiography of Jimmy O'Dea.

In *Teen Talk*, young people talked about themselves and current topics; *The Professors* sat around in leather chairs and pronounced on weighty matters. Serious music (always difficult on television) was offered a grain of incense once a month on a programme called *Music in View*. In variety there was to be *Music Hall* with Joe Linnane; the *Showband Show*; *Cover Story*, a quiz; *Melody Fair*, with the R.E.L.O., and *Jamboree*, an Irish style Country and Western programme. '

There was to be a television workshop for new actors and writers on the Drama side and a new series, under Public Affairs, entitled *Open House*, an outside broadcast programme for local communities with a politicians' panel to answer questions. Weekly Current Affairs were handled in depth in '64. *The Changing Face of Ireland*, an occasional series, was intended to look at the economics of the country in its social context; and a series—*As Others See Us*, would provide films about Ireland made by foreign companies, with a panel of Irish people to comment.

The *Late Late Show* was coming back, with Frank Hall in the chair. Gay Byrne, its first Chairman, was working in London, first with Granada, then with the BBC. He was to bring his loved-and-hated touch back to the show the following Spring.

\* \* \*

> *I withstood him to his face.*
> —ST. PAUL

The station now got itself into hot water with the Government over a Public Affairs programme in the '64 series on the turnover tax. Mr. Lemass insisted that the programme had shown an anti-Government bias and that a 'make-good' programme be devised.

Kevin McCourt went to see Mr. Lemass and stood his ground. The Taoiseach was told that if he insisted on this McCourt would call the Authority into emergency session immediately.

The matter was dropped and no 'make-good' programme was in fact transmitted.

\* \* \*

# CHAPTER 1: A CAUTIONARY TALE

*These are glorious times for
the engineers.*
—JAMES NASMYTH C1850

During 1964, Mr. McCourt and his executives had been taking a close look at the organisation of the service. Staff figures now ran at over a thousand and this inevitably posed problems, many of which had not been satisfactorily solved.

During 1965 the Director-General decided to call in the services of Dr. Bill Murray, a research consultant, to investigate the existing structures and their relationships and make proposals for change and improvement where it might prove necessary.

A long investigation in great detail ensued.

The main outcome of his proposals was to move all of those services and facilities which were most immediately related to programme-making out of the Engineering Division into the Programme Division.

This was done under a Steering Committee comprising Vincent Finn, the Financial Controller, and Tom Hardiman, Head of Studio and Outside Broadcasting Operations, working with a firm of independent consultants.

This new Engineering group was called 'Production Facilities'. Hardiman was in charge of it. He had the title of Assistant Controller—Production Facilities, reporting to the Controller of Programmes (Television).

The Production Facilities Group was to have five departments for actual programme servicing and a sixth, Planning and Control, which would be, as its title suggests, a centre for assessing the implications of programme decisions in money, production resources, manpower and scheduling. The Group would also maintain administrative cost control procedures for the whole Programmes Division.

All the services, artistic and technical, that were needed to make a programme were incorporated into this Group: design, lighting, cameras, floor-managers, vision-mixers, contracts and casting, film production, studios and outside broadcasting unit, etc.

The investigation, proposals and planning for these changes took almost two years to implement fully. They continued, in the interim, to exercise an influence on the conduct of events.

The new system worked well, partly because it was logical, partly because the Controller of Programmes was a strong man, partly because his new assistant was gifted in organisation, had long contact with programme-makers in both services and knew the plan inside out; partly because the News Division's demands on resources were at that time confined to four film cameramen and some part-time freelance 'stringers' around the country. There was, in those days, a predictable duration for Newscasts, either in the small Studio 3 or in the Newsroom itself. This was also being used as a News studio. These film cameramen continued to operate under the direction of the News Division. One cameraman who had been working for the Sports Department remained in that capacity.

The only part of the operation which was untouched by any new system was the 'creative' side of production. Here, to be sure, changes had already taken place and the groups, in principle, remained.

With the passage of time, and the comings and goings of Producers and their swapping over from group to group, the 'vertical' system began to revert, over the next couple of years, to a semi-departmental system. The group edges became blurred. The specific identity that each night's programming was intended to have, ceased to be clear. In any event, the consultant's work stopped short of a re-organisation of the Producers. The Irish passion for formlessness was well under way. The artists' splendid disregard for fixed organisational structures permitted the administrators' need for departmentalism to grow where the Executive Producer was an administrator, and to collapse where he was an artist.

To the Producers it didn't seem to matter; the programmes were made. The girl Production Assistants kept order and calm. The Programme Controller kept up the impetus of the attack on the real target, production.

There were, during 1965, a number of wage claims and strike threats (as well as an actual, if brief, strike, again by the Newsroom's journalists). There were demands by Producers, Production Assistants and film editors. In one case conciliation machinery was put into effect. But this was all done without rancour in the Programmes Division. It was even found difficult to get sufficient numbers to a meeting in order to back the vigorous wage claims that were being made by Jim Plunkett Kelly and the usual small number of public-spirited enthusiasts.

A report by Eric Spain, manager of Engineering Planning and Equipment, on foot of a visit to three Scandinavian television stations, made a number of invidious comparisons between the scale, size and kind, of their operation and our own.

Spain's report suggested:

1. the use of joint industrial committees for management and staff;
2. the use of close working committees for building development;
3. the wide use of large specialist technical departments, based on the idea that RE is the basis for any future national electronic industries;
4. regular meetings with formal minutes and questions;
5. proper rest facilities;

6. the provision of an engineering information officer to keep the public informed about new transmitters, reception difficulties and so on;
7. the provision of safety engineers and committees—to ensure the protection of staff and members of the public who came into the studios.

Some of these recommendations were implemented, many were ignored.

\* \* \*

What were known as 'brain-storming' sessions were held by the Controller in the Montrose Hotel with key members of the programme staff. Secrecy is traditionally difficult among communicators. These were, in the cliche phrase, 'both frank and open discussions'.

RE's agricultural adviser, Paddy Jennings, had been on secondment from Local Government by way of protracted leave of absence. He was to help to lay the foundations of RE's agricultural policy. His relaxed studio manner and ability to deal with rural people and his great personal charm made him popular both inside and outside the station. His return to his duties in his original professional role was a matter of real regret. He continued to be associated as agricultural adviser to *The Riordans* for the remainder of the season.

By the middle of March 1965, Justin Keating had been appointed editor of agricultural programmes. He was a gifted and original research scientist in the agricultural field and he already had an established reputation in TCD. He had a deep social commitment and was to prove a brilliant acquisition as a creative television programmer. Four days later, Joe Murray was appointed as his assistant.

Plans which had been under discussion between Telefís Éireann, the Department of Agriculture and various farming groups around the country were reversed by a new plan which Keating put forward and which, after some resistance, was agreed. This was *Telefís Feirme*. It was to become one of RE's most brilliant social programme experiments. It had an almost immediate and deep effect on Irish farming attitudes and practice.

Meanwhile there was the General Election of April 1965 to be handled. Politicians, extraordinarily touchy at the best of times, tend to become even more sensitive around election time. However, all the arrangements were finally hammered out for the party political broadcasts: who should get how many programmes, in what proportion, on what nights.

Predictions of television dullness and disaster were common on political broadcasting. The critics had an even more depressed anticipation of this event. Ken Gray wrote:

> My own guess is that we will have a series of party political broadcasts as dull and unexciting as anything we have seen to date, with potential T.D.s stolidly using the electronic camera and teleprompter in much the same way as they have used the back of a lorry and the crumpled, rain-sodden bundle of notes in elections of bygone, pre-television days

As Fianna Fáil's seven, Fine Gael's five and Labour's two campaign broadcasts on television wore inexorably on, the predictions were fulfilled. The only politician discovered as having any flair for the medium was Mr. Charles J. Haughey, Minister for Justice. He was described as relaxed and informal: 'he must have won a few votes with the only touch of humour yet introduced—the prefacing of his message to vote for his party with the phrase "And now the commercial..." '

The election itself was given full coverage in News and Public Affairs comment. The first of the marathon election programmes was mounted, John O'Donoghue unflappable in the chair, with results coming in through the night.

This time the critics were pleasantly surprised. 'The whole mammoth programme—all ten hours of it—was full of interest, never dull or boring. Most important of all, it cannot have failed to increase the political consciousness of the nation.'

The results were foreseeable and were foreseen. Fianna Fáil came back to power. There was a new Minister for Posts and Telegraphs, Mr. Joseph Brennan.

The first Authority ended its undistinguished legal life in May.

> *Soldiers of the Legion of the Rearguard!*
> —I.R.A SONG

Four of its members, Ernest Blythe, Charles J. Brennan, Áine Ní Cheannain, and George Crosbie, were replaced by Mrs. Sean T. O'Kelly, wife of the former President Seán T. O'Kelly, Ruairí Brugha, son of the Republican hero, Cathal Brugha; Michael Noonan, a former President of Macra na Feirme, and Donall Ó Morain, Chairman of Gael-Linn.

Much criticism had occurred about the use of the Irish language in programmes, both from private citizens and from public national institutions. Dónall Ó Móráin had more than once criticised this aspect of the service—and his appointment, too, was seen as a concession to this point of view. At least he was now assimilated into the system and would himself be at the receiving end and be responsible for whatever Irish policies the Authority adopted.

The new Authority was to have a life of one year. This was in order to allow a review of the Broadcasting Authority Act. Legislation, it was believed, was in draft form.

In the event, there was no legal change of any great importance. An amendment in 1966 changed the name of the service from Telefís Éireann to Radio Telefís Éireann and made some changes in the arrangements for yearly audit and for the distribution and exchange of programme material, including the provision of services 'for and on behalf of Ministers of State'.

Eamonn Andrews remained Chairman of the Authority.

*The House of Peers, through-*
*out the war,*
*Did nothing in particular.*
*And did it very well.*
—SIR WILLIAM S. GILBERT

At a meeting with this Authority in June 1965, Mr. Brennan the Minister, complimented the outgoing Board on the success of its broadcasting over the past five years and made special reference to the really successful way in which they had handled revenues and expenditures. The more a State body depended upon the Government and on the Exchequer for assistance, he told them— particularly financial assistance—the more the Government and the State Departments would seek a voice in its affairs.

He enjoined strict impartiality upon them. The Government sometimes felt that the Authority was not quite aware of this responsibility. They must beware of allowing their interviewers to put the wrong answers in the mouths of persons being interviewed.

On the cultural side, he was not looking for 'crash' Irish programming but rather would prefer to see television brought to the stage at which it was processed with a distinctive Irish tone and character. This kind of service, he explained, could have been given if the Government had decided that there need be no commercials on television.

But, for good reasons, he said, advertisements were necessary.

Nevertheless, it was the duty of the Authority to arrange programmes so that they did not play up to commercialisation. He saw the difficulties all right but felt that the members of the Authority, who had his complete confidence, would not fail to surmount these difficulties.

He congratulated them on what they had done in this regard in the past and said that they had made some lovely programmes. Their task would now be to fuse two objectives; independence in money matters, and culture.

He recommended to the Authority absolute co-operation within itself, outspoken opinions, collective decisions and the tying up of all loose ends. Cabinet decision-making was, he remarked, of this kind and he commended the thought to the Authority. He hoped always to be able to work in harmony with the Authority and undertook not to interfere in their very responsible work.

On this admonitory note of reflecting a dynamic, progressive Ireland, without plunging into any major changes which might be dangerous, the Minister's participation in their meeting ended.

*  *  *

If the Authority was disconcerted by this extraordinary discourse from their Minister, they failed to keep it to themselves. Everyone knew all about it within twenty-four hours.

An Authority which accepted and even reflected views such as these and advocated the pursuance of them, views which charged it with the task of fusing the incompatible into a coherent programme policy, was obviously going to split from stem to stern.

That they remained together, at least on the surface, was largely due to the teamwork of Eamonn Andrews, Kevin McCourt and Rugheimer—and below them, to the ingenuity, nerve and hard slogging of production staffs and crews. There were now open divisions within the Authority. Mr. Eddie McManus and Mr. Ó Móráin became mutually surprised allies in opposition to their Chairman. Professor Moody was also occasional make-weight. Ó Móráin pressed for Irish popular programmes and Moody for serious culture—particularly music and history.

Irish radio and television was now producing an output comparable, roughly, in quantity to that of its British competitors on routine evening schedules; but at one-tenth the cost. None of this prevented the public from continuing to fling brick-bats, many of them cranky, some constructive and well-founded. Most Producers are self-critical anyway and almost childishly anxious to know what the people think of their work.

*\*\**

Imagine a distraught Producer, his discussion programme carefully organised, coming in to his desk in the studio block. He would push past Frank Hall with a bundle of provincial newspapers on his way to the carpark to write his script, in his car, for that evening's Newsbeat. He would enter a room about fifty by thirty feet. At one end, a group of intense and concentrated people would be beating out the time to a Showband tape-recording, stopping and starting it again and again, in search of a good 'cut-in' point for a programme. The noise would be unbelievable. At another desk, another Producer would be conducting a telephone conversation in Irish with a shy piper in Kilrush. Three or four other production teams would be trying to concentrate on their special problems. Everywhere, Production Assistants and clerk-secretaries would be typing out incomprehensible camera-scripts, replies to complaints, financial estimates, prop lists and polite postponements of programme suggestions about the emigration habits of wild duck.

Our Producer would make his way to his own desk, riffle through the desperately urgent messages beside his telephone while his Production-Assistant was informing him that his star performer for that night was down with tonsillitis. Not to worry; she, with the characteristic calm and resource of her kind, had short-listed three experts on thatching cottages on the Western seaboard. Three rapid telephone calls added to the pandemonium. Could Mr. Exe come to the studio? Yes, yes. Straight away? Terribly sorry but that is the way television is made. Yes, they could meet in the main hall and discuss it over a cup of coffee in the canteen. Of course, of course, a taxi could be sent down straight away.

Our Producer would say three quick 'Hail Marys' that Mr. Exe was as talkative as he was learned and that he had no ambitions as an amateur Producer himself.

At the reception door of the studio block Mr. Sean Exe would turn out to be a modest, scholarly man. They would make their way up the spiral staircase into the canteen, throwing a startled glance to three nuns sitting on bentwood chairs in the lobby, their skirts drawn up to their green-stockinged knees, smoking like chimneys and arguing about a straight flush.

A troupe of girls in glittering tights mingling inconsequentially in the doorway with a group of Swedish folk dancers would cause a momentary blockage in the traffic. On entering the canteen, which had no windows, a queue, three-deep, stretched from the door to the service counter as it shuffled animatedly forward.

Mr. Exe and the Producer would already have begun their conversation on thatching patterns and means of securing the roof-tree against Atlantic storms.

At one table Jim FitzGerald, fresh from producing a play in the Gate Theatre and now planning a drama for television, would be engaged with the Rev. Romuald Dodd, O.P., and Tony Barry, senior cameraman, in an argument on the five proofs for the nonexistence of God.

Luke Kelly of the Dubliners at another table would share fish and chips and views on the validity of eighteenth-century political ballad forms with Christy Killeen, Mike Slevin and a bevy of girls from Accounts. Mike would inevitably bring the conversation round to the success of streamer-flies for trout-fishing on Loch Sheelin.

At a top table, three Cavaliers and two ladies in crinolines would eat sausage and mash with baked beans while Producer Peter Kennerley, in cavalry twill trousers and a knitted cardigan, would hold a ferocious conversation with Stuart Hetherington about some film stock that had been temporarily mislaid at Dublin Airport and finally turned up in the Drama Department in Airfield House.

The queue was now passing a rumour back about someone who, it was alleged, had been beaten to death by cocktail glasses the night before. Mr. Exe laughed uproariously—but completely missed the point.

A floor manager would break his way through the queue, scoop up the Cavaliers and their ladies from their baked beans, and exit.

John Cowley and the cast of *The Riordans*, away from rehearsals in town for a costume fitting at the studios, mixed incongruously with the cast of *Tolka Row*, let out from the bowels of Studio One for a tea-break, around a table presided over by Charles Mitchel.

Mr. Exe and our Producer, coffee sloppily in hand, would now be ensconced at a half-vacated table. Mr. Exe suddenly declared his adamant opinion that the slides that the Producer had shown him would not suffice. Eddie McEvoy (with thirteen photographs of thatched cottages) materialised; a graphic artist busily sketched the method of tying down thatch in a gale; the Production Assistant noted busily what was being decided; a designer drank coffee busily and the lighting director altered his lighting plan busily. Mr. Exe was now developing his thesis on the migratory habits of thatchers in the nineteenth century at alarming length, in what he evidently saw as a fourteen-part serial.

A cool floor manager would politely break up the discussion and lead a bewildered Mr. Exe to the make-up room for 'a bit of a dust'. Mr. Exe's egghead shone somewhat.

He would suddenly find himself in a studio that looked like a mausoleum converted into a filmset, with suspended lamps and huge artillery-like cameras bearing down menacingly on three empty chairs. Men with lighting metres shouted incomprehensible instructions to someone who seemed to be in heaven. Sound men tinkered with microphones between the chairs. The Producer had totally disappeared. The floor manager introduced Mr. Exe to the chairman of the discussion, Mr. Brian Cleeve, and to Mr. 'Patch' Wye, the famous thatcher.

The floor manager would then ask them to take their places. Brian would try to keep them both relaxed. For some reason, everybody seemed keen to prevent them from discussing the programme before the recording started; this was just a technical rehearsal, you see. Mr. Exe and Mr. Wye would be asked to say a few words to test their voice levels. The 'top' and 'tail' of the programme would be rehearsed. Disconcertingly, then, the floor manager would ask them to go for a walk while further technical adjustments were made.

Returning to studio half an hour later in a state of delicately controlled nervousness, Mr. Exe and Mr. Wye would take their seats on each side of a bland Brian Cleeve. Brian would watch the floor manager who would begin a countdown from ten seconds to programme commencement. Mr. Wye would remind himself to sit upright in his chair; Mr. Exe would be careful not to kick the microphone, while Brian calmly and with awful relaxed casualness introduced them to their hundred thousand accusers, packed in serried ranks with sneering hostile faces—somewhere out there.

Somehow, and suddenly, the discussion was launched. Two lifetimes of close study and experience in the arts and sciences of thatching cottages seemed to be put through a meat grinder. Odd fragments of learning, detached from their vast sociological context, would somehow get caught up in the machinery. Within what seemed an outrageously inadequate time, the programme was over. Everything worth saying had been left unsaid, of course, but it was too late. The opportunity had passed forever. It was sadly obvious to Mr. Exe that the Producer had failed to realise the importance of the subject and had given it unworthy treatment. 'Was it all right?' he asked, however.

Mr. Wye was innocently astonished to discover that he was to be paid £5 for his trouble.

\* \* \*

For the Autumn schedule of 1965 new programmes were necessary. *Telefís Feirme* was finally launched, as was *The Course of Irish History* ,a bow to Professor Moody, maybe. A detective thriller, Ó Dúill, was launched in Irish—perhaps a reflection of Mr. Ó Moráin's new voice—or with the intention of pleasing him.

The Autumn schedules were always designed to open the new season with a flourish, to bring viewers back from their Summer sleep, increase audience ratings, and so increase advertisers' interest.

It was reported in a Dublin newspaper on the 24th September 1965 that an attempt to increase the cost of advertising by a scale ranging from 10 per cent to 25 per cent had been successfully resisted by two groups representing the advertising interests. These had made a joint delegation to the Director-General and got a promise that the increases would be reduced by 10 per cent until the end of the year.

The set count, upon which the advertising rate is based, had risen by almost 100,000 and, as the Authority was to say in its report for 1964-65, 'the increased advertisement charges are still lower than warranted by this growth'.

\* \* \*

> *Wheresoe'er I turn my view*
> *All is strange, yet nothing new;*
> *Endless labour all along,*
> *Endless labour to be wrong.*
> —SAMUEL JOHNSON

In a creative organisation, the administrator gradually forms the impression that he has his finger in a hole. If he takes it out for a moment, the deluge will pour in. The slow war of attrition to rationalise the organisation, to bring it up to date, to give it shape and a contact with the public, went on. Kevin McCourt had pioneered a number of changes and was to institute others, with the intention of ordering without destroying. In 1965 he set up an Audience Research Unit to amplify and give some qualitative assessment to the merely statistical TAM-rating system, and to be of assistance to Producers and programme planners. As he said at the inauguration of the Unit:

> No audience research can replace the need for creative thinking about programmes, and professional skill and judgment in planning and producing them. But it is a

unique link between the public and those who provide the programmes and, as such, it should be fully and wisely used.

It was well done but poorly used. Mr. Fred Littman and his staff have fashioned a fine instrument. RTE needs training to use such tools.

If programming stretched the studios beyond their capacity, the demands on the use of film cameras and the Outside Broadcast Unit were also enormous. In fact, RTE's experiments with the Unit pioneered new techniques in the use of electronic cameras and video-tape, in programmes like *The Riordans, Location*, etc.

It was frankly amazing that so much was possible with so little. During the 'vertical' programming schedules, an ancillary unit described by broadcasting people as a 'lash-up', using two cameras which had been removed from one of the studios, did an out-and-about type of programme series around Dublin. The need for more mobile equipment of this kind was clearly seen. In spite of suggestions to start with single camera-units, which would provide more mobility and flexibility, the tried and trusted was again reverted to. It was decided to buy another Outside Broadcast Unit, larger than the last, but with a greater range of equipment. Mr. Eric Spain, Project Engineer, and some Producers, had questioned the wisdom of this purchase on the grounds of its immobility. Time proved them right.

\* \* \*

*Having organised and trained her manhood through her secret revolutionary organisation...*[11]

---

[11] Proclamation of the Irish Republic, 1916

The spring of 1966 was the fiftieth anniversary of the 1916 Rising. It was now only six months away and planning was already advanced to celebrate the events. Again, the real cost had to be estimated. With the demands on time, resources and manpower that programming would make, some areas had to suffer. The chief victim was the Drama Department whose normal output of plays, about one a fortnight, was now cut back. Drama production was merged into an effort to achieve the most ambitious possible commemorative production. This was to be Hugh Leonard's scripted documentary drama of the Week of the Rising. It ate up huge amounts of money and facilities. Filming was directed by Michael Garvey. Studio and outside broadcast recordings were produced by Louis Lentin.

> *... having resolutely waited*
> *for the right moment to reveal*
> *itself ...*

It was in November 1965, while these plans for Easter 1966 were in preparation, that the criticisms of Rugheimer, already publicly voiced by Irish Actors' Equity, the Gaelic League and some Dublin newspapers, who had spoken darkly of 'foreigners' and 'foreign influence', began to be actively prosecuted by members of staff within the station.

A group of Producers, some at senior level and some Heads of Department, including James Plunkett Kelly, Maev Conway, Aindreas Ó Gallchóir, Jim FitzGerald and Padraig Ó Raghallaigh made representations to the RTE Trade Union Group who sent a memorandum to the Authority on 18th October. It complained about staff conditions, lack of facilities, overwork, the debasement of professional standards, and, in particular, the personal and professional qualities of the Controller of Programmes. The memorandum was published in part in The Irish Times on 4th November. 3

> *... strikes in full confidence of victory.*

The Authority ignored the letter and refused to have anything to do with it. They handed it to the Controller to deal with it in any way he saw fit.

The rot, however, had set in; there was an anti-Rugheimer lobby and it was to become increasingly effective.

He was naturally annoyed. He might justifiably have been surprised that his Producers had not made their corporate criticisms directly to him, particularly as these criticisms voiced complaints about his undue influence as a non-national; that he 'can and does dictate the content of our programme-schedules without the leavening influence of those who have a life-long understanding of national ideals and the Irish way of life'.

Some of the statements in the document were, he was advised, libellous.

Rugheimer's contract of employment, which had been for a three-year period, had been due to expire in June of 1966. It had had six months to run. He had indicated to Mr. McCourt his intention to leave Telefís Éireann, on expiry of his contract. The intervention on the part of his staff strengthened this resolve.

There were rumours and malicious gossip in the Dublin cocktail circuit to the effect that Gunnar Rugheimer was the man who really ran the station. These rumours which Rugheimer believed to be, and McCourt knew to be, false, nevertheless affected their working relationship. They may have unnerved McCourt. From Rugheimer's point of view he could see that such sentiments and attitudes were unlikely to improve the morale of the station.

A suit for libel, which he was being urged to take, would wreck the service both inside and out, and permanently damage working relationships among production staffs. Philosophically, he regarded it as part of the price he had to pay; some of the locals would get together and form a cabal. He was being paid to ride out that sort of affair. It was also clear that not all the staff was involved and that relationships must be mended rather than further marred. This proved in great measure possible. The hard core of the Producers who were active in complaining about their Controller, had transferred from radio at the outset of the television service. They continued to mutter about 'high-handed tactics', but this 'push' collapsed—for the moment.

\* \* \*

Jim Plunkett Kelly had been a Trade Union official in the Workers' Union of Ireland, and a member of the old Radio Éireann sound broadcasting staff. He is a short story writer, a playwright, novelist and musicologist. He is a man of wide and deep culture and very great talent.

Of complex character, he has simple and unaffected manners. In normal social and work intercourse, his style is gentle, even shy, although never aloof.

From his earliest years, he was a passionate admirer of the great Labour leader, 'Big' Jim Larkin, and a close friend and confidant of his son of the same name, who was also General Secretary of the Workers' Union of Ireland. Jim Plunkett Kelly is a man slow to make friends but with a great capacity for close and loyal affection where he can discover grounds for trust and a common area of sympathies.

His mind is that of an artist. Circumstances and his great compassion for the inarticulate and the defenceless often turned him, one feels reluctantly, into the field of action as a Trade Union militant. In such circumstances he was of resolute and often obstinate character.

In moments of crisis in the station, the years of back-breaking and painstaking work that he had devoted to the good of clerk-secretaries, Production Assistants, Producer-Directors and others, commanded their immediate and instant loyalty and respect. They simply knew him in action to be a man of principle, and they followed him.

No respecter of rank, he was intimidated by none and utterly indifferent to the personal consequences, on his own standing and fortunes, of any action that he thought it right to take.

He was capable under provocation, or in the presence of intellectual dishonesty, of a sudden blaze of frightening anger. It was followed almost at once by a remorse that invariably found expression in a generosity of withdrawal so evidently sincere and so respectful of the dignity of those he had offended that in a long career in broadcasting, packed with incident and conflict, it is true to say that he has few lasting antagonists and no enemies.

If he suffered a disadvantage of temperament, it was that of the novelist—a tendency to live and re-live and to flavour and assimilate the past into the pattern of his present experience.

* * *

In the debate on an administrative Amending Bill (to the Broadcasting Act) in the Senate in February 1966[12] there were, yet again, references to Telefís's pandering to what was popular for the sake of advertising revenue. There were critical references to drink and cigarette advertising, the revenue from which in the previous year had been £184,000 from drink and £176,000 from cigarettes.

---

12   Debate on the Broadcasting Authority (Amendment) Bill, 1966.

*The Hurler on the Ditch* came in for comment; political commentators shouldn't be allowed to make or break politicians and Governments, the way Telefís Éireann had allowed them to do. Far too close a tie-up was seen by some perceptive members between this programme and Backbencher.

In the Dáil debate, the same issues were raised. On the question of the filming or recording of Dáil debates, the Minister said he was totally opposed to this.

* * *

> *Knight to Queen's Bishop.*
> —CHECK

February was a busy month. There were 'incidents' on the *Late Late Show*. One such incident has passed into our folk mythology and is known as 'The Bishop and the Nightie'.[13]

The item had occurred on the programme on 12th February 1966, As part of a game, a husband was asked, among other things, to name the colour of his wife's nightie worn on their honeymoon. The husband replied that his wife's had been transparent. She, having been out of the studio while he was questioned, said when she returned, that she hadn't worn one at all. She discreetly changed her mind and said that it was white.

'Vigorous protests' arrived.

The Bishop of Clonfert asked members of his congregation to add their protests to his telegram, sent to Gay Byrne after the show on Saturday night.

---

13  Title of The *Irish Times* Editorial on the incident.

CHAPTER 1: A CAUTIONARY TALE

The nation was agog again a few weeks later. Brian Trevaskis, a student, on the *Late Late Show* abused both Galway's Cathedral and its Bishop, referring to the latter as 'a moron'. The studio audience waded in. Some didn't want to listen to degrading remarks about 'both our Church and our Bishops'. Another said that he was glad to see Trevaskis was not afraid to express his opinion, even if 'he spoke a bit harshly'; another thought Trevaskis was right in his criticism and agreed that Ireland had developed little since the Proclamation of 1916. A man in the audience told Gay Byrne that it was up to him to stop characters 'coming up here to slag the clergy'. Gay replied that he didn't bring people on to the programme to 'slag the clergy'. The programme was one in which free speech was allowed and the audience was entitled to disagree with anything that was said.

\* \* \*

*Knight to Bishop 2.*
—MATE

Trevaskis had objected to Galway people having to pay for a new Cathedral when they lacked such things as theatres or art galleries. He also criticised the Catholic Archbishop of Dublin over the dismissal of the Dublin school teacher and novelist, John McGahern.

The blandness of the Dublin Diocesan Press Office comment should take some beating:

> It would appear from newspaper reports that during the show Mr. Brian Trevaskis expressed his personal opinion on various subjects, including architecture, our primary schools' educational system, and social

services. The Archbishop of Dublin would have no comment to make on such personal opinions.

The Bishop of Galway was, as usual, more forthcoming. He would expect no more, he said, from a student of Trinity College.

Mr. Oliver Flanagan thought the *Late Late Show* was now 'an objectionable programme'.

Kevin McCourt said that he regretted remarks made on the show about the Bishop of Galway and the Archbishop of Dublin. There had been few such lapses during the four-year run of the programme. The show's whole essence depended on its being spontaneous. Those invited to take part were chosen in the belief that they would contribute in a fair-minded way. Without discounting their undesirability, such breaches as had been referred to had been few.

Trevaskis came on the show the following week and publicly apologised to the Bishop, in a stimulating programme which ploughed the same ground again!

The reactions of public groups, revered institutions and letter-writers had been righteously intense during both incidents, particularly over Trevaskis. It is interesting to compare that reaction with the outcry which followed another, a few years later on the same programme. This time it was the John Feeney affair, with Feeney saying much the same things as Trevaskis had said. It is a reflection of the changed times that it was not now Mr. Feeney who was unanimously castigated for his views, but Gay Byrne for his attack on Feeney's.

On this occasion, it was Mr. Byrne who was thanked by the Archbishop of Dublin.

Perhaps it is not unfair to suggest that the public was not as mindless as officials thought in their reaction to these affairs. It might simply be that the public will tend to defend *whoever* is attacked, whether he advocates murder or charity, cowardice or courage, integrity or depravity.

This may be deplorable but as the practical men say: 'it's a fact of life, let's face it'

The *Late Late Show* had been, since Michael Barry's era, a place where anybody could discuss virtually anything. The show had been planned as open-ended, spontaneous, topical and involved with the community. It has erratically but regularly done all these things. Without exaggeration, it can be said that the show has let some healthy air into dank and mouldering corners of Irish life. It has always been viciously criticised and lavishly praised. One hopes that it always will be. Its critics are its most ardent viewers.

> *The large corporation has been the leader in the retreat from risk.*
> —J. K. GALBRAITH

The felt-lined caterpillar tracks of order and administration moved inexorably on.

A Management Appreciation Conference held in a hotel in Greystones at the beginning of February was the second of its kind. The Irish Management Institute had been asked to run these courses by Kevin McCourt. It was certainly a useful idea to provide creative programming people with some grasp and insight into the techniques of management.

There were fifteen RTE participants drawn from Engineering, Administration and Sales. Four came from the radio and television Programmes Divisions. Subjects ranged from management techniques and the need for clearly articulated objectives to motivation theory. There were lectures on management control systems and quantitative methodology, group discussions and working groups—all of this over a weekend.

The four production people thought it was an Orwellian nightmare. Their characteristic defence-reaction was an amused 'sending up' of the whole mentality of 'scientific management'. They were profoundly wrong.

What is not clear is whether methods of business management developed by the Irish Management Institute, largely concerned with business and industry in the private sector, was readily adaptable to the needs of a broadcasting public service. Of course, RTE's commercial bias may have compounded the problem, since one could hardly have argued that RTE's work was a public service operation, except in the spirit of its professional broadcasters.

The manipulative methods of the management 'ethos' should not have seemed so out of place after all. Indeed, a list of the objectives of RTE seems to have emerged from these conferences. A dissertation, in 1967, on the allocation of resources for television programmes by Mr. George Waters[14] (then Head of Production Facilities), lists them in the following way:

a. from the broadcaster's point of view :
   1. maximise audiences
   2. maximise quality of programmes (*sic*)
   3. entertain
   4. inform
   5. educate

---

14   *The Allocation of Resources in the Production of Television Programmes* (unpublished dissertation), George Waters, 1967 (see Appendix II)

b. from the audience point of view:
   6. obtain maximum satisfaction
   7. minimum cost

The dissertation goes on to say that in the particular case of Radio Telefís Éireann the following objectives might be added to (a) above:

8. to maintain financial viability
9. to be impartial and objective in the presentation of programmes

If this was the order of priorities, it might be argued that RTE had already given up the ghost of the old Hag of Beara and was firmly planted in the commercial sector.

Creative people, always chary of systems, despite amused scepticism, were intrigued.

The truth is that the station's professional broadcasters *needed* skills for the management of complex machines and staff. A television programme, unlike a painting, is not made by a man working alone in a garret but by one who has at his fingertips the ability to handle intricate machines and even more complicated humans. Such courses, had they any sensitivity to our special problems, might well have been a means of liberating RTE staff from hindrance, time-wasting and drudgery. We did not need these techniques like a set of scalpels to be picked up and used mechanically. Above all, we did not need the neatly packaged and philosophically unexamined assumptions about man, work and society which this management 'philosophy' purveyed. It was horrible in its second-hand pretentiousness.

The greatest single blockage between the 'management' mind and the 'creative' one seems to be this: because the creative person decries quantitative managerial solutions, it is concluded that he is an anarchist with no regard for order. The truth is the opposite of this view. The raison *d'etre* of a creative person is the *organisation* of material—always of a conflicting kind—into an organic unity. As Virginia Woolf said: 'the artist consumes all impediments'[15].15

There is another fundamentally important characteristic of the creative person. His work is built on the concept of *communicating* with others, not *transmitting* at them. Again, this is a difference of approach from that expounded by conventional managerial theorists: to the artist, the communication is *always* multiple and complex, and always essentially ambiguous; never a refined one dimensional me-to-you transmission.

Of course, management theory will admit this: it will insist that communication is never brought about by one-way transmission. It requires, the manager would say, 'feedback' before communication can take place. What he doesn't seem to realise is that his idea of communication is really two transmissions on a me-to-you-you-to-me basis. Two transmissions don't necessarily make one communication. In short, he doesn't understand communications, but explains them. The artist understands but can't explain them.[16]

Communication for the artist in all its ambiguity and multiplicity of intention and reception only exists when it adds a new dimension of awareness to a community. The manager's notion is like a game of tennis: the artist's is like a flight of birds changing direction.

---

15   See Appendix I, *Leonardo and the Leviathan*

16   'Stradivai *knew* every detail of how to make a perfect violin- but this knowledge was tacit. He was not able to specify the details of construction, to be explicit about them, and could only pass them on *by example*. He knew, in other words, but could not tell' (*The Tacit Dimension*, Michael Polanyi) This philosopher is undoubtedly right, but it will no longer suffice for the artist working in television. If he has no muscularly worked out philosophy of his work, the management institutes will not be shy of providing him with one!

If, as we suggest, creative techniques are community-forming techniques and that these differ from the transmission techniques of managers, it obviously follows that a broadcasting service must replace transmission by communication in its managerial thinking if it is to implement the purposes for which it was set up. Mr. Ivor Kenny, Director of the Irish Management Institute, regards television as being a 'commentating' medium.[17] Something happens; television provides a means of transmitting somebody's view of it. This may evoke a response—what he might call 'feedback'. This is an oddly Marxian notion of the mass media. We've no doubt he would deny this, indignantly. Nonetheless, this is a view of communications as an ideological superstructure, reflecting the 'real' causes of action within the body politic.

The professional broadcaster, when he concerns himself at all in reflections about his work (he seldom does), would see it in quite different terms. Art, television, radio and the newspapers are, in themselves, the community's attempt to bring the whole complex of its beliefs, feelings, fears and hopes to a level of consciousness that need never be conceptual at all.

The *Late Late Show* may provide no comment that anyone can articulate in a transmittable message on, say, the revival of Irish. It represents a great and internally contradictory uprush of thought, feeling and desire. In Mr. Kenny's sense, it conveys nothing. In the communicator's sense, it brings the community to a tacit but intense awareness of its own nature and attitudes. For this reason, it has always seemed to us that Gay Byrne's judgment in progressively including substantial religious, political, social and cultural topics in the *Late Late Show*, is of vital importance for the healthy development of the community's

---

17   After-dinner speech to IMI Business Management Programme II '68/'69

self-communication. Otherwise, these topics will tend to be transmitted *at* the viewers by experts. This will, inevitably, inhibit and wither the thought, feeling-habits, and engagement of viewing audiences with real life. Serious matters must be discussed gaily and spontaneously. This is communication. It cannot be managed. When it is achieved it is, in abstract rational terms, a 'miracle'. When it fails, it is a mess. The principle of its 'organisation' lies in the creative, aesthetic judgment of its makers—not in the 'principles' of management. These are there, discreetly, in the wings. If they dominate or obtrude—the butterfly dies upon the wheel.

* * *

> Billy the Music here broke in:
> 'The person I would have liked to hear more
> of is Cuchulain, for he is my own
> Guardian Angel and it's him I
> 'm interested in. The next time
> I meet him I'll ask him questions'
> —JAMES STEPHENS

Perhaps, again, owing to the presence of Dónall Ó Mórain there was, at that time, a statement from the Authority *For the Guidance of its Staff in Regard to the Use of the Irish Language in Broadcasting* (January 1966).

The Authority had not uttered a word on its policy on the language to staff before this time, although there had been a memorandum from the Controller of Programmes two years previously. This had been brief and merely stated that Irish should be introduced, where it fell naturally into programmes, by those who were proficient in its use. This had resulted in such programmes for adults as *Club Céilí, Labhair*

*Gaeilge Linn*, the Irish thriller series Ó Dúill, and magazine items in *Newsbeat*. The new Authority policy was introduced to staff members by the Director-General in Studio 2 at a special meeting in January.

Based on the thesis that restoring the language was a feasible aim and that television programmes were going to throw in their weight, in an unexamined way the document laid down certain broad, and certain specific, requirements.

RTE was to nurture the language by presenting it in a sympathetic, positive and imaginative way.

It was to build a better public consciousness of national identity by means of programmes on Irish history and culture.

We were to try to see to it that:

- the boat was not rocked by presenting 'unbalanced' discussion on the national aim of restoring Irish;
- localised vocabulary and pronunciation would be avoided by announcers and newscasters and standards of pronunciation, grammar and diction would be at least equal to those required in English;
- Nuacht would go on carrying the main News headlines but would have secondary News items of its own;
- Irish be extended in Children's and Sports programmes, that Producers and interviewers in information, magazine and light entertainment programmes should include items in Irish; they should lose no opportunity to encourage members of the public to use the language 'in part' when being interviewed; at least one programme in Irish of special interest to adult viewers was to be broadcast weekly on television; the Guide and other publications were to assist in the extending of bilingualism;

- quantitatively, more Irish was to be introduced into sports commentaries, but in such a way 'as not to diminish general communication'.

The last paragraph of the document is a classic piece of self-contradiction, the kind of contradiction that seems to be a guiding principle of Irish broadcasters' lives. It said, simply, that jobs which required bilingualism should be carried out by bilingualists, even if they had to equip themselves after recruitment.

> But it [the Authority] is anxious that those who do not know Irish should feel secure in their positions, *while recognising that bilingualism cannot but make their usefulness and access to opportunities appreciably greater* (our italics).

Questions and comments from those present ranged from sheer bewilderment to polite rage. A rather uneasy gathering left the studio after the meeting and one colleague was heard to say: 'my next trick is impossible'. Out of this welter of expedients, one adult programme in Irish was to emerge—and one quiz. Those who loved the language despaired; those who were indifferent shrugged: a qualitative problem was to be solved quantitatively.

The Editor of Irish programmes, who had had nothing to do with the formulation of the 'policy', made recommendations on the extent to which Irish could be introduced in running programmes such as *Home for Tea, Jackpot, Teen Talk, Melody Fair, Ballad Session, '65, Cine Club, Spectrum, Discovery, Cover Story,* the *Late Late Show, Pick of the Pops, School Around the Corner,* Sports programmes, *Newsbea*t,

1916 programmes, Children's, Agriculture, Drama programmes, and continuity announcements.

In the jigsaw, the Irish pieces could be identified: they were marked 'Security'.

These recommendations were implemented, in part; most of them never saw the light of day again. Another pinch of incense had been rubrically burned.

\* \* \*

In May 1966 the first phases of the plan already mentioned to move Production Facilities into the Programmes Division as a new major unit under the direct supervision of the Programme Controller, was initiated.

The production crews welcomed it. By temperament and inclination, they were programme people. Many of them were fine artists. From the earliest days when the crews, operators and Producer-Directors had been trained together, through the hectic scramble to get programmes on the air, Producers and their crews had managed to maintain an identity of purpose. There was not a programme in the schedule that did not owe its flashes of style and imagination to their contribution. Designers, graphic artists, photographic stills men, prop men, wardrobe and make-up, cameramen (both film and electronic), lighting men, film editors, film processing personnel, sound-men, vision mixers, floor managers, carpenters—all have the same orientation as Producers: to do that little bit extra; to try it another way; to, somehow, make the damn thing work.

Revolutionary as the Production Facilities move must have seemed at the time, it may not have been quite revolutionary enough. Inevitably, after a time, those structures of line management which had been set up to regulate crew proceedings—section heads, supervisors, managers—tended to draw Producers and crews apart again. The Producers then began to see these managers and supervisors as blockage points.

Some Producers, in their assessment, even went so far as to confuse the issues by lumping the crews in with the managers, as a target for their frustrations.

What they did not realise was that the crews felt their own frustrations just as keenly. In some cases they had to work with Producers who had been insufficiently trained—some of them by the very technical staffs who were now supervisors or managers in the Production Facilities Department. Others were frustrated because the facilities necessary to realising the Producers' intentions were unavailable, inadequate or broken down.

Some crew members found ways out by applying for appointment as Directors; others did work outside the station in their own time which they found more rewarding—and there were some who left.

*Arrivals, Departures, Delays.*
—HEUSTON STATION

By the end of May 1966 the one-year-old Authority was due for retirement or renewal. The Authority was not renewed; it was re-instated. It lost its Chairman.

Eamonn Andrews resigned at the end of May. His comment at the time was that the station was going too far too fast.

It was trying to be self-sufficient, without enough experience.

He felt, he said, that output was dominating the staff's energies instead of trying to create standards of professionalism. The aimless and quantitative insistence on Irish was not successful. It was lowering the quality of programmes without increasing the status or use of the language, meaningfully. The following day the Authority publicly expressed its regret at his resignation. The staff was amused.

There were hints that Dr. C. S. Andrews might succeed him and a newspaper editorial of the same day urged that a strong independent man should be selected to chair the Board.

Dr. Andrews was appointed as predicted. The newspapers announced it on 3rd June 1966. It is reported that the unseemly wrangles that had gone on in the Authority during the previous years ceased and that they were a well-disciplined group soon after Dr. Andrews' arrival.

Gunnar Rugheimer was to have left at the expiry of his contract on 1st June 1966. However, no suitable replacement had been found. In April, it was said by Irish Actors' Equity at their annual general meeting, that RTE should have an Irish Controller of Programmes. It was incongruous, Equity said, that a non-national should be trying to evolve a philosophy of Irish consciousness. The Gaelic League backed them up in May, protesting that the Controller of Programmes did not understand the Irish way of life. They did not say who did. Whatever history is finally written on this period of Irish broadcasting it will have to consider these accusations. It seems to us that Gunnar Rugheimer had more insight into the Irish mind than many a native and had done more to reflect it than those who employed him. It would be less than honest on our part not to say this. His great defect was not that he did not know the Irish mind; rather he had an uncanny gift for exposing it to its own gaze. The gift was attributed to him as an arrogant vice. It is therefore hardly to be wondered at, that in spite of repeated attempts on the part of McCourt (and Eamonn Andrews, while he was there) to have him remain, Rugheimer was to leave. The Authority had demanded an Irish national.

On 13th December 1965 the post of Controller of Programmes had been formally advertised in Irish newspapers. The announcement, also published in many newspapers abroad, yielded no acceptable result. Mr. McCourt travelled extensively to interview applicants but by the following June there was still no one in prospect. Rugheimer stayed on and gave what assistance he could in the finding of a new Controller.

The earlier affair of the eighteen Producers' complaint to the Authority was an unfortunate one, not merely because of the course adopted, not merely because it lacked support among the rest of the staff; it represented the frustrated aspirations of a group of people whose vision of the role of a national broadcasting service, though well-intentioned, may have lacked insight and a full realisation of the commercial and cultural contradictions which govern the Authority but are borne by the Directorate.

The Controller, as the strongest man in their immediate orbit, whose forcefulness they daily experienced, was the natural target for their anger. It may be a reflection on the accuracy of their aim that the shots went wide and landed in the cotton-wool bed of the Authority.

The saddest aspect of this matter was that it partially cut off from the main body of Producers a valuable group of colleagues who remained in virtual 'exile', though they continued to carry on their duties in the making of programmes. Like most exiles, they lost touch with the changes among new and incoming programme staffs and tended to lapse into a nostalgia for the days and ways of the station's beginnings. It was not until the 7 Days row that the majority of the programme staff and this group came together again in any full sense to make common cause. More than one of them has since expressed regret at their having to take a course which, at the time, they felt it their duty to pursue. Jim Plunkett Kelly, Maev Conway and Aindreas Ó Gallchóir have done this generously in our presence. We believe that others would concur.

Gunnar Rugheimer did not finally leave Ireland and the station until December 1966. In the meanwhile he carried on.

# CHAPTER 1: A CAUTIONARY TALE

*The President shall be elected by direct vote of the people.*
—CONSTITUTION OF IRELAND ARTICLE 12

The Presidential Election was due in June 1966. Mr. Tom O'Higgins of Fine Gael was contesting it. The incumbent was Éamon De Valera who also stood for election.

The Controller and the Director-General decided that this was a political event in the sense of the Act and that a broadcasting service had a duty to cover it as such. Rugheimer accordingly wrote to the Directors of Elections of Fianna Fáil and Fine Gael in these terms, so that each could see that the other had been invited; stating that RTE intended to cover this as a political election and that time was therefore offered for party political broadcasts on behalf of the candidates.

There had been no consultation with either party prior to the sending of the circulars. The station had simply taken the initiative, which it deemed to be its right.

Fianna Fáil was not pleased. The President, their Director of Elections, Mr. Charles J. Haughey, said, could not campaign. To this the polite reply was that in that event there was no objection to his having people to speak on his behalf.

Mr. Haughey rejoined that the President was above politics and that Radio Telefís Éireann was committing itself to a political act.

RTE was sorry that the Director of Elections should feel like that but it was a matter for Fianna Fáil to accept the invitation or not as they felt inclined. The invitation to the other party would, in any case, stand.

The service carried the campaign on the basis of party political broadcasting under Section 18 (2) of the Act, which permitted departure from impartiality—by the parties. An appearance was made on behalf of Eamon De Valera, not by the Fianna Fáil Party as such, but by the friends of Mr. De Valera—among them Nora Connolly.

Mr. Haughey may, by now, have realised the mettle of the man he was dealing with. In the event, it is ironical to note the bitterness with which Fine Gael attacked RTE for what it called a biased coverage of the campaign.

* * *

Notwithstanding the fact that no new Controller had been appointed, plans for the Autumn schedule were brought under way by Rugheimer. There were to be new programmes, and a shake-up on the Current Affairs side.

Three of these programmes were to have important consequences for RTE—and involve the present writers. We feel it necessary to deal with them at the expense of other, equally pivotal, programmes—like *Newsbeat*, the *Late Late Show*, *The Riordans*, *Telefís Scoile* and *Telefís Feirme*.

The weekly programme '66, which had finished its season in June, was to be replaced by a new programme with more scope—*7 Days*.

*Home for Tea*, a chatty family programme, was to go in favour of a family advisory programme in depth, Home Truths.

*The Hurler on the Ditch* and *Strictly Politics* were to be replaced by *Division*, a programme which would concern itself with Irish politics and to which politicians and others would be invited.

> *... patiently and unremittingly to sustain the vigilance of reason in the presence of failure and in the presence of that which appears alien to it, philosophy is the principle of concentration through which man becomes himself, by partaking of reality.*
>
> —KARL JASPERS

As Gunnar Rugheimer was to say to the present writers prior to their taking up these new commitments: it might well be that we were not ready for such a departure. The station, however, must grasp the nettle of its Irish commitment. It had to face the Irish realities and it had to take the consequences, even in the teeth of resistance or possible failure.

The ground that had been rough-dug and planted each year with a sturdier growth had to be prepared for the new crop. A letter from the Controller to the three Party Whips in the Summer of 1966 had stated that RTE did not feel happy about the party political broadcasts in the form in which the parties wanted them. The station did not think it desirable in the interests of good political broadcasting to institute party political broadcasts again, except in an election situation. Instead, it intended to cover politics in a programme, entirely produced and devised by itself, for which it would select both the topic and the participants.

The station would invite politicians to take part.

The object of this departure was to take political television out of the party-line. Under the old scheme, any Deputy selected by his party merely reproduced the official party view. He spoke with the dull solemnity of any man required to enunciate ex cathedra.

The new scheme, being the responsibility of RTE, would leave any participant free to speak informally. Since the responsibility for impartiality was now the station's, everyone would force the pace and liven the proceedings—it was hoped. It might also encourage politicians to take television seriously—as part of the nation's debate with itself. The success of the programme '64, '65 and '66 nourished this hope.

The three parties were agreeable to the new arrangement but Fianna Fáil wanted the invitations to Deputies to continue to go through the Whips. Gunnar Rugheimer and Jack White on behalf of RTE argued against this arrangement, pointing out that in, say, the event of a split in the Fianna Fáil Party some members might refuse the Whip and RTE would be bound by an agreement not to approach them.

At length, after more discussion at a higher level inside the Fianna Fáil Party, RTE agreed to be responsible for the invitation, naming the particular member it wanted but passing it through the Whip. However, if the Whip declined to produce the member, RTE would consider itself free to invite him direct. The other two parties agreed in the amendment.

The notorious 'Whips' Agreement', often referred to darkly by political correspondents, never, in fact, existed. The only written document was a joint memorandum about this agreed method of approach. There was no reference to the number of politicians that should be invited or whether the programme should be restricted to politicians. This memorandum was not published.

The fact that any agreement with politicians, *for normal programming*, was entered into, was to prove, in the long run, unfortunate.

What appeared to be bothering the Whips was that RTE would deliberately select Deputies who were 'characters', in order to increase entertainment value. This argument was a little thin in view of the kind of programmes that Telefís Éireann had already been doing in that area.

What finally transpired was that the parties wanted to keep the discipline of their members firmly in line. Rugheimer pointed out (as he had pointed out to the Bishops' Interim Committee at an earlier stage) that RTE did not wish to interfere in the disciplinary affairs of other bodies.

Division was to have its problems and its triumphs in the following season's programmes. But inevitably, the old form of the party political broadcasts, unadulterated, was to return in The Politicians.

During the Summer, on the Chairman's providing himself with an office in the station, an advertisement appeared for the post of Secretary to the Authority. Mr. Oliver Maloney was appointed to the post early in September. Shortly afterwards, the selection of a Controller of Programmes was finally made.

* * *

The man chosen was Michael Garvey. He was a graduate of U.C.G. He had produced in the theatre and had worked in radio for several years as a Producer before moving into television in 1962 where he had become one of the outstanding Producer-Directors in the service. He had not applied for the position but had been approached by Mr. McCourt with the concurrence of the Authority. He agreed to serve.

This appointment was made after a protracted search by Mr. McCourt, both at home and abroad, for a candidate who was both an Irish national and an experienced programme administrator. The Authority was made fully aware by Mr. McCourt that Michael Garvey's inexperience in executive administration would create great difficulties for him. They were aware, too, of the modesty and shyness of his temperament, often disguised by a certain airiness and even flippancy of manner. Having consulted with Gunnar Rugheimer, Mr. McCourt is believed to have made this recommendation in the conviction that, with a strong supportive Directorate, Michael Garvey's qualities of orderly production methods, so clearly evident in his own programming, his high intelligence and almost encyclopaedic erudition would make it relatively easy for him to develop the necessary qualities of leadership.

From the point of view of the Authority, he had other qualities of great worth. He was an artist whose distinction was not confined to theatre, radio or television. He painted and had a really profound sympathy with architectural, painterly and sculptural idioms. His command of Irish was both fluent and scholarly. He had an extensive knowledge of Irish, English and European literature and a passionate attachment to music, in the production of which he excelled.

An essential characteristic that facilitated television programme control, and which Michael Garvey had to a supreme degree, was a tolerance of characters foreign to his own mental temperament. He had worked successfully with some of the most difficult people in both radio and television. He is a man of great charm.

The staff were astonished and delighted. He was 'one of their own'. At the time of his appointment, announced on the 24th September, he was engaged in the production of The Real Charlotte—a serialisation of the Somerville and Ross novel, the first venture of this kind that RTE had undertaken. It was being recorded by outside broadcast on locations near Dublin and he was occupied with it well into October. His 'take-over' period under Gunnar Rugheimer's guidance was, unfortunately, less than two months. He was to take up office officially on 31st December.

> *It is not sufficient to make a hole in the ground, bundle in the roots of the tree or plant, cover them with soil, and stamp on it. A plant so treated may grow, but it will be in spite of the treatment and not because of it.*
> —GARDENING MANUAL (1913)

The Autumn programmes opened with an insistent clash of cymbals which resembled the sound of a telephone bell. It originated in the Newsroom but it affected the whole Public Affairs area.

Programmes there were in a state of intensive reorganisation and were undergoing the normal daily pressures.

*7 Days* had opened, as had *Division* and *Home Truths*. They were to have a close inter-relationship not only because of their material, which was social, political and economic, but because of the personal relationships of their Producers, Directors, reporters and research teams.

The three approaches were different. *7 Days* aimed to give an Irish view of the larger public issues, at home and abroad, which affected the people's lives and thought: it intended to broaden the viewer's outlook and intensify his involvement.

Lelia Doolan, its Producer, had, apart from a spell on *Newsbeat*, worked predominantly in Drama—on the production of *The Riordans* in its early days. She believed that Public Affairs on television were intrinsically dramatic and only extrinsically technical. Her two young Directors, Eoghan Harris and Dick Hill, had mutually opposite and complementary qualities.

Eoghan Harris was intensely interested in social and political affairs with a sharp, incisive and constructive mind.

Dick Hill was organised, scientific and methodical with the Anglo-Irish sense of dedication and concern for the public wellbeing.

A brilliant team of reporters, John O'Donoghue, Brian Cleeve, Brian Farrell, were already well-known to the public, and trusted by them.

*Division* was devoted to trying to get the Irish public interested in its political institutions, personalities and issues.

Under Muiris Mac Conghail, who had extensive knowledge of the Irish political scene from his excellent work on *Newsbeat* and *Headlines and Deadlines*, a new attempt to bring the nation and the station into a stimulating dialogue with the Oireachtas and Local Government bodies was launched.

He was ably served by Paddy Gallagher, Ted Nealon and, (characteristically associated with The Politicians) David Thornley —all tremendously well-versed in the detail of their subjects and experienced political commentators.

*Home Truths* operated with a totally new staff. Forty-three economists and social scientists were interviewed, from whom Mary Murphy and Tomás Roseingrave were chosen. Jimmy Flahive, executive chef of

Aer Lingus, was chosen from a panel of chefs suggested by the Trade Unions. The Minister for Health promised the co-operation of his Department and provided medical advisers. The Institute of Research and Standards undertook to carry out scientific research on household products. Mary Leland became Home Truths Munster correspondent.

230 members of the Irish Housewives' Association and the ICA acted as purchasing agents throughout the country.

Jack Dowling, the Producer, had just finished his Producer-Director course, as had Eoghan Harris and Dick Hill. Dowling's previous experience had been in scripting and interviewing in religious and socio-religious programmes.

*7 Days* aimed at the greatest possible extension of interest; *Division* aimed at the greatest possible intensity of involvement; *Home Truths* aimed at being as particular as possible.

Their styles might be put like this: *Home Truths* might trace the cost of *this* mackerel; *7 Days* might investigate food prices in the cost of living index; *Division* might mount a programme on the Department of Fisheries.

Programme pressures in these three areas were particularly intense. Every programme had to be planned in the knowledge that it might have to be abandoned in favour of a new idea in the face of a new event. Research by experts was the keynote of the three programmes. A slip in *Home Truths* could result in a Court action for libel; a mistake in *7 Days* in a controversial storm; an error in *Division* could bring about a confrontation with a 'pride' of politicians.

There were no working hours or days. People rested when they could.

Each programme had its special and its common difficulties.

The common difficulties were lack of time and experience.

The special difficulties were that in *Home Truths* research and checking facts was endless and exhausting. The unit worked in a constant atmosphere of threat, recrimination and influence.

For instance, a programme on patent tin-openers had been prepared for a particular Wednesday night. Script, research and production arrangements were more or less complete. Jack Dowling, Mary Murphy and Tomás Roseingrave decided to take the Sunday off. On Sunday afternoon, a member of the Irish Housewives' Association telephoned Jack Dowling at his home.

She asked him why the slump in cattle prices, about which the farmers had been complaining, had not been reflected in a reduction in the price of meat. He noted this for future reference. His interest was immediately alerted when she went on to add that she had just paid eight shillings a pound for round steak during her weekly Saturday shopping. The previous Saturday it had cost her six shillings a pound. Jack Dowling asked her if she had any reason to believe that this was anything more than a local phenomenon. She said yes. there appeared to be an agreement among the master butchers to raise the price of meat. The Housewives' Association was concerned. Could he do anything?

Jack Dowling telephoned Mary Murphy and Tomás Roseingrave. He sent word to Mary's assistant, Noelette Gannon. They met in a pub in Baggot Street within the hour and drew up a sketch plan for a replacement programme for the following Wednesday. Tomas undertook to spend the night reviewing the Stock Market prices for beef for the three previous months. Mary undertook to meet officials concerned with the compilation of the cost of living index. Jack Dowling went to the station and cancelled the arrangements for the can-opening item and set up new design, graphics and presentation methods with Sid Neff, who arrived in a Land Rover with his hat full of fishing flies. Jack Dowling explained the scheme. Sid was a graphic artist of extraordinary ingenuity. He was required to provide a means of showing the price of meat by townlands from Belfast to Dingle; to devise some means of comparing the profits to farmers, wholesalers and retailers and, at the same time, show the average cost of the previous three months, now being researched by Tomás Roseingrave.

Jack Dowling rang Rickard Deasy in Tipperary, who immediately placed an N.F.A. statistician at Roseingrave's disposal. Dowling rang Mary Leland in Cork and his agents in Galway, Longford, Belfast and Dundalk, instructing them to have the I.C.A. and I.H.A. panel each buy one pound of round steak in butchers' shops wherever they had members throughout the country.

Arrangements had to be made to reimburse them.

On the Monday morning, every telephone in Group C was manned. Michael Johnston of Group B co-operated by putting the telephones of his group at *Home Truths'* disposal.

Tomás Roseingrave was installed, with Noelette Gannon, also a social scientist, to analyse the incoming data and feed it down to Sid Neff, who incorporated it into a Heath-Robinson contraption that he had constructed during the night. It looked like the marker board on the London Stock Exchange.

Denis O'Grady procured a camera crew out of thin air. Dowling, Mary Murphy and the crew conducted filmed interviews in butchers' shops, bus queues, the abattoir, the N.F.A. office, the meat wholesalers' headquarters, and with the President of the Master Butchers' Association.

Tuesday was spent editing film, collating the figures, writing the script, rehearsing the whole programme, of which this was one item. A production conference with design, graphics, floor manager, lighting, sound, vision mixer and technical operations manager, rearranged the programme in minute detail.

The conference was interrupted by a group of angry butchers who had got wind of what the programme was up to.

By the time recording took place on Tuesday evening, everyone was exhausted but triumphant. Tomás Roseingrave was able to assure the Producer that the figures were accurate to what he characteristically described as 'point five of a penny'. The crew was mesmerised and entered into the spirit of the project with great enthusiasm. A verifying procedure had been arranged, in which the buying and analysing operation was virtually repeated on the day after transmission. It was discovered that the price of meat had fallen by an average of tenpence[18] per pound since the previous purchase, three days earlier.

The team slept for twenty-four hours. Then the grind began again.

In *7 Days* the endless flux of events made planning enormously difficult, and the conservative and Establishment view—whether business, religious or political on any issue—was almost impossible to find defenders for. This made balance a critical and exhausting matter.

Last-minute change was here the rule rather than the exception. The programme was transmitted on a Monday night and its subject matter was never finally chosen until Sunday or even the Monday.

Obviously, then, segments had to be pre-planned and stockpiled with an eye to what was coming up on the national and international scene. For example, the farmers were in dispute with the Department of Agriculture. It might or might not develop into a major political crisis. Clearly, one couldn't be caught napping. Internationally, the tensions in the Middle East were beginning to warm up; there was Aden, as well. Elections in Germany were in the offing, and at home the L.F.M. were becoming vociferous.

---

18    *2017 note:* There were 12 pence in a shilling.

Some sort of line of development had to be aimed at. The availability of experts had to be traced and a visiting pundit had to be utilised—perhaps from the mere fact of his being in Dublin— anticipating a future transmission. We had to find and instruct reporters and contributors abroad who still had sufficient awareness of the Irish scene and an insight into their local milieu.

Always one had to be prepared for the 'special' programme to cover an unpredictable event. These were generally hour-long programmes. Many of them had to be compiled at short notice in addition to carrying on the routine weekly transmissions.

The deployment of the team was a continual organisational nightmare. Stretching and leap-frogging was the order of the day. Travel down the country and, on rare occasions, abroad, consumed time and frustrated communications.

A sudden opportunity-programme might well find all the staff dispersed and all the facilities engaged. Yet the opportunity could not be ignored. Lelia Doolan became a temporary Director on these occasions. Facilities were borrowed from Division. Help was sought from Home Truths. Telegrams and telephone calls attempted to find experts and speakers on the topic and to recall one of the harassed reporters, perhaps calmly discussing co-operatives in Connemara. Cameramen, film editors, sound-men, designers, crews, changed course in midstream and threw their help in. Somehow, the thing just got done.

Often, the most hastily assembled programme came off with unexpected brilliance; sometimes it was ghastly. The most riveting talker on a telephone might turn out to be a dummy in the studio. An expert flown in from, say, London, would give no one else a chance to get a word in edgeways.

But there were two lines of dependability and unrufflable calm: Brian Cleeve, Brian Farrell and John O'Donoghue worked endlessly and painstakingly; scripting, interviewing, researching. Whatever the mayhem that may have preceded the floor manager's countdown, they could always be depended upon to give the programme an air of thoughtful deliberation and authority. Behind them, Eoghan Harris and Dick Hill coaxed, cajoled, organised, wrote and calculated, week in week out, with unflagging energy.

It was television at its most exhilarating and its most exasperating.

*Division*'s particular difficulties were of a similar kind, sharpened by the Irish resistance to frank talk in public—on matters which involved close scrutiny of its own accepted political attitudes, institutions and leaders.

Perhaps the man who carried the burden of this reputation was Mr. Charles Haughey. The fact is that *all* politicians of any party *anywhere* have an almost paranoid conviction that they are being done down.

The Minister for Agriculture was not peculiar in this. It's just that he was singularly un-shy.

\* \* \*

> 'You do not like that woman?' Caeltia enquired.
> 'She's a bad woman', replied Patsy.
> 'What sort of a bad woman is she?'
> 'She's the sort that commits adultery with every kind of man', said he harshly.
> Caeltia turned over that accusation for a moment.
> 'Did she ever commit adultery with yourself?' said he.
> 'She did not', said Patsy, 'and that's why I don't like her.'
> —JAMES STEPHENS

SIT DOWN AND BE COUNTED

\* \* \*

The clash of cymbals:

The telephone rang on 2nd October 1966 in the Newsroom.

Mr. C. J. Haughey was on the line, complaining about the juxtaposition of a statement from the National Farmers' Association with one of his own. The N.F.A. had advised the farmers to sell the cattle which Mr. Haughey had advised them to hold.

The complaint was in vigorous terms, no doubt. Mr. Haughey does nothing by three-quarters. Both statements had appeared in the main News bulletin. The Duty-Editor telephoned the Head of News at his home and the N.F.A. statement was deleted from the following bulletins. 'All hell' broke loose.

The National Union of Journalists met to discuss the incident which was reported in the following morning's papers. The Minister for Agriculture said that he had felt compelled in the public interest to protest that the N.F.A. statement should have been carried immediately after his. 'I gave specific advice to farmers in reply to questions from Deputies in the Dáil... and I felt that to have my advice followed by a contradiction from a [farming] organisation could only lead to confusion and damage the industry.'

The N.F.A. said it was amazed at the Ministerial intervention. The *Irish Times* was amazed that Mr. Haughey's telephone call had succeeded. It asked whether he had any right to ring the Newsroom at Montrose. RTE, it pointed out, had immediately complied with the request.

The N.U.J. was amazed. It was already considering what union action it could take.

Staff generally were not amazed. They were uneasy and disturbed. On 4th October, speaking at a Dublin Chamber of Commerce luncheon, Mr. Kevin McCourt said that an editorial error of judgment by a junior member of staff had been made and then rectified. He denied any intrigue: 'I have never known that a programme has been changed or withdrawn as a result of political or any other kind of pressure.'

There is no record of any amazement among the members of the Chamber of Commerce. Mr. Haughey must surely have been mildly astonished.

The staff was outraged at McCourt's so unashamedly washing his hands of responsibility for one of his own journalists in public. The 'junior member' had behaved with professional propriety: he was now left holding the bath in order to save the Authority's face on their discovery that the baby, like the bathwater, was on the floor.

> *'The Dormouse is asleep again',*
> *said the Hatter,*
> *and he poured a little hot tea on its nose.*
> —LEWIS CARROLL

The N.U.J. issued a rebuke. They defended their colleague's right to make editorial decisions independently. They expected their Chief Executive to support them.

The newspapers complimented the N.U.J. for standing up to be counted and said that McCourt should have admitted that there were in fact pressures, even if he wished to claim that they had been resisted.

This was a new Kevin McCourt. What, the staff wondered, was happening to him?

Two days later Mr. Haughey withdrew from a planned interview on Division in which he had agreed to appear some days previously knowing that the N.F.A. leader Mr. Rickard Deasy had also been invited to the programme. The N.F.A. was in dispute with the Department of Agriculture.

> *Fivepence, you dumb-bell,*
> *shouted Shorty.*
> *I will double that, said the*
> *Good Fairy. Tenpence ...*

Jack White and Gunnar Rugheimer went to Leinster House to discuss *Division* with the party Whips. This was on foot of a telephone call from the Fianna Fáil Chief Whip, Mr. Michael Carty, who said that RTE had broken the agreement about *Division* (presumably because Mr. Deasy was not a politician). His real purpose, it was felt at the time, was to ensure that Mr. Deasy be withdrawn from the programme—in which case Mr. Haughey would go on. This was a political foxtrot. Rugheimer knew that there was no such agreement. He suggested that since Mr. Carty believed that RTE had broken the agreement it must be a very serious matter. Why did Deputy Carty not call a meeting of the Whips?

> *I will see you for one and sixpence,*
> *said the Good Fairy ...*

Deputy Carty did; he called the meeting at Dáil Éireann.

Gunnar Rugheimer and Jack White went to Leinster House to meet the Whips. Their visit was picked up immediately by the newspapers.

They produced the memorandum from the meeting which had agreed the procedures for Division. It simply stated that politicians would be invited through the Whips. They read this aloud and then enquired what Mr. Carty's complaints were? If the other two Whips did not know what was going on at the beginning of the meeting, it slowly began to dawn on them. Mr. Carty was trying to make it appear that the Whips had understood *Division* to be a programme for politicians only. His co-Whips weren't having any of this nonsense. They said there was no such agreement. Things rested so.

The broadcast was to go ahead without Mr. Haughey.

The Authority was in a state of high nervousness and had probably been undergoing pressure to back down, or to talk the Director-General and Controller into backing down. There were rumours, later substantiated by the Minister for Posts and Telegraphs, Mr. Joseph Brennan, that there had been attempts made from within the Cabinet to have him intercede and use his power to stop the broadcast.

The programme went off without sensationalism. There were no grounds for an action on the impartiality clause. It was a high moment for the station, though probably only a few people realized it at the time. Rugheimer's and White's staunchness had given the staff a sense of the potential integrity and strength of the service. Clarity and fearlessness had done it, while higher authority had quaked in its boots.

The Fianna Fáil Party boycotted Division. The programme survived it and continued without Fianna Fáil.

> *None of your bloody miracles, shouted Shorty, we're playing for money! None of your trick-o'-the-loop, none of your bloody quick ones! If you try that game I'll take you out of that pocket by the scruff of the neck and give you a kick in the waterworks!*
> —FLANN O'BRIEN

Mr. Lemass then said in Dáil Éireann:

> RTE was set up by legislation as an instrument of public policy and as such was responsible to the Government. The Government had overall responsibility for its conduct and especially the obligation to ensure that its programmes do not offend against the public interest, or conflict with national policy as defined in legislation.

The Division-N.F.A. row obviously rankled. The claim for independence of broadcasting was evidently causing the Government alarm.

Mr. Lemass continued:

> To this extent the Government reject the view that RTE should be, either generally or in regard to its current affairs programmes and news programmes, completely independent of Government supervision.

This statement caused the broadcasters alarm. The interpretation of impartiality under the Broadcasting Act required the station to sit in judgment on the Government's claims on its services as much as upon its opponents'. It could not view itself, therefore, as an instrument of Government without betraying its obligations.

The Public Affairs sections of the Programmes Division threw their weight into the fray. For example, *7 Days* devoted the whole of a week's programme to freedom in broadcasting. It was intended as a Swiftian fable and looked at Government interference and resistance to it, in the BBC and continental broadcasting services, and at Government and commercial attempts at interference in America. Walter Cronkite of CBS and Chet Huntley of NBC gave *7 Days* immediate interviews when they learned the subject matter. So did Grace Wyndham Goldie, a champion of the rights and freedom of broadcasting in her years as Head of Talks and Current Affairs at the BBC. The *7 Days* team was encouraged and stimulated by the support of Gunnar Rugheimer and Jack White and by technical, Newsroom and programme staffs. There was, evidently, plenty of fight in RTE Programmes Division. They did not fear accusation of recalcitrance.

Things were not so clear in the News Division, however.

Pearse Kelly, Head of News, isolated by lack of sympathetic understanding from his own chagrined staff, and by lack of support from those in authority over him, resigned. On leaving, he put a notice (which we print in Appendix III) in the Newsroom saying that he could not disclose the reasons for his resignation but thanked the staff for their loyalty. His resignation was announced on the same day as the appointment of his successor.

It was a nasty business. Mr. McCourt's standing among the staff was now dubious. Dr. Andrews was widely believed to be responsible for the new tone of management.

On 13th November 1966 Mr. James P. McGuinness took over as Head of News. He had been the first Public Relations Officer of the Authority and had later become Editor of the RTV(now RTE) Guide and other Authority publications.

In a leader in a Dublin newspaper of the following morning the RTE Authority was described as 'the most discredited body in Ireland… in the recent disgraceful happenings they have not piped one note'. The editorial remarked that rumours are inevitable and urged that the tantrums of politicians should be forgotten and a sharp watch kept for Government interference. The great danger, it went on, was that politicians in general should reach the stage of believing that RTE was their play-thing.

\* \* \*

In the meantime, a fundamental struggle of another character had been determined within the ranks of the Fianna Fáil Party leadership. Mr. Lemass retired as Taoiseach in the early days of November. The station followed the contending 'claims' of Messrs Haughey, Colley, Blaney and Lynch. On 9th November the issue had been decided and announced. Mr. Jack Lynch was the new Taoiseach.

The party's quarrel with RTE over the *Division* incident was closed. The programme was able to offer Mr. Lynch a platform for his first appearance as Taoiseach, and a graceful way out of an impasse to the Government party.

There was now a new Minister. Mr. Erskine Childers replaced Mr. Brennan in Posts and Telegraphs in Mr. Lynch's first Cabinet.

\* \* \*

This was the atmosphere of the station and public opinion when the new Head of News took over. The dust of battle lay thick on the ground. Mr. McGuinness was a new broom.

He had had wide editorial experience in Ireland, Britain and America. He had worked for The Irish Press, both in London and later in Dublin, as Editor. He was known to be an old protege of Dr. Andrews, whom he had first met in Bord na Mona.

In the uncharitable Irish tendency to suspect 'pull', wherever personal association could even remotely be established, it was widely held that Mr. McGuinness's appointment was due to the influence of the Chairman. Unfortunately, this kind of charge has haunted RTE's appointments from the beginning. Certainly, in this case, there is not a grain of evidence to support it. It is, in fact, quite out of character with Dr. Andrews' reputation and with the undoubted professional ability of Mr. McGuinness. Perhaps the fact that he was appointed without the usual procedure of advertising the vacancy was responsible for the suspicion.

Of quiet personal manner, he almost immediately revealed himself to be a man of strength of will and of clear vision. He showed, however, little obvious gift for personal warmth or camaraderie.

He began the reorganisation of the Newsroom with firmness and encouraged his subordinates to view their role in the station's life as one of primary and growing importance. The Producers of the Programmes Division became aware of him as a new force in the station's management.

We later had occasion to oppose the extension of his influence and ideas with what must, at times, have seemed a disproportionate vigour. He always showed himself tough, courteous and without rancour.

\* \* \*

Michael Garvey gradually took over as Controller towards the end of December. He had been working closely with Mr. Rugheimer during this period and this must have given him an insight into the awesome responsibilities of the job.

Gunnar Rugheimer finally took his departure on 21st December 1966.

> *The cook was a good cook,*
> *as cooks go; and*
> *as good cooks go*
> *he went.*
> —SAKI

\* \* \*

SIT DOWN AND BE COUNTED

Michael Garvey had had experience of Producers' problems at every level, as they had come to Rugheimer's desk. Among these was a programme already referred to: it had been making its own headlines during the Autumn season.

Home Truths was produced by Jack Dowling. In discussion with Gunnar Rugheimer during the preparation of the programme in late Summer of 1966, the Producer had drawn up a list of seven objectives which had been given the imprimatur of the Controller. We quote them here in full:

1. To provide a family magazine for viewers whose incomes (per head of household) is £13-10-0 or lower. This will take account of family multiple incomes of the estimated national average of 1.75 of the basic head of family income: £23-12-6.
2. To entertain as large a section of the community as possible.
3. To promote standards of family and personal health and hygiene.
4. To inform viewers of their rights in law and custom and their opportunities of availing of voluntary and private means of improving their standards of living.
5. To help viewers in the above income groups to use their incomes rationally and get the best possible value.
6. To promote an interest in a varied and pleasant diet of well-cooked food.
7. To discover and investigate any malpractices in administration or commercial practice which have a direct bearing on the foregoing and to right them as far as fair comment and publicity permit.

*Home Truths* from its very first transmission in September ran into trouble with the business community.

## CHAPTER 1: A CAUTIONARY TALE

There were threats of civil action which were ignored; they turned out to have been bluffs. These were from a canning factory, from a meat merchant, from a fruit and vegetable merchant, from a solicitor, from a builder, from fish merchants, from butchers— and a threat of a High Court order of restraint from the manager of a co-operative. Far from wilting under these threats, Gunnar Rugheimer had insisted upon one occasion that Jack Dowling take up a case afresh against inflated fish prices by wholesalers and retailers. In order to nail the story clearly to the masthead, he ordered Dowling to trace the cost of a mackerel from the moment of catch to its arrival on the housewife's table, thereby clearly pointing up the malpractice in a wholesale-retail profit of 280 per cent!

There had been an early Summer meeting with Mr. Jack White and Mr. Robert Gahan, Advertisement Sales Manager, about the effect of the programme on advertising. Arrangements were made by Jack Dowling to avoid the display of 'brand' names as it might be a 'free' advertisement. It would be necessary to disguise the names of products on the programmes. The only reason for showing a product would be if a firm were:

1. breaking the law, or
2. behaving in an unethical or grossly deceitful or unfair manner.

This situation changed in mid-December.

It had always been Jack Dowling's procedure to check in advance with the Legal Department for advice and to use this advice in making up his own mind whether or not to do a particular item in a particular way. Now, in connection with an item on building malpractice by a contractor in a Cork housing scheme, which he intended to expose, he was told that he could not transmit the item.

This was some five hours before the actual transmission was due to take place. Jack Dowling was told by the Deputy Director-General that, since the Attorney General on being advised of the transmission said that his office was proceeding against the miscreant, the matter was now sub judice. The item was cut. The programme ran under time. An apology was made to the public.

Jack Dowling waited to read announcements of proceedings in the newspapers. He had to wait for two years.

The new Controller, Michael Garvey, shortly afterwards sent for Jack Dowling. The Director-General, he was told, had become worried about the policy of *Home Truths*.

In the case of advertising, he was accused of carrying out a 'Which?'-hunt.

This had never been the intention of the programme; its policy was a sociological one. It would include items concerned with commercial marketing.

Dowling had lately been subjected to pressures from inside the station—not only from his own Executive Producer, Denis O'Grady, who was apprehensive; but also from the Advertisement Sales Manager, now supported from the Controller's office.

The Controller suggested that Dowling should go on a short holiday. The pressures of the programme were such that he might be nervously exhausted! Perhaps a rest might give him a chance to reflect on the policy of the programme. He did so and wrote to the Controller on 1st January 1967. His letter[19] gave Mr. Garvey a 'brief' on the policy for *Home Truths*, stating that it was essentially an *advisory* programme, listing the items it included from week to week, and showing the sociological bases for these. It was, frankly, a working-class programme for

---

19   Letter to Controller of Programmes (Television), Jack Dowling (see Appendix III)

working-class households and families—and partisan on their behalf to the extent that they were underprivileged and imposed upon by business, Government, administrators and, regrettably, the 'mass' media. Jack Dowling could read the signs; he ignored the warning.

The programme went on exposing the excessive profits and claims of pharmaceutical preparations—particularly cosmetics— which it was then pursuing in a series of items each week.

The Controller appears to have found this policy unpalatable. Early in January, Mr. Gahan protested that the policy of *Home Truths* was resulting in a loss of revenue. While the programme said nothing untrue, he agreed, the station could not afford to expose the kind of truth the programme was transmitting. We had a duty to our advertisers. There was pressure from an advertisers' advisory council, Mr. Gahan said. If the policy continued, he would take further action. He would discuss it with the Director-General or even with the Authority. This was during a telephone call from Mr. Gahan to Jack Dowling.

Dowling's Executive Producer had a meeting with the Controller and told Dowling later that an item for a forthcoming programme was objected to. This was about a free gift scheme—to be examined by Mary Murphy. Dowling was told to alter the packet to make it unrecognisable—and the 'free' gift itself should be altered. Dowling refused to disguise the evidence.

A meeting was then called at which the Controller said it had been decided to change the policy of *Home Truths*. A script of the previous programme and a script for the next programme were reviewed. Mr. Gahan had a copy of this script and he conducted the meeting from it. There were four items found unsuitable:

1. A smoking item by a medical representative of the Department of Health.

2. A cosmetics item by Mary Murphy.
3. A 'free' gift item by Mary Murphy.
4. A comedy verse comment.

Mr. Gahan said that these must be removed or substantially altered. The Controller agreed, except for the smoking item. As this represented the policy of a Department of Government, it was decided to retain the smoking script and cancel advertising for cigarettes for that night. Helena Rubenstein had cancelled their contract, Mr. Gahan said. He had lost Christmas advertising from the food interests. Mr. Jack White gave a short lecture to Dowling on the economic benefits of advertising in keeping prices down.

The Controller summed up:

1. There was a moral objection to Jack Dowling's conduct of the programme—one could not accept advertising and then 'slay' the advertisers.
2. That he would have to 'gut' *Home Truths*. The expression was his.

Jack Dowling refused to depart from his brief and asked to be relieved as Producer of the programme. He was relieved with effect from that moment.

Mary Leland, the programme's Cork correspondent, resigned immediately. Jack Dowling pleaded with Mary Murphy not to resign.

It was then announced that any new policy for the programme would have to make the scripts available to the Advertisement Sales Department a week in advance, in order that Mr. Gahan could re-arrange his advertising for each transmission night.

Any doubts remaining about the workability of the Authority's aims were killed once and for all by this incident. It was clear that the national aims could be promoted by RTE only to the degree that its financial dependence on advertising allowed.

Production staffs were in a dilemma. So powerful was the double-think: 'we are taking their money, so we can't knock them', that most people had replaced a question mark about the system with a reflex response. Nobody liked the station's dependence on advertising sales, but what could you do about it? Mystification reigned. There were some among the Producers—but more especially among production staffs, clerk-typists, canteen staffs, who didn't have these deep moral qualms about advertisers' rights or problems. These people did not have to keep the middle-class myths going: they knew them to be a fraud; their reaction was actively skeptical—one of disenchanted mockery—but always with the rider: 'they'll get you in the end'. Yet others, seeing the significance of the incident, wanted to do something about it.

There were Union meetings, and letters exchanged with Management. The official reaction was more or less expressed in a letter of Mr. Gahan's to the Controller, part of which was released to the Union concerned—Irish Actors' Equity:

> It has come to my notice that there is a rather strong anti-Sales lobby in the Programmes Division following the *Home Truths* problem, and there is also the suggestion abroad, and being fanned, that this is the first step in Sales control of all programmes!
>
> It is easy for you and I to see this is nonsense based on ignorance of the facts, but at the same time in order to maintain the level of co-operation that has up to now existed between the Sales and Programmes Division, I would appreciate you making it clear that apart from the fact that you personally would not tolerate the idea,

> the Sales Division has no desire to be involved with programme content, but on the other hand, advertisements represent more than two-thirds of our income and programme producers have a responsibility to keep this Division informed of items likely to affect the Sales effort. This is almost exclusively to ensure that the placement of advertisements is not a source of embarrassment either to RTE or an advertiser .

The hope that middle-class Producers, held in fee to the system by the system's most powerful weapon—job security—would stand together and refuse to service the newly orientated programme was perhaps idealistic and foolhardy. In any event, it proved vain.

The programme continued and it was produced by Gerry Murray. Resistance fizzled out slowly and uneasily. The Executive Producer, Denis O'Grady, omitted to recommend Mary Murphy's contract for renewal and she left. The Assistant Controller was kind enough to offer an apology for this oversight. He said that he hoped that she would work for RTE in the following season. The station lost a great broadcaster. Jack Dowling was transferred to Art programmes.

> *... the triangular person has got into the square hole, the oblong into the triangular, and a square person has squeezed himself into a round hole.*
> —SYDNEY SMITH

There was still enough disquiet, however, to make people want to protect programme makers in their professional rights in this kind of situation. Union intervention, on a matter of ethics and morals, was obviously difficult. Their traditional role—to seek for better wages and conditions—while not making it impossible for them to be involved in matters of professional conduct nevertheless raised problems in the specialised and complicated field of television communications.

It was decided to see whether production personnel had any interest in the formation of an association whose concern would be the professional and ethical standards and conduct of broadcasting. It was felt that these would best be formulated and implemented by broadcasters themselves, on the principle that self-discipline is better than outside strictures.

It was also felt that, apart from worthy declarations on the role and function of 'mass' communications, broadcasters went on with their daily work amid a clutter of ready-made ideas that acted as corks to stop up leaks in the system.

Many of the corks were the wrong size for the holes.

These concerns became all the more urgent when, in April 1967, the News Division's Vietnam expedition was cancelled.

The News Division, headed by Mr. Jim McGuinness, was broadening the scope of direct news-gathering by Irish journalists to replace, where possible, foreign comment and a foreign point of view. The news agencies from which the Newsroom derived its main sources of non-Irish news, were American or British. The Vietnam reporting enterprise was an ambitious one for a small station. However, in view of the seriousness of the war, both in its conduct and in its consequences for small nations, and in view of the sources available to us for information on it, it can hardly be argued that the undertaking was unnecessary. Because of our reputation in the Congo, Cyprus and the Middle East, ours was one of the few European stations that could get a North Vietnam visa.

It was up to the Authority to govern the use of its own finances. The Authority knew of the enterprise and approved it. The Director-General, Kevin McCourt, who had given support and encouragement to the idea and its planning, also approved it. In fact, he was thought to have conceived it. The News Division had journalists of professional capabilities to undertake it. In the event, they didn't get an opportunity to exercise them.

> *... if anybody in this country does not know the issues in Vietnam, somebody could go at his own expense, or a group could go at the expense of people who send them out. They would be able to go out there, learn the language, live there for a couple of years and describe it fully with their pens ...*
> —MR. FRANK AIKEN, 13TH APRIL 1967

Up to that time Ireland had been supporting in the United Nations the rights of small countries to work out their own destinies without power-bloc interference. Our new relations with the USA would not allow this to continue. Things had changed. We could not afford to embarrass them.

The Minister for External Affairs, Mr. Frank Aiken, pointed out that we did not have to be on the spot to know what was happening. We could always be told. Had we found out for our-ourselves, RTE might even sell its reports to other stations. They might edit them as they saw fit without Irish supervision! This could have international consequences of unimaginable proportions. The Holy Ghost Missions in Nigeria might be picketed. The whole thing really wasn't necessary at all. The Government would be embarrassed. Anyway, RTE reporters could not speak Vietnamese. Better stay at home.

The Authority caved in. Once again, it failed to pipe a note. The woods of Arcady were dead. Mr. Frank Aiken did not resort to invoking the veto-powers of the Government under the Act. He did not have to. A telephone call was enough—or a few personal words of warning.

The staff were dismayed by the Government's action; they were shamed by the Authority's inaction. 'What', some of us asked one another, 'has happened to the Director-General of four years ago, who withstood Mr. Lemass to his face and threatened to call an emergency meeting of the Authority when his rights were interfered with?'

The Newsroom was enraged. The Opposition parties in the Dáil were enraged. They suggested that a service which had been set up to be impartial was now being turned into a Government Information Bureau.

The newspapers frowned on the Minister's activities in the matter and the Authority's craven behaviour in giving in. Members of the public wrote letters saying that of course the Minister was right. The whole undertaking was a shocking waste of money, anyway, and the Authority were a pack of spendthrifts; others wrote that the Minister was wrong and that the Authority were a weak-kneed crowd of political 'hacks'. The bulk of letter-writers being middle-class, it is a fair guess that the weight of letters went in favour of the Minister.

The television critics were mixed in their views. Some thought the enterprise may have been overly ambitious—but on the other hand, who was supposed to be running the station: the Minister for External Affairs, the Minister for Posts and Telegraphs, or the Authority? The fact is that from that moment we no longer knew. We suspected that really nobody was running anything anymore, except the Chairman.

One hundred and twenty-seven members of the staff wrote a letter to the Taoiseach protesting against the Government's action[20] They did this in the belief that Mr. McCourt, their colleagues in the Newsroom and the need of the public for a service of integrity had been dealt a heavy blow.

Mr. McCourt replied with a letter to staff on 1st May 1967 saying that the Authority had taken its decision after 'very careful consideration' of the 'new circumstances brought to its notice' (our italics) and that there was 'no question of any infringement of the Authority's independence'. Protests by staff on behalf of the integrity of the organisation were 'inadmissible'. There were channels of communication and they had a duty to use them[21].

The staff felt they had been given a slap in the face. They had hoped that their open support would enable the Director-General to push the Authority into standing up for their rights.

If the Government wished to interfere they had the legal instrument of the Act at their disposal. They did not use it, because they could not. They had no power to stop anyone going anywhere. Their right under the Act extended only to transmissions of programmes. The very people who had been appointed to protect these rights now rejected the support of their staff in exercising them.

If the *Home Truths* affair had left a small pockmark, this incident left a major scar on the whole organization.

Attempts at intervention in the case by the N.U.J. foundered. In these circumstances it was all the more necessary for professional broadcasters to examine the principles which governed their work.

---

20   See Appendix III

21   See Appendix III

CHAPTER 1: A CAUTIONARY TALE

\* \* \*

As a result of a mandate from one of the largest meetings ever held among programmes staff, representing programme editors, scriptwriters, newscasters, reporters and Producer-Directors, it was agreed to consider the formation of a Guild for professional standards and conduct in communications. It was also resolved to improve internal lines of communication in the RTE Programmes Divisions (both sound and television) insofar as this could be effected by staff.

It was urgent that television programme people make common cause with their colleagues in the radio service. This was to prove very difficult. They were geographically remote and largely demoralised.

A drafting committee was elected to begin work on a constitution which would take both these professional objectives and our Trade Union obligations into account.

Further meetings were held and in mid-May the draft constitution was ready for discussion.

A weekend seminar to debate, amend and finalise it was held on Saturday and Sunday, 27th and 28th May 1967.

This seminar founded a Guild which was called The Television, Radio and Film Guild of Ireland.

The preamble of the constitution reads:

> Conscious of our duties and rights in the creative functions of communicating information, education, entertainment and comment, and conscious of the social character and importance of these functions and of their moral and aesthetic value to the community and to ourselves, severally and collectively we bind ourselves together by these articles of professional solidarity and association.

In the hope that other groups in the station would form their own professional associations—one group already had—the Guild resolved:

> To recognize the creative and artistic functions of associated and professional skills and to work at all times in closest relationship with those who practise them and their representative associations. Further, the Guild shall instruct the executive committee to establish the fullest working relationship with such associations (Article 2).

Later in the same article there was a reference to the Trade Unions. A fear had been expressed that such an association would run counter to the interests of members of Trade Unions. This was never seen as part of the Guild's intention, as the constitution makes clear.

Odran Walsh became its first Chairman and the Guild was launched.

> *And when they were up they were up,*
> *And when they were down they were down,*
> *And when they were only halfway up,*
> *They were neither up nor down.*
> —NURSERY RHYME

The Programmes Division's organisation had remained unchanged since the departure of Rugheimer. The old groups remained, though in a state of disintegration. One or two production teams had grown up, such as *Division* and *7 Days*, outside the orbit of the Group structure. Executive Producers still had charge of groups of programmes and Producers. The 'vertical' scheduling system— programming for special interests on special nights—had disappeared. With it went the

Executive Producers' need to organise their teams to specific deadlines. This removed, in great measure, the functions for which they had been set up. They tended to hang in mid-air.

Executive Producers were still answerable to the Controller for Producers, whose natural tendency was to form small work-teams. The fact of their being together with other work-teams in the same room was often no more than a physical relationship. No Group effort required them, any longer, to take one another's plans into account. The Executive Producers tended either to exercise executive control, or just float about, trying to keep up with the play. Some went back to producing programmes, keeping an eye from time to time on the administrative needs of their teams.

The Executive Producers, with the Heads of Departments, still attended the Controller's weekly meetings of the Programmes

Division, which was, ideally, a forum for the exchange of ideas, up and down in the organisation. Communications from, and to, this meeting tended to atrophy. When communications falter, confidence usually falters too. This was no exception.

In early Summer the Producers had met with the Controller and expressed their concern about the role of the Executive Producers in the communications chain. A lack of candour is a hindrance to work in a television organisation and Producers wanted to know what was going on, straight from the horse's mouth, so to speak. This was the new Controller's first major meeting with his Producers en masse. Two things were clear at the end of it: the Executive Producers' days were numbered and Michael Garvey, whatever his virtues, was, as an administrator, going to have a lot to learn—and quickly. He had everyone's support.

The Autumn schedule for 1967 had been almost totally finalised before Michael Garvey took up office, it being the practice to schedule for September (the start of each year's work) during the Winter of the previous year. This allowed time for the logistics of money utilisation and resources to be worked out, amended, rearranged and changed again. It permitted Producers to be allocated programmes or departments for the following season's work.

The new Controller, therefore, faced a schedule which was, by mid-Summer, in fairly trim shape and ready to go. He knew that he had a problem of communications.

Garvey was, by temperament and outlook, a very different man from Rugheimer. Those who had opposed what they regarded as the foreign influence and 'rail-roading' tactics of his predecessor, saw in Michael, as he was still affectionately called, the fulfilment of their hope. This was for a truly Irish station. They pledged him their backing.

He had already shown a flair for programme mix—the placing and juxtaposition of programmes in a night's transmission schedule. His creative intuitions and the support he enjoyed made him, therefore, an ideal man from the programming point of view. He wanted an open, Producer-involving, participative kind of organisation. He tried to get it. He lacked physical stamina, political awareness and experience to handle the administrative demands made by the job. Like most creatives, he was essentially orientated to the work at hand and tended to see every side of every problem, reaching his conclusions by intuition rather than by a conceptualised analysis. In a job demanding constant decisions in 'grey area' problems this was a disadvantage.

> There was an old woman
> Who lived in a shoe.
> She had so many children
> She didn't know what to do.
> —NURSERY RHYME

CHAPTER 1: A CAUTIONARY TALE

Numbers of staff had risen and the accommodation problem had become acute. A new office block was nearing completion. The Director-General had already moved to a suite of offices on its top floor. The Controller, who up to that time had maintained the closest physical contact with his own people, was to move there also. This was viewed with apprehension by some of the programme staff. The new building was largely to be occupied by administrative personnel. It was said to have plush carpets and to be very fancy. In programmers' minds, living in squashed quarters in the old studio block,²² in one or two older houses in its vicinity, and in caravans parked along the colonnade, this new building was the symbol of the 'other' world. It had become identified, however erroneously, with a shift in emphasis to administrative primacy. Whatever the physics, the Controller was now psychologically distanced from his Producers by light years.

These imaginings were dismissed by commonsense men. They were in fact very real and seriously affected the situation. That there was a situation was not yet recognised. People who live in glasshouses assume that other people will be careful about throwing stones.

Tom Hardiman, Assistant Controller of Programmes, was now appointed Director of Engineering. He had been an important bridge for the new Controller because of his experience and close association with Rugheimer. Jack White, another support left to Michael Garvey from the previous administration, had remained as Assistant Controller to give his knowledge and guidance to the new man.

---

22  This had been designed, Michael Scott has told us, to accommodate ten hours of home production per week. In an organisation which has produced from eighteen to twenty-two hours of home-made programming per week since its first year, it is little wonder that this accommodation is strained to bursting-point.

| Controller of Programmes: **Michael Garvey** <br> Assistant Controller: **Jack White** ||
|---|---|
| **Liam Ó Murchú** <br> Editor, Irish, Social and Educational Programmes <br><br> PROGRAMMES WITH HEADS OF DEPARTMENT <br><br> 1. Telefís Scoile <br> 2. Telefís Feirme: <br> 3. On the Land <br> 4. Mart and Market <br><br> PROGRAMMES WITHOUT DEPARTMENTAL ORGANISATION <br> Buntús Cainte <br> Labhair Gaeilge Linn <br> Home Truths <br> Garda Patrol <br> Folk Music <br> Modem Art <br> Astronomy <br> Youth Programmes <br> Religious Programmes <br><br> **Jack White** <br> 'Special' responsibilities for: <br> PROGRAMMES WITH HEADS OF DEPARTMENT <br> Sports <br><br> PROGRAMMES WITHOUT DEPARTMENTAL ORGANISATION <br><br> 7 Days <br> Division <br> The Politicians <br> Newsbeat <br> Into Europe <br> 1916-1937 Documentary | **Lelia Doolan** <br> Editor, Drama and General Features Programmes <br><br> PROGRAMMES WITH HEADS OF DEPARTMENT <br> 1. Drama <br><br> PROGRAMMES WITHOUT DEPARTMENTAL ORGANISATION <br> Céilí <br> Ballad Programmes <br> Quicksilver <br> On Your Mind <br> Céim Ar Aghaidh <br> Kino <br> RTELO <br> Late Late Show <br> Bláithín's 'Let's Draw' <br> Murphy agus a Chairde <br> Junior Magazine <br> Special Projects <br><br> **Denis O'Grady** (not a member de jure, attended meetings de facto) <br> Head of Planning (reporting to Assistant Controller) <br> Transmission scheduling <br> Presentation <br> Eurovision <br> Information <br> Audience Research <br><br> **Bill Harpur** <br> Head of Film: In charge of editorial selection, buying and preparation of imported film material. |
| **George Waters:** Head of Production Facilities <br> Contracts and Casting; Programme Services; Film Production; Studios; Outside Broadcasting Unit; Production Planning and Control. ||

The Controller had made a plan for the Division. The essentials of this were the improvement of communications. He dissolved the role of the Executive Producers as titular heads of programmes. The Heads of Department remained. The Controller was now forming a small group around himself to be called the Editorial Group.

It was to be responsible for 'all the productions of the programme area'. It was to provide 'a fast and open communications' channel between the Controller and the Producers and technical planning-and-control personnel. It was to take part in planning programmes and in policy-making decisions. There were to be five members.

Two new Editors, Lelia Doolan and Liam Ó Murchú were offered appointments with responsibilities for programmes on the Editorial Group as shown above .

The new Head of Production Facilities, George Waters, did not have the status of Assistant Controller that his predecessor, Tom Hardiman, had had.

Lelia Doolan had some misgivings about this plan.

Jack Dowling had gone to her about a Trade Union matter involving the Production Assistants, who had sought his advice. He was anxious to discuss this with the new Controller whom he knew only professionally, through the unhappy *Home Truths* affair.

In an attempt to overcome some of these difficulties, the three of them had dinner together. This had two immediate and important results.

The first was that Lelia Doolan told him that her acceptance of the appointment, involving what she considered to be equivocal relationships with Heads of Department and with Producers who had no Departments, had been contingent on his clearly recognising that initiative in programme making and planning lay with the Producers. He immediately agreed and confirmed that the role of the Editor was to stimulate, facilitate and advise the Producers, to ensure communications and to help in the evolution of his own policies.

He told Jack Dowling, on hearing the case for the Production Assistants, that he would attend to the matter instantly; in fact, the next morning. He thought it disgraceful that so valuable a group should be forced to contemplate strike action on a matter in which their claim was so evidently just.

This was a hopeful occasion and, in fact, the Production Assistants' case was expeditiously and tactfully concluded to everyone's satisfaction.

> *King James he pitched his tents between*
> *The lines for to retire;*
> *But King William threw his bomb-balls in*
> *And set them all on fire.*
> —SONGS OF RESISTANCE

With the promotion of T. P. Hardiman to the post of Director-of-Engineering there was, as the Controller's memorandum announcing the new organisation stated, a 'serious temptation to move the Production Facilities in the same direction. I was loath to do this as the liability and quality of service which has been coming from this section is of cardinal importance to all programme making. Mr. George Waters will now be Head of Production Facilities and for a short period *will report to both myself and the Director of Engineering on a personal level*' (our italics).

The Director-General's Newsletter of the same date, however, stated: 'Mr. George Waters has been appointed Head of Production Facilities and will for the time being, report to the *Director of Engineering*' (our italics).

Who was the Head of Facilities to report to? The matter remains a mystery to this day. There was the tendency, since Mr. Hardiman had been an able leader of the Group's destinies inside the Programmes Division, to continue to look to him as their old head and patron rather than to a new Controller—to whom they, nevertheless, felt a loyalty was due.

It was a classic piece of organisational ambiguity.

It was guaranteed to make Mr. Waters' job difficult.

It was, certainly, to make the Controller's effectiveness precarious.

Its results were to become evident almost at once.

It was the busy time of year. The Controller, with the encouragement of the Editorial Group, met with all the Programmes Division personnel early in September 1967 and spoke to them of the new organisation and of the plans for the Autumn schedule prior to announcing these plans at the Press Conference.

It was decided to amalgamate *Division* with the old *7 Days* programme, under the latter's title. It was to run as a twice-weekly Current Affairs programme dealing with national and international affairs. Muiris Mac Conghail, who had produced *Division*, was to be Producer of the new *7 Days* and was also responsible for *The Politicians*, the monthly party political broadcast. The new team included reporters and interviewers who had worked on both programmes and the two young Directors who had carried *7 Days* during the previous season, Eoghan Harris and Dick Hill. Two trainee Directors from a group appointed during the Summer, were posted to the team.

> *Casey Jones, he mounted to the cabin,*
> *Casey Jones, with his orders in his hand!*
> *Casey Jones, he mounted to the cabin,*
> *Took his farewell trip into the promised land.*
> —CASEY JONES

The new *7 Days* opened with the Autumn schedule at the end of September and continued to delve into matters of public controversy boldly and, some people in high places thought, brashly. Like most human organisms which are vital and involved, it sometimes made mistakes, and it was often in hot water. When a cold bath was administered by the Director-General in February of the following year, it was to cause the biggest television row in the history of the station.

The evidence that this row was inevitable had been there for everyone to see from the start. In the Dáil debates over the formulation of the Act it had been foretold. In every succeeding debate on Posts and Telegraphs Estimates, in the appointment of the Authority itself, in newspaper comment, letters and editorials, the fact which all could see and none would face was revealed again and again: the Government wanted an independent broadcasting service in theory, but found the practice unbearable.

Inside the station the evidence was equally clear: in attempts to set up working groups of Producers whose interest in and judgment of their material would grow through experience and exercise; in endless discussions about their need for support, encouragement, criticism and candour.

It was clear too in the administrators' need for order and predictability; in treating certain matters as 'confidential', in being too busy about particulars to think about what the station was doing or what it ought to be doing. Contradictions uneasily coexisting in the station were gathering the forces of conflict into a pressure chamber.

These forces of conflict and contradiction were potentially productive.

The pressures of Government can, and did in many cases in the past, lead to an increase in fortitude among professional broadcasters.

## CHAPTER 1: A CAUTIONARY TALE

The conflicts between 'creative' people and administrators were solvable and in the past had, to some extent, been solved. As long as the station remembered that its first task was making programmes for Irish people, its problems were a sign of health—conflict being inevitable among dedicated and intelligent people.

The Vietnam disagreement was the worst management-staff rift so far. It might have been examined and investigated; it might have been made fruitful by the Director-General's standing firm, as had happened in the past; but increasingly his resistance seemed to weaken.

People had not been hired as automatons. They had been employed to think. The fact that nobody owed his soul to the Authority never seems to have been acknowledged. Confidence in top management continued to ebb.

Programme people were awaiting the effects of the new Editorial arrangements.

The weekly Editorial Group meeting had difficulties from the start, mainly because it lacked a common notion of its purposes. There were differing views as to the role and function of the Editors. Some regarded them as virtual Heads of Programme-groups, with delegated authority from the Controller, and executive responsibility for the conduct of their work. Others understood the Editors' functions to be primarily those of communication and advice; to keep the Controller and his group informed of the sentiment, difficulties and plans of Producers and the Departments. Above all, they were to orchestrate all the ideas and initiatives, from above and below them, into a realistic unity that would at once execute the Controller's policy and facilitate the Producers' ideas. In this sense, they were truly executives.

There was much talk but the methods of programme control remained unclear. Producers were beginning to think that ambiguity and vagueness were instruments of programme administration.

Nothing that was decided ever seemed to stick; increasingly, the production teams found it more conducive to do their work and just ignore 'decisions'. At least, the job got done.

A not unamusing aspect of the situation was that quite ordinary people, with whom one would, a short time previously, have argued in a public house or canteen, felt that their senior positions conferred upon them a certain sudden and sober wisdom which entitled them to obedience and loyalty. This is, of course, a common pitfall in hierarchical organisations which tend to seduce even the most democratic executives. It gives them a paternalistic attitude towards subordinates of intelligence. This is often unconsciously amusing. Alas, it is not a joke that can often be shared!

Pressures there certainly were, and the higher executives of RTE were feeling them that Autumn. *Newsbeat* had always had its quota of 'admonition' and 'abuse'. Programmes which had sought to test the public's maturity inevitably increased the testiness of national leaders.

*7 Days* did such programmes and underwent such pressures, not only from enraged public servants but from within the Authority itself, whose political and temperamental predilections favoured the status quo. They seemed to be saying: scrutiny of public and current affairs, persons and events is a responsibility of the service. At the same time, such scrutiny must be 'responsible', predictable as far as possible and, above all, defensible. Lucky is he who can have it both ways: official bodies must.

Ken Gray wondered if it would last. An Irish Times leader had to defend 'young lions' on *7 Days*.

This Janus-like stance filtered down through the Director-General, Controller and Assistant Controller to the Producer and the Directors and the reporters on the *7 Days* programme in thinner and thinner trickles.

## CHAPTER 1: A CAUTIONARY TALE

Jack White, who had an ill-defined 'responsibility' for Current Affairs programmes, had asked to be made Editor of these programmes at the reorganisation in September. His request had not been granted. He had the instincts of a programme man. With Gunnar Rugheimer, he had gained great experience of work relationships with Producers in these pressure areas. He had experience of the need for complete candour with programme staff; he had taken part in the resistance to outside groups and persons who had attempted to restrict the freedom of broadcasters. His own experience as a journalist and broadcaster, his integrity and grasp of the complexity of production problems gave him an unequalled insight into the work of the *7 Days* group. He knew that a mutual trust formed the basis of any workable relationship.

At the time of Rugheimer's departure, he might have been regarded as a man most suitable and well-fitted to take over the Controllership. It was owing to the curious temper of the Authority, reflecting in their turn the feeling of a nation which regarded itself as Celtic first and Anglo Irish whenever it felt the need, that he was not even granted an interview for the job. A Jewish Lord Mayor of Dublin is a thing bizarre enough to pay lip-service to social tolerance. A Controller of Programmes, however gifted, who had been to Trinity College, had worked in the Irish Times and belonged to a Protestant minority— growing ever more minor —is quite another matter. His position in the ensuing events was to be fateful.

As the months of tension pressed on, nobody knew whether the temper of the Authority was reflected in its Chief Executive, or whether the temperaments of Michael Garvey and Jack White were not allowed to mesh because the Director-General saw a need for the new man to stand on his own two feet. At all events, the relationship between the Controller and his Assistant, though friendly, was less close than was sensible in view of the demanding nature and interdependence of their two roles.

Mr. White became, to some extent, isolated. This was to be a disaster.

Perhaps this isolation was not altogether a product of the circumstances or of his background. A certain withdrawn and wary aloofness characterised his manner and, to some extent, his methods. He disdained self-defence and therefore sometimes ignored the need for self-explanation. The sense of propriety in the Anglo-Irish tradition, with its post-revolutionary need for survival, may have been at the root of this. He was, in fact, a warm friend, and in need of friendship in his working relationships, but shy of disclosing the fact.

It is not without interest, in trying to understand his role in RTE, that he had occupied positions of secondary executive authority both in journalism and in television. This calls for very special qualities. Where a second-in-command has a strong and decisive principal, men of Jack White's qualities—his ability to think problems systematically through, his calm, his artistic sensibilities— are invaluable.

In short, he was not equipped to work in a jungle, unscathed. He was working in one.

Mr. McCourt's position was not a happy one either. After a strong start and years of development, through steady pressure, aided by the stimulus and thrust of the Programmes Division, he had undergone changes himself.

The broadcasting experience of Eamonn Andrews was no longer available. Nor was the strength of Rugheimer. Nor was the confidence of the staff. The corridor joke was: Dr. Andrews is the Director-General; Mr. McCourt is the Controller; the Controller ...

The News Division under Jim McGuinness had been undergoing changes. Des Grealy, who had been assistant to Pearse Kelly, had resigned. The new Deputy Head of News was Desmond Fisher, an experienced writer who had been Editor of the Catholic Herald.

The News Division was broadening its scope and range, both in its main News bulletin and in *Nuacht* which now went into the schedules at the prime time of 8 p.m. Attempts had been made to provide it with a news comment programme—the first of which was *Newsview* in the early days, then *Ceamara na Cruinne*, and finally *Féach*, all of which, in due course, had been terminated or moved into the Programmes Division. Newsmen, always questing and inquisitive, had ambitions beyond simple news gathering.

Since the early days, journalists in that part of the house had been less than happy about their work prospects and regarded themselves as being in something of a straight-jacket.

News got the scoops. Programmes Division got the comment.

Nonetheless, morale in the *7 Days* team was at its height. In December 1967 they could look back proudly on a series of programmes which had closely tested the public's appetite for officially unpalatable truth. The public had shown it wanted more.

A story on the closedown of the Electra factory had revealed the 'other side' of foreign-backed industrialisation. The IT&GWU was not happy, its role having been vigorously handled in the programme.

Then Patrick Gallagher's tough interview with a property speculator, Mr. Matt Gallagher, had revealed the gross inequalities of Dublin's affluence. His accountants were revealed as having close Establishment connections. Mohair-suited gentlemen were dismayed.

A *7 Days* film on emigration had provoked the wrath of the Archbishop of Dublin because some Irish labourers in Britain said they didn't go to Mass. Shortly afterwards a survey by London priests confirmed the accuracy of the programme.

The Government had announced a Referendum for June to amend the Constitution. This raised questions that called for public comment. There was little. The electoral boundaries and the whole issue of P.R. had, naturally, first been reported by News. *7 Days* had analysed the Fianna Fáil propositions, dispassionately and scientifically. In a programme in December, David Thornley and Basil Chubb had shown that Fianna Fáil would secure ninety-seven seats, if the straight vote system were adopted. This enraged the Fianna Fáil Party. They felt that *7 Days* was accusing them of a gigantic national confidence trick.

Despite the atmosphere of official disapproval, the team was determined to pursue its tough policy of enquiry. Early in December they put up two programme suggestions, confident that an aroused public opinion would support them. They underestimated the power of the men in the saddles.

The first of these suggestions, from the reporter Brian Cleeve and the Director Eoghan Harris was that the activities of the Special Branch should be investigated. Their starting point was the involvement of police officers in events leading to the eviction of a newly-married couple, Michael and Georgia Murray.

It was suggested to Brian Cleeve, in the course of researching and making the programme, that it would never see the light of day and that *7 Days* should avoid appearing to defend Communists like the Murrays. He replied: 'Look here, I hold no brief for Communists or Fascists or any other political convictions of that kind. We're professional broadcasters: people have a perfect constitutional right to be Communists. It's absolutely irrelevant what they are; if they are being done a violent injustice by the forces of the State, it's the duty of this programme to expose the fact.'

On 20th December 1967 a film interview with the couple was shown as a pilot-run to Jack White in the presence of Rory O'Farrell, film editor, Brian Cleeve and Muiris Mac Conghail. Jack White said that the charges made in it against the Special Branch should form the basis of a full-scale documentary. He thought that as a short item it might perhaps do less than justice to the importance of its subject. *7 Days* was not, of course, equipped to do full scale documentaries.

Around the same time Patrick Gallagher and the Associate Producer Dick Hill began research into a dispute at Mountpleasant Sq. Planning permission, already refused by Dublin Corporation, had been given by the Minister for Local Government, Mr. Kevin Boland, to a Mr. Lahart. This man wished to build a petrol station. The area was scheduled as an open area under the draft Dublin development plan. Objection to the permission was widespread from bodies like An Taisce. Rumour had it that the profit to Mr. Lahart, if he should wish to sell the site, would be in the region of £60,000. From Thursday 18th to Monday 22nd January 1968 the *7 Days* film unit worked in Mountpleasant Sq., interviewing among others Mr. Michael Mullen, T.D., Prof. Kevin Nowlan and Mr. Joe McCullough, Secretary of An Taisce. The item was to be transmitted on Tuesday 23rd January. That day the item was deferred by general consensus of the team to make way for a more topical issue.

On Wednesday 24th the Producer, Mac Conghail, left for Lisbon on his way to Biafra, leaving Dick Hill in charge with instructions that the item was to be transmitted on Friday 26th without any cuts.

For the next two days there was constant agitation among the team.

It began on Wednesday evening when Jack White viewed the Mountpleasant film, expressed concern, but ordered no cuts. On Thursday the film was again viewed. This time the Controller, Michael Garvey, attended. He suggested cuts but left the final decision in the hands of Dick Hill.

Around the same time Dick Hill told Eoghan Harris that Jack White was beginning to show nervousness about the Special Branch film.

On Thursday evening Jack White rang Dick Hill to say that the Mountpleasant story was not to be transmitted but could become part of a later omnibus programme on planning.

On Thursday, too, Eoghan Harris told Jack White that he could view the 'rough-cut edition' of the Special Branch programme on Sunday 28th.

On Friday morning there was an angry meeting of *7 Days* staff. They asked Dick Hill to enquire if the Mountpleasant Sq. story was going out that night as part of an 'omnibus' programme. Jack White agreed to this, as it seemed to meet his objection to what looked like an isolated swipe at a Minister. Throughout Friday afternoon Patrick Gallagher and Eoghan Harris frantically assembled the 'omnibus' part of the programme. At 7 p.m., less than three hours from transmission, Michael Garvey phoned Dick Hill to say that the Deputy Director-General, John Irvine, had viewed the film. In the absence of the Director-General, he would not make a decision to transmit it. The Director-General had left for the international rugby match in Paris. That night the bored public watched a meandering discussion with three municipal Councillors. An embarrassed Gallagher had to stretch this by eight minutes to cover the gap.

There was now widespread talk about the developing situation. The debate was drawing in many who were concerned about the programme's freedom of enquiry.

As Jack Dowling was to write in a note to Lelia Doolan:

> ... everyone is becoming suspicious of everyone else: I hope that I'm not being morbidly imaginative in thinking that Michael [Garvey] may be building up a complex of misunderstandings in this situation. It seems to me that his obligations to Jack White involve frankness with him—and with the *7 Days* team.

## CHAPTER 1: A CAUTIONARY TALE

The team was too busy to be engaged about such speculations. Their concern was with practical effects. All that was now clear to them was that since Wednesday something heavy had been leaning on the programme echelon.

Mr. Boland has not since denied that he telephoned the Director-General for 'information' on the Mount Pleasant Sq. programme. Jack White's worry about the Special Branch film was not an isolated one. He was then unaware that an effort by members of that force in RTE to bribe a film editor for information had been rebuffed. Clearly they had gone to higher authority. Determined efforts were made by the *7 Days* team to come to terms with the vague weight of repression.

The Controller of Programmes was asked if the Producer, Muiris Mac Conghail, had not sent him a memorandum before leaving for Biafra. In it, he had said that he intended to transmit the Mountpleasant Sq. programme on the Tuesday and the projected Biafra programme on the Friday of the following week. The Controller subsequently told them that he had not replied to the memorandum but had taken it merely to be a document of information.

The expedition to Biafra, in which the 7 Days team were to be flown from Lisbon by a plane chartered for international newsmen by a private firm, was agreed in advance with the Assistant Controller, and later with the Controller. It was stopped by the Director-General before it left Lisbon.

The war in Biafra was regularly reported in Newscasts. News reporters must have nodded in sardonic resignation when the *7 Days* team was recalled, remembering their own Vietnam experience.

Nonetheless, *7 Days* produced a programme on Biafra, made by a foreign company, but with a *7 Days* voice commentary. It was deemed to be pro-Biafran.

The Nigerian *Charge d'Affaires* described the programme as 'shocking'. It 'gave an unfavourable and unfair impression of the Nigerian Government', he said. There was, however, he made clear, no major diplomatic row. He had not made a formal complaint to the Irish Government but had simply requested that the Minister for External Affairs 'exchange views' with him on the programme. Mr. Aiken in turn referred the matter to the Minister for Posts and Telegraphs and he asked the Authority for a copy of the film in order to view it privately.

Rumours and counter-rumours, whispers of interference from everywhere and increasing disquiet at exhortations to play safe and be 'responsible' harried the Producers' days. They began to wonder whether anyone wanted the truth told about anything. They were pressing for the transmission of the Mountpleasant Sq. programme.

This was conveyed through the Producer, Muiris Mac Conghail, but by this time Mac Conghail seemed to have withdrawn into himself and began to disturb the confidence of certain members of the 7 Days team. Clearly some kind of approach had been made to him by senior Management and he did not feel free to tell the team.

On Sunday 28th January, as arranged by Eoghan Harris, Jack White viewed the Special Branch film, expressed satisfaction, but said he would like to show it to the Director-General.

On Friday 2nd February the Director-General viewed the film privately. Through an alleged technical error it was also seen in the Newsroom and its contents became common talk. This is probably not unconnected with a 'Red-scare' story in the Evening Herald.

From now on, events within the station were being 'leaked' to the newspapers as fast as they were happening.

Following this viewing, the Director-General requested some cuts, especially of pictures showing Dr. Noel Browne being attacked by police dogs during a demonstration. Nevertheless, Mr. McCourt said he regarded it as a public service programme and that the Minister for Justice, Mr. Brian Lenihan, should be represented on it.

That evening, following a programme in which he was appearing, the Minister informally told Muiris Mac Conghail that he would be available for comment. The atmosphere was cordial.

On Monday 5th February at 10 a.m. the Chairman of the Authority, Dr. C. S. Andrews, viewed the film with the Director-General. Later with his entourage he came to the *7 Days* office and surveyed the staff inside. He did not speak to anybody.

Repeated requests to the Producer from his staff for a decision on transmission got no satisfactory reply. Again and again it was asked what the Chairman of the Authority intended to do with a forty-five minute documentary that had cost £400 to make. Sources close to him said he didn't like it. But we understand he did not forbid its transmission. The remainder of the Authority said nothing.

It was in this atmosphere that Sean Egan had begun a film on Father Michael Sweetman, S.J., and the Dublin Housing Action Committee. It, too, disappeared. Neither it, the Mountpleasant Sq. story, nor the film on the Special Branch were ever transmitted.[23]

> *With just their heads above the ground*
> *They bade a fond goodbye,*
> *With all the people shouting out*
> *'Here's mud into your eye!'*
> *(And there certainly was).*
> —JOHN LENNON

---

23  Another film on the Housing Action Committee was transmitted by *7 Days*, after it had moved under the control of the Head of News.

Producers, like other human beings, will only become recalcitrant and devious if they find themselves being treated as children. An insidious fear for the integrity of the work creeps into staff relationships. It ends by destroying them. Muiris Mac Conghail had a group of lively, fearless and committed people working on the programme; the growing official caution affected work relationships. Directors and Reporters were likely to take out their frustrations on the responsible man above them.

The team suspected Mac Conghail; Mac Conghail suspected White; White lost touch with Garvey who knew that McCourt suspected White. The Authority suspected everybody and everybody suspected it.

Always, the suspicion from below was that those above were "trimming the truth'; from above that those below were trying to 'embarrass' the Authority *vis-a-vis* the Government. In the corridors there were mutterings that Jim McGuinness wanted a Public Affairs programme and that Muiris Mac Conghail was doing a deal with the Management about the transmission of the Special Branch and Mountpleasant Sq. programmes. Few took these seriously.

There was genuine uneasiness among supporters and opponents of the programme. Some of the criticisms were harsh; the team was going too far in a hurry; they had a death wish; they were trying to push a tottering Management.

Others felt that this kind of surgical Public Affairs operation was precisely what the nation needed. This type of critic was responsibly aware that grave mistakes of judgment or emphasis could be, and were in fact, made occasionally (in fact twice), but that as long as the impartiality of the team was sincerely exercised any criticised person or institution would have the right of open and public reply, thus keeping the situation healthy.

The team's sympathetic colleagues had one fear: the pace was so hectic that the standards of research and detachment—so vital to its integrity—might begin to suffer from sheer physical and mental exhaustion. Once again, RTE was doing a job comparable to its competitors but without their resources.

The consensus of both hostile and sympathetic opinion was that *7 Days* was doing a first-rate job and deserved the vigorous support of Management.

Lelia Doolan, because of her old association with *7 Days*, had kept in touch with the team. Jack Dowling was also kept in touch by Eoghan Harris and Paddy Gallagher. Lelia Doolan had urged Michael Garvey to be open and frank with Jack White about pressures to which Garvey was subject from the Authority through Mr. McCourt. She had similarly urged Jack White to see the Controller at once and ask him what was going on at Director-General and Authority levels. There were others who appealed to Muiris Mac Conghail to be candid with Jack White and with his own team. Michael Garvey's stock with the Producers was high; the Editorial Group was in its early days and it was at least attempting to open up communications throughout the house.

Jack Dowling returned from a filming assignment in England on Saturday 10th February 1968.

On Sunday 11th February Eoghan Harris and Paddy Gallagher telephoned and asked him to meet them during the evening.

> *Necessity is the plea for every*
> *infringement of human freedom.*
> *It is the argument of tyrants.*
> *It is the creed of slaves.*
> —WILLIAM PITT

They spent three or four hours together reviewing the situation, teasing out its different strands. Jack Dowling arrived at an alarming conclusion.

Taking into account the Authority's attitude to the kind of controversy which was permissible and that which was not; the physical strain which was obvious in Michael Garvey; a lack of candour which the team was now experiencing from its own Producer; the prospect of a Referendum on P.R. about which the Government and the Authority were touchy to the point of absurdity; the growing strength of the Newsroom headed by Jim McGuinness; the meetings recently between Mac Conghail and McGuinness and finally Michael Garvey's political *naivete*—Kevin McCourt was going to move *7 Days* into the editorial safety of Jim McGuinness' bailiwick.

They telephoned Lelia Doolan at her home, and told her of this conclusion. She was incredulous. She rang Michael Garvey and told him what she had heard. She asked him if he thought there might be any truth in it.

He told her that that afternoon at about 4.30 p.m. he had, upon the request of the Director-General, gone to see him in his office at the studios.

Mr. McCourt had informed him that he intended to transfer control of *7 Days* to the Head of News.

Michael Garvey said he was still in a stunned condition. He had just arrived home.

He intended to see Jack White.

Lelia Doolan then informed Jack Dowling, Eoghan Harris and Paddy Gallagher that, unbelievable as it might have seemed, their analysis was correct.

The Programmes Division was going to be neutered in order to quiet the Authority's fears. We were about to realise Dr. Andrews' philosophy of the Government's being master of all semi-State company policies.[24]

---

24   Cf. *State-Sponsored Bodies*, Garret FitzGerald, p. 53

> *Officers will send in their swords*
> *to the cutler for sharpening.*
> —ARMY ORDER (1914)

At 8.30 a.m. next morning Jack Dowling, Eoghan Harris and Michael Slevin called in their Trade Union officials.

Lelia Doolan, having consulted with some of the production staff concerned, telephoned the Controller of Programmes and told him of the intentions of the Union shop stewards to effect Union intervention. He said he was to see the Director-General again that morning. He was extremely unhappy about the situation and said that he wished to prevent, if he could, the transfer of the programme. Lelia Doolan asked him to come to lunch with herself and Jack Dowling, in order that he might get out of the station, have a respite, and reflect upon the situation in reasonable calm.

Meanwhile, the two Union officials, Liam O'Dea of W.U.I. and Dermot Doolan of Actors' Equity, had telephoned to the Assistant to the Director of Personnel in the early morning in order to request him to delay the posting of the notice of transfer until they should have time to consult with him about its effects on their membership. They were faced, they told the Assistant, with the task of preventing an unofficial mass walk-out of staff.

Michael Garvey, at luncheon, said that the Director-General had intended to post the notice of transfer at 12.30 that afternoon but that he had agreed to delay it until 3 p.m. He had, in his discussion with the Director-General that morning, offered to resign on the grounds that the transfer of the programme evidenced a loss of confidence in 'his ability to lead the Programmes Division'. Lelia Doolan and Jack Dowling reviewed the possible developments with him. Aindreas Ó Gallchóir telephoned during lunch to say that the Workers' Union would support Equity in resisting the transfer. He was calling a joint Union meeting of production staff at once. Dowling told the Controller. The whole thing, Michael Garvey said, had been a complete shock to him. The programme, he said, would be transferred over his dead body.

On returning to the station they discovered that the notice was to be posted. The place was in a hubbub. Michael Garvey had been officially informed by Kevin McCourt at 3 p.m. that the transfer was to take place. In a conversation with Michael Garvey that afternoon, Lelia Doolan told him that in the present circumstances it would be wiser for him not to resign. This was for two reasons. One: he had obviously opposed the transfer of the programme and would therefore more readily support and be supported by staff who similarly opposed it. Two: if he now resigned, the new man appointed could, in the circumstances, be expected to support the transfer of the programme. Michael Garvey said that he would not resign. Senior staff colleagues had also urged him not to do so, as had the Trade Unions.

The official Union requests, both by telephone and in person, to have the notice of transfer delayed, even by thirty-six hours, were refused. These requests were made in order to enable the Unions to consider the implications of the transfer in its effects on the working conditions and interrelations of the staff concerned.

The notice of transfer was posted on the notice boards at 5 p.m. It said:

NEWSLETTER From: Director-General To: All Staff

With effect from today, responsibility for public affairs programmes in television at present covered by *7 Days*, will be transferred to the Head of the News Division.

(Signed) Kevin McCourt
Director-General.
12th February 1968.

A *7 Days* programme was due to be transmitted on the following night. There was a joint Union meeting that evening at which the production staff concerned were instructed not to report for duty to the Head of News Division. They would remain subject to instructions from the Controller of Programmes until such time as changes in the nature of their employment could be properly discussed between the Unions and the Management. This meant, in effect, that there would be no transmission of the programme until such time as production staffs concerned were satisfied, through their Unions, of their future status and conditions.

> *History is neither mere action,*
> *nor vertiginous freedom, nor*
> *frivolous creativity, but it is*
> *the persistent attempt to do*
> *the best we can with the*
> *knowledge of the moment.*
> —J.-P. SARTRE

Of course, the issue was one of freedom of speech; the freedom of professional broadcasters to exercise their responsibility to viewers and to the general public: but this was not an issue upon which Trade Unions could carry on a negotiation. Some Producers, who simply wanted to stop the programme being transferred, had difficulty in understanding this point. But the facts of the case were that the Authority had every legal right to transfer any programme it wished to any part of the house it wished or to any officer or to any servant.

What it could not do was to transfer staff outside the terms of their contracts. This was ground upon which the Unions could stand and upon it they took up their position.

Through the refusal of the Producers and the Production Assistants to transfer, without consultation, to the Head of News Division, the programme was effectively 'blacked'—that is, kept off the air.

The Guild, whose object was to do nothing to interfere with Trade Union negotiations but had, at the same time, to consider the professional and ethical implications of the situation, met together on Tuesday night and subsequently issued the following:

> Conscious of an impression which has been spread among our members that Michael Garvey, Controller of Programmes, and his Assistant, Jack White, had by dilatoriness or indifference allowed the structure of the Programmes Division to be altered without opposition, we have investigated the circumstances ...
>
> This Committee is satisfied that the interests of programme integrity and the professional freedom of Guild members have been actively protected by Mr. Garvey and Mr. White to the limits permitted them by their own professional obligations to the Authority.
>
> We wish our membership to know that they enjoy the full confidence and respect of this Executive Committee.

This was signed by: Odran Walsh, Jack Dowling, Patrick Gallagher, Celestine Rooney, Romuald Dodd, o.p., Lelia Doolan, Eoghan Harris, Pan Collins.

There were questions in the Dáil and comments in the newspapers. Arthur Noonan of the Irish Independent said that he had given hints of the transfer many weeks before. He couldn't understand how the programme could be transmitted by the News Division without breaking the impartiality obligations of the Act.

On Wednesday afternoon, 14th February, the Unions' representatives and shop stewards finally met with the Director of Personnel, Mr. Hugh McNeill, for over four hours, fruitlessly.

Bluntly he told them that if the Producers made the trade dispute into a 'free speech' issue the Authority would expose 'those whom the Producers most wished to protect'. One of the Producers rejoined: 'That is a most improper remark. You mean Mr. Garvey and Mr. White.' Mr. McNeill did not reply. These two men, nominally leaders of the Programmes Division, became little more than spectators in the upper-Management/Union discussions which were to follow, and in which they took no part whatever.

It was obvious to the Union delegation that Mr. McNeill had no plenipotentiary powers and that the Director-General had altogether lost touch with staff sentiment and intention.

On the same day the newspapers reported Muiris Mac Conghail, the Producer of the programme, as saying: 'I discussed programme content of future *7 Days* productions with my new boss. I am hoping the situation will resolve itself and that there will be no more trouble.'

In a dispute which made newspaper headlines every day for three weeks, there were bound to be a number of rumours, misstatements and apparent inflammation of tempers. In fact, the conduct and the demeanour of staff was unhysterical. The Authority, Mr. McCourt and

RTE 'spokesmen' made long statements every few days. The staff made no rejoinders. Mr. McCourt and his Authority were evidently looking for rope. They got all they wanted.

> *I'm not arguing with you— I'm telling you.*
> —JAMES MCNEILL WHISTLER

Management had internally published an eighteen-point memorandum which stated, among its other conditions to resolve the dispute, that unless the 'blacking' of the *7 Days* programme was lifted by Friday, 16th February, the staff involved would be automatically suspended. A Trade Union meeting of production personnel considered this memorandum and resolved to continue the 'blacking' until the Management sat down and talked.

Management countered by suspending the Producers, Directors, Production Assistants and one Reporter, Paddy Gallagher. Muiris Mac Conghail was required to suspend his staff and then himself!

Bunny Carr and Joan Birthistle proposed that a Fund Committee be set up for the support of the suspended members. They were given powers to co-opt a committee. They worked like trojans and raised the money.

This time, the Authority had piped a note: it filled the woods of Arcady:

> It is noted that since the controversy arose, consultation with union officials has taken place, from which it is clear that the real matter at issue is whether the Director-General or the staff has a right to decide who is to be in charge of any programme, or where in the

organisation management of a programme should be located.

In view of the fact that no authority, public or private, could yield on such a *basic issue of management*, the Director-General will suspend those members of the staff who now refuse to carry out their duties (our italics).

The Authority denied outside pressure and re-asserted its independence.

The Unions did not rise to the fly. They expressly denied any formal opposition to the transfer of *7 Days*. They wanted to discuss only their workers' conditions of employment. Management could see no reason to do this. A Producer, they said, could be ordered to sweep the floor.

*  *  *

In the midst of all the brouhaha and Union negotiations, a notice appeared in the canteen. It said.

To All, Whether It Concerns Them Or Not:

The Director-General wants to inform the staff that following controversial statements by Daithi Lacha, in the current series of programmes, he has decided to transfer responsibility for the series to Mr. Michael O'Hehir, Head of Sport. The reason for this change is a logical one in that the animals concerned have been known to run on occasions and would, therefore, fit more easily into the Sports Department. There was no question of interference with the Head of Children's

Programmes, who would still have full freedom to play the National Anthem at 5.30 p.m. every day.

In regard to Quicksilver, it is confirmed that this programme will now be under the direct control of the Archbishop of Dublin, following the unfortunate slip of a competitor in using the word 'feck' on the programme. The Director-General wishes to deny that this change-over from money prizes to indulgences is an unwarranted intrusion in the affairs of the Producer.

The fact that the Late Late Show is now being transmitted without sound is one more example of the technical daring which makes Montrose the courageous leader of the Irish people. Fury without sound is a far more civilised form of entertainment. Should panelists continue to use untoward facial expressions, it is eventually intended to dispense with vision also ...

... all those who still have opinions are advised to cash them in at the Chairman's office before 28th June when a Referendum will be held.

The Friday night, 16th February, was a transmission night, not for *7 Days*, but for *The Politicians*. Its position in the transfer operation now came under question.

It was raised by Deputy l'Estrange in Dáil Éireann, who asked whether this programme, too, was transferred to the Head of News. It was realised, with some amusement, that the question had not entered the minds of Management at all!

The Director-General's notice had said 'Public Affairs programmes'; it was, therefore, our intention to 'black' *The Politicians* also.

There would have been considerable confusion if this party political broadcast were to be transmitted under the control of the News Division.

Mr. MacNeill had told us that it was to be transferred with *7 Days*. He now said that this had been a mistake. Would we please produce the programme? We would. We did. It remained in the Programmes Division.

Jack Dowling addressed the annual general meeting of the Irish Transport and General Workers* Union Branch in Studio One and explained the W.U.I. and Equity case. The meeting was sympathetic and supportive in mood and expression. It was made clear to him privately that active back-up would be difficult because of Mr. Fintan Kennedy's membership of the Authority, but that, of course, this mighty Union would not pass our pickets.

Also in Dáil Éireann, Deputy Sean Dunne made reference to a memorandum, of which he later produced a copy, which, he alleged, was a directive stating that the pros and cons of P.R. were not to be discussed on News bulletins. The existence of such a directive was denied by Kevin McCourt and later by a statement issued from some executives of the Newsroom staff. Jack Dowling saw the memorandum. It was not signed by Mr. McGuinness but by the Duty-Editor. Where the Duty-Editor got his instructions remains a mystery.

The Sunday Independent had reported that Mr. Jim McGuinness issued the directive to staff banning 'all criticisms of the Government's plans to abolish P.R.' It published an apology.

The Authority continued to publish statements throughout the period of the dispute. The Unions devoted their statements and questions to formal negotiating sessions.

Jim Larkin and Dermot Doolan, of W.U.I. and Equity, now took formal charge of the dispute.

On Monday 19th February Producer-Directors, Production Assistants, reporters, clerk typists, etc., voted for strike by seventy-four votes to three, in support of the action of their suspended colleagues.

The following day, after a meeting of the RTE Union Group, Equity served strike notice of fourteen days. It was followed by the W.U.I.'s notice of strike two days later on 22nd February 1968.

The strike, said a statement issued by the latter Union, would take place on 7th March, 'if by that date the suspensions have not been wholly cancelled and our members reinstated in their normal employment'. On the same day, the Authority, locked in the headlong rush of their own curious logic, countered by suspending three N.U.J. members, Brian Cleeve, John O'Donoghue and Ted Nealon. This Union, too, announced strike notice on 23rd February.

In accordance with Trade Union practice, Equity called on Conciliation[25] immediately after serving strike notice. The W.U.I. and the N.U.J. also took part in the conciliation tribunal between Unions and Management which was held on 26th, 27th and 28th February 1968.

The Conciliation Board consisted of a Chairman, Mr. T. K. Liston, s.c., Senator D. F. Murphy and Mr. Fachtna Ó hAnnracháin.

The Union negotiating teams consisted of Dermot Doolan, General Secretary of Equity; Jack Dowling and Michael Slevin, representatives of the Equity House Committee; James Larkin, General Secretary of the W.U.I.; James Plunkett Kelly and Aindreas Ó Gallchóir, representatives of the House Committee of W.U.I.; and James Eadie, Irish organiser of the N.U.J., with Joe Fahy, staff representative of the N.U.J.

---

25    RTE (the Authority and its staff) is committed, in order to obviate a strike to three preventative stages: (i) direct negotiation between Management and the Unions, (ii) a Conciliation Tribunal, which hears the cases of the disputants and (iii) the arbitration machinery of the Labour Court.

CHAPTER 1: A CAUTIONARY TALE

In Dáil Éireann there were exchanges. The Minister for Posts and Telegraphs, Mr. Erskine Childers, said at Question Time that 'no kind of instruction was given whatever' to RTE about 7 Days and 'I have not done anything to suppress any programme at all. I have not taken any action. Action was taken solely by the Authority.' RTE, he said, was responsible to the Government who appointed the Authority and provided the capital—a statement which rammed home the truth of the situation better than all the disclaimers.

Mr. Kevin McCourt issued a Newsletter to all staff on 20th February 1968. It set out his reasons for the transfer of the programme. Explaining his views on impartiality and on the need for editorial back-up in the Division, for which he had set up the Editorial system, he wrote: 'the changes, however, still failed to provide me with sufficient advance information about key programmes. In particular, I had frequent concern about *7 Days* programmes which at times tended to lack impartiality.'

The shock for staff came on the last page of the letter.

It said:

> Both the Head of News and the *Controller of Programmes* were informed in advance of my publishing the decision and both agreed to the change (our italics).

The Newsletter, in the main, had pointed the finger fairly strongly in the direction of Jack White as failing to provide sufficient advance information on *7 Days* projects and treatment.

It was the question of the Controller's having agreed to the transfer of the programme in advance, however, that really shocked the Programmes Division staff. They had issued, through the Guild, a statement in support of the Controller, whom they had believed when he told them that he had not concurred in its removal to the News Division. They were faced now with a direct counter-assertion by the Director-General.

Lelia Doolan, as a member of the Editorial Group and a Trade Unionist who supported the action of her Union, went to the Controller and asked him whether he would publicly rebut this statement. He could not see his way to do so. She suggested to the Controller that he should consider resigning if he were unable to clear up the discrepancy between Mr. McCourt's account and his own. He said that he would consider this.

On behalf of the Equity Trade Union delegation, Jack Dowling wrote to Mr. Garvey calling on him to deny the Director-General's allegation or resign. Dowling repeated this vigorously on the telephone pointing out that it was on his word that the industrial action had been initiated, because he had believed Mr. Garvey. The Controller claimed privilege.

Odran Walsh, as Chairman of the Guild, convened a meeting of the Executive and invited Mr. Garvey to it.

The Guild's public statement in the Controller's defence would now appear to be untrue unless Mr. Garvey could enlighten the Committee.

He accepted the invitation.

The meeting was held in the RTE Club in Ely Place. There was only one absentee. Those present were Odran Walsh, Jack Dowling, Patrick Gallagher, Celestine Rooney, Romuald Dodd,

o.p., Lelia Doolan, Pan Collins and Eoghan Harris.

The Controller was reminded of the assurances given to Lelia Doolan and Jack Dowling that he had not agreed to the transfer of *7 Days*. He was invited to reconcile these assurances with the Director-General's statement that he *had* done so. The Guild was now in an embarrassing position, having publicly expressed its belief that he had not.

Mr. Garvey agreed that, having told Jack Dowling and Lelia Doolan that he had not agreed to the transfer and had threatened to resign rather than concur, he had placed the Guild in an embarrassing position. He still did not agree to the transfer. He did not feel required to say so publicly. Pan Collins asked him, since he had already told Lelia and Jack that he had not agreed, why did he not now say so? There appeared to be some doubt in his mind as to the dependability of his memory on the exact events. In whatever way they had taken place, he was, he said, now quite confused.

Odran Walsh, on behalf of the Guild, wrote to the Director-General, asking for clarification. Mr. McCourt maintained a discreet silence on the point. The staff were now left with two statements. They had, perforce, to make up their own minds.

Subsequently, the present Director-General, Mr. T. P. Hardiman, told Jim Plunkett Kelly and Jack Dowling that Michael Garvey had, in fact, both known about and agreed to the change of the programme in advance.

The Conciliation Tribunal work went on remorselessly. On the Management's side of negotiations Hugh MacNeil, the Director of Personnel, was a gifted and tough-minded negotiator with Jim McGuinness. Members of RTE Staff Relations office attended in a secretarial capacity.

This was one of Jim Larkin's last great negotiations. He was in epic form. Dermot Doolan's cool, humourous style, his meticulous homework and quiet tone, were a perfect antiphon to Larkin's power of logic and driving energy. It was evident after the first day's session that Management were lost. Everyone's sympathy was with Mr. MacNeill. He argued a hopeless case with great resource and unfailing courtesy.

He was hamstrung. His principals just did not know what the case was about and would not be told.

On 29th February, a week before strike notice was due to expire, the Chairman of Conciliation, Mr. T. K. Liston, gave his judgment.

The claims of the three Unions were:

> (a) withdrawal of the Director-General's directive to transfer staff to News Division until negotiations take place and proper written agreements are concluded on conditions of employment for the staff concerned.
>
> (b) Immediate cancellation of suspensions.

Mr. Liston's main recommendation ran as follows:

> 1. The Authority should forthwith suspend, for a period of fourteen days from notification of such suspension, the continued implementation of the Director-General's direction of the 12th February 1968 transferring as from that date to the Head of News Division responsibility for public affairs programmes in television covered by *7 Days*...

The staff was to be reinstated, strike notice withdrawn and a settlement negotiated.

Every item for which the Unions had argued was upheld. On 1st March, the three Unions issued a joint statement accepting the recommendations and saying that they were immediately available to meet Management in order to implement the recommendations. RTE Management also accepted.

## CHAPTER 1: A CAUTIONARY TALE

The settlement talks lasted for three days. Agreement was reached and ratified. The settlement document was known thereafter as 'The *7 Days* Agreement'.

The programme, of course, was to be transferred, but its personnel were not to be integrated with News Division staff. The programme team would remain as a group. RTE reserved to itself the right to transfer 'functions' within the organisation.

Management could not say what degree of permanence was seen in the transfer. It was not intended that it be temporary.

Further, it did not, at that time, intend to transfer any other programme.

The retention of the programme team would not inhibit RTE from having contributions made by News staff to the programme if required.

The scheduling of Producers to work on the programmes would be done by the Controller of Programmes 'in consultation and agreement' with the Head of News.

Members of the team could go to the News Division or not, as they wished; or could go for a trial period of three months, which could be extended by mutual agreement.

The Head of News was also empowered to recruit Producers directly to the News Division to work on *7 Days*.

The Production Assistants on the team would not be liable for work in any other part of the News Division. The same conditions of transfer as applied to Producers would apply to them.

The functions of staff, in this case, would not be affected by the change, nor would the concept of Producers' duties as expressed in the job-specification. This latter was written by Michael Garvey. It was the only official part he played in the whole affair.

It stated :

> A Producer is responsible for the concept, preparation and presentation on air of whole programmes. A Director is answerable to a Producer for the physical preparation, and presentation of programme material for transmission.
>
> A Producer-Director with RTE combines these two functions. He or she may initiate the programme idea or be presented with it by the Programme Controller. Thereafter he or she is charged with the responsibility of research, treatment, preparation, administration, rehearsal and transmission of the finished programme subject to the instructions of the Programme Controller or through his executive subordinates be they Editors or Heads of Departments.
>
> To fulfil these duties the Programme Controller authorises the Producer-Director total control of the programme and the personnel and services necessary to its achievement.

To those who had conducted the negotiations and those who had supported them, the cause had been worth fighting. The outcome, given the limited objective which it was possible for the Unions to pursue, was entirely successful. While understanding this, the Programmes Division staff nevertheless felt the loss. However well this strategy had been outlined; however well the tactics had been played; however much dedication, intelligence, stamina and courage had been shown by their colleagues, it was still the Authority that had its will. As Jack White was to describe it at the time, a heart transplant from a living donor had been made. The Programmes Division was never really to recover from it.

## CHAPTER 1: A CAUTIONARY TALE

*Exit, pursued by a bear.*
—SHAKESPEARE (STAGE DIRECTION)

Due to retire in March, Kevin McCourt left the station abruptly. His wildest nightmares could hardly have envisaged such an end. He left an organisation on which a job of superficial patching had been done. The loose stitching from this patch-work was to be placed in the hands of his successor, Mr. T. P. Hardiman, who took up office on the eve of St. Patrick's Day, 1968.

*God bless us, is it wounded y'are or what?*
—SEAN O'CASEY

Why did Kevin McCourt go so quickly: why did the Authority choose Tom Hardiman?

We can only surmise. Mr. McCourt had effected an organisational change in order to bring about a firmer control of Public Affairs by the Authority. They knew that the Government, facing a Referendum, was restive. Staff reaction had been violent and unexpected. The object had been to hand over to his successor a neatly-tied package with the last knot carefully pulled. The parcel burst.

It had been a rough few weeks; many individual persons, as well as the station's morale, had suffered deep wounds.

Mr. McCourt, undoubtedly, had a few sabre-cuts too; he probably wished to bind them up in private—and as quickly as possible. He made his last round and said goodbye to a rather silent staff.

Whatever he left behind by way of pain, frustration and crushed hopes, he departed, it is said, with relief: a relief, perhaps, at ceasing to be the object of target practice for authoritarian outsiders, a temporising Authority and a defiant staff.

The Authority now needed someone who would be familiar with the peculiar problems of RTE at that particular and difficult moment of time. He should be capable of inspiring confidence: someone to keep the shop open, in fact. In a situation of disquiet they may, in their prudent way, have believed that an outsider, from among the number of distinguished Irishmen who had applied, might engender further excitement.[26]

In these circumstances, the choice of Mr. Hardiman who, as Director of Engineering, had been in their highest counsels and knew the situation thoroughly, had a kind of inevitability about it —once it was made.

He had come through the television organisation from bottom to top: he was an able administrator, a highly intelligent and resourceful man, a shrewd negotiator and well-known and liked by staff. He may, indeed, have had certain shortcomings—particularly as the Chief Executive of a great cultural organisation. His training and education were scientific, as was the cast of his mind.

He delighted in argument to a point of garrulity. He was not a great listener although he knew to a nicety the value of tactical silence in a discussion. His manner of address was pedagogic but always clear and incisive. He had a prodigious memory for facts but never allowed himself to be intimidated by them— always a mark of high intelligence. He had built up a strong personal loyalty among his engineering and administrative colleagues based on a real consideration of their welfare and appreciation of their values. In hammering out policy he was concerned primarily with logistics, not logic, and had an accurate appreciation of the forces of power in human affairs. He had a certain boyishness of manner and was without social pose or pretence.

---

26    Conor Cruise O'Brien applied for the post. He was not interviewed.

# CHAPTER 1: A CAUTIONARY TALE

He had one further great advantage: he was the one man on the technical side who had continual contact with production personnel. It was generally considered that he knew their problems.

The new Director-General took up office officially on 1st April.

\* \* \*

> 'Your stirabout is on the hob'.
> 'Are there lumps in it, my
> dear?' said the Philosopher.
> 'I hope there are', replied the
> Thin Woman, and she leaped
> into bed....
> 'Finality is death. Perfection is
> finality. Nothing is perfect.
> There are lumps in it', said the
> Philosopher.
> —JAMES STEPHENS

A scientific manager making an assessment at that time, on the back of a capacious envelope might have come out of a forward-policy meeting with a set of notes something like these:

**Main Weakness: Radio**

*Problems:* present deficit quarter million per annum; requirements: increase transmission hours in order to gain advertising; revenue must increase by quarter million; Symphony Orchestra: £100,000 a year?

*Means:* recruit staff; apply to Minister for increase in transmission hours; step up sales; start building radio centre; form steering committee: under whom?

*In General:* concentrate main effort on rehabilitation of radio until it is self-supporting; hold *status quo* on television until this is completed.

**Main Strength: Television**

*Problems:* morale bad; organisation shaky; priorities?; equipment deteriorating.

*Engineering:* good; colour by '71-'72; set up forward project studies for this; new outside broadcast unit £130,000; coverage: 98 per cent of the country; Ballymun wired scheme almost complete; VHF cover complete: push final back-up of whole radio system.

*Personnel:* recruit necessary staffs (radio); arrange training; employ training officer (engineer); arrange familiarisation courses into production process for Authority and senior staff; build up Michael Garvey; rationalise situation of Jack White *vis-á-vis* Public Affairs.

*Advertisement Sales:* good on television; poor on radio; increase in revenue near ceiling on television; prospects of increase: poor until introduction of colour; set count increase levelling off.

*Finance:* study capital investment; radio centre; increased accommodation for other staffs; press Minister for increase in licence fee: prospects?; prepare estimates study for capital grant or loan for colour and current equipment replacement; study phasing of turnover to colour.

*Interim:* television retrenchment on capital expenditure; but maintain transmission hours to retain advertisement revenue level.

These notes might be given direction by a descriptive assessment.

The internal organisation, in its two key areas, was in disarray.

Radio programmes were under-staffed and undernourished, both creatively and financially. The increase in hours to fill the morning 'gap' had been a merely quantitative improvement. The service was running a quarter million pound annual deficit. Staff strove manfully but could not help feeling like second-class citizens.

Television programmes, in their seventh spring, had almost been uprooted by the recent gales. Their future growth was now a delicate matter. It required imaginative tending. Trust and leadership must be restored; and a sense of purpose.

The News Division had a new programme acquisition and its old problems: *7 Days* would not be integrated with the Newsroom. An air of expansion formed a scab over old sores.

In the other Divisions, matters were more manageable, and were managed.

Engineering Division had an efficient, workmanlike organisation. There was the prospect of colour television, however. It could not be delayed forever. It would require planning and money. The Production Facilities Department, logically organised, had divided loyalties: to Programmes; to News; to Engineering itself. Should this be rationalised, or lived with?

Sales Division was in good order. It had delivered an increase of more than a quarter million pounds—most of it on television. Advertisement sales for radio were low, though.

The Personnel Division had taken its first big strain in the *7 Days* row. The morale of its senior members was not high. Staff numbers had risen to just on thirteen hundred. A new two-year phased Agreement which would introduce a forty-hour week was nearing final negotiation. This would mean a 2% per cent drop in man hours for all staff who worked overtime. Training at all levels was inadequate.

The Financial Control Division had more money, and increased demands on it. Sixty-eight thousand new licence holders had brought in another two hundred and twenty thousand pounds. There was, in fact, a surplus of three hundred and seventy thousand pounds in all. But danger signs were ahead.

Programme costs would continue to rise. Revenue had no such prospect. Saturation point was approaching in the set count— further increases in the advertising rate would thus be hazardous— at least before the arrival of colour. Pressure on Government to raise the licence fee had yielded no result.

Expenditure had been pegged back from a 17 per cent increase to less than half (7 1/2) per cent in the previous year. Belts would have to remain tight.

In short, to ensure maintenance of revenue, transmission hours would have to remain at current levels. If revenue was to be increased quickly, it could only be done in the radio service, where both hours and advertising were capable of expansion.

This purely managerial assessment was in the true spirit of the Broadcasting Act. The activities of the national spirit would be attended to in due course.

> *I always do my best thinking on my feet.*
> —T. P. HARDIMAN

CHAPTER 1: A CAUTIONARY TALE

The story pauses in order to gather together the forces that were to erupt again in circumstances of almost incredible similarity to the *7 Days* dispute.

In an interview issued on the day of his taking up office, answering a question about the difference between his job and that of Controller of Programmes Mr. Hardiman said:

> The Controller of Programmes has specific responsibility in relation to television programming, but broadcasting is about programming, and as Director-General of RTE I am, of course, concerned about programming in all its aspects.

On the day-to-day involvement of the Director-General in particular assignments of broadcasting personnel, he said:

> By the very nature and size of RTE the Director-General cannot hope to be in intimate touch with all day-by-day activities of the organisation, but I would expect to be in touch with all significant activities.[27]

On his relationship with the Authority, Mr. Hardiman is not on public record. But he has expressed to the present writers and others the view that he regards himself as responsible for providing policies which the Authority would ratify.

These he now proceeded to formulate.

The new Director-General held policy meetings twice weekly. These were attended by the Deputy Director-General, the Director

---

27   The Irish Press, Interview with Tom O'Dea (Part 1), 1st April 1968

of Engineering, the Controller of Programmes (television) and his Assistant; the Controller of Programmes (radio) and his Assistant; the Head of News and his Deputy. The Director of Personnel later became a member of this group.

These meetings were intended to have no executive function: they were to be consultative and informative and would evolve policies from experience and practice.

Policy, obviously, has to come from somewhere. Mr. Hardiman had said to Tom O'Dea: 'What is policy, anyway?' O'Dea then asked: 'If policy might be reduced to a set of personal rules to which you would refer when the chips are down, how would you define your policy?' Hardiman's answer was: 'If you push me in those terms, I simply say that my policy is to develop Irish broadcasting so as to provide a better and more effective service within in terms of reference to the Irish people'[28].

This meagre and guarded comment might be thought understandable from a man whose training was specialised, who had just arrived in a new and exacting job and who could, at the outset, give no more than general terms of reference. This, in our view, was Mr. Hardiman's defect; it was to grow worse rather than better as his views gained particular and concrete form. Bluntly, we have become more and more certain that it was not his lack of a broadcasting philosophy that was to be feared but his strange conviction that he was evolving one.

Where, then, should policies come from? The broadest measure of 'common attitude and belief' comes from the people who actually make programmes. They turn ideas into physical objects, like tape and film. These reach out to the nation and affect or reflect its view. These people are placed in the very eye of every storm.

---

28    Irish Press Interview with Tom O'Dea, (Part 2), 3rd April 1968

CHAPTER 1: A CAUTIONARY TALE

In fact, the Director-General's Policy Committee of senior managers was to evolve a philosophy of broadcasting!

\* \* \*

*In nearly all television organisations,*
*the higher you go the fewer people you*
*find who have a 'creative' background, and*
*at the highest levels of policy and*
*decision-making you will commonly find*
*very few people who by nature, experience*
*and conviction represent the 'creative' attitude.*
—BARRY BAKER

A survey, carried out by Evelyn Quinn of the Department of Psychology of U.C.D. the previous Autumn, had indicated that typical Producer-Directors were exceptionally intelligent (seven out of ten classified as being 'very superior', a category into which only 2.2 per cent of the world's population falls; the other three falling into the category of 6.7 per cent of world population). Producers are, she reported: 'sensitive, imaginative, forthright and deeply involved in their work'. On page 21 of her report she goes on to write:

> If we agree ... that in the end the programme-makers are the broadcasters, that they are the programmes and the programmes are the station, then insofar as we are considering television as a creative medium, our attention must focus above all on the contribution of the producer.[29]

---

29  *The Personality Structure of Television Producers*, Evelyn Quinn Report of Survey

It is the basis of the present book that the programme-makers are the broadcasters—and this in no narrow sense: the cameraman, the lighting-man, the sound-man, the wardrobe people, the makeup girls, the prop-men, the designers and graphic men, the stills-photographers, the researcher, the script-writer, the reporter, the interviewer, the performer or artist, the Production Assistant; are all in their varying degrees programme-makers drawn together by the Producer's magnet to face the common task; fired and guided along the necessary trajectory by the Director's vision. The working lives of everyone in the station, whether inside the production area or outside it among the administrators, accountants, secretaries, librarians, engineers, drivers, canteen staff, receptionists; must all properly be orientated towards the single function of the station: to make television programmes and to make them well.

The policy then, ideally, would come from the Producers, Directors and other programme-makers, each in his own area. But the difficulty was that the tendency to say, 'why not?', uncommon among administrators and strongly felt by the programme people, lost the emphasis on its second word and gained weight on the first the further away from the point of production it went. Whether sideways or, in the curious mode of modem organisation, upward, the question became: 'why?'

An incident of late March 1968 might help to make this point clearer. In the light of the policy, 'why not?' the station had taken the responsible step, during the Presidential Election of 1966, of covering it as a political election.

In March 1968, a volume on the life of Éamon De Valera was published. The Producer of the *Late Late Show* decided to discuss the book on the show. This was planned for 23rd March. The item was deleted by the Assistant Controller of Programmes in consultation with the new Director-General, and the Deputy Director-General, on the grounds that it would be 'inappropriate in the context of the Late Late Show'. This was done against the arguments of the Producer, Gay Byrne, and the Editor responsible, Lelia Doolan.

The precedent had been established that the President was not 'above politics'—as his party wished to suggest—but a national leader putting himself forward for popular election to that office. He is, therefore, a political Head of State. He is responsible to the people who have elected him for ensuring that their rights are protected under the Constitution. Why should the people not talk freely about him? They do in pubs; why not on the telly? Above all, why not on the *Late Late Show*? As our only really international figure, he is certainly of interest to the widest possible section of our audiences.

There would probably be no objection, it was replied, to a dispassionate discussion of the book as a contribution to history, or even to an objective discussion of the part played by the President as a figure in Irish history before 1922. The trouble was, really, that the discussion might lead on to 'what kind of a man is De Valera?'—the *Late Late* being interested in human topics. There was a danger that it could become 'personal and embarrassing'. The audience might want to talk and that would be a risk.

What kind of view of the role of television, and of the role of the President, did this 'policy' reveal? In our view, a distorted and diminishing one. The President thus was reduced to the dimensions of a holy puppet to be trotted out on national occasions or handled with care in minority programmes by persons with straight faces and wrinkled brows. For all human purposes, the President was to be treated as if he were dead.

Anyway, it was implied, the *Late Late Show* was supposed to be *light* entertainment and if it didn't stay in its place nobody would know where he was!

It is to the credit of the show's Producer, Gay Byrne, that it has continued to thrust forward a host of different points of view to the nation's mind. It has done 'serious' subjects more justice than many more 'serious' programmes. It was to the detriment of the show, and the viewers, that it often lost the battle to do the normal human thing in a free and adult society—to talk about anything on earth. 'Why not?'

Sadly, the deletion of these debates reveals fearfulness, on the part of senior executives, of actual or anticipated criticism. The source of such troubles was a hypersensitivity in the station's relationship with the public, as when, in June, the Producer was refused permission to debate on air the motion That RTE Has Failed the Public Trust—'partly', it was said, 'because the same motion was being debated in County Councils'!

On other occasions, it was a deadening anticipation of Government displeasure, as in the deleted programme on the Referendum; the rehashed Criminal Justice Bill discussion, or the Rates discussion.

On complaint from the Editor and Producer to the Assistant Controller, they were encouraged to reflect, with gratitude, upon all those topics which had not been censored!

By bowing to the will of the Government party when they refused to take part in a debate with the other political parties on the *Late Late Show*, the precedent so valuably set in the Division-Haughey incident was repudiated. Management was passing power from the hands of the Authority into those of politicians.

It is the business of the station, and *not* of the Government, to exercise impartiality and balance under the Act. No party can be allowed to exercise the station's function in this. It is a particularly acute problem when the Authority is a Government-appointed body well-stocked with its own supporters.[30]

It is difficult, therefore, to see where a policy for broadcasting, or any philosophy about it, was to come from—one, that is, that was not committed to the view of a trouble-free broadcasting service. In theory it would come, so the tale still went, from the Producers via the Editors to the Controller and thence, for ratification, to the Director-General. The Programmes Division generally, and the Editorial Group in particular was, however, in bad case. It was very sick indeed.

\* \* \*

In surveying the implications and the aftermath of the *7 Days* affair Jack Dowling and Lelia Doolan put forward a plan to the Controller and his Assistant in March of that year. The plan was an attempt to restore a sense of confidence and purpose to programme staff, particularly since they regarded the continuation of the Editorial Group system as a blockage to future development. It envisaged a number of programme departments, on the old system, and an additional Assistant Controller who would be (as Tom Hardiman had been) responsible for all programme services. This was to be an interim measure to give the Programmes Division a chance to gather its dissipated forces. Shortly afterwards, on the 31st March, Lelia Doolan put forward an amended form of this plan with diagrams and explanatory notes. She attached a memorandum which tried to draw some conclusions from the *7 Days*

---

[30] The present writers are not so naive as to believe that a change of Government will bring about a cessation of Government pressure. The Fianna Fáil Government figures irritatingly and frequently in this book. It is the only Government RTE has known. It is wise to remember the case of the BBC. It was berated in the days of a Conservative Government for being ardently pro-Labour. On the night of the election when Labour came to power, Hugh Carleton Greene was very pleased. When Barbara Castle was elected he said delightedly, 'She's the only Minister I've ever kissed.' The kissing stopped soon afterward.

affair and foresee what measures were now needed to meet the problems it had raised. On the following day, Liam Ó Murchú, her fellow-Editor, made a submission to the Controller about the Editorial Group system, at the end of which he said:

> 1. You have an Editorial Group which is supposedly responsible for the whole programme output, which, in important programme areas, is not recognised;
>
> 2. Your authority to make editorial appointments and to assign programme areas to them has been questioned and you have not in fact upheld your right;
>
> 3. This is now public knowledge within the Programmes Division and the erosive effects on discipline generally could well become progressively worse, as the bad precedents become talked about and their implications fully realised.

Of the role of Editor and the confusions it engendered, Lelia Doolan's memo said:

> ... three levels of decision-making united in the one job and the inevitable tendency for too many decisions, which belong at programme level, moving up and away from there. The sad part is that removal of a decision removes the responsibility for it too, and so delegation of authority is stymied by the system itself.
> Add to this that the Editorial Group has never even begun to work properly: that there are two Heads of

## CHAPTER 1: A CAUTIONARY TALE

Department and one Senior Producer who refuse to work the system; neither you nor the Editor has found a solution; that Producers themselves work across Editorial Group lines, some of them to two Editors simultaneously—and you get a blurred picture: we are in a state of confusion bordering on chaos.

The memorandum also suggested that work should be undertaken by a small group of Producers, Production Assistants, technical people—to investigate and put forward proposals for organisational development of the Programmes Division. The need for training, re-training and refresher courses was also urged.

Liam Ó Murchú's suggestion was that the Editorial Group should simply be *made* to work, Lelia Doolan's was that it *could not* work and should be phased out. In the event, the Heads of Departments suggestion, as an interim solution, was filed. The Director-General and, in some cases, the Controller of Programmes, talked to the dissident elements. The system *was* to be made to work.

> 'Yes, I have a pair of eyes', replied Sam, 'and
> that's just it. If they was a pair
> o' patent double million magnifyin' gas
> microscopes of hextra power, p'raps I might be
> able to see through a flight o' stairs and a
> deal door; but bein' only eyes,
> you see, my vision's limited.'
> —CHARLES DICKENS

The Producer-Directors' job specification was their first charter. The part of it which gave them, subject to the Controller of Programmes or his executives, total control of all the resources necessary to the making of a programme, had caused some concern.

It perturbed those of the Editorial Group who regarded their own role as an executive one; it caused concern also among the managerial grades in the Production Facilities area. Yet this total control was a necessity if the Producer-Director was to get the work done. There were major anomalies. One was that the Producer-Director controlled his own budget at a remove. A previous system, by which his Production Assistant administered his budget, had been abandoned.

The data now came from a costing officer working centrally in Programme Facilities. Officially, his cost reports were records of money spent. In fact, due to time-lag, many of the figures were derived from estimates or forecasts. They were guesses, in short. The 'information' on costs, therefore, tended to be alarming, due to over-estimation.

This did not worry the Producer, since he knew. It did not worry the cost officer since he knew that the Producer knew.

The Heads and Editors, at a remove from this knowledge, were often alarmed.

It was not a helpful system, although the cost office was always helpful, within the limits of a method that just could not keep up to date. The near-impossible always takes somewhat longer than the obvious. The obvious was immediate budget-control, where a Producer knows his facts because he makes them.

> 'And if you take one from three hundred and sixty-five, what remains?'
> 'Three hundred and sixty-four, of course.'
> Humpty Dumpty looked doubtful. 'I'd rather see that done on paper', he said.

CHAPTER 1: A CAUTIONARY TALE

> *Alice couldn't help smiling as she took out her memorandum-book, and worked the sum for him:*
>
> 365
> 
> <u>1</u>
>
> 364
>
> *Humpty Dumpty took the book, and looked at it carefully.*
> *'That seems to be done right .. ' he began.*
> *'You're holding it upside down!\* Alice interrupted.*

\* \* \*

Another anomaly was the fact that Producer-Directors were, in many cases, not sufficiently trained to work the extremely tight production schedules. The technical crews and floor-staffs complained that the burden of getting the show on the air was devolving on them. Recently, Producer-Directors had come to think that some of the newly recruited technical and floor-staffs were insufficiently trained and too heavily over-worked to handle the concentrated load of getting a programme rehearsed and recorded in the time allotted. Because of these conflicts—each with sufficient truth in it to make it worth investigating—'over-runs' increased or quality fell.

Producers do not work to set hours. Floor-staffs and technical crews do work in shifts. There are two shift-systems. They do not mesh. The two affect different grades and types of technical and artistic workers.

If this seems crazy to the reader, it is not surprising. It is crazy.

Crews began to see that overtime was now the order of the day rather than the exception. In the past, they had always been willing, as most of them still are, to 'pitch-in' in order to get the work done. Now they felt that the organisation was using their goodwill as an instrument of normal scheduling. They began to resist this, through their Unions.

A two-year phased agreement had been negotiated during the year and came into operation during the Summer. This meant a two and a half hour weekly drop in crew availability for the servicing of Autumn programmes. Alpho O'Reilly, Head of Design, had on numerous occasions drawn the attention of programme-planners in the Controller's Group to this prospect. It was duly noted, strenuously discussed for some weeks, but finally evaded. The practical step of cutting back production by 2 per cent, or increasing facilities and staff numbers to bridge the gap, was never taken. With no one to stop them, the Editorial Group, planning for the new schedule, simply went ahead on the assumption that someone, somewhere, would manage to make ends meet. Nobody could.

Two suggestions had been put forward to meet the case. One was that an Executive Production Assistant in each Department should provide a liaison between Producers and Planning and Control, in order to keep the flow of information going back and forth quickly and in detail.

The Production Assistants are among the jewels of the broadcasting service. A group of devoted and dedicated girls, their intelligence and administrative abilities have got their Directors out of many difficulties. They are one group of programme people who understand the implications of time, machines and money. They do, at the same time, work with both creative and technical mentalities.

The other suggestion concerned the danger of technical personnel using the limitations of machine-loading to determine the kind of programmes the Producers could make. This was, in great measure, a fault of the programme planning system.

\* \* \*

## CHAPTER 1: A CAUTIONARY TALE

*Go make yourself a plan*
*And be a shining light.*
*Then make yourself a second plan*
*For neither will come right.*
*In such a situation*
*Men aren't bad enough or vile.*
*Human aspiration*
*Only makes me smile.*
—BERTOLT BRECHT

With the agreement of the Controller of Programmes, three members of the Editorial Group sat down during the Summer to try and survey the existing mode of planning, and make some forecasts for future programme developments. The Group, consisting of Jack White, Liam Ó Murchú and Lelia Doolan, submitted a report on their first findings in July of 1968.

The report, as a set of guide-lines, suggested that there were two phases of forward development. The first phase covered about four years from October 1968, during which much the same technical base as presently used would continue to exist. The second phase, from 1972 on, foresaw the introduction of colour television, satellite distribution and electronic camera developments.

In the phased overlap that would be necessary, the report saw the need for an information pipeline to be built into the system, whereby engineers and programme-makers could keep in close touch.

Training was seen as a vital need during this phasing-in period. The report noted that staff and resources were extended to the utmost to keep home-originated programmes at 50 per cent of the total transmission output. While noting that this would seem to indicate that home production ought to be held at its present level or even reduced, the

Group felt that RTE was, in fact, likely to be forced to thinking terms of a gradual increase of home production. On the one hand, the station was not yet satisfying the needs of the community; on the other, there was increasing difficulty in getting quality television material from American companies.

An Audience Research report of that time showed that four of the six 'most disliked' programmes were imported films, disliked equally by urban and rural viewers. The report drew attention to this important aspect of the enquiry. The Head of (imported) Film, Bill Harpur, was absent at the time.

In programme terms, the Group made recommendations for policy and long-term planning in the Current Affairs, Sport and Presentation areas; for Irish, Social and Educational programming and in the areas of Drama and Light Entertainment.

In the field of Documentaries and Current Affairs, it was suggested that the removal of *7 Days* to the News Division had solved one demarcation problem but created another. It was a waste of resources (and demoralising for staff) to have the two Divisions fighting over the same territory. At the same time, it was recommended, members of the Programmes Division should not be prevented from using the experience and skill which they had built up in the area of Public Affairs. This could be developed in Documentary programmes in specialised areas. Further, a treatment in depth could be given to such subjects as industry, agriculture, and social matters.

For Irish, educational and social programmes, the report recommended several changes of policy. Reviewing the progress of *Buntus Cainte* and *Labhair Gaeilge Linn* and the limited possibility of their continuing under their present form, the proposal was that some *reason* be given to people for wanting to revive the language—and more real, adult programming to those who had Irish.

CHAPTER 1: A CAUTIONARY TALE

For drama and light entertainment, it was recommended that existing policy needed to be experimentally tested. This might be done by abstracting one or two programmes from the conventional production-process and, in each Department, running these on a workshop basis in order to test the validity of their policy assumptions. This would involve employing the services of technical production groups, the Audience Research Unit, and outside critics and writers.

These ought to be gathered together to work as a group, constantly reviewing their own procedures, productivity and work-quality.

This suggestion was put forward after unofficial study-discussions which had been going on between Jack Dowling, Dick Hill, technical production personnel, and Lelia Doolan.

It was to be put forward by Jack Dowling to the Director-General in a more refined form at a later date. Mr. Hardiman would not discuss it on the grounds that such an experimental organisation would need too sophisticated a data-processing unit.

The report of the two Editors and the Assistant Controller was never formally discussed by the Controller. If it informed anyone's thinking, there was little public evidence of it. It was, by and large, wasted time.

> *If once a man indulge himself in murder,*
> *very soon he comes to think little of robbing*
> *and from robbing he next comes to drinking*
> *and Sabbath-breaking, and from that to*
> *incivility and procrastination.*
> —THOMAS DE QUINCEY

Two incivilities and a procrastination now broke out. Traced with mischievous hindsight, they led back by inexorable logic to the originating murder of the Programmes Division.

The planning of the new Autumn schedule was uncivil in the extreme. The demands of the expanded News Division on technical resources was a continual civil commotion. The procrastination in rationalising the situation was blithe and bland.

The Controller announced the Autumn plans to a meeting of his Division on September 9th.

Instead of doing less, we were to do *more* production than in the previous Autumn. In fact, about 2£ per cent more. This, with the reduction in available working time of 2 per cent, made for an excess of production over capacity. This may not seem much of a stretch. One must, however, take into account the generosity of staffs that had been driven to breakpoint for seven years in order to set up the station and increase its output. The workers of all grades had set 'norms* that no longer allowed for any 'stretch* at all.

There were time-clashes in studio between *Newsbeat* and *Garda Patrol*, and, on another afternoon each week, between *Mart and Market* and *Newsbeat*. There were clashes between *Wanderly Wagon* and *Sport in Action*. There was not enough time, in these cases, for sufficient rehearsal to keep the quality of programmes to a proper standard.

The new Outside Broadcast Unit was delivered late, and a number of programmes which would have been made possible by the provision of the new Unit, still had to be made despite its absence. This overloaded the Unit already in use.

Continuous and serious technical troubles, even when the new Unit finally came into operation, occurred. These were 'due partly to bad equipment or design, and partly to lack of spares'[31] and support equipment.

---

31   Report of the Television Production Committee, January 1969

*Bring Down the Lamp*, *The Riordans*, *Like Now*, dramatised short stories, sports and other occasional outside broadcast projects vied with one another for priority.

Although dedicated engineering and technical crews pitched-in and worked long hours to keep the system going, the strain began to tell.

It began to show, too, on Producers and their work. Efforts to meet deadlines and to get their productions 'in the can', while at the same time keeping quality high, became increasingly difficult. Health break-downs began to occur. There were five in as many weeks. After a Producers' meeting, Jim Plunkett Kelly and Jack Dowling complained to Jack White. He was helpful and sympathetic, as always. He pointed out that desperate remedies could not be applied unless the Controller knew that there were desperate cases.

If the schedules had been designed with the station's capacities in mind, there would have been no desperate cases.

In mid-Autumn, after much urging, a committee was set up to investigate the problems. Its very useful report did not appear until January, by which time many of its recommendations were out of date.

The difficulties had been pragmatically solved on the spot through direct intervention by the Assistant Controller of Programmes, and by intervention on behalf of the Unions by Alpho O'Reilly and the two house representatives for Workers' Union of Ireland and Actors' Equity, Jim Plunkett Kelly and Jack Dowling.

If procrastination was the child of murder, robbery was the posterity of mulishness. The *Work* team was stubborn. The Director-General was insistent ...

*Work* was the old financial programme, *Exchange*, expanded to a half-hour and revitalised by a larger team. It included Brian Cleeve and Paddy Gallagher as interviewers. Eoghan Harris was the Director.

These men had, with Seán Egan, opted out of the transfer of *7 Days* to the Newsroom under the terms of the Union-Management agreement.

Aindreas Ó Gallchóir was its Producer.

*Work* was designed as a Current Affairs programme which would treat specific social topics *in depth*. Its first difficulty came with a programme investigating the Gulf Oil refinery at Whiddy Island. Film had been made, gathered and edited for a trenchant programme on the subject. The Minister, Mr. George Colley, was to come to the studio to be interviewed.

Suddenly, the team was told that they must not complete this project; *7 Days* intended to cover the subject.

Perhaps the *Work* material could be used later? No!

*7 Days* did cover the subject—in a small 'spot' item, using imported film, at the end of one of its programmes.

The *Work* team was informed that as the subject had been dealt with in *7 Days*, there was no need for further television investigation. The team was rocked.

One of its members said to Jack Dowling: 'Good God, is the old *7 Days* pattern emerging again?'

Specials were planned and executed. The second of these was on the University merger. The Minister, Mr. Brian Lenihan, faced a panel of interested persons and gave an affable and forthright performance.

Venial sin proliferates where mortal sin is condoned. After murder, Sabbath-breaking was inevitable.

The 'Cautionary Tales' syndrome emerged again.

\* \* \*

On 27th July 1968 Monsignor Cremin had held an historic Press Conference on the Irish Hierarchy's interpretation of *Humanae Vitae*. The national debate which followed purported to be about birth control; in

CHAPTER 1: A CAUTIONARY TALE

reality it was about the nature and exercise of authority in the Roman Catholic Church in Ireland.

It was this latter issue that moved Eoghan Harris and John Horgan to propose to Jack White that a special programme should be devoted to this crisis of authority in the Church. It was conceived as a Public Affairs programme in the Specials series. Jack White agreed. Observing the courtesies of protocol, Eoghan Harris went to Father Romuald Dodd, o.p., for advice.

A meeting between Jack White, Fr. Dodd, Eoghan Harris and John Horgan took place. Jack White (as a Protestant) confined himself largely to the programme aspects of the project. He made very helpful suggestions on points of emphasis; perceptively agreeing that sensitivity on birth control among the Irish Catholic community was such that the issue should be avoided if the more fundamental question of authority was to hold the public attention without distraction.

Throughout September preparations went ahead. Jack White was kept closely in touch. A meeting was held at Portlaoise to ask the two new Bishops, Dr. Lennon and Dr. Harty, to take part and put the Hierarchy's view. Father Dodd, Eoghan Harris and John Horgan outlined the programme's approach. The Bishops agreed.

Questions from 'the Top' had been raised; requests for advance information. Admonitions to caution increased. Nervousness was very evident all down the line. It stopped at the Producer, who had no qualms. But this kind of apprehension was now usual. A date had been set in studio. Final arrangements and last minute preparations were almost completed when Father Dodd approached Eoghan Harris with a strange message.

Fr. Dodd intimated that the Director-General would be happier if editorial control of this programme was transferred from Jack White to Jim McGuinness, Head of News!

Eoghan Harris could not decide whether this was a reflection of Jim McGuinness's determination to keep all Current Affairs under his control, or whether someone on the Authority had taken exception to the programme's being produced under the supervision of a Protestant, Jack White.

Either reason was unacceptable to him. He told Father Dodd, who was clearly on a 'sounding out' mission, that, as Producer, he would not accept this change.

Later Jack White, deeply depressed, told Eoghan Harris that the requirement to change the editorial responsibility for the programme was now an instruction from the Director-General.

Eoghan Harris expressed his regrets, refused, and went to his Trade Union.

> *There is no terror, Cassius, in your threats.*
> —SHAKESPEARE

The Director-General insisted. The Producers gathered to support Harris. In view of the intention expressed in the *7 Days* settlement agreement—not to remove any other programmes from the Division without prior consultation—the Producer-Directors requested an interview with the Director-General, the Controller of Programmes being absent.

In a discussion with Lelia Doolan to arrange this, the Director-General requested that the meeting with the Producers take place on a non-Union basis. He asked that it consist of a 'representative' group of Producers from the affected areas. He also asked Lelia Doolan to ensure that the discussion should not be dominated by Jack Dowling. Dowling then refused to attend. The Director-General said that this was not what he had really meant.

The meeting was arranged. The Assistant Controller of Programmes, Liam Ó Murchú and Lelia Doolan were present with the Director-General. Twelve representatives of the programme-makers, Gay Byrne, Seán Ó Mórdha, Michael Slevin, Jack Dowling, Paddy Gallagher, James Plunkett Kelly, Aindreas Ó Gallchóir, Eoghan Harris, Bill Skinner, Gerry Murray, Dick Hill and Father Romuald Dodd, met Mr. Hardiman.

In a lengthy discussion which went on for almost four hours, the Producers had an opportunity, for the first time, to put their views to the Director-General, face to face. They expressed their concern about the quite extraordinary caution being shown by the Administration in its conduct of this kind of programming.

They vigorously reasserted the right of Programmes Division personnel to continue to treat in depth subject matter of a topical and controversial nature. In particular, they resented the use of *7 Days* as a means of preventing treatment of any subject in depth, merely by doing a 'spot' item on it in advance.

They rejected the Director-General's view that 'Current' Affairs was proper to *7 Days* and that 'Public' Affairs could be handled by the Programmes Division.[32]

They also discussed the Director-General's continual last-minute censoring of the *Late Late Show* serious items, particularly with political figures.

Finally, they stated that they would have to consider industrial action if he persisted in his intention to transfer the programme.

---

32 'Current' Affairs, described by the Director-General as any theme requiring 'continuing editorial supervision', would be removed at his discretion to the Head of News. 'Public' Affairs he described as 'one-off studies of public problems in the community'. Mr. Hardiman was, we have suggested, stronger on logistics than on logic. If his definition of 'Public' Affairs held, why then was he transferring the Church programme (certainly a one-off study) to the Head of News? The origins of the distinction seemed to owe more to Oliver Twist than to Thomas Aquinas.

Mr. Hardiman was visibly shaken when Mike Slevin told him that our experience of him as a man of clarity, courage and programme sympathy was no longer recognisable in his conduct since he had taken up office. Sean Ó Mórdha told him bluntly that he had condemned the Programmes Division to death. Eoghan Harris said that it was clear that he seemed to have no view of broadcasting other than the 'filling of time-slots'.

The Producers, with their experience of the *7 Days* affair in mind, presented an implacable front. Their first duty, they made plain, was to the truth, their second to the public, their third to him and the organisation. This may have sounded very noble but it was necessary to say it.

The confrontation may well have been a useful exercise for the Director-General also. It revealed to him, for the first time and at first hand, the concerns and frustrations of the production staff— and their undeviating determination to engage on real issues, upon which the public had the right to every possible point of view. They would not, he could plainly see, back down on this. They did not.

The discussion was lively, intelligent and courteous although, at times, blunt. It ended with a formal exchange of sincere compliments. The Producers thanked the Director-General for having met them. Such a meeting had never happened before. The Director-General assured them that he would give the matters discussed his thorough and grave consideration.

Whatever else could be said for or against T. P. Hardiman, he proved himself one who could take straight talk.

On the 11th November the twelve representatives reported on their discussion with Mr. Hardiman to a joint Trade Union meeting of their colleagues. Two resolutions were passed, one asking the Director-General to rule that the programme on the Church entitled: *Church in Crisis—By What Authority?* was a proper one for the Programmes

Division. A second resolution was framed specifying the industrial action that would follow in the event of his insisting on the transfer.

The following day James Plunkett Kelly and Jack Dowling, on behalf of the two Unions, saw the Director-General and presented the first resolution. His attitude was cordial, conciliatory and, as always, gravely courteous. They formed the impression that he was decided upon returning the programme to Mr. Garvey's Division but that he wished to delay announcing the fact because of some commitment of courtesy. He promised to let the Producers know his mind 'very quickly'. He did. The next day he returned the programme to its original management and policy.

There was general relief.

The decision was accepted as an indication of Mr. Hardiman's good faith. An expression of the Producers' appreciation of the generosity of the decision, both as a gesture and as a confirmation of policy-intention, was sent to him.

Producers also asked that an attempt be made to set up machinery for a thorough examination of their difficulties in programming matters generally, and in the organisation of their Division particularly.

James Plunkett Kelly and Jack Dowling met Mr. Hardiman and his Director of Personnel, Mr. Oliver Maloney. The latter was also Secretary to the Authority and had been responsible for implementing the Director-General's policy for radio.

The Controller of Programmes was away.

Jack White, his Assistant Controller, was in charge of the Division. Jack Dowling, in courtesy and as duty-bound, went to see him. Mr. White had not been invited to the meeting. He wished to attend. Dowling asked Oliver Maloney if the Director-General could have this invitation issued. It never was.

Once again, at a critical meeting for his Division, the Programme Controller was not present or represented.

> *Shut, shut the door, good*
> *John! fatigued, I said;*
> *Tie up the knocker, say I'm sick,*
> *I'm dead.*
> —ALEXANDER POPE

The purpose of this meeting was to prepare the ground for further discussion with Mr. Hardiman on the development of programme management. As a result, a consultative group was formed. It consisted of six elected representatives of the Producers, the Director-General, the Director of Personnel, the Programme Controller, a and the Head of Production Facilities. The group was to be non-Union in character. It was regarded as a tentative exercise and was, as the Director-General said, 'an experiment in participative management*.

Actual programmes management was not flattered. Members of the Controller's Editorial Group were extremely confused about their status and function. The Director-General was entering into direct negotiation with their subordinates and they were being ignored. Liam Ó Murchú wrote a memorandum to the Controller to this effect. He was later appointed to the Consultative Group.

There was some apprehension felt by Producers about negotiations taking place with Management on a non-Union basis. This view was particularly advanced by Jim Plunkett Kelly. However, because of the Director-General's gesture, it was decided to give the thing a try.

The first meeting was held on the 4th December 1968. Its terms of reference, previously agreed, were four:

1. The development of Programmes Division organisation.
2. Producer-involvement in programme planning.
3. Day-to-day problems in the Programmes Division.
4. Initial and continuation training.

There were six meetings in all of this consultative group.

From the first meeting, two things clearly emerged in Jack Dowling's consciousness: one was that there was complete unanimity among the Producer representatives that the Editorial system was just an obstruction. It must go. This was made painfully plain.

The other was that Jim Plunkett Kelly, Aindreas Ó Gallchóir and Maev Conway were mentally back in the days of the Rugheimer dispute. They wanted to reinstate the old Departmental system, as a first concern. Dowling went along with this as an interim solution. He pushed for an experimental production unit to run concurrently with it. They supported him in this, loyally, but he felt that their hearts and real interests were elsewhere.

A ferocious exchange on the needs and nature of authority took place at the second meeting. As a result, Dowling and Lelia Doolan wrote a memorandum on the subject for the Director-General. It was never acknowledged and had no influence on the debates.

The meetings dragged on.

Dowling proposed a specific scheme for an experimental production group. It was an attempt to evolve a system of organisation for programme production which would bring all of those concerned in the production process into the closest possible relationship. It was not an attempt to do 'experimental' work in the sense of *avant garde* or *risqué* programmes; rather it was intended to be of practical value in discovering the sources of frustration suffered in the production of a programme. It was intended not to interfere with the output which the station would have to keep up during the period of the experiment.

The aim was to organise a production team consisting of every element of production from Producer to floor staffs, give them a block of series-programmes (such as quiz shows, *Outlook*, *Garda Patrol*, discussion panel shows or programmes with a fixed format) and allot them a studio. It was hoped to weld them into a mutually co-operative and mutually critical team; streamline their scheduling and measure their increase in output.

After three months, the format and quality of their programmes would be re-designed and a six-month quality improvement experiment would be conducted, with the 'worst* programmes being given to the experimental group and the 'best existing' programmes to a conventional production team. The results could then be comparatively studied.

If an increase in output and quality resulted, progressive adjustments of the Department system to a Production Group system could be undertaken without disrupting the work of the station.

This plan was merely proposed as an experiment. It was rejected on the grounds that it would require an electronic computer to operate the data-input and analyse the results. Jack Dowling had spent six years in England on data-processing and knew this to be unfounded.

Suddenly at a meeting of the Group held on 11th January, a reorganisation of the Programmes Division was announced by the Director-General.

It was outlined and detailed by the Controller of Programmes at a further meeting on 20th January.

The plan was for a Head of Department system as the final solution to the Programmes Division difficulties.

No experimental group was provided for; no strengthening of the Controller's position by the appointment of two extra Assistants, as had been asked for; no budget-control reforms; no institutional recognition of the Producers' notion of delegated authority; no structural changes in the relationship of programmers to technical personnel; no clarification of the conflicting claims on facilities and programme subjects between our Division and the News Division.

Everything had been solved—except the problems.

A list of programme Heads and Senior Producers was to follow. Four of these Department Heads would have control in both radio and television: Sport, Education, Agriculture and Religion. There would be five output departments in the Television Programmes Division—(i) Features, (ii) Irish and Children's programmes, (iii) Light Entertainment, (iv) Drama, and (v) (imported) Film.

The Producers' representatives, Aindreas Ó Gallchóir, Dónall Farmer, Jack Dowling, Gay Byrne, Seán Egan and James Plunkett Kelly had certain reservations about this scheme. As a non-union group merely representing Producers and without plenipotentiary powers, they could do no more than raise questions.[33]

Mr. Hardiman had stated at the first meeting that the group would move to a consensus as a basis for the re-organisation. This did not now seem possible. He said that he had thought deeply about the re-organisation. The Editorial system now being dissolved, the new Heads of Department system would have to go into immediate operation. There were to be job-specifications for Heads of Departments.

---

33  The Producer representatives had agreed with the Director-General not to discuss the subject-matter of the meetings until such times as a conclusion (or a 'consensus' as he called it) was reached. This seemed reasonable at the time; no deliberative body can work calmly on difficult and emotion-charged problems, if it has continually to debate them with two parties at the same time. We soon realised that we were wrong. Our colleagues roundly castigated us for this. Whatever the difficulties might have been, we now acknowledge they were right.

He agreed that the system was hierarchical but, he said, it could be humanised.

At this final meeting, Jack Dowling recorded his dissent from the new plan. He said that he could not bring it back with recommendations for acceptance by his colleagues. He would not actively recommend its rejection by the Trade Union meeting. This, under the *7 Days* Agreement, must ratify the plan as affecting conditions of employment. He doubted if the Producers would accept it in its peremptory form.

It appeared as if the re-organisation was a fait accompli. The Unions were to be notified the following day, and the plan was to go into operation on 1st February 1969, nine days later.

In order to prevent the hopes expressed for the future of consultative machinery as a basis for democratic decision-making from deteriorating, Jack Dowling asked to see the Director-General.

This request was not granted, so Oliver Maloney arranged for an interview with the Controller. Jack Dowling saw the Controller and explained his apprehensions to him. He asked that the discussions be kept open in order to allow for amendments from the general body of Producers.

The main amendments from the Producers, he thought, would be three:

1. At least one further Assistant Controller, in order to strengthen the Division's administration.
2. The adoption of some kind of production group for experimental investigation, as a token of forward thinking; the Head of Department system, by itself, being a senseless return to a method proven useless eight years earlier.

3. Recognition of real delegation of authority. This would require some institutional way of giving the Producers control of the resources and budgets necessary to make their programmes.

The Controller of Programmes opposed these suggestions, in an amicable way, but said that certainly they were open to further discussion and amendment—in other words, the ball was still 'in play'.

> *Queenie-I-o! Queenie-I-o! Who*
> *has the ball?*
> —PLAY SONG

Three lengthy Producer meetings followed upon receipt of this information from Jack Dowling.

Ten proposals, either by way of amendment or as requests for clarification, were adopted. These included amendments to delete a separate department for religion and a department for Irish from the system, on the grounds that Producers felt that each of these interests should pervade all programming.

The Producers proposed, instead, that there should be an Adviser appointed to each of these areas, *with a budget*, in order to give him independence and flexibility.

Children's Programmes, it was also felt, should have a Head of Department in its own right, as it tended to be inadequately financed and staffed.

The power struggle developing between News and Programmes Divisions, in which the Director-General had, increasingly, to play the role of Solomon, should be rationalised by the provision of two new Assistants to the Controller of Programmes.

There should be some final and rational solution provided to the problem of allocating facilities between the News and the Programmes Divisions. It was suggested that this might most effectively be done if each of the Departments, including News Division, should have a facilities-budget in its overall programme budget—an attempt to institute budgetary control.

The experimental, or pilot production unit, to investigate the needs of the Programmes Division, should be adopted along with the organisation plan. If it proved useful, it could be implemented on a phased basis.

A job-specification for Programme Heads should be agreed with Producers.

Senior Producers or Deputy Heads should be appointed to act with authority, in the absence of Programme Heads.

At the final meeting of the Consultative Group, these proposals and amendments were put. They were turned down, excepting the last two.

Jim Plunkett Kelly was promoted Head of Features Department and was now in the embarrassing position of representing the workers' case as a member of senior programme management.

When Mr. Hardiman was told of the assurances given by the Controller that the matter was still open for discussion, he said that he could not admit to consideration any assurances given outside the machinery of the Consultative Group.

As a formal, legalistic interpretation of management practice, such a statement was probably fair enough. In the actual circumstances, it appeared nothing more nor less than a repudiation by the Director-General of his own Controller and of one of his Producers.

If the Controller was offended he kept it to himself; he denied having given the assurances.

## CHAPTER 1: A CAUTIONARY TALE

Jack Dowling did mind; he resigned from the Consultative Group. The Producers' representatives then broke off consultation with Management, as being in bad faith.

Jack Dowling had a spell in hospital, and during convalescence was asked by the General-Secretary of his Trade Union to comment on a curious statement made by Mr. Oliver Maloney, Director of Personnel, during Dowling's absence. The Director of Personnel had invited Producers to continue the work of the consultative committee and a meeting between him and the Unions' representatives had taken place. It had been somewhat acrimonious; some of the Union members making it clear that management's anxiety about consultation was now designed to use the Producers to 'rubber-stamp' unilateral Management decisions—in short such 'consultations' as had already taken place were fake. Some had remonstrated with Mr. Maloney about Mr. Garvey's denial that he had told Dowling that 'the ball was still in play'. Mr. Maloney replied that the whole thing had been a misunderstanding between two men who were singularly likely to misunderstand one another. He would, he said, 'shanghai' both of them, if he could, for having prejudiced the prospects of consultation.

On the day of his return, Dowling presented himself in Mr. Maloney's office for shanghai-ing. Mr. Maloney seemed somewhat embarrassed and said that he hoped that nothing that had been said or done would prevent the process of consultation so unfortunately begun from continuing, nevertheless, on a non-Trade Union-Management basis.

Dowling replied that the Trade Union policy, now determined upon by his Producer colleagues, would be the only basis on which Management negotiations or consultations would be conducted again with the present Management.

He added that in his view, which he believed to be commonly shared, the Management could no longer be trusted. Only Trade Union officials, working under the formal protocol of negotiation, could treat with such Machiavellian opportunism.

He asked for an interview with the Director-General to put this view to him. He also wanted an opportunity of rebutting Michael Garvey's denial. The Director of Personnel replied that this would not be possible since it would be tantamount to asking the Director-General to sit in judgment upon a conversation at which he was not present. He recommended Dowling to have the matter out with the Controller himself.

Dowling did so. On returning to his office he immediately telephoned Mr. Garvey and asked for a personal interview on the grounds that Mr. Garvey had done him a grave personal injustice and that Mr. Maloney was evidently pressing for a continuance of the consultative relationship. The charge of having misinformed his colleagues hung over Dowling's head as one of the Producers' representatives.

A meeting of Irish Actors' Equity shortly afterwards passed a resolution, sent to the Director-General, confirming Dowling's attitude as expressed to Mr. Maloney. It excluded any further contacts except through Trade Union officials. Jack Dowling and Michael Garvey, in fact, never met formally again.

> *miranda: O! brave new world, that has such people in it!*
> *prospero: 'Tis new to thee.*
> —SHAKESPEARE

A brave new experiment had wound up in ashes. A sense of emergency; a sense that Producer unrest which had gone on for three years must be stilled, that a new system must be evolved, had led, as in the case of the new radio set-up, to an expedient solution which solved the superficial managerial problems but left its core of programme-making untouched.

The very possibility of reaching other than pragmatic solutions was now looked upon by Producers with lack-lustre eyes. It seemed as if Management wanted, not to consult, but to have a chat with them and build some of their wishes into Management structures, if they could conveniently do so.

As the Director-General had revealingly said about the Consultative Group, it was not an executive group.

A forum for talk might still have been useful, if the talk had been prepared to delve into every nook, to winkle out every idea, to absorb every impediment and faulty vision and to think things through thoroughly, before hastening into action.

This, one had been taught on Management Institute courses, was an essential element of good management procedure. There was no evidence that such theories of structure or man-management had any place in Radio Telefís Éireann's immediate internal policies. 'We are in an emergency situation', Mr. Hardiman had said no less than four times during the course of negotiations. 'We must provide immediate emergency solutions.'

Jack Dowling had been trained in the military tradition and had spent sixteen years in the study and practice of man-management and a further six in the study and practice of business administration on an Organisation and Methods basis. He had been taught and forced to practice the maxim that emergency situations were precisely those which needed cool and careful thought. *All* our problems were recurring crises. The same strains and forces were continually building up in similar pressure chambers. The same kinds of detonators were chronically causing them to explode. We were, in our view, preparing the dispersed forces for a new concentration.

Both Michael Garvey and Lelia Doolan were then taking part in a senior management course at the Irish Management Institute. Nothing that had been taught there was practised in this 'solution'. The separation of theory and practice, according to the classic Marxist analysis, is characteristic of the dying liberalism of the West. Whatever about such speculations it was certainly characteristic of RTE in our experience—although the 'theory' was somewhat eclectic. Bits of management theory hung like rags round a holy well.

Resentment of management efficiency is silly: fear of its thoughtlessness is unnerving. One can only estimate these things but we felt that even those who found the 'new' solutions acceptable had no real faith in them.

* * *

The radio 'reorganisation' had had much the same air of hasty improvisation. Staff was not consulted until after the master-decision had been taken: this was to close the afternoon 'gap', to start earlier in the morning and finish later. Sponsored programmes would be phased out in favour of 'spot' advertisements. News coverage was to be extended in time and scope. The consultation was limited to the practical matter of filling programme schedules.

Altogether there was an increase in programme hours of 17 per cent. Production staff was hastily selected and given crash training. The augmented staff was still insufficient to meet the increase in hours.

Daytime programming had to be light and 'popular' so that advertisers would buy time. The evening programmes, when advertisers and audiences had switched over to television, were materially better in quality. Who they were for is another matter. Listeners have so far not responded as favourably to the 'reformed' radio as had been expected.

There was a diminution of adult Irish language, programmes but, following the Authority's stated policy of 'diffusion', there was more 'use' of Irish in and around programmes. The incense was acrid to those in the radio service who had a commitment to the language.

The Steering Committee set up by the Director-General to plan and implement the whole shoddy affair was headed by Mr. Oliver Maloney, Secretary to the Authority and Director of Personnel. He was an economist, an ex-Civil Servant, and had come to RTE from a post as Chief Administrative Officer of the Agricultural Credit Corporation. He had no experience of broadcasting but was an administrator of thoroughness and stamina.

The reorganisation had to be pushed through by 2nd November 1968—six months after the Committee was set up. What magic may have been in this date is not known. The Authority had obviously learnt nothing whatsoever since, in September 1961, it had instructed Michael Barry to get on the air by the end of the year 'even if it was the last day'.

A demoralised radio staff had its hopes raised by Mr. Maloney's Steering Committee and by the freshness of his approach, in much the same way as Producers had had theirs raised by Mr. Hardiman's offer of a Consultative Group. Both sets of hope proved to be balloons.

> *The People in Between*
> *Looked underdone and harassed,*
> *And out of place and mean,*
> *And horribly embarrassed.*
> —HILAIRE BELLOC

The new Heads of Department system in television, in this atmosphere of unease and distrust, got off to a flabby start.

An informal meeting of Heads of Department discussed certain procedural principles to govern their conduct:

In their relations with the Controller they would expect candour and clarity.

They would be clear and candid with him and with one another.

They would support one another in the exercise of those duties and rights which their job-specifications acknowledged.

Curiously, these sentiments were not conveyed to the Controller!

Although the artistic quality of its individual members was considerable, the Heads of Department, as a group, floundered in indecisiveness. They suffered the prevarications from above which had ruined the old Editorial system.

The fundamental factor which undermined the new Heads of Department system from the beginning was this: the Director-General's Policy Committee, nominally consultative, had in fact become a decision-making group. Jack White, a member of it, later admitted this to be the case.

Its decisions bore mainly on controversial programmes. The censorship of the *Late Late Show* and the News/Programmes Division wrangles over Public Affairs, already referred to, are instances of the Director-General's tacit acceptance of its real executive role.

This had had a curiously concealed divisive effect on the Heads of Department Group. Only those Heads whose programmes were affected were actively aware that the real principle of programme-decision in these matters lay not with them nor with the Controller of Programmes but with the Policy Committee. These Heads frequently felt ineffectual: the remainder carried on their work unaware.

The programme-makers were, of course, affected by the radical ambiguity of this situation.

On more than one occasion, decisions which the Heads had taken were reversed without consultation. They were to be repudiated again by senior authority when an RTE spokesman stated publicly that its members were 'being given more authority each day'. What they were to do in the meantime was not explained.

The Autumn schedules were being planned later than usual. This year, 1969, an estimated budget allotment was given to each Head, with the number of hours programming required. It would be possible, therefore, to institute, despite Management's official unconcern, a budgetary-control system of some sort.

There was, the Controller said, to be an increase in emphasis on Light Entertainment, involving the whole country.

Lelia Doolan had become Head of Light Entertainment. She was interested in it as an area which had been neglected for a long time by the station. It was one about which there were enormous assumptions current, many of them dubious. It might now be possible to test some of these in actual programming, and to evolve policies which could be verified against the international commercial format of Light Entertainment shows which, up to then, had been largely accepted as the norm.

One of these assumptions was rather neatly summed up by one of the Producers as 'a laugh in a vale of tears'. This was, frankly, an escapist view. It was worth examining.

Another, perhaps more thoughtful, was summed up in a note from Bil Keating, Producer of *Like Now*, when he said: 'light entertainment is something that requires no background knowledge of the subject matter'. This, too, would need to be tried out.

Our unclarity on this subject had been revealed to Lelia Doolan when she represented the station at the Montreux Light Entertainment Festivals. Most of the other delegates were quite clear: Light Entertainment was anything that sold music sheets, discs and copyright. This, of course, didn't apply to all the delegates but to the battalions of commercial hangers-on who increasingly formed the character of the Festival.

The Irish delegation suggested closing down the 'Festival' in its tenth year, 1970, and substituting a study-week. This might show typical *national* work rather than the 'international-appeal' diet that was draining the concept of Light Entertainment of any meaning.

In RTE, many of the Producers in Light Entertainment had already been working to her during the past couple of years, and she had tried to respond to their programme needs but in a formless and probably unhelpful way. She hoped that through examination of the whole notion of Light Entertainment in group discussions, seminars and 'Teach-Ins', and by buying programme *ideas* from Producers with her budget, it might be possible to work out an interim policy which could be developed, through practice. With the involvement of the Producers, this work was commenced.

> *Cheer up, the worst is yet to come.*
> —P. C. JOHNSON

In other areas, programming plans went forward too. In Current Affairs, now located in the Features Department under James Plunkett Kelly, there was evidence again of pressures to keep snugly to trouble-free programming. This was equally true of Public Affairs in the Irish Department.

Eoghan Harris, the stormy petrel of the *Work* programme, was asked to transfer to *Féach* to work with Breandán Ó hEithir. It was an understandable transfer in view of the lack of fluent Irish speakers among Producers. Committed to the idea of Irish language programming, he believed (with the concurrence of Liam Ó Murchú) that the station had done less than service to Irish language speakers.

Capable in the imaginative and forceful handling of Current Affairs programmes, Harris was naturally loath to leave the *Work* programme area, particularly in view of past pressures upon it and the likelihood of their continuing.

*Work* was to be replaced by a new Autumn programme: *Wednesday Special*, to which Breandán Ó hEithir had requested a transfer. Ó hEithir had been the mainstay of *Féach*. He had had many Producers. He was disgusted with the Management's attitude of indifference to it as the only really mature Irish language programme in the schedule. He and Harris discussed the situation.

They decided that working together they could make *Féach* a first-class programme. Accordingly, Harris agreed to his transfer without further demur and Ó hEithir withdrew his own application.

In a memorandum to his Head of Department, Liam Ó Murchú, in mid-May, Eoghan Harris outlined what seemed to him the two basic requirements to effect a substantial change in the status of the programme and thus of the Irish language in the station.

Firstly he said that he could not see in the case of a Current Affairs programme like *Féach* that there was 'any explicit or implicit reason why (it) … should not receive parity with similar programmes in English*.

The particular application of this would be to remove *Féach* from the tiny Studio 3, the limitations of which had, for example, prevented the large-scale discussions which the report of An Comhlacht Comhairleach required. He pointed out that if adequate Current Affairs could be done from Studio 3, *7 Days* would not need the larger studio they, in fact, occupied.

His second point was that the transmission time should be changed from 'the euphoria of Sunday mealtime' and given a more authoritative quality by a late-night transmission. Knowing that advertising revenue increases as the night goes on, he pertinently inquired 'if the relationship between advertising and the Irish programmes militates against giving Féach a late transmission slot'. He concluded 'if there are advertising problems how was this to be reconciled with our commitment under the Broadcasting Act?'

On the same day he supplied a brief for the programme, as follows:

> To provide Irish speakers with an intelligent and authoritative Current Affairs programme. The quality must be high enough to satisfy both good Irish speakers and encourage those whose intellectual curiosity will transcend their poor Irish.

This was an explicit statement of his intention to aim *Féach* at adult viewers and to shun the 'lá breá' diffusion 'policy'.

Meanwhile, James Plunkett Kelly, who had made strenuous efforts to retain Eoghan Harris on *Wednesday Special*, asked Jack Dowling to join the team. The programme was to be produced by Aindreas Ó Gallchóir with Patrick Gallagher and Brian Cleeve as reporters. Michael Monaghan was to direct it.

The team set out to write a policy for the Autumn. There was some disagreement on this notion of writing a programme policy.

Some members of the team felt that one should be written in order to test the Management's sincerity in advance. They were convinced that Management would never allow the series to become a Public Affairs programme in any real sense, but would try to divert it into safe channels.

The others agreed but thought that by *not* writing a policy, the team would be more likely to get real Public Affairs material through the watchful screen of the Director-General's Policy Committee.

The situation was complex. Jim Plunkett Kelly as Head of the Department, and late leader of the Workers' Union of Ireland militants, naturally felt that he could deal with the obstructions which, he acknowledged, were likely to be met.

During these policy discussions, the first confirmation of the team's fears came. The Assistant Controller informed the Department that eighteen Documentaries (and not a weekly Public Affairs programme) were acceptable to Management.

Kelly and Ó Gallchóir protested and carried their point. The team, however, was convinced that this had only been conceded at Programme Controller's level and not at the level of the Policy Committee.

Paddy Gallagher, Brian Cleeve and Jack Dowling were now openly skeptical of the possibility of getting a Public Affairs series through at all. They said so.

Jim Plunkett Kelly was angry at this scepticism of his ability to force his policy through.

From this moment on, the close friendship and trust which he had shared with Jack Dowling began to give way to a slow process of withdrawal.

> *You may have the engines painted any damned colour you like as long as they are black.*
> —CHIEF ENGINEER OF L.M.S.
> (TO HIS BOARD)

Politics now seemed to obsess the Authority. A document entitled *Staff and Politics,* circulated without prior consultation with the Heads of Department, or even notification to the Trade Unions, came from the

Director-General. It set out lists of 'Restricted' and 'Unrestricted' staffs. It specified additional requirements on staff during an election.

A particular section required members of staff in the 'Restricted* category to obtain advance permission from their Divisional Head before engaging in 'minor political activities* such as canvassing for a candidate.

The good sense of staff as adult citizens, to say nothing of their Constitutional rights, did not seem to matter. The Unions rejected this document and members were instructed to ignore it.

The prospect of the General Election seemed to have made everyone in the upper echelons of staff extremely touchy.

Gay Byrne revolted.

On Friday, 9th May, he was directed to delete from the following night's *Late Late Show*, an item about Local Government rates in which two politicians were to take part.

The item had been approved by his Head of Department, Lelia Doolan. The instruction came from the Director-General via Jack White, via Lelia Doolan, after a Policy Committee meeting on the Friday morning.

Gay Byrne, invoking his rights as a Producer under the *7 Days* Agreement, decided to include the item.

He was supported in his view by a group of Heads of Department who were hastily called together by the Assistant Controller to deliberate on the problem. Their unanimous agreement was that the *Late Late Show* was a perfectly proper place for politicians to discuss matters of current interest.

Nevertheless their professional judgment was reversed by the Director-General. He had, it appeared, decided that the station was in an Election situation, even though the writ for the Election had not been moved!

Heretofore, the Constitutional practice in the Republic of Ireland was to reserve this right to the Head of Government.

Of course, the picture was not glum all over, nor glum all of the time. Television people are a gay and resilient lot. Like the Irish generally, they love-hated one another and cultivated one another's' company assiduously. They were used to failure and delighted in the occasional success. The oddities of Management, most of the time, merely bored them; their interest was aroused only when Management became so obtrusive and arrogant as to distract them from their work—or their distractions.

The Director-General had attempted during the late Autumn, by inviting a number of famous communications experts to talk to selected staff members on social and broadcasting matters, to develop debate. These lectures tended to become a bit like Mass on Sundays. There was still the rest of the week to get through— and no obvious connection between prayer and practice. This is not a snide remark. The fact is that there was no framework of common experience which would have permitted this new knowledge to be meaningfully assimilated—and issue in action.

In April 1969 the Guild, hoping to give the debate some purpose, and thereby, perhaps, broaden its own membership to include the technical people, held a public seminar in Dublin on the topic 'Broadcasting—What Can We Do?' Raymond Williams, the Welsh writer and don who had so valuably contributed to communications in Britain, was the guest of honour.

Williams' main thesis in this discussion was that there are no 'mass' media, for the simple reason that there are no 'masses' but intricately overlapping structures of audience-interest. The whole notion of the 'masses', in his view, was an unconscious conspiracy on the part of manipulative Elites. They were an invention that permitted the transmission of control ideas in a one-way traffic. Often, television and radio as they are *actually* used, prevent communications. Potentially, they *are* communication.

The seminar was regarded by the Director-General as a splinter movement.

> *There's a good time coming, boys.*
> —THE GOOD TIME COMING SONG

Why should programme-makers be bothered about anything other than making programmes? Why should they concern themselves with management, structures and policy?

The answer, we hope, is now plain: it is policies that programmes are about. Internal policies of the station are but reflections of larger policies of the nation. If programme-makers confined themselves to programmes there would soon be no programmes to make outside the area of distraction, edification and a thinly disguised party-line.

Radio and television are nothing other than the people talking to themselves in public. Every piece of pragmatism, every sort of defence-mechanism, whether by way of management jargon or engineer's technique or administrator's conservatism or artistic twaddle, stultifies, distorts and constipates this conversation.

It is a difficult conversation to hold anyway, interrupted as it continually is by the repetitious noise of advertisers' jingles. We were losing viewers: 15 per cent in the last year. 'A worldwide phenomenon' we were told. The question 'why?' was shied away from.

We needed to loosen up, to get out and about, above all, to *think* about what we were doing.

*Thinking?* We were building a new radio-block at a cost of a million pounds; probably because it had been promised in 1947. The fact that conditions might have changed by 1969, that the whole question of ground-station transmitters and large Dublin-based studio-blocks needed close examination in the light of satellites and future developments in radio, was thought to be an 'interesting' question—but not really relevant here. In the words of our Head of Technical Development, Eric Spain: 'The Radio Committee, by simply existing, tended to regard its own survival as a prime reason for continuing the work. It simply could not seriously consider the suggestion that it had really no reason to do it'.

Technical advances were making it irrelevant: but we were going to have a Radio Centre—at £1,000,000. Mr. Spain did not propose to know the answers: he simply wanted to raise the question. He was politely listened to: he was ignored.

*Thinking?*

The prospects for television in its inevitable development towards colour were being examined by a group set up by the Director of Engineering, Mr. George Waters. This group consisted solely of engineers. One of its members noted:

> Very early in their discussions, they realised that they could not really make any clear recommendations unless programmes policy in relation to colour was decided upon. Once again, the idea of talking to Programmes Department was 'taboo'. When, at last, they did manage some sort of contact, the Director of Engineering asked what they were doing talking to Programmes Division—they should be concerned with equipment!

The Colour-group's contact with programme people included Lelia Doolan, Liam Ó Murchú and Jack White. It ended abruptly.

Was it to be the case again, as at the start of the station, that programming thinking would *only* be done *after* the technical changes had been decided?

If so, we will, like most other broadcasting stations, in our pragmatic way, go into colour programming feet first.

The BBC's Head of Design, Mr. Dick Levin, at a seminar with our Producers and Engineers, had already warned us of the dilemma that this kind of 'thinking' had landed the BBC in. Designers and Producers needed a soft, clear colour image. The Engineers had already decided on a sharp resolved one. They made do. So, will we?

*Thinking?*

The one performing art in which our country excels is drama. We have a fine professional tradition. Per head of population, we probably have the highest and most intense amateur drama involvement in the world. The role of drama on television is something that demands the most careful and systematic thought. It uses about sixty per cent of our workshop capacity, a huge chunk of our facilities and a massive section of our total programme budget. What has eight years of effort done for Irish drama, playwrights, actors, the improvement of standards of performance and taste among our people either as amateurs, professionals or audiences?

Chloe Gibson had proposed a Drama School to give training to young actors (also to such performers as commentators, newsreaders, floor-managers, stage managers, continuity girls, Directors) because, as a national body, RTE had, she felt, an obligation to give some of its resources and time to training those who would work in the artistic and communications fields, even outside the station. The plan had first been put forward by her in 1966, again in 1968 and finally in 1969. It remained, at the time of our resignations, filed.

Incentive to come forward with ideas tended to wilt, yet Mr. Oliver Maloney, commenting on talk about 'creative people', thought fit to say that he did not notice much sign of their creativeness in their work.

*Thinking?*

The greatest single need in the country is education and re-education. Enormous changes have been taking place since Donogh O'Malley lifted the whole problem into the forefront of public consciousness.

RTE has made important contributions on certain fronts: *Telefís Scoile* once promised to bring the organisation onto the main axis of the nation's educational advance. It now acts as little more than an electronic service to officials of the Department of Education. Despite the fine ambition, interest and energy of Maev Conway, the programmes tended, increasingly, to reflect the Department of Education's, rather than the station's, initiatives.

The tremendous task of providing technical education to farmers, so well initiated by Patrick Jennings and expanded into a national asset by the flair and drive of Justin Keating, is now, on the eve of our entry as a primary producing country into the EEC, in need of expansion on an unprecedented scale. The thought devoted to this by top Management in RTE for the coming year's television programme is reflected in this table issued to Heads of Department in February 1969:

|  | Estimate | Hours |
|---|---|---|
| Drama | £90,000 | 66 |
| Light Entertainment | £86,800 | 143 |
| Irish and Children's | £68,500 | 170 |
| Features | £67,000 | 190 |
| Sport (without Outside Broadcasting) | £52,000 | 85 |
| Religion | £19,100 | 80 |
| Agriculture | £11,500 | 20 |

In what possible sense could this be said to take 'the national aims' into account?

*Thinking?*

The transfer of *7 Days* to the News Division in February 1968 marked a subtle but definite shift in the station's 'thinking' on Current Affairs coverage. The old programme had happily contained two different ways of thinking on matters of public importance. On the one hand, the Producer, Muiris Mac Conghail, with David Thornley, Brian Farrell and Ted Nealon, tended to see politics in terms of who was saying what in Dáil Éireann. The academic cast of mind of Thornley and Farrell, orientated towards political science, intensified this general attitude and gave it intellectual form and direction.

Another approach to politics was represented by Dick Hill and Eoghan Harris and the two reporters, Patrick Gallagher and Brian Cleeve. Hill was a science graduate and Harris a lecturer in modern history; Gallagher a professional journalist and Cleeve a novelist, archaeologist and artist. These tended to be more interested in the particular; in social and economic movements which they believed to be of more enduring importance than personality struggles in the Dáil.

In programme terms the difference could be very significant. For example, industrialisation to Patrick Gallagher or Brian Cleeve would mean the plight of a redundant worker, the father of a family. Conclusions would not be shirked; inarticulate workers would be helped to speak. Impartiality was interpreted as a balancing of the scales between silent poor and articulate rich. The same issue to Brian Farrell or David Thomley would be interpreted, quite properly, in terms of Government statements on industrialisation. The resulting programme might mean the close interviewing of a smooth Minister. Very often it made good television but, without the other approach, the social contexts would often have escaped through holes in the net.

Until the transfer, these differences made an invaluable synthesis. Gallagher or Cleeve might, on film, investigate the socioeconomic background of a problem: Farrell, Thomley or Nealon would follow up the responsible politician.

The transfer ended this. Harris and Cleeve together with Seán Egan—a new Director who shared their approach—resigned from the programme. Not long after, Dick Hill left active production to take up a management position. By the end of the Summer, Patrick Gallagher had found that the programme did not any longer offer scope for his aptitude for digging persistently into issues, composing the result into a script and laying it before the public, starkly.

The decisions of Cleeve and Gallagher to withdraw from *7 Days* represented a large professional sacrifice for both men. Instead of that regular 'exposure' on a positive programme which is the broadcasters' lifeblood they were relegated to that graveyard of Current Affairs—a fortnightly programme.

Despite limitations of money and facilities, the *Work* programme showed flashes of the old style of approach. When both *7 Days* and *Work* decided to tackle the same subject— Gulf Oil—the result not only illustrated the difference in 'thinking' but had led to a confrontation between the News and Programmes Divisions. The item transmitted by

*7 Days* consisted of film of the arrival of the ship 'Universe Ireland' at Bantry Bay. The only commentary was that provided by a foreign voice.

In the *Work* programme, Patrick Gallagher and Justin Keating were meticulously researching the profit and loss to Ireland of the arrival of Gulf Oil in Bantry Bay. Their findings were not reassuring. They prepared to lay them before the public.

A series of delays resulted as the Management fretfully queried whether *Work* was not exceeding its brief. The *Work* team believed that Jim McGuinness, Head of News, was using the Director-General's Policy Committee to advance his own programme interests without effective opposition.

Finally, during the confrontation between the Director-General and twelve programme-makers on the Church programme, an undertaking was given that the Gulf Oil programme could be made and transmitted. It was transmitted and, according to an Audience Research report, the public recognised that some thinking was being done and that the truth was being told.

Meanwhile the *7 Days* programme was reflecting more and more the bias towards political coverage in terms of the parties and their personalities.

There was something else too—an unconscious censorship. Not censorship from outside but, more dangerously, self-censorship: the short-cut to thinking. This might have been no more than a reflection of the new team's lack of interest in such matters. At first, the difference in thought and feeling was so subtle that only professional broadcasters and journalists would comment on it. There was, for example, a programme on Ballymun. Technically skilful, beautifully photographed, it somehow failed to deal with the small matter of a wall dividing middle-class from working-class in Ballymun.

Directors are men with visual sense; failing to deal with this barrier was like going to Berlin and not showing The Wall. *7 Days*, later, went to Berlin—and showed the Wall! In the Ballymun programme John O'Donoghue inexplicably managed to ignore a member of the audience who seemed determined to discuss the wall. The public could see this, and protested. The following evening Frank Hall was given the task of 'restoring the image' by interviewing the man John O'Donoghue had not noticed, but to a different audience.

One could not imagine the old team ignoring the Arigna strike. A remote mining village, whose entire population was locked out of work for three months, is material for the kind of theme that no film-maker would ignore. In the hands of John Horgan, in *The Irish Times*, it became epic journalism. As film, it would have said more about master and man in modem Ireland than all the speeches made by Mr. Ivor Kenny or Dr. Hillery. Somehow, *7 Days* ignored it, although we know that individual members of the team wished to tackle the story.

Thoughtful programming invites the viewers to think: viewers saw film of striking dustmen throwing rubbish on the streets; it produced outrage among citizens of suburbia. No attempt was made to explain the minds of men who must rear families on £11 per week. No digging into the social causes of their action was done nor was the need for it even suggested.

*Thinking?*

In the early coverage of the Northern crisis there was little systematic thought evident on the socio-economic *causes* of unrest; what was reported was uncovered rather than dis-covered. It was shown rather than analysed. The result was impression rather than thought. This is the News, not Current Affairs, technique.

To the casual viewer, it was a long time before the programme discovered that Eddie McAteer was not the leader of the Civil Rights movement; he was belatedly replaced, as father-figure, by John Hume, just at the moment that leadership in Derry was passing into the hands of Eamonn McCann and the Housing and Unemployed Action Committees.

In *The Irish Press*, Joe Carroll had explained how such committees really controlled the Derry movement. *7 Days* never seemed, now, to grasp who did what. It continued to reflect the descriptive policy of the News Division. No hint of the vast changes of thought taking place in the North was conveyed to the Southern viewer.

The Chairman of the Northern Ireland Civil Rights Association, Frank Gogarty, was not interviewed in the programme; neither was the Vice-Chairman, Vincent McDowell, who lives in Dun Laoghaire! Both of these men could have pointed out that John Hume and Ivan Cooper were not the leaders of the Derry militants. Cooper had denounced as hooligans the Bogside 'mobs' who later defended Derry. The moderates' policy, in Cooper's *own words*, had failed.

*Thinking* is a 'first-hand' activity—not a second-hand transmission of other men's thoughts.

The Chief of Staff of the I.R.A., Cathal Goulding, lives in Dublin. Yet *7 Days* was content to use a BBC interview—confirming *Sunday Times* reports that the Irish Government had ordered a clampdown on coverage of that organisation.

*7 Days* did nothing to counter the systematic campaign of vilification against Bernadette Devlin, carried out by the British press. They seemed to be unaware of it. It was left to *Féach* to screen the first interview with her. *7 Days* gave the impression that 'sensible' men like Hume were in charge.

Did Management really think that we opposed the transfer of *7 Days* to the News Division out of jealousy, or because we feared this kind of treatment and 'thinking'?

CHAPTER 1: A CAUTIONARY TALE

When Fr. Jerome O'Herlihy spoke about the need for Current Affairs programmes to look behind mere News reportage, his *Outlook* was refused transmission.

But self-censorship is more difficult to detect; sins of apparent commission may really be sins of omission. Professional broadcasters are men who can read the signs writ small. They were writ large: the public knew. A special Audience Research report of 10th May reported regular regret at what was expressed as a 'softening' of the programme's thinking.

Somehow the public had found out.

There were good programmes still being made. Tragically, there were many more that could be made.

A programme like *Newsbeat*, *Let's Draw*, episodes of Telefís Scoile, *Right of Reply*, *Brogeen* for children, some *Bring Down the Lamp* programmes, the *Late Late Show*, episodes of *Like Now* and of *The Riordans*, and often *7 Days*, *Buntus*, and *Féach*, the experimental drama series and an occasional Special— still did the job that broadcasting was really about. They did it with skill, imagination, humour and courage; it was a core of wonderful potential to cherish.

The Authority deliberated monthly and kept a Skibbereen Eagle's eye on what the nation's leaders were doing. Whether it had given up the battle to rid itself of its commercial arm is not known. We know that Professor Moody was disturbed. The Authority had little prospect of ignoring established institutions, being itself an Establishment Institution. Its ability to spancel political comment was still able to command the confidence of the Government. Mr. Erskine Childers was able to say in the Dáil in his statement on the Estimate (1968/69) for his Department:

I understand also that the Authority has taken steps to modify the recent trend in interviewing persons of all political and social opinions in a manner which has aroused the strongest criticism.

* * *

*Our defence-lines are penetrated at many points; we are in danger of being over-run. Our ammunition is running out. Our casualties are heavy and my troops' morale is sinking fast. We have nowhere to which we can retreat and no shipping by which we can be evacuated. The situation is obscure.*
—U.S. WAR REPORTS (1943)

The detonator went off; a slow, soggy explosion followed.

Bob Quinn's letter was written on 14th May 1969.[34] It arrived in the station two days later. Many people had left before, quietly. Quinn did not. He accused the station of selling its birthright, of demanding loyalty from those to whom it gave none; of systematising its artistic life out of existence. He did not resign; that was 'playing the game'. He just walked away.

An informal meeting of Bob Quinn's friends and a few other interested members of staff was held on Monday, 19th May.

These people were all concerned about the truth of what he had said but confused about what they could do.

---

34  See Appendix III for this letter and other resignation correspondence.

Some thought his statements too general to be useful, too vague; some felt the style was regrettably extravagant and the tone intemperate. Besides, the manner of his leaving had been abrupt and unprofessional.

But nobody thought the substance of what he had said about the station was untrue.

The younger people present felt that in fact the issues he raised were important enough to concern staff generally and senior Management particularly. Various courses of action were talked over; there should be a meeting of all staff; there should be a 'teach-in'; a 'sit-in' might be organised in the administrative block.

One group felt and said plainly that Bob Quinn's leaving a camera crew in 'mid air', so to speak, was a signal act which high-lighted the logic of his basic conviction: that he was engaged in a fraudulent contract with a national organisation whose only reason for existence is to nourish the mind and spirit of the people. This organisation in practice was engaged in warping and withering that mind and spirit—starting with its own staff. No polite and professional 'bowing out' would make this point clear.

Others thought this was not permissible, even if the point was sound. The ethic of our commercial society was an ethic of loyalty to one's contract—and so on.

At length, Jim Plunkett Kelly, supported by Maev Conway, pointed out that whenever the Heads of Department had acted resolutely and unitedly, the Director-General had proved himself receptive and reasonable.

Jack Dowling took up this point: the Heads were the structure created by the Director-General through which the sentiments of staff were to be conveyed. Jack Dowling asked the Heads, of whom four were present, to meet the Director-General and express our concern.

He decided to put the viability of the new Head of Department system to the test.

It was agreed that the Heads would meet and Jim Plunkett Kelly then left.

The next evening (Tuesday) the Heads met and discussed the problem for three hours. On the grounds that their meeting was not plenary[35] and formal they postponed it until their next official meeting with the Assistant Controller.

The Controller was absent on sick leave.

At this next meeting, held the following Thursday, the matter was postponed again, after fifteen minutes discussion. It was to be talked about at the next week's session. It should be realised that they were not being asked to support Quinn. *They were asked to see Mr. Hardiman and give him a message of concern.*

The next morning (Friday), Jack Dowling told Jim Plunkett Kelly that it was now evident that nothing decisive was going to be done by the Heads of Department Group. He gave Jim his letter of resignation (unsigned) at 1 o'clock. He then went to Lelia Doolan and asked her if six people, who had expressed willingness to go to the Director-General, would do so. They agreed.

Lelia Doolan then asked Jim Plunkett Kelly during lunch-time if, as Jack's Head of Department, he would come with her and the group. He refused.

At 3.00 p.m. Jack Dowling signed his letter of resignation. Jim Plunkett Kelly said he reserved the right to hold it in his private possession until he had time to think about it.

---

35  A beautiful example of what Seán Ó Faoláin has described as the 'theologising' Irish mind conditioned by Canon Law attitudes to moral problems.

Lelia Doolan then telephoned the Director-General and asked *him* if he would see the group—which included Producers, Reporters and a Newscaster. Since both the Controller and the Assistant Controller were absent, he said he would prefer to see no one below Head of Department level.

She then asked to see him alone, and informed Jim Plunkett Kelly that she was going to do so.

Liam Ó Murchú, on his way to Yugoslavia, telephoned the Director-General to express Eoghan Harris's alarm that Jack Dowling should be forced to resign in order to move the Heads to do what they ought to do.

Lelia Doolan saw the Director-General immediately afterwards. This was his first knowledge, he said, that anything serious was amiss. After a long discussion, she asked him to give the whole matter his gravest and most urgent attention. She also asked for a gesture that would quickly quieten the house in its concern.

\* \* \*

> *He had been years upon a project for*
> *extracting sunbeams out of cucumbers,*
> *which were to be put into vials hermetically sealed,*
> *and let out to warm the air in raw*
> *inclement Summers.*
> —DEAN SWIFT

The Director-General's gesture, on the following Monday, was to accept Jack Dowling's resignation in spite of Jim Plunkett Kelly's attempt to withhold it.

All through Monday morning, staff members from production and administrative areas, singly and in groups, telephoned, telegraphed, called and attempted to call upon the Director-General for interview. Some wrote letters. Their names were noted. Chloe Gibson had gone to see him on Sunday. Two Producers had walked into his office. All had tried to bring him to some realisation of the disproportionate consequence of the Departmental Heads' failure to communicate that the House was disturbed by the substance of Bob Quinn's letter.

In justice to the Director-General we should say that he had a nicer sense of the proportion between accepting Dowling's resignation and acknowledging the ineffectuality of the Department Heads than anyone else in the station.

Mr. Hardiman knew their ineffectuality: they were, in his own words 'an emergency solution to an emergency situation'.

He would, in the words of his own spokesman 'give them more authority each day'—that is, when he thought them ready.

He knew that Dowling had tried to bring Jim Plunkett Kelly to a realisation of this and had failed.

He knew that, in tendering his resignation to Jim Plunkett Kelly, Dowling had made his last attempt to bring his old comrade to face the fact that he had been assimilated into a masquerade.

More pathetically, Mr. Hardiman knew what Jim Plunkett Kelly could not bring himself to acknowledge: the Heads of Department were now preoccupied with justifying their continued existence. This brute truth could not be faced. They did not even have the moral authority to deliver, face to face, a message that might displease him. Consequently, the Director-General knew that Dowling's resignation was an accusation that must be buried if the system was to survive. He buried it.

At a Teach-In in the canteen on Monday evening, organised by members of the technical production staff and others, Jack Dowling read his letter of resignation. Lelia Doolan and other speakers expressed support for him and alarm at the situation.

The Heads of Department met again that night under the Assistant Controller's Chairmanship. Lelia Doolan urged them to go to the Director-General. They refused to be moved. She told them that while she did not intend to resign, she would carry on exposing the situation inside and outside the station. They were undoubtedly concerned; they could do nothing but talk.

Jack White, however, did explain the gravity of the situation to the Director-General at the Policy Committee meeting and told him that Jack Dowling's resignation might be followed by others. It was this Committee and not the Heads of Department Group that was the real source of power.

The next Heads of Department meeting was two days later. Jack White reported raising specific causes for concern with the Director-General's Policy Committee. These, he said, would be taken up and discussed again in that group. In other words, those who were being accused of blocking the work of the Department Head were to be their own judges.

This Heads' meeting talked for two hours about a document circulated by Lelia Doolan analysing the contradictions of the Management's statements to the Press[36], without reaching any new conclusion. They asked her to refrain from speaking publicly on the delays and prevarications of the system.

She said she would consider this.

> *But they that held through*
> *Winter to the Spring,*

---

36   See Appendix III.

> *Despair as I do, and, as I do,*
> *sing.*
> —BELLOC

A second Teach-In was to be held in the canteen on Thursday evening. Jim Plunkett Kelly conveyed a threat of suspension from the Director-General to Eoghan Harris if he spoke at this meeting.

That afternoon, the Director-General handed an ultimatum to Lelia Doolan. It required her to keep silent in public on the issues and to confine her protest to the proper channels.

These had clearly proved ineffective and were being used by him *because* they were ineffective.

The Director-General's determination to hold the status quo at any cost was now clearly evident. Had she remained silent in the face of this threat, the House would have been intimidated. She felt she must speak. She resigned.

> *Today an accusing memory*
> *passed by. Supposing, now,*
> *the accusation came to light?*
> *I could go far away, live in a*
> *foreign country, a new life far*
> *from every possibility of its*
> *being revealed. I could live*
> *hidden.—No, I must remain*
> *on the spot and continue to do*
> *everything as usual without a*
> *single prudential measure.*
> —SOREN KIERKEGAARD

## UNSCIENTIFIC POSTSCRIPT

Throughout the week of Teach-Ins and of Jack Dowling's and Lelia Doolan's resignations, a certain euphoria gripped those who supported Quinn's critique. It had seemed certain that the public interest which was evident heralded a national debate, and positive action to deal with the issues raised. Among RTE staff, operational crew-leaders in particular showed great courage, despite warnings and hints about job prospects and promotion. Throughout the week men like Peter McEvoy, Fergal Costello and Michael Morris spent every spare moment interpreting the issues to their colleagues. Essentially, they were attempting to cross what amounted to a kind of professional class-barrier. The initial reaction had been that this was a Producers' problem; by the end of the week, it was everybody's concern.

Typical of the mood was the invitation by clerk-secretaries to Eoghan Harris, Chairman of the Workers' Union of Ireland (RTE section), to come to a meeting and explain the issues to them. The lowest paid workers in RTE, these girls showed that they were not just passive observers of the scene and adjuncts of their typewriters. Everybody seemed to be removing their role-masks, to become human. Above all, the threat to suspend Eoghan Harris had quickly given the dispute a Trade Union form. Shop stewards from all Unions rallied to his support. As the weekend approached it seemed as if strike action was likely and industrial dispute was inevitable. Before publishing a sixteen-page refutation of our accusations[37] the Director-General, for the first time since his appointment, began to appear among the studio staffs and was conciliatory. Every facility was extended to Harris. The services of Father Jack Kelly, S.J., were acceptable to Mr. Hardiman in order to discover the temper and tone of the staff.

---

37   See Appendix III for this, and also our reply to it.

The appearances were of course deceptive. From the beginning Management had been totally in control of the one group of people who could then have produced change—the Heads of Departments and their Producers. Throughout the week, most of those who, in the public view, might have been expected to be most keenly involved stood back and watched the technical crews' efforts with detachment. The reasons why only a handful of Producers made a stand are many and complex. The most important had to do with the position of Jim Plunkett Kelly.

In the early days in television, a small group of Producers had tended to give general leadership not only to the Producers but to the whole Programmes Division. This circle was distinguished either by having a radio background or by their commitment to the Irish language. They were the dynamo which, with Jack Dowling and the twelve Producers, had driven the Director-General to set up consultative machinery. They had stood fast and fought hard and skilfully when *7 Days* was transferred. They were committed Trade Unionists and their leader was Jim Plunkett Kelly. Their common characteristic was and is moral courage. They were prized by the underprivileged in a society where such a quality is rare.

At this critical moment and for the first time in his career, Jim Plunkett Kelly hesitated. He decided that as a newly-appointed Head of Department he could now effect reform from within the new structures of Management. Remote from the passion of the staff Teach-Ins he demanded order and stability. Reforms, he declared, would come. The station was, for the first time, open to the influences of those who had for so long represented both the interests of the workers and of the nation's culture. It must be said that no man in the station represented these more typically and deeply than Jim Plunkett Kelly. Our only reservation was that he was two years behind the actualities of the situation and could not see this. We would make it clear that Jim Plunkett Kelly was not suborned by Management promotion. He was incorruptible. We believe that he was profoundly wrong, being locked into the logic of a system that was wrong. No doubt he thought us wrong and obstinate.

Time was all that Management needed. The Producers already knew that Kelly would not fight nor see any need for fight—except in his own well-tested way.

Carefully avoiding the mistake of suspending Harris, the Management allowed the long Whit weekend to produce its 'common-sense' cure. On Tuesday, this process was given a few artificial injections. We regret to have to say this, but we have first-hand evidence that certain staff members set about a deliberate campaign of vilification. It was said that Jack Dowling had ordered studio crews to address him as 'Captain'; with what sincerity could he, then, talk about carpenters' rights? It was said that Michael Morris in U.C.D., where he was a student in his spare time, had put up inflammatory posters. It was said that Eoghan Harris had not *really* been threatened with suspension or that it was only to be implemented if students had marched from UCD: Oliver Donohue was 'accused' of having organised this. It was said that Lelia Doolan had master-minded the whole affair in order to embarrass the Government party; that she had been responsible for the Teach Furbo programme, yet defended Irish culture! It was asserted that it had been a plot by Dowling to promote the interests of the Labour Party. Ridiculous as these rumours were, they helped further to corrupt the atmosphere. The crews knew that Producers were doing nothing as a body. Once more they felt that professional snobbery was at work.

But if Jim Plunkett Kelly's attitude had calmed the Producers' will to resist, nevertheless a substantial body of people among them wished to make some gesture. Equity[38] met and passed a resolution, helplessly. The Workers' Union of Ireland was to become the scene of an exorcism of ghosts. From the outset, Eoghan Harris, its new House Chairman, had few illusions about what could be expected.

Harris is a complex, subtle and even discursive character. He had made an impact on the station almost from the moment of joining it as a trainee Producer-Director in 1966, at the age of twenty-four. He had had a brilliant scholastic career and had taught history at University College Cork. His early and lasting pre-occupation was with the revitalising of the Irish spirit—at first romantically under the influence of some of Corkery's students. This gradually gave way to a reflective realism that many of his former associates found harsh and unpalatable. He had a social commitment to the underprivileged of such intensity that it often frightened his friends as much as his opponents. Any injustice seemed to trigger that 'savage indignation' of which Yeats speaks so movingly in his description of Dean Swift.

Of extraordinarily high intelligence among men who were themselves markedly above average, he had nothing of the intellectual bully in his make-up. He had, however, a habit of speech that was most disconcerting. His thought ran far ahead of his ability to articulate it; this was considerable. Speaking in public, in moments of high tension, what he was *about* to say ran to meet him with such precipitancy that what he was *actually* saying, in the interim, became an obstruction. He consequently tended, towards the end of a speech, to gabble his words at an alarming rate of acceleration in a fine Cork accent. This gave him a reputation for excitability which, indeed, was often well-founded. Yet his friends and opponents were continually struck by an

---

38   Both Irish Actors' Equity and the Workers' Union of Ireland represented Producers. The WUI also represented Production Assistants and clerical workers. Designers, newscasters and scriptwriters were members of Equity.

incisiveness of insight and language that could cut into a confused issue like a scalpel and, with deft and witty verbal strokes, lay bare the skeleton of a situation.

His influence in the Trade Union movement within the station, was great and often commanding. His intense nervous energy made it difficult to keep up with him. He had that unusual gift of being able to switch his mind, without any apparent internal shock, from one subject to another, and to treat each with the freshness and penetration that other men can give only to the first subject that engages them each day.

He quickly gained a reputation as a hothead—a frightful thing among the new Irish *bourgeoisie*—second only in horror, according to Patrick Pearse, to being seen walking down Grafton Street with a brown paper parcel under one's arm.

Fearless of personal consequences, a master of savage irony in both Irish and English, he disturbed the complacent, amused the dilettante and alarmed the plodder. He was born to be a leader. He would always have followers. He lacked only training and experience to give him the kind of calm to deal with a crisis among the respectable whose only concern was, not to hide the truth but rather, to admit its existence and, avoiding it like a bunker, keep the ball on the fairway.

In the debate which followed the resignations, he suffered one insurmountable disability; the removal from the scene of two of his closest friends, who had asked him not to join them, had affected him deeply. This led those who trusted him to suspect the balance of his judgment in these particular issues. In fact, it had given him a stripped and sharpened vision of the issues. People, increasingly insistent on not understanding them, found this unbearable.

It has been one of the curiosities of our situation since retiring from RTE that we have been receiving reaction reports from every shade of opinion within the station.

It will be evident that Harris's position as Chairman of the WUI House Committee was regarded by some as biased to the point of partisanship. Jim Larkin, the only Irish Trade Union leader who might have translated the issues into Trade Union language, was dead. An ex-branch secretary, Jim Plunkett Kelly occupied the supreme moral position in the WUI, so far as RTE was concerned. It was inevitable that the Union's Head Office would look to him for guidance. His declared position was that he didn't know what all the excitement was about.

A Special General Meeting of the Union saw matters reaching their inevitable pathetic conclusion. Eoghan Harris, young, the nominal Chairman, was confronted by the spiritual veteran leader of the Union. It was—as Seán Mac Réamoinn sadly remarked— like listening to an argument between Daniel Cohn-Bendit and an old guard French Communist during the Paris riots. Nothing caught the atmosphere in the bitter exchange between them like Kelly's remark that he considered the Teach-Ins 'undignified'. In view of Jim's own reputation for sudden anger and his known attitudes in times of crisis towards Gunnar Rugheimer, Adrian Cronin, Tom McGrath, Burt Budin and Michael Johnston, this remark was somewhat surprising to Harris.

Despite the confusion, the meeting unanimously passed a resolution recognising the 'truth of the substance of criticism' made by those who had resigned. It instructed Harris and his Executive Committee to identify grievances and formulate claims for their rectification.

Five meetings of this committee followed. It was a grim and thankless task for Harris. He knew that Sean Mac Réamoinn was correct in describing the committee as a 'shadow cabinet' without Jim Plunkett Kelly's moral support. And he knew that Management knew this and would treat any claims accordingly. Nevertheless, the claims were speedily formulated; there were six in all. Two bore upon programme-makers' representation on the Director-General's Policy Committee; two upon an investigation committee on advertising. The two central claims were for an investigation into the Engineering Division's relationship to Programmes Division and the setting up of decision-making consultative machinery.

This time Harris was determined not to let the theory of consultation which had led to the charade of the previous Producers' group operate again. The claim was framed in the light of the 'origin, operation and breakdown of that group'.

Finally, there was a meeting with Management. Mr. Oliver Maloney, Head of Personnel, predictably described the consultative claims as 'doctrinaire' and refused them in the sense of decision-making participation. He was at that time busily engaged in setting up 'non-Union' consultative committees which somehow managed to contain Union shop-stewards! Jim Plunkett Kelly's ambivalent position as Trade Unionist and senior manager was evidently to be multiplied in little—across the entire organisation from studio crews to News Division.

Mr. Maloney made it clear that the Director-General would not countenance an investigation into the Engineering Division. This is understandable, especially in view of the fact that Cumann na nInnealltóirí interests at that time were under challenge from the non-University technicians. This was the first time that the tensions between graduate and non-graduate engineers had publicly surfaced in RTE affairs. 'The Engineers' had always managed to put up a united front. Divisions, resentments and disappointments now began to reveal themselves.

Mr. Maloney was prepared to do *something* about advertising.

He assured himself of a warm place in the Union's Head Offices by warning the meeting of the dangers of overwork attached to consultation in the form advanced by the House Committee.

The Union House Committee returned with the results of this encounter to a Special General Meeting. Broadly, the Management had said No! This meeting, well aware that nothing further could be done, effectively, without the concurrence of Jim Plunkett Kelly, was disconcerted. It required a focus to express its tensions. It fixed on the fact that Management had made an offer of consultation to Producer-Directors the previous April. This had been for non-decision-making consultation, restricted to Producers.

Vainly, Harris tried to explain that the proposal had been a red herring and that the Producers had then known it to be so. He reminded them that he and Michael Slevin, Equity shop-steward, had told the Head of Personnel at that time, with the Producers' approval, that his proposals on consultation were only a rehash of the system that had just broken down. The Unions' present claims, in any case, subsumed Management's previous offer.

It didn't matter. Logic was at the bottom of the lake. The sword of division—Excalibur—had surfaced. The meeting demanded that a claim for consultation for all staff be set aside until the Producers decided on their own offer.

Harris was not placatory. He was conscious that he was now holding down an empty honorary position and yet was expected to face a Management which knew that the Union would not fight without Jim Plunkett Kelly.

This business done, the meeting went thankfully home. The ghosts had been laid.

* * *

Union activity in other parts of the house appeared to be sporadic.

The internal affairs of the National Union of Journalists have so far deteriorated that their monthly meetings have not taken place during the past few months, regularly.

In other cases, they were concerned with routine particulars. Nonetheless, even some of these reveal staff dissatisfaction and the readiness of the Director-General to keep the peace at all costs, even to the point of over-ruling his own senior executives. He clearly realises the explosive delicacy of the situation among technical staff.[39]

For example: Vans in use for Outside Broadcast radio had proved dangerous and unsatisfactory in the past, in terms of roadworthiness when equipment-loaded and in technical performance. Nevertheless a Production Services executive ordered new ones of the same kind, despite warnings from the Sound Operators, and the Union (Irish Transport and General Workers'). On delivery of the new vans, a senior Sound Operator refused to work them. He was suspended without warning on 23rd August by a decision of the Head of Radio Production Facilities and the Director of Engineering. The Union blacked all the programmes which he would have worked on over that weekend—including the All-Ireland Semi-Final and the Sunday Mass on location. A transmission of a studio Mass was also vetoed. By immediate and direct intervention of the Director-General, the vans were withdrawn and the Sound Operator reinstated. Mr. Hardiman can read the signs and, on occasion, move with despatch to meet them.

\* \* \*

The Workers' Union of Ireland meeting with Mr. Oliver Maloney had requested that "a joint committee of management and staff be set up to investigate and report on the relationship between the Engineering and Programmes Divisions', with reference to the 'structural control

---

39   On 15th September last, his Director of Personnel informed the Secretary of the Forum Discussion Group, who had invited RTE to debate with us in public , that this would be inadvisable as the staff was in a state of 'trauma'.

and authority in each'. Mr. Maloney had a particular objection to this request.

He was adamant that such investigation was undesirable in the Engineering Division. Some of the Union representatives shrewdly suspected that he was anxious to see that the interests of Cumann na nInnealltóirí should be protected. The point is that the Cumann is not a Trade Union. It is a professional association of university-graduate engineers. Although small, its members occupy key positions in RTE as they do in most semi-State bodies. Its record during trade disputes in RTE has been, in the eyes of the Cumann members, one of loyalty to and co-operation with Management. Trade Unionists see it as an Establishment organisation.

Naturally, Management has a keen regard for the interests of the Cumann.

Mr. Hardiman was one of its earliest members. Most of the Engineering Division, not being graduates, find it difficult to share its exclusive esprit de corps. Those operational engineers, many of them with high qualifications from Colleges and Institutes of Technology and with long experience in Communications, feel that all key promotional outlets are controlled by Cumann members and that a member of that organisation will normally be promoted in preference to one of them. A recent vacancy in the Engineering Division of radio showed both sides locked in struggle.

Earlier this year the 'soldering iron' men, as they deprecatingly described themselves, came together to form a non-graduate association in the *B* and *B-plus* grades, that is, the Trade Union grades. Many of these showed strong sympathy with the attitudes and convictions of those who had resigned.[40] These non-graduate engineers were particularly interested in circulated notes and talks addressed by Jack Dowling on 'control and authority' in the organisation. His idea for an experimental production unit was immediately intelligible to them and the possibilities for reorganisation of the Engineering Division grasped.

It was probably the formation of the new non-graduate association and the restlessness of the Engineering Division which caused Mr. Maloney to show concern that Trade Unions might wish to bring the existing structures of authority into open discussion.

*  *  *

We have been asked repeatedly since leaving RTE why our Producer colleagues did not corporately support us and why, in particular, we seemed to represent a 'splinter group' on an issue in which the press and the public seemed to offer more support than those who had heretofore shared our stance and attitude.

It is natural, indeed in one sense it is inevitable, that outsiders should interpret our action in the light of a 'throw' in which we had supposed that we would be supported actively by our immediate colleagues. On this interpretation, we would simply have miscalculated.

It is extraordinarily difficult to be self-critical in circumstances of this kind. It is equally difficult to be just in the assessment of the activities or inactivity of others. But if there is one shred of truth behind this way of posing the problem then we have not merely misled ourselves

---

40   It was reported to us that Eric Spain, Head of Technical Development, probably the most imaginative and artistically sensitive of the senior engineers, said at the presentation gathering given at his departure from the station in July that he had felt an accumulation of dissatisfactions over the years, not the least of which was the treatment of Jack Dowling and Lelia Doolan.

and others, we have gravely deceived ourselves. Our action was not a 'throw'.

At no time did we make an appeal for corporate support to our colleagues. At no time, then, did they fail us. We do not feel any resentment towards our late colleagues. Above all, we do not feel that they should have done what we did. Both Lelia Doolan and Jack Dowling persuaded friends not to follow their example.

It would be foolish, however, to deny that we have been disappointed in the action or inaction of the Producers and Heads of Department in the events that have taken place since our departure. There was evidently a ritualistic character to Eoghan Harris's attempts to use the Trade Unions to stop the further extension of a fake consultative concept across the range of the station's staff structures.

It seems to us from the outside that the Producers, having resisted Management concepts for three years and having obtained a 'settlement' apparently acceptable to their senior members, had simply had enough. There were, of course, notable exceptions but this seems to have been the general tone. The initiatives may well be passing into the hands of other staff grades.

It must be borne in mind that the Summer doldrums had set in. Holidays, Summer filming and Autumn planning made it possible for most Producers to move these matters quietly to the periphery of their attention. Increasingly, we would hear from friends that Producers were at loss to understand precisely what the whole thing had been about. The continued interest of the newspapers and journals now bewildered or irritated them—a classic collective defence syndrome against accusations that were never made. Perhaps it was this that led them to stand by with such extraordinary detachment during the attempts of the *Féach* team to get a fair deal for their programme, the suppression of Fr. O'Herlihy's *Outlook* programme on television, the serious questions raised about News coverage, in particular of the events in the North, the 'banning' of expelled Fine Gael 'young tigers' from programmes, on the grounds that they were 'controversial figures'[41]. There was also a letter of complaint, we understand, from Mr. Gerard Sweetman, TD., to the Director-General about the participation of Mr. Vincent Browne on a radio programme with him, prior to the expulsion of the 'young tigers' from their party.

Perhaps the most sinister of these instances of regression from an adventurous programming policy was the handling of the *Outlook* incident. Fr. Jerome O'Herlihy, o.p., had made an extraordinary impression on the viewing public. Religious television had, evidently, made a find. The Reaction Index[42] for *Outlook*, the last item in an evening's schedule, normally runs below sixty points. As his early talks gained in momentum, this leaped to seventy-nine. The *Late Late Show* runs at about sixty-eight, at peak-viewing time in Winter. Fr. O'Herlihy's *Outlooks* were transmitted in August.

* * *

> *There was a frightful, appalling row.*
> *As a matter of fact the Pope told us all to go to hell.*
> *He threatened to silence Fr. Fahrt.*
> —FLANN O'BRIEN

On Wednesday, 13th August, Fr. O'Herlihy interviewed the Head of Religious Programmes at RTE about his arrangements for the week's

---

41 The is reminiscent of the withdrawal of an invitation to Jack Dowling for radio's *Later Than Late* show in June and of the failure of the Director-General to allow Gay Byrne to include Lelia Doolan and Jack Dowling on the *Late Late Show*, at that time.

42 An indicator, used by RTE's Audience Research unit, of a programme's popularity.

recordings. He intended to analyse RTE's output from his particular point of view. Mr. O'Grady must have had a premonition of the priest's forthrightness and intellectual convictions. Humorously, he asked for some reassurance on Fr. O'Herlihy's treatment of the station and its role.

The Producer of the programme was Alan Davidson who, on the following morning, examined the script notes for a talk on RTE News coverage. Davidson is an Englishman who, understandably, in the current climate of RTE's hypersensitivity about itself, may have been nervous when he saw the direction in which Jerome O'Herlihy's thought was moving. Fr. O'Herlihy proposed, in his notes, to cover the problem of viewers' critically examining RTE's News coverage. The programme was recorded but not transmitted. It may be of interest to the reader to examine this material for himself. We quote from *The Irish Press* (22nd August 1969) report and transcript of a tape of the programme. The tape had been smuggled out of RTE.

The following is the text of the talk that was prepared for last night. (Fr. O'Herlihy introduces it with a quotation from a typical news bulletin.)

> 'Hundreds were injured in Derry on 5th October when clashes broke out between 500 civil rights demonstrators waving banners and chanting civil rights songs, who tried to force their way past police blocking the main road. The Civil Rights Association has in recent weeks been vigorous against the Government's Special Powers Act.'

Then he goes on:

'That's a typical comment you could get from all news coverage of the North. Because it's a particular point of view and the words we hear change the picture we see.' (Here there was an insert of Derry riot film and noise of crowd.)

Fr. O'Herlihy then introduces another quotation:

> 'Young trouble-makers are causing bigger problems today than ever before. They should be dealt with quickly and harshly.'

Then he says:

> 'That idea comes across from a few of the comments we hear from time to time. Another way of talking about the same picture from Germany, of course, would be to say that police, through over-reacting and manhandling people they don't like, cause much of the disturbance in city streets. What we see here on television presents a particular point of view, just as I present my particular point of view.
>
> 'All news coverage plays an important role in forming public opinion. It's important to remember that there's another point of view in presenting the same facts.' (More riot film and sound effects occur here.)
>
> 'By making speeches telling of their concern for civil rights and by taking to the streets, the civil rights movement causes the automatic breaking down of law and order. To their opponents, the protest march becomes a mob. Words can change pictures.
>
> 'Television news coverage is limited by certain things. You must have action. So if we have a protest march, in which there is one incident of trouble, you

can be sure the cameramen will get there if it's at all possible—that is, of course, provided the protest march is in the North.

'So you have a striking difference between the film coverage of public trouble in places outside Ireland to that which we get at home. If there's a protest march in Dublin, for example, say a family are evicted from a house, you get merely a picture of the house—after the event. We don't get the live coverage that we seem to get from the North.

'Another way in which coverage should be viewed critically is Vietnam, for example. We continually get the American viewpoint, the film we see is film of Vietcong aggression. We seldom get anything from the North Vietnamese point of view. We can't even get there, not to mind getting film back.

'I was struck a couple of weeks ago by the 6.15 news coverage of a farm in Meath which was blown up. It was quite an extensive coverage. But by the time the 9.30 news came along there was a lot of film from Belfast of trouble there, and our farm in Co. Meath was barely mentioned.

'Another way I feel the news is limited is because it just describes what has happened. It can load the dice. If there is a strike in a factory tomorrow morning, you hear that so many workers went on strike. And this always makes it appear as if the worker is always the aggressor. That's because the news is purely descriptive.

'News coverage can sometimes be shallow and superficial. We should be aware of this in watching news coverage. I *think* that's why it is important to have current affairs programmes—programmes which don't just tell you what happened, but tell you why it happened.

'If there's trouble, for example, in a factory, let it not just say: so many men belonging to so many unions went on strike, but that it tried to get behind the facts, to the reason for the situation. Sometimes television news cannot get behind the facts because it's limited.

'Then, it's up to you in your viewing to try to get these facts, to realise the limitations of television so that you can get behind the facts—the fact, too, of the limitations of news by activity, and the limitations, too, of whom we get our news from, because we can't always go where we like. Goodnight.'

* * *

A history of the suppression and its consequences is contained in a circular, Correspondence One[43] issued by an anonymous group inside the station who have declared their intention of keeping the public informed about the station's efforts to keep the public misinformed. We were assured by an *Irish Press* reporter that he had checked the assertions contained in the document and found them to be true. We have since tried to check these facts again with Fr. O'Herlihy who

---

43  We do not wish to get involved in a discussion of the ethics of 'leaks', either signed or anonymous, beyond saying this: until RTE's information service deals frankly, fairly and unambiguously with the public, this kind of 'leak' is inevitable. The document's anonymity has led to its being distrusted as an instrument of argument with Management- also inevitably. This kind of think as gone on, anonymously, since the 7 days affair. The brute fact is that anonymity is the response to repression. The documents being useless, the facts of the incident should be openly examined.

informed us that we had all the facts and that he 'did not wish to be further involved'.

Commenting on the document, Mr. Garvey said, inter alia:

> I was the one who cancelled the programme because of what it said about Northern Ireland, not what it said about RTE news. On the basis of what was happening in the North at that time, I decided not to allow the programme to go out. If I knew then what I knew yesterday about the Northern situation, I might have allowed it to go out. But in view of the latest events in Belfast, today [8th September], I would stand by my original decision. One will always have to make such judgments at particular times.
>
> Fr. O'Herlihy was telling people to be critical about what they see on television; I just feel that in this situation, people might not be as critical as he would like.[44]

We have had the bad taste to collate Mr. Garvey's statement to *The Irish Times* reporter, Sean Carberry, with the events in Northern Ireland for the date of the recording, 14th August, for the proposed date of transmission, 18th August, and for the date of his explanation to Mr. Carberry (8th September).

The first thing to be noted about Mr. Garvey's statement is that it refers to a programme about RTE News reportage on Northern events which had reached crisis point in Derry during Thursday, 14th August (the day the recording was made) and continued in Belfast until

---

44   The Irish Times, 9th September 1969

Saturday, 16th August. On the night before Fr. O'Herlihy's recording, the Taoiseach had broadcast to the nation.

The reader of Mr. Garvey's statement to the papers may well have forgotten that Fr. O'Herlihy was advising his viewers to be critical of the dramatic treatment of this Northern news while 'home' news was being treated with a deliberate sobriety.

It would seem therefore in the logic of the case that if Michael Garvey was expressing the motives for suppressing the programmes, two factors would have been taken into account by him. (1) the station would be anxious not to exacerbate a situation that was dangerous for the Northern participants, and (2) the Irish Government would wish to keep our people in a mood of calm that would permit the Cabinet to take the coolest and freest action possible.

In these circumstances, assuming that they *were* the circumstances which were in Mr. Garvey's mind on the day the programme was due for transmission (18th August), Fr. O'Herlihy's *Outlook* should have been a godsend to him. Nothing more helpful could have conceivably presented itself to ease emotional tension than his warnings against uncritical viewing of dramatic material in Newscasts.

Yet the very suitability of the programme to Mr. Garvey's statement of policy was given by him as the reason for not transmitting it!

The developments in Belfast, on the 19th, 20th and 21st August where tensions remained high, and among our people in the South, where apprehensions were still present, might have been somewhat relaxed by the transmission of the programme on any of those dates.

Alas, the situation is even more hopelessly absurd than this. Mr. Garvey made his statement to the Press on 8th September, the day upon which a Protestant had been reported shot dead in the streets of Belfast. Most readers of newspapers would have assumed that the effect of a transmission on that date would have had the same dangerous emotional effect as a transmission on 18th August. In fact, as we have just shown, the effect should have been the diametric opposite.

Mr. Garvey gives the impression that Fr. O'Herlihy's *Outlook* was mainly about Northern Ireland news coverage. It was about general news coverage on television.

It can therefore be safely accepted that whatever his reasons were, they are an extraordinary rationalisation. On the other hand, it should not be too hastily assumed that they had nothing to do with the quality of RTÉ's News reportage on Northern Ireland.

We cannot claim any special knowledge of what was in Fr. O'Herlihy's mind when he pleaded for a critical attitude to the News, but we do know that Mr. Jim McGuinness, Head of News, had both said and indicated at News Conferences that in treatment of Northern reporting he did not propose to be impartial.

This is borne out by two incidents which caused profound professional disquiet in the Newsroom. The first was Mr. McGuinness' refusal to sanction the use of a filmed interview with a 'B' Special of the RUC on his own responsibility as Head of News. In this, as in other News bulletin items, the decision was pointedly left to the professional conscience of subordinate officials who had raised objections to the line indicated by their Chief. The interview was, in fact, transmitted. It is evident that a News staff that must in such circumstances exercise its responsibility against the policy of its Head is in a delicate position.

One member of the staff whom we approached, Myles O'Farrell, had begun to take so much exception to the general tone of news coverage by RTE that he wrote a letter of complaint to the Director-General. He instanced the editing of a piece of film on the night of 20th April, on the personal direction of Jim McGuinness, Head of News, as an example of biased reportage which, whatever their personal political convictions, outraged the sense of professional veracity of good newsmen. We quote from his personal account to us:

> On that night a film of an interview with an RUC officer in Derry was cut, on the direction of Jim McGuinness, Head of News, contrary to the advice of the newsmen responsible, so that the bulletin led with a small piece cut from the whole film.
>
> The interview concerned the visit of an RUC officer to a hospital to see his wounded men. One of his sentences which said, in substance, 'From what I have seen here today I have every reason to be proud of my men' was snipped out, and was made part of the short opening to a News bulletin that dealt mainly with the Northern troubles in Derry and elsewhere. The other part of the opening of that News was a woman from Bogside saying the police had beaten many people.
>
> For all the public knew, the RUC officer was saying he was proud of the conduct of his men in the Bogside, and not of the deportment of his men in hospital, or even in general.
>
> In my opinion the only apparent reason for doing this was to colour the whole News bulletin that followed with an anti-RUC bias. The fact that the interview with the RUC officer was shown in a much later and less important part of the bulletin appeared to me to be merely a sop to the professional outrage committed at the outset of the bulletin.

The Director-General did not reply. The newsman concerned went further and sent a copy of the letter to the Taoiseach. As far as is known, he got no reply.

The growing anxiety for the preservation of their professional integrity was contained in a letter of remonstrance from thirty sub-editors, reporters, newscasters and news cameramen protesting against the policy of not covering General de Gaulle's visit to Daniel O'Connell's house in Derrynane, this year.

That General de Gaulle's family holiday should be treated with a decent respect for his privacy, RTE's professional newsmen found quite proper. This particular event, however, was a departure on the General's part from his claims on privacy and was evidently intended as a public gesture of interest in an Irish historical figure with French connections. Their remonstrances were in vain; the General's visit to Derrynane was not transmitted by RTE. Further, and in view of the concourse of home and foreign newsmen who had attended the visit, six men of Chief Sub-Editor rank sent a vehement protest to Mr. McGuinness pointing out that 'within the framework of a dignified reference' the Irish people had been entitled to a report on this historic compliment to an Irish patriot.

These protests were left unanswered. A number of News Division staffers are now convinced that there is no point in making any protest to anybody.

Not the least surprising aspect of this is that News reports of the General's holiday were, in fact, being gathered and sold to international news agencies.

> *You have the facts;*
> *I'm left with the problems.*
> —EOGHAN HARRIS (TO THE PRESS)

On 6th June, Eoghan Harris inquired of Liam Ó Murchú whether the Controller of Programmes had granted requests for a better time slot and facilities for *Féach*. Liam Ó Murchú replied that there would be an 8 p.m. Monday evening transmission, but that in the matter of improved facilities the request for a larger studio on Thursdays would mean the curtailment of the time available for a light entertainment 'personality' show. Blandly and ironically, Harris thought, Ó Murchú said that such a show was 'regarded as a most essential element in the schedule'!

At this point Harris and O Murchú enjoyed each other's confidence and were aware that the ritual memoranda which they were exchanging were but formal statements of a strong personal effort to have the programme improved.

Thus on 25th June, when Harris received a note informing him that *Féach* would have to alternate, week-about, between the largest and smallest studios in the station, he took it for granted that Liam Ó Murchú expected him to protest and that his insistence would be used by Ó Murchú to effect reforms.

Their case was powerful—any Producer would reject the notion of doing a Current Affairs programme from a different studio each week. The simple fact is that a set built for Studio One simply would not fit into Studio Three. *Féach* would have to 'make do' with an undesirable alternative: manipulable design 'elements'. Accordingly, Harris and Ó hEithir wrote to Liam Ó Murchú stating that unless these matters were immediately rectified, RTE would be asked to allot them to other work.

At this stage, in mid-June, they were armed with the absolute confidence that the Broadcasting Act would not permit such a blatant second-class treatment of the one adult Irish programme in the schedule. As they put it: 'we cannot believe that the Authority would condone this second-class treatment of an Irish-language programme'.

By 'the Authority' they mean, of course, Donall Ó Móráin. They were to be disillusioned. On 8th August the Irish programme group met the Controller. The situation was unchanged; indeed it seemed to have deteriorated. Not only would the *Féach* team have to put every second programme on film, whether Irish events dictated this or not, but in the weeks when Studio One would be available they would be obliged to rehearse and record topical items in the early mornings only. This was restriction to the point of impracticability.

Nevertheless, Harris rang the Director-General for an interview about the situation. He was told he must go 'through proper channels.' Every channel right up to Ó Morain himself was, of course, by now firmly blocked. The Director-General was aware that Harris, Ó Murchú and Ó hEithir knew this. Lelia Doolan had been treated in precisely this way for the same reasons. The Director-General had all means of effective protest barricaded and was no longer shy of having it seen to be so. Indeed, he was in a strong position. The Heads of Department, having seen no need to protect their own member, Lelia Doolan, were not likely to do much to protect Harris or Ó hEithir. The Director-General knew their strength.

It seemed evident to the Management that working members of the general public who wished to discuss topical matters in Irish should be prepared to do so in the early mornings. It also seemed evident that since *Féach* had been 'satisfactory' over the past two years, Harris's attempts to give it, in reality, the place it had, nominally, in the schedule would be construed merely as trouble-making.

None of these things was clear to Eoghan Harris with his tendency to see every issue of principle as if it were seriously intended to be used in practice. Following the meeting he wrote to the Controller of Programmes and Liam Ó Murchú stating that the facilities offered to *Féach* in his opinion did not achieve the aims set out for Irish in the

Authority's statement of January 1966. This claimed that RTE would provide a programme 'of special interest to adult viewers'. He attached to this a lengthy memorandum pointing out the technical and professional reasons why the facilities offered prevented the execution of the Authority's policy. Once more he asked to be released from his production responsibilities. The treatment of his programme was not only a sham but was known to be one.

On 15th August the Controller of Programmes wrote to him restating the position and refusing to release him. That avenue being closed, he and Ó hEithir decided that it was now squarely in that area for which Liam Ó Murchú was responsible, namely the implementation of the Authority's policy in relation to the Irish language. Harris wrote to Ó Murchú inquiring formally whether, as Head of Irish and Children's Programmes, he agreed with the Controller 'that the facilities offered are adequate to the major Irish programme for adults coming from your area'. In his reply Liam Ó Murchú remarked 'specifically' on *Féach*: 'I must hold that the facilities at present offered to the programme are adequate'. Then, following the Management's line, he added: 'It has worked on facilities that were no greater over the past two years and neither the Producers nor myself have expressed major dissatisfaction'.

It was thought by Harris and Ó hEithir that Donall Ó Moráin understood the Management's predicament and that this 'understanding' had communicated itself to Liam Ó Murchú. This proved to be mistaken. Eoghan Harris's reply to Liam O Murchú did not put a tooth in it: 'Your acceptance of a practice in conflict with this principle [parity] makes it clear to me that your position has now changed ... the facilities for such a programme must be assessed in relation to similar programmes in English. Any other criterion reduces our area to *beal bochtary*. Ó hEithir also wrote, if anything in a tougher vein. It was given point by the fact that he had never before, in a distinguished broadcasting career, found it necessary to request release from his contract. He began by indicating the surest sign of programme neglect, the frequency of Producer changes. *Féach,* in under three years, had had no less than thirteen Producers! He went on to say 'go raibh sé thar am clár ... Gaeilge a bheith ar an aer a bhéadh ar aon chéim [le] clár Béarla'. He put a question: 'Ar caitheadh mar seo ariamh le clár cúrsaí reatha Béarla do dhaoine fásta sa staisiun seo?' He had a request to make: 'Iarraim ort, dá bhrí sin, malairt oibre a cur ar fáil dom i do Rannóg'.

The requests were, of course, refused. After all, something in Irish has to go out on the air. *7 Days* had announced that it might use some Irish! Arthur Noonan of the *Irish Independent* believed it to be evidence that the Current Affairs programme in English could do anything but come to grips with real political issues. As for dealing with such matters properly in Irish—well that could wait! Donall Ó Moráin had not yet met Cú Chulainn. He discussed the complaints with Ó hEithir and let it be known that he would take the matter up with the Authority 'vigorously'. As we go to press there is no indication that this has had any effect.

Harris and Ó hEithir had asked the Unions to take legal opinion on whether the Authority's directive on Irish had any sanction under the obligation imposed by the Broadcasting Acts, 1960-1966.

The Unions did so.

The result was a shock. This provision of the Act could not be legally enforced!44[45]

> If I have got him right, Mr. Garvey intimated that if RTE didn't in fact, have to cater for the undoubted demand that there is for the kind of television that

---

45  The Irish Press, 6th September 1969.

comes from the BBC and ITV—the cowboy films and the comedy shows—it would be able to devote more time and energy to minority programmes, to programmes, presumably, that would reflect more accurately our separate culture, to purely Irish affairs, even to the Irish language.

I have elaborated upon what Mr. Garvey actually said. But I hope that I have done him no injustice. It is an interesting pipe-dream. Wholly impracticable, of course, without a complete re-casting of the basic premise upon which Irish television has been built.

—KEN GREY (on the 1969-70 programme schedules)

All of this must seem a cumulative indictment of management of affairs. There are no evil men in RTE, if by evil we mean those who are unprincipled and deliberately violent; but evil is not a matter of commission only. More often, in our time, it is omitting to do what ought to be done, 'falling asleep', being too busy, letting the thing happen.

Great public organs determine the type of men who will be selected to administer them: they will also determine that curious sub-alternation of human motives which allows true development and actual distortion to proceed together as if they were out of personal control. This is a mark of the growing impersonality of our technological institutions.

Radio Telefís Éireann, it must now be clear to the reader, is sick at heart. This is not primarily an indictment of its officers but of its structures, the ambiguities and ambivalences that reflect the divisions within the nation's psyche.

With such organs as RTE, men must do what they can, while they can. There is then a choice for each one. This is a record of ours.

# 2

## COUNT ME OUT

## THE CULTURAL EVOLUTION OF A TELEVISION PRODUCER

*By*
*Bob Quinn*

## CHAPTER 2: COUNT ME OUT

STATISTICS

'Those Platonists are a curse', he said,
'God's fire upon the wane,
A diagram hung there instead,
More women born than men'.

—W.B. YEATS

... for the world which seems to lie before us like a land
of dreams,
So various, so beautiful, so new,
Hath really neither joy, nor love, nor light,
Nor certitude, nor peace, nor help for pain;
And we are here as on a darkling plain Swept with con-
fused alarms of struggle and flight, Where ignorant
armies clash by night.

—MATTHEW ARNOLD

B*ob Quinn first showed* signs of 'instability' at the age of twenty-one. In the bleak year of 1957 he left the pensionable womb of the Civil Service to tour the world.

Intending to make his fortune, he got as far as working on a farm in Bavaria. There he learned some earthy phrases.

In the following four years before he joined the embryo RTE, he engaged in seventeen different occupations. He became proficient at two: pub-pianist and bus-conductor. In addition he had been a commercial traveller, English teacher, travel courier, freelance journalist and, not least, washer of Coca-Cola bottles. When occasion offered he involved himself in the theatre.

His social background had been 'improving working-class'. He had a mystique of this class which was, perhaps, pardonable. If allowed, he would tend to talk rather vaguely about the essential worth and dignity of the individual person. Even to those people who had not the ability or the desire to conform to middle-class standards, he attributed a meaning which transcended their social status. Any ordinary man could think as imaginatively or even as metaphysically as any theologian or philosopher. At least their conclusions, he felt, were equally worthy of respect.

Burdened with these simple ideas he joined Radio Telefís Éireann as a trainee studio operator in 1961.

He was one of thirty young men, drawn from many occupations, selected as the raw material from which the operational staff of the new service was to be moulded. Everybody had their own fantasy about this new, complicated world of television. A common one was that television was simply an extension of show-business; another held that it was a sort of parlour game. There was also a powerful view that it was going to 'educate' the nations.

Quinn's particular fantasy was a combination of all three. Television was a place where theatrical people could get a regular salary for trying out ideas that hadn't worked in the theatre, either; balancing this was the view that television was a vehicle for cosy discussions about fashion, flying ducks on the wall, plastic fruit arrangements and holidays in a place called 'Barthelona'.

Whatever their separate fantasies may have been, many of the young men felt a lack of fulfilment and started doing 'nixers'. These were part-time jobs like private recordings, freelance filming, wiring houses, etc. There was even one excellent chimneysweep. Quinn's outlet was writing ponderous satire for the press and occasional radio-writing.

Two years after he joined the service he was offered three jobs: Programme Assistant in radio, trainee continuity announcer in radio and Producer-Director in television. The glamour of this last appointment claimed him.

Now his unresolved adolescent idealism came to the fore. He had a chance to articulate the views and attitudes of the Silent Majority. This, he thought, was the great mass of intelligent working-class people who were just waiting for the chance to speak. He aimed to give them their long-denied opportunity.

There gradually dawned on him a realisation of what his Producer colleagues had long known: television talent in a country of this size is in short supply. Put a witty, even brilliant, docker in a studio and he shrivels up into his Sunday suit. Some of Quinn's colleagues were equally frustrated by this discovery; but they were aiming higher. They were looking for Sammy Davis in Ballyferriter.

In the course of producing shows like *The Late Late, Club Ceili*; *Open House*; *Ailliliu*, etc., this depressing fact was borne in on him: that the studio atmosphere had a lot to do with this striking-dumb effect. He tried Outside Broadcasts, where at least the participants were comfortingly near their own environment. But again the oppressive paraphernalia of television cameras and lights ultimately inhibited the very people he had hoped would be encouraged to speak.

Meanwhile he was learning other and harder facts of life, this time about politics. While organising the original *Open House* forum programme, he discovered that not he, the Producer, but the Party Whips were to choose the participants. When, in his innocence, he mildly objected to this his views were dismissed as melodramatic.

In another, the first *Ailliliu* with Seán Ó Riada, he associated the United Irishmen's Charter, the U.N. Declaration of Human Rights and the first Selma march with a photograph of Jim Larkin. It was conveyed to him that the basic philosophy underlying this association of ideas was not approved.

However, being an a-political animal, he was concerned with other things: such as how he might help the real owners of the national television service to use it themselves. He still had the apparently quaint idea that the docker should have his say.

Quite by chance he made a film. It was about new methods of kindergarten education and, because children are invariably box-office material, it was well received. Quinn was assigned to *Discovery*, a documentary film series.

Film was a godsend. A 16 mm. film camera is less obtrusive and consequently less inhibiting than the electronic television camera. Physically, it is smaller and its lightness means that a dexterous operator can use angles and capture moments that would require hours of preparation for the electronic camera. At this stage RTE seemed to be unaware of the existence of equally flexible electronic equipment.

However, Quinn learned that the film camera did not dominate the environment as much as the television cameras. Not that it was a passive recorder of 'magic moments'. It created its own version of reality. But at least it didn't frighten the life out of performers. If used with a certain kind of humility towards the subject it could, at least as well as words, imaginatively evoke the essence of that subject. And if the camera appeared to lie, it was because its Director was lying.

Quinn, then, had a most flexible instrument of expression. It allowed him to escape the studio strait-jacket. It was, also, a more personal medium. In the studio, any personal contact a Director might build up with a performer ran the risk of being bludgeoned by three cameras, third-degree lights and the deathly spell of a countdown. Using film in, say, the performer's home, the Director and crew entered into an intimate relationship with him.

There was a grave danger here of course: it was much more difficult to preserve that distance so apparently necessary for 'professional' objectivity. Quinn found it impossible not to get involved in his subject. This became a problem when he was expected to churn out a half-hour documentary film for *Discovery* every fortnight.

After a number of films he decided that justice could not be done, at least by him, to a serious subject under such limitations. In 1964 he requested a transfer to the gentle pastures of religious programmes. The consensus was that he must be out of his mind. The prevailing attitude to religious programmes considered this area to be a sort of limbo to which erring Producers were sent for their sins.

His desire coincided with a request for his services by the Religious Adviser, Romuald Dodd, o.p.

Fr. Dodd was, and is, a man of wide humanity. He gave Quinn his trust and a freedom to make programmes which was unequalled in any other area of the station. As a direct result of this intelligent use of authority, Quinn's subsequent work was considered good enough to represent RTE internationally on at least six occasions. Quinn noted with surprise that when a position of Head of the Religious Department was created in January last, Fr. Dodd was ignored.

Apart from directing the studio Mass, *Horizon* discussions, *Word in Action* and *Outlook*, his main work was in documentary films. In his first effort for the department—a series of films on *The Psychological Development of the Normal Child*—he made a discovery. Discussions with a psychologist, Francis Forde, OMI., and a script-writer, Jack Dowling, introduced him to the relationship between subjectivity and objectivity. Given the distinct possibility of his having misinterpreted these men, he understood it thus:

A child of three years sees a bus coming towards him. To the child, that tiny dot moving in the distance is actually growing into an immense and noisy monster. The bus literally grows, and not in any adult's metaphorical sense. The child is believing its eyes. As the bus departs it actually grows smaller. To the child, that is the simple truth of the matter. Every other visual thing has the same quality. Even the child's parents are small at one end of the room, large when they move up close. Only the child has the good sense to stay the same size! In order to survive in this chaos, to reduce objects and people to the same consistency as himself, the child is eventually forced to perform a rational act.

Stated crudely, he forms a mental 'picture', then an abstract concept which he calls 'bus'. This bus stays the same size because his intellect abstracts a consistent idea from the welter of changing sense-impressions.

In this way the child has started to organise his world into a manageable system. As he develops this capacity he will realise that each time he meets an object he need not go through the laborious process of correlating his sense-impressions and forming his own concept. There is a short cut. There are people around to supply him with these concepts. He discovers one of the functions of his community.

He is, of course, forced to qualify to a large extent what his eyes and ears, his individual and subjective senses, tell him. There is thus a tension set up between what he subjectively knows and what he objectively learns to know. The child is, in part, learning not to believe his eyes. But the reward is survival.

The only difficulty about this arrangement is that what he objectively learns (even this secondhand information) comes through these same 'deceitful' eyes and ears. Further to compound the awkwardness is the fact that the people from whom the child learns must be similarly handicapped.

Quinn, strangely, derived some personal reassurance from this phenomenon. He had often had grave reservations about the validity of his personal opinions. This new knowledge gave him some confidence. However he decided to ignore for the moment its social implications.

He resolved to find out what kind of perceptual disability could cause a child to think and say 'The Emperor has no clothes'.

In collaboration with a fine audiologist, Mother Mary Nicholas, O.P., and the script-writer, Jack Dowling, he produced a film called *The Silent World*. This was a study of deafness and its implications. It is still used in the training of teachers of the deaf.

In this study of the deaf, what was emphasised again to Quinn was the fact that all the informations that are the basis of our ideas, come through our senses. This was not to say that we understand things by means of our senses. It simply meant that before we understand anything, we have to receive it sensibly. This was a revelation to somebody who had been led to believe that the ultimate truths were conveyed to us by a mysterious system of communication called Revelation. The latter consisted, in his mind, of an image of the Holy Ghost cutting a hole in one's head, so to speak, and pouring truth into it. Long afterwards he was introduced to the difficult notion of the truth contained in metaphor and analogy, but at this stage he had no access to such ideas. The only hole in the head which Quinn could see was the earhole.

This was an introduction to the process by which we learn. There was also the problem of expression.

If you can't hear words, he learned, you can't speak. If you can't speak you can't express yourself verbally or musically. And if you can't express yourself you are locked into a silent, 'atomic* and individualistic world. Quinn saw evidence of the amazing extent to which verbal and visual interplay between human beings as potentials is realised. They derived their personalities from others. Without this mutually creative interplay people would remain vegetable or, at best, animal. What price then the blossoming of the Human Spirit?

He saw the deaf as a dramatic symbol of the predicament in which the majority of people could find themselves individually and collectively if, as he thought, they did not have access to the media of group expression. If most people were regarded as the 'great unwashed', or the 'masses', incapable of grasping the finer points of human aesthetics, they were surely in the same quandary as the deaf. And the deaf were regarded traditionally as gesticulating dummies. They obviously couldn't speak in their own defence.

However, in Mother Nicholas' Clinics, Quinn saw the dumb open their lips and speak!

He saw children who had hitherto been taught a primitive set of signs—the 'dummy sign-language'—actually communicating with words. He saw how they grasped complex ideas, impossible to master with signs. He actually saw them experiencing the aesthetic pleasures of music. They literally 'felt' the music by means of its vibrations on relatively simple equipment.

Human beings, up to now considered inadequate, could be introduced to dimensions of human exhilaration and imagination previously considered totally beyond them. Applying this to the 'mass' of people, Quinn realised their eminent educability. There seemed to him to be some sort of parallel between the work of the speech therapist he had met, and the professional business in which he was involved.

He realised now that the problem of educating people was not fundamentally one of educability. It was a question of: who is considered worth educating? It comes down to the esteem in which the human person is held.

He continued to make religious and social programmes, among which were: *Why Don't They Shoot People?*, the second of two films about disabled persons.

In another, he examined the mental processes of a poet in the consumer society. In this society, the presence of a God was intuited rather than evidenced. The title of the film was: *Missing, Believed Dead*.

A film called *The Island* considered, perhaps somewhat romantically, the worship patterns and attitudes of an isolated community. In *Many Hands Make Life Work*, the principle of co-operation was examined as a means of restoring rural confidence in the small farmer and one's neighbour, as the basis for community building and economic salvation.

By this time his original concern for the 'Silent Majority' had become an 'obsession' with the under-dog, the socially deprived, the have-not and the deviant. The 'norm', as advertised on telly, he decided, did not exist.

Quinn next turned to the subject of autism. This was a form of mental illness considered at the time to be peculiar to the children of intelligent middle-class parents. Its more dramatic symptoms were absolute withdrawal from human relationships and an obsession with the manipulable world of objects. It was suggested that the seeds of this condition were latent in everybody.

A further film attempted to describe the tensions of living in a Corporation housing estate. It was called *The Flowerpot Society*, which indicated the problem of young people transplanted from organic communities in central urban parishes like City Quay to the fresh air of Finglas, Co. Dublin. It mentioned that the last thing considered worth erecting was a community centre. In an effort to describe the personal costs of a worthy, but shabbily carried out, social plan it featured house-wives attending a local psychiatric clinic. One of these interviews, in which the lady was visually and vocally well disguised, constituted the climax of the film. It was excised before transmission, without Quinn's knowledge or consent, by well-meaning authorities in RTE.

One of the images retained by Quinn from his preparations for this film was a housewife watching television with her five children. They were attentively watching commercials for the affluent society. He wondered at the time if it was seriously held that that woman could or should aspire to the goodies so tantalisingly held out to herself and her children. A psychiatrist he had consulted in connection with this film introduced him to the concept of 'cognitive dissonance'. He used it to describe the pathological tension set up in that woman's mind by the discrepancy between the way 'normal' people were expected to live and her personal experience of what she could expect.

Like many of his countrymen, Quinn at this point was slightly confused. None of the tendencies he had noted fitted peacefully into the traditional concepts of community and society. Television was obviously contributing to the situation in no small way; so rather than go ahead blindly 'getting on with the job', he decided to declare a personal inquest. Principally he wished to acquire a frame of reference with which to study the 'Consumer Society' towards which we were heading. He also wished to see if it worked for others. He decided to go to the source.

In September 1967 he was given generously subsidised leave of absence and spent the Winter in a University in Nova Scotia, Canada. There he attended courses in sociology and read voraciously.

In the course of his studies he was impressed most by:

1. Role Theory- The 'I'm only doing my job' syndrome.
2. The effect of institutionalism on good ideas. (He particularly noticed the assessment of the fate of charisma and personal integrity in different kinds of organisations. It helped him to understand the condition of Christianity as well as the secular world.)
3. The discrepancies between manifest and latent function in enterprises.
4. The relationship between culture and personality.
5. Anthropological descriptions of 'primitive' verses 'civilised' cultures.

As was his habit he tried to relate all this to the reality around him. Canada was described as the second richest country on earth. In the 1961 census it was established that the wages of 47.9 per cent, of the labour force were below the officially-defined poverty level. They had, apparently, learned how to create wealth but the technique of distributing it evaded them.

Canada was also described as a Cultural Mosaic. In 1965 *The Vertical Mosaic* by Porter, was published. It detailed precisely how the power complexes, interlocking directorships and corporate monopolies made, not only individual aspirations, but even the concept of 'private' enterprise appear as simple lip-service to an ideological strait-jacket. It also gave figures showing the control, through outright ownership as well as in blocks of shares, that the United States exercised on the Canadian economy.

As far as the respect for ethnic and cultural idiosyncrasies implied in the 'cultural mosaic' idea was concerned, Quinn saw the French in Quebec so enraged with the situation that they were on the verge of civil war with the Federal Government.

In the same predicament, but reacting differently, were the Indians. The Micmacs were a tribe Quinn visited often. In their school (State-run) there was not a shred of evidence to indicate to the children that they had a group identity quite different to the white man's. They knew nothing of their history and their language was not a formal school subject. After school they watched the television cavalry making mincemeat of their television ancestors. This was on the same programme that carried endless commercials and other items that urged them: 'You have no existence as a separate group. Forget your identity, jump into the melting pot and become white, clean homogeneous consumers like the rest of us'. The Micmacs, however, seemed to find this difficult. The average life expectancy for a male Indian was 33; for a female 36.

They had developed the habit of making their own moonshine and drinking themselves to death.

Quinn decided he would inspect the other half of this Continent. With a Dominican priest, he drove to New York, across to Chicago, down to New Mexico, westwards to California, up the West Coast and returned across the 4,000 miles of Canada. They spent three months and 12,000 miles driving, looking and listening.

They discussed and argued all the way on the various aspects of the culture they were experiencing.

They noted that New York had the highest proportion of walking schizophrenics in the world. The Manhattan Survey of 1965 indicated that four-fifths of the population of that part of the metropolis was emotionally disturbed. They experienced the four-hour physical and mental strain of driving across rush-hour Chicago. They noted how the auto freeway 'Howard Johnson Eatery' Motel complex made it difficult to actually encounter the land or its people. It sealed off from the casual observer the 10 million people who lived in squalor, the many others living in poverty. They remembered the President's 'Council of Economic Advisers' assessment: 33-35 million Americans were 'living at or below the boundaries of poverty in 1962—nearly one-fifth of our nation'. America seemed to have the same problem as Canada: how do you share wealth? But one rarely saw evidence of this state of affairs. It was all camouflaged in a plastic efficiency that tended to whisk them from one chromium environment to another. It was a smooth, comfortable non-existence.

At the end, both agreed that it was all very worrying and casual imitators would best be wary. Quinn had walked through Harlem, Berkeley, Albuquerque and Seattle; he had listened to cold discussions by police chiefs on the latest in anti-riot weapons; he had spoken to the people on whom these weapons would be used. He had previously, in theory, learned about the cultural arrogance and egocentricity that enabled the richest country in the world to rationalise its destruction of one of the smallest countries in Asia. Now it was preparing to act similarly on its own citizens. He didn't wonder, then, at the despair of a journalist who said to him in a bar in San Francisco: 'The Great Experiment has failed'.

\* \* \*

Quinn returned to Ireland in August 1968 to resume his work with RTE. He noticed that a certain apathy had settled on the station. He also noticed the flowering of business terminology, the increased emphasis on systems-analytic descriptions of 'problems', the obsession everybody had with costings. The station had all the verbal trappings of a factory, as well as the alienation of the employees of such an enterprise.

He noticed, with a sharpened sensibility to such things, the Americanism of the service's output, both sound and television. This was especially noticeable on radio, possibly because it had always been evident on television. The crudely inserted commercial jingles produced a remarkably accurate impersonation of the many brash, small-town radio stations he had heard in the U.S. There seemed little indication that it was the sound of an Irish broadcasting service. The occasional interpolations in Irish seemed to him to have all the authenticity of Bing Crosby singing *Top O' the Mornin'*.

The main midday News bulletin was so patently and unsuccessfully an attempt to simulate the synthetic excitement of America that he felt the Head of News would have done better to have employed actors rather than misuse the talents of excellent journalists. He noticed that the majority of European Continental news reports were spoken by Americans. It seemed to him obvious that English-speaking Continentals might have had a better insight into the workings of their own internal affairs. On enquiry in the Newsroom he was told that a better and more economic service was provided by American agencies.

Quinn was to start work on a new series which was to be orientated to home-making. It was natural that he should think the social, cultural and economic contexts in which people make their homes to be relevant. This series would have been the natural successor to *Home Truths*, as no other programme in the schedules covered this area.

However, the Programme Controller (TV) made it quite clear that this programme must discuss nothing more complex than do-it-yourself gardening, home-making etc. It was to avoid controversial topics of consumer interest. He recommended the Irish Countrywomen's Association as a valuable source of material, which indeed it was.

Quinn felt that if we were aiming at a full-blooded consumer society in the American style, and RTE was actively, through commercials and canned films, endorsing this, the least it might do was to provide a consumer advisory service. This could play a valuable part in educating our viewing public into the intricacies of such a society, with open discussion of possible pitfalls. This was of course assuming that the public had voluntarily decided to become such a society. However, he learned that there was to be no place for these wider considerations in the proposed programme.

Assessing his impression of the television organisation, Quinn decided that it had moved into a new phase, far removed from the fairly open atmosphere in which he had worked before. It appeared now to see its function as a passer-on of policies and decisions formulated somewhere 'up there', rather than an investigator and commentator on the texture of Irish life. Quinn was happy neither about the latter nor about the sort of society RTE was permitting and assisting in bringing about. He decided to withdraw his formal professional support from the Organisation rather than acquiesce in a process which he did not like. He resigned his stall status, indicating clearly that he would be available in the future on a freelance basis, to do work he felt moved to do. He left on quite amicable terms, at no time having expressed his disquiet in terms of personalities.

He then bought an old car and drove to Iran and back. He experienced the way of life, or culture, of eight different peoples and was able to compare their richness with the sterility of our adoptive one.

Returning in January 1969 he offered his services to RTE and was given a contract. He was assigned to produce a history series for schools. This was to be done in conjunction with the Department of Education who finance and who largely control the operation of *Telefís Scoile*.

Through reading and conversations with the experts he eventually grasped an idea of the nature of history, particularly its subjective nature. Any historical account is intended by somebody to make somebody else think something. Value-free history is impossible.

Hitherto, he knew that Irish history had been taught as a series of woeful anecdotes showing how we had suffered under British Imperialism. This was because we were a small country struggling to preserve our identity and sense of nationhood. Very properly, the new line for schools was to play down the emotional aspects of our history and to concentrate on the texture of Irish life in the past. At that time Quinn saw nothing sinister about this, although he did find it remarkable to be told that, really, the Famine wasn't the major catastrophe we had been led to believe; anyway, its worst effects were felt mainly in the West. The Pale was relatively healthy. Further, the viciousness of the landlords had been greatly exaggerated. They weren't all bad; nor was life in the Empire too bad either.

Since then Quinn has often speculated on the possible reasons for such a *volte face*. He thinks it is probably a coincidence that our revolutionary past might be a bit of an embarrassment to a country which now openly aligns itself with the counter-revolutionary countries of the Western World.

However, he proceeded with the task of organising an educational series. This was the point at which he met The Organisation, whose formal orientation was towards efficiency and which was openly applying the techniques of business management to broadcasting.

He requested film facilities informally, was asked to put it in writing, did so and waited. After a fortnight he contacted, in the appropriate department, the people who had asked for the early requisition of facilities. They could not allocate facilities yet. They were awaiting a decision from above. Quinn noted that bureaucracy was making inroads and thought it paradoxical that this was happening in the name of systematisation.

Quinn started to apply the principles of education, on which he was actually working, to the social phenomenon of television itself.

He was aware that we in Ireland were emerging from the stagnation of a traditional academic concept of education. This formal, functional process had often obscured the true nature of the educative process. A person is educated by everything that enters his mind, captures his attention and retains his interest. Everything that entertains, educates. If it is entertaining, television will educate. If it is entertaining, the worst canned rubbish or the most insidious commercial will educate and form the mind of the viewer. In an environment increasingly influenced by television, it seemed likely that few would escape this mind-forming effect.

Quinn considered the sort of consumer mind, the absorption in trivia that would be the result of viewing RTE over a long period. It could do little damage to those who already thought superficially or those who could afford other forms of entertainment. There were some who do not fall into these categories: the Irish communities in the

West; the lower-income urban groups; the many people who have not the desire or, perhaps, the means, to achieve immediately the form of affluence presented as desirable on RTE. Quinn speculated that when a voice as authoritative as the national broadcasting service urged on its viewers a particular way of life, it was likely to be believed. The viewer's subjective assessment of his own aspirations would be rather shame-facedly repressed. If this happened often and to enough people it would surely result in a national state of cognitive dissonance; we would rapidly approach the stage where all of the people would be fooled all of the time.

Quinn considered other aspects of the broadcasting situation. He was familiar with the conventional wisdom, the 'common sense' rationalisations that made discussion of the problem difficult. By pretending that audiences were unappreciative, that there was no 'television talent' in the country, that engineers were unimaginative, Producers unreliable; by advertisers pretending that they financed the service completely, by bureaucrats pretending that new forms of accounting were the answer, by all of these and many more, everybody was excusing the bad programmes and avoiding the necessity for considering the effect of the service on the community. Everybody was simply getting on with the job. This was a reasonable reaction because the problem was so complex it made the mind boggle.

Quinn tried very hard to ignore it, to persuade himself that somebody somewhere was sorting it all out. He failed.

Quinn was one of many people whose concern had been to keep the television organisation human. He had seen the efforts (and supported them when possible) of people like Jim Plunkett Kelly, Jack Dowling, Lelia Doolan, Aindreas Ó Gallchóir and many others, to keep the system sensitive to the needs of the programme makers. Despite major eruptions like the *7 Days* affair, he felt that a condition of progressive atrophy had seized the station. He felt that the main barrier to the making of good programmes was the commercial strait-jacketing of schedules. The frustrations always experienced in making programmes had intensified and were a logical outcome of trying to work within a programme schedule dictated by a commercial framework.

This framework appeared to be the only aspect of the problem, the only given premise, that was not considered open to change. Quinn sounded out some of his colleagues on the possibility of forming an internal group to study the effect of commercial advertising. The reaction was a wry: 'And accept Government control? Where would the money come from? Don't be daft!' Quinn had personally decided that the social costs of continuing the present commercial broadcasting set-up were probably infinitely greater than any loss in revenue.

He remembered reading a book called *The Politics of Experience*, by R. D. Laing. In it the psychiatrist author suggested that '… in this age of senescent capitalism can we do more than sing our sad and bitter songs of disillusion and defeat'.

So what could he do? What could anybody do who wasn't good at sad and bitter songs? Shut oneself in a comfortable £2,500 p.a. job and make 'safe' programmes? The alternative was to publicly draw attention to one's misgivings and show that, at least, one could personally withdraw unquestioning support from the process. There was really no choice. He just counted himself out.

# 3

## COMMUNICATIONS AND THE COMMUNITY
## TECHNOLOGY AND NEUTRALITY

*'Reeling and Writhing, of course, to begin with the Mock Turtle replied; 'and then the different branches of Arithmetic—Ambition, Distraction, Uglifcation and Derision*
—LEWIS CARROLL

*Locke sank into a swoon;
The Garden died;
God took the spinning-jenny
Out of his side.*
—W.B. YEATS

*Who is the villain of the new serial? The System? That will depend on how Deirdre Friel, the producer, sees things. Who is to be the hero? Society? The Community? The individual? I don't know, but I have been noticing that my friend, the individual, has been getting the rough end of the stick from many RTE people of late.*
—TOM O'DEA

## COMMUNICATIONS AND THE COMMUNITY

*'This kind of thing is all very well in theory. It's not much good in practice'*
—MR. T. P. HARDIMAN,
DIRECTOR-GENERAL, RTE

## THE INTERNAL COMMUNICATIONS CRISIS IN RTE

There is an inside and an outside to every problem.

The 'outside' to our problem in RTE was Bob Quinn's accusations that we were injuring the public mind by advertising and by the kind of programming that advertising and politics forced upon our superiors and they, in turn, on us.

He saw these as aggravated by the use of intimidating organisational structures and procedures on the participating public; he charged us with having no adequate philosophy of broadcasting which would allow of a decent relationship with performers and audiences.

The 'inside' was a quarrel about authority and the effects of systematised managerial techniques on creative people. He had studied a confident technological system on the North American continent, and was shocked. On his return to RTE he found that, through the introduction of Irish Management Institute methods, we were launched on the same course but without any apparent awareness of its dangers.

Since our resignations from RTE we have publicly insisted that these are simultaneously the concave and convex aspects of the same problem: outside, there is a crisis of national culture while, inside, there is a crisis of authority. The root of both is that ours is an increasingly technological civilisation, at once resisted and desired by our people. Some hold that we are dominated by technology; others hold that this cannot be so since technology is a neutral[46] phenomenon; its cultural effects simply depend on how it is used.

---

46  By 'neutral' is meant that technology has no cultural or moral effects proper to its own nature. Popularly this notion of neutrality is expressed by some such phrase as 'it all depends on how you use it'. Such effects as it in fact exercises are, in this view, not proper to technology itself as a law of its being but only to those who use it. It is regarded as being in itself neutral. As we hope the reader will see, we regard this philosophy of science and technology as the most dangerous idea in our culture. That it is breaking up in technologically 'advanced' societies, our people seem unaware and, regrettably, unconcerned.

If the technologist is able to gain control not only over our economic and social lives, but over the very life of the mind, this is, surely, of concern.

At the present stage of our cultural and political development he could not hope to do this if he announced it. He would not, we believe, even try to do it if he were aware of it. The very fact of his disclaiming any such intention for his profession or its techniques is the reason they have been so successful.

He must deceive *himself* before we can be deceived. To imagine that there 'may be something in it', that it may be true but unimportant, is the final deceit that may undo us.

* * *

It follows that, so far as RTE is concerned, if the cultural and moral effects of broadcasting technology are bad, it is not technology that makes them so but bad Producers.

## THE NAIVE VIEW OF TECHNOLOGY

The view prevailing among practical people, including the public, is that communications-technology is capable of being used by any cultural group, indifferently. It follows that, in itself, technology is only a service available to everyone alike.

The argument of technologists, seldom expressly stated but commonly implied, runs like this:

> Machines and technical systems are only rather complicated tools. They have no purpose or intention of their own. Our task as technical experts is to see that they are properly supplied, maintained and skilfully utilised by you creative people. We have no purposes

> or intentions beyond this. We merely seek a reasonable recognition of the nature and limitations of the available resources. We practice a kind of 'applied' science. It contains no value-judgments. We leave these to you, within the limits of feasibility.

This view seems so self-evidently reasonable that it hardly requires argument. Yet our contention is that it is false.

* * *

Perhaps we might begin by declaring the sense in which we propose to use our terms. Technology, according to the Oxford Dictionary, is the *science* of the industrial arts. Technology is not, therefore, the industrial arts themselves. Technologists are not technicians. The same dictionary defines a technician as 'a person skilled in the technique of a particular art'.[47]

Philosophical usages are, of course, not established by dictionary definitions. These fix only the current usages of words. Precise concepts require more precise articulation in the light of these usages.

We propose to use ours as follows: technology is the social use of tools, machines, organised manpower and particular techniques for the purpose of exploiting the potentialities of nature with the greatest economy of means.

Technology, therefore, is not the making or running of machines; this is the function of technicians.

---

47   Again, a technocrat is defined as 'an advocate of the organisation and management of a country's industrial resources by technical experts for the good of the whole community'.

## STATEMENT OF OUR THESIS

It seems, therefore, to us that communications-technology is not culturally, socially or morally negative but that it is, in itself, positive and formative of a cultural and moral attitude of mind and emotion.

*　*　*

Perhaps a case-example might help to indicate the area of concern. We remember our colleague, Father Romuald Dodd, o.p., at a producers' meeting, being asked what the considerations were for and against a separate department of religious broadcasting. Father Romuald replied somewhat along these (paraphrased) lines:

> Ideally there should not be a separate organisation of religious programmes. Religion is not a department of life; it is an essential dimension of everything human. Religious thought and feeling should find their reflection in nearly every programme and its problems should find their place in the work of every department in an Irish broadcasting service where these values are important. But the facts of the case make this view of my work quite unreal. The actual organisation work-load, programme-schedule, and budget-system determines the work which can, in fact, be done. If I did not have a budget account number, I would not get facilities and technical resources. If I do not have a department my work will be done on a 'left-over* basis. The facts of life here simply force me to organise my work like anybody else.

This is one level on which technological management is culturally formative.

The same argument, we suggest, holds for Irish language programmes, literary programmes and art programmes. These influences should permeate the entire output of the service; their departmentalisation is a rubric of respect to their 'high' value. In fact, it relegates them to a 'minority viewing' status in a transmission schedule that is mainly concerned to capture an amorphous 'mass' audience.[48] The determining factors are, we believe, technological, as Father Romuald's case clearly indicated. It seems to us, therefore, that technology is, *at least* administratively, formative. The pretence that it is neutral is a 'mystification' theory. Its purposes are to disguise the reality of what they are doing from the technologists themselves, as much as to disarm the layman.

## THE PHILOSOPHY OF COMMUNICATIONS AS CULTURE

Stated bluntly then, our counter-case is that increasingly, in extent and intensity, modern culture is technological in form and substance. Also, we hold that our technology is cultural in its purposes and effects.

---

48  The disregard of selective audience interests, the reduction of a community of human persons to the level of a 'mass' without differentiation of taste and judgment is evidenced in this statement from the Broadcasting Authority Report for 1963: "Radio Éireann is a national broadcasting organisation. It believes that broadcasting has a positive role in public life which transcends, but includes, the provision of entertainment. The service must maintain contact at all times with a mass audience, and its need for commercial revenue will ensure that it does so." The almost unbelievable arrogance and philistinism of this statement of a policy for a national institution is, we assume, unconscious on the part of Management and most of those Authority members who signed it. How as man of Professor Moody's intellectual standing failed to stop its publication, or how Mr. Fintan Kennedy could associate himself, as a Trade Unionist, with a description of this kind is surprising. Television and radio as 'a national broadcasting organisation' should aim at serving the greatest possible diversification of audiences- not the service of a 'mass' for commercial revenue purposes.

It is contradictory, therefore, to describe it as culturally neutral; as a mere means.

The 'neutrality theory' allows the managerial technologist or technocrat to regard radio (or television) as a kind of 'funnel' through which an independent content can be pushed.[49] It obscures the fact that the very character of the funnel has a formative influence on the 'content'. In reality this formative influence saturates the content until they are a unity and indistinguishable. For us as professionals the astonishing fact was that the so-called content was rarely allowed to influence the funnel. That was regarded as an absolute given thing. The pseudo-distinction between the medium and its so-called content has passed into the common pool of unexamined assumptions.

* * *

Morals are merely a dimension of culture, so technology cannot be morally indifferent either. The systematic use of the techniques of machine and man-management means that the innermost layers of human beings are touched. Man makes technology and, in turn, is *really being re-made by it*, in a most vital sense.

How is the spiritual centre of humanity touched by technology?

## THE EFFECTS OF TECHNOLOGY ON CULTURE

Take a concrete example of how the 'purely' technical and physical can bring about a qualitative change in the interior or spiritual life of man.

A television camera considered simply as a physical object is just a lump of dead metal, glass and rubber, etc.

In its ordinary sense a television camera is made for a purpose.

---

49   See chapter on Culture.

It is an instrument constructed for human use on human beings. Suitably activated by a skilled cameraman, in dialogue with a Director, it produces a very highly selective pattern of images in the mind of the viewer.

In fact, an 'image' on the screen, in the sense of a physical object present at any one moment of time, is a single white or grey dot, varying in brightness. There is literally nothing else there.

The white dot, however, moves horizontally at enormous speed along a set of parallel lines, 625 of them. In this way it 'paints' a reproduction of the object at which the camera is pointed. This reproduction is not on the screen. Only a single white dot appears on the screen. The scene is reproduced in the viewer's perceptual consciousness and nowhere else!

## THE EFFECTS OF A FALSE 'SCIENTIFIC' ABSTRACTION

Now, to return to our theme: the camera as a lump of physical matter has no meaning. A television camera is *not* a mere lump of matter. It is an intelligent organisation of physical components designed to achieve a human purpose. To think of it as dead matter is a mere abstraction.

If, by this kind of abstract thought, you think of the camera in this way, then it is intellectually neutral. It is not actually neutral. As soon as you advert to its meaning or purpose it has a cultural function. It is a *social* instrument by means of which the will of some person or group can be done.

Of course, it could be argued that this merely physiological bias does not contradict the camera's cultural or moral indifference.

The camera has an image-making meaning. Additionally, the image itself has its *own* meaning. Indeed, its whole reality is a meaning-reality. It is a cultural thing. But the image is meaning-loaded in a far richer and more complex sense than is the camera. The audio-visual image that actually enters into consciousness has emotional and imaginative *sets* of meanings which coalesce into one another and with a whole perspective of the viewer's personal and social life. He does not merely understand the image's meaning; he responds to it emotionally. He augments it, fills it out with memories and imaginings. It activates, in this sense, a whole perspective of intelligibility. It creates, also, a set of expectancies and intentions projected into the future. It makes and activates an imaginative, intellectual and emotional 'world'.

The capacity, then, of a so-called 'lump of dead metal' to vitalise this vastly complicated structure of human responses is the meaning of the camera as an instrument of technology.

Machines in themselves are not technology. As we have said:

> technology is the whole rationalised system of the human use of mechanical and other managerial techniques, in order to exercise power over nature, including human nature.

\* \* \*

The 'neutral' or cultural indifference theory is an unacknowledged mystification theory.

Can it not still be said that there is an important sense in which technology *is* culturally indifferent?

After all, the same machines can be used to create image-systems that represent cultures unintelligible or even hostile to one another. The Israelis can use the same machines and studios, the same personnel, to propagandise their border-enemies, as the Jordanians. The equipment is the same. Is the technology not, then, neutral? The answer must be boldly: No!

Why?

This way of putting the question, we would say, is precisely where the technocrat's habit of unacknowledged abstraction causes the mystification.[50] What does this question really ask the mind to do? It leads it to revert, unawares, to the mental 'trick' of abstraction. This turns the whole complex of communications once again into a system of 'lumps of dead matter'. In other words, it turns the mind from the notion of technology as the social use of techniques to the quite trivial abstract fact that machines can be thought of as simply 'lumps of matter*. In this kind of abstract thought, the machines have no social use in themselves. But the implications of the argument then carry the mind forward on the unuttered assumption that technology is merely the activity of technicians handling their machines, indifferent to their human and social effects.

The Israelis certainly have different intentions to those of the Jordanians. Equally certainly they use similar machines and techniques. They both, however, obey the laws of technology: the machines and techniques must be used to exploit[51] human nature. This is what they were made for; this is all they can do. They always necessarily and inescapably do it.

---

50  By technocrat we mean a technologist who is also a manager by virtue of his technical-logos or 'wisdom'. This is the sense in which the technologist succeeds in deceiving us by stealth; he has first mystified himself by persuading himself that his science is free of value-judgments and cultural effects. Of course, as the Oxford Dictionary implies, the technocrat does his expert work for the common good. This is a supreme value. The problem is that, logically, he can only hold it privately. Values have, he claims, no inherent place in technology. It is value-free. It is concerned only with facts.

The technocrat, embedded in a social complex, is in an essentially ambiguous position: he must take values into account but is not equipped to deal with them. His brother- the 'pure' technologist- is abstracted from the existential context of such embarrassments.

51  Exploit here has no perjorative sense as it now appears to have in common usage. It means, merely, 'to realise every potentiality'.

However much and however skilfully the Arabs or the Israelis use the equipment to widen their differences, the fact remains that their use of its peculiar culture-form does more to make them alike than it does to differentiate them, culturally.

To us, a most astonishing confirmation of our contention is that the culturally 'Marxist' USSR and the capitalist 'liberal' culture of the Anglo-Saxon bloc are more and more intelligible to one another and grow every day more alike in their ambitions and actual culture forms. Notwithstanding differences of ideology which each considers irreconcilable with the other, they are both, now, technological societies whose ambitions are to match achievement for achievement in this field. It is with a shock that one realises that to the American factory manager, Russian economic and educational systems are more readily intelligible than the Chinese systems are to the Russian manager, although they share a common ideology. The Sino-Russian 'internal' quarrel was not originally about socialism but about technology. It is, of course, now rationalised in terms of ideology. Indeed, Russian 'Marxism' is a technological State capitalism; U.S. 'free enterprise' is, increasingly, a technological military socialism.

The cultural chasm that separates India from Britain is far deeper and wider than that which separates Britain from Russia.

Identical technologies have brought the latter together, in spite of irreconcilable ideologies. Each knows, below the level of acknowledgement, that ideologies are, progressively, irrelevant.

## THE TECHNOLOGICAL 'ELIMINATION' OF VALUES

Television-technology can, of course, be used for different and even conflicting purposes but it has an over-all social dynamic that determines all its special uses and liberties. This is the 'exploitation' of nature. There is thus a common purpose in every one of its uses. Technology, as a form of social life, is precisely the organisation of a culture to ensure the control and mastery of nature. If there is something in man that exceeds nature, as we believe, then there is a problem for technology[52].

The problem is that the principle of economy requires every possible element that enters into the process of mastering nature to be rendered measurable and predictable. Technological mastery of nature depends on 'quantifying' whatever is allowed into the system. Physical nature, being extended in space, is ideal for treatment by the refined systems of measurement that modern mathematics have made possible. Even human behaviour, although subject to freedom and chance, can be measured. By the careful observation of statistical patterns of recurrence, it can be largely predicted, 'in the mass'.

The principle of economy in the employment of resources is the use of the least possible quantity of means to the maximum possible effect. This is always a matter of measuring quantities. It must, in theory, allow a sufficient 'surplus' of means to provide flexibility.

In practice, it seldom does. The practice is impracticable.

Perhaps we ought to examine the theory. Technology does not; it stretches the elements of human generosity to compensate. It then 'patches-up'.

## THE PERSISTENCE OF VALUES AND THEIR EMASCULATION

Those things in man, his contemplative intelligence and free will, that cannot be quantified can be taken into account by technology only in their physical effects, not in themselves. They are the sources of all

---

52  We are not unaware of a new almost defunct natural law theory that includes human nature. In this notion, freedom and the spirit are included in man's nature. This is certainly not the view of the later work of St. Thomas, who held that liberty lies outside the realm of nature. His insight has regained a place in the mainstream of Western though in the philosophies of existentialism. Man makes his own nature, out of his liberty.

'values'. Values solicit the individual man's freedom. They are all those things which he freely (unpredictably) chooses. They do not *determine* what he will do. They are incalculable. Therefore, they can find no place within the matrix of technology as such. They are 'allowed for' as irrational 'mass* factors when they must be; they are eliminated whenever they can be[53].

So in technological culture, freedom, contemplative intelligence, imaginative and emotional cultivation are progressively confined to the smallest possible areas; they are then assigned to the realm of the 'ideal' and the 'emotive'. Practical reason replaces contemplation; freedom is replaced by ever more flexible and refined systems of calculation. The in-calculable human activities are not denied, expressly. They are ritually honoured and practically dismissed. They are not capable of 'objective' measurement or verification.

Yet value judgments continue to obtrude themselves.

If our basic contention is well-founded, then our modem technology is essentially cultural and not neutral. It is itself founded on a value judgment. This unuttered judgment is that it is *desirable* to exploit nature according to the principle of economy.

The fact that this is a value judgment is never adverted to. It is simply taken for granted as launching and maintaining the whole system. To examine it critically would be taken as self-evidently 'romantic' and absurd. It is simply a 'fact of life'. Without technology 3,000 million people could not survive on earth. It is no longer thought sensible

---

[53] Imagine our astonishment at hearing a programme-colleague described, after a management course, as an 'unpredictable variable'. Another was described as 'non-productively orientated' - meaning lazy. Perhaps the most comical and mystifying was a description of an old-school-tie short-cut in administrative procedures being raised to the level of 'scientific' description as 'a socio-metric overlay'. There is a new jabberwocky, with its attendant ironic glossaries, that gives business administration its own kind of sub-culture. Where this is administratively dominant in a communications medium, it provides its own difficulties.

to ask: is the exploitation of nature in this way desirable? We have 'painted ourselves into a corner'! The only question left is: what is the most that we can get out of the actual and irreversible situation? Such a question is a quantifiable problem: it can be answered, in principle, scientifically. Other values may be very fine but, as values, they are not strictly admissible as objective ingredients in the situation. However noble, they must not, in the technologist's view *qua* technologist, be allowed to obtrude themselves into the real world of practice.

## THE APPLICATION TO RADIO AND TELEVISION

This general problem in the modern predicament is critical for radio and television. Ostensibly, these media are culture-forms. For technological civilisations, they belong, in their so-called 'content'-function, to the 'ideal', not to the 'real'. Actually, they are instruments of societies dedicated to the exploitation of nature for private profit (in the West) or for public power (in the East). On the modern 'principles' of practical men they simply cannot be allowed to obtrude the order of values into the serious business of life. This is just what those humanists who are dedicated to value judgments (and trained in making them) insist on doing.

Television is, therefore, in the mind of the technologist, the businessman and the politician, too dangerous a set of instruments to be left in the hands of the technically non-expert. People seeking the realisation of transcendental values would 'gum-up' the beautiful works. The 'ideal' must not be allowed to obtrude into the real until the beautiful works are finally made and running smoothly. They never are. The proper place for the 'ideal', they would say, is in the harmless theoretical world of literature and philosophy.

Technology, by virtue of the same principle of economy of means, has made a bomb which could well destroy us all. It has made a culture-form that could well destroy itself.

## THE MAIN HOPE WHICH MOVED US TO ACT

We think that neither of these is a desirable outcome. In our view, a technology that could make the H-bomb is too dangerous to leave in the hands of men who regard their techniques as morally neutral.[54] Ordinary people have an ineradicable tendency to regard the survival of their species and our 'useless' human culture as morally desirable. They will, we hope, insist that these value judgments, however hopelessly unquantifiable, will be preserved and acted upon.

Similarly, we think that the perfection of communications as universally effective as radio and television raises an equally crucial problem. It is this: since these are not passive but formative, how can they be left in the hands of men whose whole mental training leads them to regard these media as having only extrinsic moral and cultural significance? What quantitative answer can such men give to the question: 'If these media are morally and culturally indifferent, who ought to use them and for what purposes?' There is no quantifiable reply to a question which includes the ethical word 'ought', since this implies cultural and, therefore, immeasurable values. Inevitably the media will be found in

---

54  Scientists and technologists were able to justify the work which ended at Hiroshima on the grounds that they merely pursued truth. The use to which their work was going to be put, they thought, had nothing to do with their sciences. These were morally neutral. The use was a matter for moralists, not scientists. But it was politicians and soldiers who made the 'inevitable' use of their pure science. See review by John Naughton of Tongues of Conscience: War and the Scientists' Dilemma, in The Irish Press, 16th August 1969, in which he speaks of the 'increasing doubts, fears and prejudices of leading scientists about the morality of their work'. Being Irish, we wonder how different this is from the behaviour of the profit-seeking businessman from Monday to Friday compared with his religious activities on a Sunday.

the hands of those who can ask the quantifiable question: 'How much do you need in order to use them?' Technologists will serve men who ask quantifiable questions. There are no quantifiable reasons why they should not; there are clearly quantifiable reasons why they should.

If our technological civilisation is not to exhaust its potentialities *as a culture*, it must allow the instruments of communication, which it has made, to be used in order to ask the most powerful and ultimate question of all: 'What do you think *ought* to be done?' This question should be addressed to the whole community. It cannot be answered on behalf of the community either by the technologist, the politician or the broadcasting Producer. It is *their* function to raise it intelligibly in all its implications and to help the community to pose the question *to itself* and to reflect the temper of its developing answers.

What principles are available to guide all of us?

## COMMUNICATIONS AND COMMUNITY

If a young elephant trumpets a warning to his herd which sends them into cover where the hunters' jeeps cannot follow, is this warning a communication? Of course. It is a signal, an instrument of the common life of the herd.

Men, however, are not merely animals; human communications are not merely signals sent across a dividing space. They are relationships of intelligence, emotion and desire that create a community of persons. Communications consist in opening people out of their individuality. Individuality consists in locking people into themselves like atomic particles. The person, not the individual, is the principle of openness[55].

---

55   Individuality is the principle of exclusiveness. One rock essentially differs from another by virtue of its exclusive individuality. Its exclusiveness has no character. Its relationships can be merely eternal. This notion of the individual vitiated the whole liberal tradition of individualism. The person, on the other hand, by virtue of his intellectuality and free will, is an outwardgoing and inclusive centre of community.

## CHAPTER 3: COMMUNICATIONS AND THE COMMUNITY

Communications are the very relationships which allow people to be open to one another in a community. Communications are comm-union. They are not a mere unification of disparate individual members.

In a spatial sense, a pile of rocks are together. They form a heap; a kind of loose unity. Animal herds are together in a more complete way. As far as we can judge, herd-animals depend on one another to satisfy their *vital* needs: security, reproduction, growth, emotional satisfaction and play. This togetherness is possible because they have a rudimentary recognition of necessary signs. Animal intelligence seems to be confined to things present and useful for survival. Their communications are mere signals or signs with fairly stereotyped sounds and gestures for joy, fear and desire.

Men, on the other hand, live out a structured complex of full communication.

Take an example: the italicised words in this paragraph refer to means of human communication:

A man walks through an *aisle* of restaurant tables. He *signals* for his bill. He *signs* it as being chargeable to his account. He *bows* to an acquaintance. He *speaks* to the *manager*, a few *words* of *compliments and thanks*. He makes a *telephone call*; leaves the *hotel* through an *exit*; drives his *car* on the *highway* into the *city*; he enters his *office* and *writes a letter*. He then *studies* his accountant's *trading figures* for the month, and so on.

He has been moving all day on a web of communications.

These are saturated with intelligence; they are subtle and multiple. Unlike the animals', they form a system, not merely of signs, but of

---

Of course, every person is an individual—but not by everything that he is. His free intellectuality escapes nature.

symbols. The system is flexible and continually subject to change, yet it is always gaining in precision.

Like the animals', however, signs make evident to us those things that are present. Human symbols make things that are absent intentionally present to mind. By 'intentionally' we mean that kind of presence that is not physical, here and now. A symbol is the presence of something that is absent, like the portrait of a friend.

Human communications seem to transcend the here and now. They also transcend the merely useful. In this sense they are a kind of surplus intelligence. What is left over, so to speak, from satisfying *vital* needs, is available for the creation and satisfaction of new, deeper and more subtle ones.

They are a certain luxuriance in the fact that intelligent beings live together in communion.

Communities live, not by speech, nor by gesture, nor by ritual or imaginative indulgences like dancing, myth and story-telling; nor by religion, painting, music or poetry. Communities live *for* these things. Societies do not.

## COMMUNICATIONS AND COMMUNITY

We talk of the Royal Dublin Society, not of the Royal Dublin Community. Its members do not share a common life. They are associated for a common limited set of purposes.

A mountain village, or an island, holds a natural community. It has no formal rules to learn from books. It lives its rules. These are powerfully effective in the degree to which the villagers are unconscious of them in formal reflection. They could hardly say what they are, for the most part.

## THE PURPOSES OF COMMUNITIES AND COMMUNICATIONS

Communications, then, are the actual, unreflective, interpersonal relationships of a community. These are held by its members, not as mere notions but as bonds actually *achieved* and tenaciously, even savagely, lived out.

Community is the sharing, in tacit consciousness, of the pattern of a common life. It is productive of unique good.

Language is the basic example of a shared life-pattern on this level. Associations of a rationally purposeful kind are societies, not communities. If you found a society for the promotion of rose-growing, you do not create a community.

Societies presuppose, they do not create, basic forms of communication, like language. Social forms are works of reason, in the reflective sense.

Societies are founded; communities are found.

## THE PURPOSE OF SOCIETIES

Communities establish *social* organs for the purpose of extending, protecting, refining and intensifying their common good life. The State is the most important and effective of these rational societies. It, therefore, has the duty of making special use of that excess of intelligence which is the basis of community.

The community is neither irrational nor sub-rational. It is simply not reflectively rational. Its 'reason' is its culture-forms. These, by comparison with the State's organs, are rich, delicate, fragile and free; they show that merely utilitarian responses, like those of the herd, are static. They show, too, that the utilities of the State are arid and rigid.

The subordinate organs of the State (like RTE) tend to share its characteristics to the extent to which they are dependent on it. When they share the character of the community they become rich and fruitful.

When they are free of both they become parasitical and devour their parent bodies.

## THE STATE'S PROVISIONS FOR THE LIFE OF COMMUNITY

The State has the duty to provide special *means* of communication that protect and extend the community's cultural life-activity in subtlety and range. This is complicated by its additional duties of releasing the community from problems of security and providing the *means* of satisfying its vital needs. The State can promote or wither the life of the community by the very effectiveness of its technical means. Never has the human community had such powerful means for intensifying its life than in radio and television.

## THE TWO RATIONALITIES: COMMUNITY'S AND SOCIETY'S

To summarise the distinction: the community is essentially a culture-relationship of communications. It sets up the State in order to throw off the utilitarian load of its economic and political activities. The State is the community's *means* of ordering the production of its vital satisfactions and perfecting the instruments of its communications.

If the State should use these powers of refinement and extension to usurp the functions of the community, the results will be wanton. The community is peculiarly susceptible to injury from its own organs of communication. This is so because its intellectual life, although rich, is not rationalised in the same highly developed sense as the State's. Its intellectuality is tacit, creative and immersed in the imagination; it is not reflective, legalistic, conceptual or utilitarian.

The community's indifference to these qualities allows 'the practical man', whose mind is formed by them, to think that other kinds of ideas, rooted in values, are all very well in theory but irrelevant, if not impossible, in practice. This is the most dangerous characteristic of the one-sided and self-assured product of modern technical education. The up-shot is the practical subservience of an enchanted society to the 'omni-competence' of the specialist.

Practical men can pursue techniques of great utility and beauty; yet the logic of their work can defeat itself. It can destroy us. It is a logic of empirical rationality. It knows nothing of the transcendental intellectuality upon which civilised values depend. This takes the human presence and its purposes into account as essential to the truth of every situation—in ethics, politics, philosophy of sociology, of the sciences and culture. It is now recovering its place in European thought after the long nightmare of eighteenth and nineteenth century rationalism.

Out of the State's enormous increase in social rationality in the empirical sense, it has been able to develop and control vast systems of communication such as roads, shipping, airways, post and telegraphic services and 'mass' media. Logically, these ought to have resulted in a corresponding increase in the intensification of community-life. In fact, communities have tended to fragment and atrophy. They have withered in inverse proportion to the rate of growth of the means of communication. This is surely worthy of the closest and most anxious study.[56]

## THE DESTRUCTION OF THE COMMUNITY BY SECTIONAL INTERESTS

From the beginnings of political society, whenever a section, class or person within the community has been able to get a grip of the State's machinery, effective use of the means of communication has passed

---

56   Local cultures have tended to be replaced by a universal and uniform 'culture', as the very means for their growth increased in effectiveness. A friend saw eight sampans tied up at a mooring in an up-river village in the Far East. Their crews and families were watching the Lucille Ball show on television through the door of a bar. And what about the Manhattan guesthouse in the Kingdom of Kerry, or the drums of the Miami Showband on the Arigna Mountain overlooking Lough Allen? Are these any less outlandish than an Inuit putting up an Esso sign on the ice-cap?

out of the community's hands. The manners, morals and cultural idiosyncrasies of these sectional interests have been thrust upon the whole community.

When the means of communication were sparse and primitive the community could assimilate these sectional *mores* fruitfully. When communications became pervasive in range and depth this was no longer possible. The community's own voice tended to falter and lapse into secrecy and silence.

## THE LEVIATHAN-STATE AND COMMUNICATIONS

Further, if the duties of the State to provide for the common security and to order the economic life of the community are used to secure the interests of a section, there is a double distortion. The common life is being misappropriated by a subordinate part. This is a distortion because the State exists for the whole community. Worse, the very means which the community has created in order to rid itself of the clamour of its vital needs is being used, not for the extension and intensification of its life of communication, but to push it back into the condition of the herd; solidarity for immediate gratification. This is to use specifically human means in order to de-humanise the community. Even were this to be done in the interests of the common good it would be dreadful. Where it is done in the interests of a commercial section or a political party or a class it is, quite soberly speaking, monstrous—the Leviathan.

This, we believe, is our condition in both East and West. The silence of the truly human voice is now almost global. The repetitive clamour of the ad-man or the party propagandist fills the air. Of course, they provide for fun and 'high' culture—but in their proper time and place, where they will not affect profits or power. A third of mankind is sick from stimulated gluttony: two-thirds are in want. Are we to spread, over all, a ghastly cultural impoverishment?

## IRISH COMMUNICATIONS MAY BE DESTROYING OUR COMMUNITY

The problem is well-nigh universal but we can have immediate experience of it only where it touches us. Its scale in Ireland is small, its advent is recent. Its effects may be contained or even reversed. These facts may permit us to study it the better. They may also facilitate its solution.

Ireland suffered her Great Silence,[57] the loss of her native culture, in the mid-nineteenth century. For fifty years now she has devoted her best energies to reviving what many believe to be her most authentic voice.

For the past two decades these faltering accents have fallen away into what, we can only hope, is a Little Silence.

This book is a small attempt to break the silence. The fact that it is being written at all is an admission of a breakdown in communications between professional communicators. They broke down between, on the one hand, those in the communications field who regard their problems as technological (in their abstract sense) and, on the other, those who regard even technology as a cultural phenomenon.

A culturally detached technology, we have tried to show, is false; yet it remains the single great cultural problem of our time.

In Radio Telefís Éireann, the technologically-trained managers and the creative programme-makers became unintelligible to each other. The managers hold power without insight; the programme-makers have insight without authority. The breaking point was reached when the technologists refused to recognise a problem and the programme-makers were unable, we believe, to recognise a solution.

---

57   *The Great Silence*, Seán de Fréine.

# 4

## THE MEDIUM IS THE MATTER
## CULTURE AND COMMUNICATIONS

> *Mr. Dillon: Why can we not avail of that apparently immensely valuable advertising revenue which is pouring into the coffers of Radio Luxembourg?*
>
> *Mr. Sherwin: They have very good bands on Radio Luxembourg.*
>
> *Mr. Dillon: I am not prepared to venture an opinion as to the quality of the material broadcast.*
>
> *Mr. Sherwin: They have good bands. That is the secret.*
>
> *Mr. Dillon: I believe in letting everyone judge for himself. I know a great many people in this country listen to Radio Luxembourg for reasons that do not carry conviction to my mind.*
>
> *Mr. Sherwin: They have very good bands and good singers.*
>
> *Mr. Dillon: I am sorry to have to tell the Deputy that that is not the reason recommended to me.*
>
> —DÁIL DEBATES

*The Battle of Waterloo* made a vast fortune for the Baron Rothschild. He knew what communications were about—at least in one of their aspects.

The story is an odd one. Rothschild was a banker, very rich and very imaginative. Napoleon's armies were marching on Brussels. The British army and its Prussian allies were separated. Napoleon hoped to attack and defeat the British before the Prussians could arrive. He had no money.

Rothschild lent him twenty million pounds. This shook the confidence of the market. British stocks and shares fell in value— to rock bottom. Rothschild sent his agents to the French coast with a pair of carrier-pigeons. There was a primitive line of semaphore signalling stations from positions near the battlefield to the coast. Rothschild's pigeons came home to roost with the news that had been flashed on the semaphore telegraph—Napoleon had been beaten!

At once, Rothschild bought up all the British stocks and shares he could get—dirt cheap.

The official news of the victory arrived some hours later. British stocks and shares soared in value.

In a sense this cynical and sad little story sums up the greatest change in human culture since 7,000 years before Christ. The Industrial Revolution had not only been launched—it was triumphant and politically safe for a 100 years. The balance of power in Europe was held by Great Britain from that moment until 1917. By then the effects of the Industrial Revolution were virtually universal and local cultures were under sentence of death. Some had temporary respite but almost all were eventually to succumb, in some sense, to the technological culture that had originated in the North of England; in Leeds, Manchester, Birmingham, Newcastle and Glasgow.

Its values have now penetrated into the Aran Islands. They are breaking up the tribal cultures of Central Africa; they have revolutionised the USSR; China is being convulsed in trying to assimilate them. The USA is disseminating them even to the surface of the moon.

Human cultures have always been subject to change. Some have slowly adapted. Some have changed cataclysmically through military exhaustion, conquest or great natural disaster. Some have died through a mysterious inner failure.

There have been two great periods of change that have proved irreversible. Somewhere between 10,000 and 7,000 BC, communities of men ceased to be food-gatherers or hunters and began, systematically, to cultivate roots and the seeds of wild grasses— corn. They used controlled fire, invented or discovered cooking and began to make pottery. These facts forced them to give up their nomadic habits and live in villages. Social life underwent a fundamental change. If you plant corn you must wait for it to grow. You learn to live with it.

There followed, of course, a long slow period of development and improvement. The next comparable leap forward *in kind* was in the hundred years 1750 to 1850 AD. In this hundred years the Industrial Revolution was launched. It established power-technology in such a position of dominance that literally nothing that opposed it could withstand it. Technology was the application, by capital, of Renaissance science to the division of labour.

We opened this chapter with a symbol of its power over military force and politics. Everything seemed to be suddenly in motion in a new way. This great change was made possible by communications—efficient shipping and navigation. The first really important practical application of 17th century science had been made to the arts of navigation and ship-building. Fast, dependable shipping established England as a great ocean-going and colonial nation.

In 1750 she began to import cheap cotton from India. She made it into cheap cloth. Her ships carried and sold it all over the world. Shipping lines of communications were quickly followed by others: mail services by coach in 1784, regular postal services in 1840. McAdam, Telford and other brilliant engineers laced England with roads and canals. Railways began in 1827. The electric telegraph had been known since 1737; by the invention of Morse in 1844, 'instant' communication was possible over the whole island. Newspapers and news-sheets proliferated, beginning in 1702. The steam-ship had been in use on the paddle principle since 1788. The discovery of the screw propeller in 1845 doomed the sailing ship, just as it had reached perfection of design and performance.

The Universal Education Act in 1870 extended literary and elementary communication in simple form to virtually everybody.

Britain's working population were uprooted from the land, their place in the structure of her culture destroyed; her people's ancient ways abandoned.

In the USA the culture of the Old South went down. It had depended on the great south-flowing waterways of the Missouri, Ohio, Cumberland and Mississippi river-system. The North built a railway westwards across the Allegheny Mountains and into the Western plains. Her own Industrial Revolution began, was propelled by the needs of the great Civil War, and now dominates half the globe.

Other nations began to imitate the British: Germany and France, the Japanese, the Americans. As each nation adopted the new technology its old culture began to change and eventually withered.

In the early 20th century Russia followed; in the late 20th century China began. India, South East Asia and the new African states are making efforts to do likewise. So are we, in Ireland.

Now the third great technological leap is upon us: the electronic world of automated production and space culture has been inaugurated. We are already using it. It has already begun to use us.

We Irish shared in the first 'leap'. We missed the second. None, it seems, can escape the third.

Is our culture to be similarly affected?

* * *

In the middle ages, because education was virtually confined to the clergy and since they were mainly recruited from the lower orders, learning and the cultivation of the arts was socially 'open'. Even the aristocracy were often illiterate. In ordinary usage we speak of the cultured man as one who is educated and well-bred in manner and tone. This is a modern usage; it has had currency since the Industrial Revolution. It is really a class concept since 'it happens' that the educated and well-bred are middle-class or upper-class, for the most part. For the most part, also, only they have had unrestricted access to the means of educating themselves in the techniques of literary and scientific culture.

Of course, there are 'nature's gentlemen'. They, without these advantages, have been able to imitate the manners of their betters and are admitted into their affections if not always into their society.

This notion of culture is essentially literary in origin. From about 1830 it has increasingly become scientific in character. Since the early 19th century it has run concurrently with yet another theory of culture. This envisages the development of a classless man, springing from the dispossessed, the unprivileged and the exploited—socialism.

There are three basic attitudes involved here. They have interacted and have had profound effects upon one another. In a sense they have been present together since the Industrial Revolution was launched. They are with us now. Their attitudes and ideas are struggling for control of the 'mass' media. They are: (1) the notion of culture as the sensibility and achievement of an elite; (2) the notion of culture as the area of the 'ideal', in principle open to all but in fact limited to what the individual and society 'can take' at any given moment in its evolution; (3) the notion of culture as the expropriation by a class of the whole field of ideas and sensibilities and their organisation into an ideology expressive of that class.

We propose to touch upon each of these in turn and conclude with some observations of our own.

\* \* \*

We have said that these three views have been current together all during the Industrial Revolution. Television and, to a lesser extent, radio and film have brought their relationship to crisis-point.

The first is frankly the philosophy of an élite. It recognises that the things of the spirit are difficult. It asserts that men and women of the talent, energy and sensitivity to acquire and promote them are rare. For the élite, literature and the spirit are essentially a criticism of life, a continual testing of the commonly accepted against the touchstone of their cultivated sensibilities, special knowledge and experience. This minority constitutes the heightened and refined consciousness of the race. Its critical vigilance protects the 'people's' values. Its detachment and intellectual discipline, its command and custody of the common language at its most refined and nervous level of expressiveness and analytical penetration, equip the élite to provide a set of criteria and to give the community (with an inevitable time-lag) moral and intellectual direction. At the heart of the minority is the creative nucleus—the poet, the philosopher, the composer, the critic, the saint and the sage. Around these, sharing in their creativity, is the receptor group, passively appreciative for the most part, capable of firsthand judgment but unable to create. It is the élite.

Around this centre of spiritual dynamism lies the great 'mass'; animated by it, deriving its values from it, experiencing its experiences at second, third and tenth remove. This 'mass' in our technological society spends its 'life' in grinding, repetitive and inhuman work in order to gain leisure in which to be truly human. But the leisure is empty. The 'mass' has neither the means nor the will nor the sensibility to fill it with anything but beer, small talk, spectator games and spectator surrogates for the life of the intellect: radio, film, television, cheap journals. The 'mass' are, in the words of one such critic, Stuart Chase, busy in providing themselves during their working lives with the means of 'de-creating'[58] themselves in their leisure hours.

This view is not necessarily cynicism, in intention. It is often a sad resignation to 'the facts of life'. It is a philosophical pessimism.

Its paternalist and protectionist function towards the 'mass' is at best to provide a high popularisation, to subject the press to its gadfly sting, to expose to ridicule the 'un-values' of advertising, to deplore the triviality, meretriciousness and vulgarity of television, to provide criticism of revered institutions and contrived values. In general, it makes 'civilisation' ashamed before the gaze of 'culture'.

We have described this view somewhat more starkly than most of its adherents would do. It finds expression, however, in the refined view of culture as art—meaning Mozart, Beethoven, etc. —implicitly advanced by Mr. James Dillon at the beginning of this chapter, and in the sensibilities of the Anglo-Irish ascendancy both

North and South. It is shared by their imitators—a growing band of middle-class, urbanised Celtic ex-peasantry.

The view has been most unapologetically stated by Dr. F. R. Leavis and Mr. Clive Bell in Britain. It is the dying fall of 19th century liberalism. It goes back through Wilde, Pater, Arnold and Coleridge to the Romantics: the withdrawal of the spirit from the mechanical and brutish progress of industrialised man. It is usually characterised by a pastoral nostalgia for the golden days that, truly, never were. The paradox of the urban élite lies in their bucolic memories.

It is a defence reaction to industrialised man and the coarseness of his technologically industrialised civilisation.

Now let us state at once in the interest of candour that our personal sympathies lie with this 'brutish technological civilisation'. Our dilemma

---

58    Quoted in Principles of Literary Criticism, I.A. Richards, 1924

is that we wish to repudiate its explanation of itself. Its dilemma is that it has the better case but has consistently advanced the worse argument. Let us now consider it.

\* \* \*

The Industrial Revolution was not merely an economic event but the creation of a culture. Its component elements were capital, science and communications, devoted to the development of the division of labour.[59] Communications, among other functions, have provided the necessary supplies of raw materials and access to the markets. Technology is the social application of scientific method to the management of the other elements: the exploitation of nature according to the principle of economy. In its early stages it did of course result in the creation of an ugliness that was brutish. The criticism by the cultured minority has been in large measure justified. Technology has been slow in providing an adequate intellectual theory. It should not be assumed that it has none.

It may be necessary to remind ourselves that the basic postulate of the scientific method is that nature is not mysterious in any religious or superstitious sense. It is not governed by occult forces. It is simply there. Human power to manipulate and exploit it was, in the past, obstructed by a tendency to project man's own psychological drives, needs and desires into nature. The progress of scientific thought has depended, in this view, in 'de-mythologising' nature, in removing the subjective and the emotional, in scientific methods of handling a purely secular and objective world. By the device of 'neutralising' nature, including man, all power in heaven and earth has been given to us.

---

[59] The repetitive function of manufacturing the smallest possible component units, the assembly of which make up the whole product.

This is the philosophy of Positivism: that the positively actual[60], stripped of subjective judgment, the animism of nature and 'magic', is the only source of truth and certainty.

What place have the arts, philosophy and literature in such an intellectual construction?

For science, any proposition with a claim to be true must be analysable into its component axioms, which either are tautologies, or must claim to be verifiable propositions that can be confirmed in sense experience, actual or possible.

Since art is evidently not a set of propositions at all and since literature is verifiable only in the imagination and not in sense experience or experiment, there seems no place for them in the mental schemes of the Positivists or the technologists who use them. We said earlier[61] that 'values' are relegated to the realm of the 'ideal', given ritual honour as being noble, and practically ignored.

Here we must press the question: what does it *mean* to relegate the life of the spirit, in the sense of art, literature, mythology and religion, to the realm of the 'ideal'? Where does this realm of the ideal actually exist? Not in the real world of nature, evidently. Nature is just there: positive, massive and impervious to anything but force—supremely, the refined forces of technology. The 'ideal', then, can exist only in the psychological recesses of man's consciousness; lie below the level of conceptual scientific reason.

I. A. Richards, the clearest and most systematic exponent of the view, frankly admits this. Values, he concedes, are purely psychological and subjective. They are the consciousness of what we want. Their criteria are the degrees of success with which we can find, fix and assimilate

---

60   As against the negatively possible.

61   See chapter on Technology [Communications and The Community]

them without destructive disturbance. Those things that we want are good which we can assimilate without creating chaos within ourselves, personally or socially. Those are evil, which, on the level of action, would destroy the pattern of our relative stability.

But man wants to have and to do and to believe in all sorts and degrees of things which would destroy him if they really happened to him. He wants to accept, with a desperate yearning, the beautiful simplicities of the Sermon on the Mount. If he actually did them, that is if he actually lived them out, they would destroy all the complacencies, ambitions and patterns of his real life. Yet he cannot let them go, they are 'so various, so beautiful, so new'.

Never mind. For Richards and the cultured technologist or scientist there is a way out! Literature and art are ideal principles by which our imaginative experience can be so organised by the intensity, perfection and beauty of the work that the human psyche can play with that which it dare not assimilate on the level of reality. It can be so conditioned and stimulated by this imaginative play that the real ego engaged in practice and science, the ego of business and affairs can be prepared, little by little, to realise these ideals in the future. Art is a play routine of the imagination that prepares us for a *future* expansion of life on the plane of reality. In the imagination, everything is possible, now. In action, everything has to be *managed*.

So for this view also, the Industrial Revolution resulted in a separation of the brutally real from the artistically beautiful. It is perhaps more humane than the élitist view—at least in the sense that the artist and the 'masses' are all in the same boat. It has, perhaps, the additional attraction for the 'masses' that in real life, the skipper is a technologically competent navigator. To change the metaphor, they know from experience that he regularly delivers the goods.

## CHAPTER 4: THE MEDIUM IS THE MATTER

On the level of the imagination the 'masses' are not in fact, whatever the principle, in much better case than in Dr. Leavis' view. The actual state of technological achievement has not yet so realised its priorities that it has been able to open up the avenues of education equally to everyone. The efficacy of works of art and literature to organise imaginative experience as preparatory play, assumes this experience itself to be organised—at least to the point where it can *imaginatively* assimilate without inducing the collapse of our life-patterns.

Indeed, the division of labour has now extended through the actual mechanisms of technological production *into the very processes of education itself*. This educational specialisation requires not that education will be open to the whole 'mass' but that a whole structure of *educations* shall be made available to them. Men will be educated not for the reception of a unifying cultural experience but for their functions in the process of production alone. In short, their experience pattern will be so circumscribed and fragmented by training in special disciplines that any real art experience would bring about collapse into chaos. If this specialisation should ever become universal then, on Richards' principle, art and literature would be destructive. We should be justified then in describing them as evil!

In the meantime, only a bad realism in art, at once a 'photographic' and idealised reflection of reality, can be accepted by the 'masses' without reducing their real world to chaos.

Curiously enough, the intellectual honesty of I. A. Richards[62] concedes this point. Since poetry is a kind of psychical therapy, it can be accomplished by a bad poem as well as by a good sonata.

So, in fact and in the end, the 'masses' in this theory too, must make do with such thin diets of imaginative play that they may be

---

62   *Principles of Literary Criticism*

assimilated by the whole social structure of disparate and differently conditioned specialists in a thousand fields. These 'play' experiences will come not from painting, poetry, literature and religion, all of which would be too intense, esoteric and disruptive, but rather from the thin film of popular pseudo culture provided by the radio, television, the *Daily Mirror* and Metro-Goldwyn-Mayer. In principle, this view is an optimism. In fact, it is a cynicism.

What a strange cycle is closed in European culture! Plato had written over the doors of his Academy: 'Let none ignorant of mathematics enter here'. In his dialogue, *The Republic*, he regretfully announced that, however charming his rhapsody, the poet was destructive of good order and must be driven from the city.[63]

We have been considering two opposed and, in a sense, complementary notions of the role of culture in European civilisation, each a reaction to the other pole of its dynamic. The élitist notion of 'high' culture is a reaction—at once escapist and defensive— to the economic objectivity of the scientific technology of the Industrial Revolution. Positivism, on the other hand, upon which this technology was historically based, finds a place for the values of 'high' culture in the area of subjective consciousness—but at the price of regarding them as merely 'ideal'.

Marxism, the third modern view of culture that we are considering as typical, would declare these theories to be idealist mystifications— rationalised flights from reality.

For Marxism, art is, in the transitional stage of the dictatorship of the proletariat, the propaganda of the masses. It would criticise the

---

63    The modern technologists would, on I.A Richards' principle, have found a way in which the poet could have been safely allowed to stay.

elitist view as an *idealist*, fascist aesthetic. It would characterise the Positivist view as a bourgeois escapism.

The whole difficulty about trying to discuss a Marxist theory of art is that there is no such theory to be found in Marx's writings. Marxist 'theories' have been attempts by his followers to reconcile two 'elements' of Marx's notion of social life. He saw these as consisting in the basic socio-economic structure of productive forces with their *superstructure* of law, politics, religion and culture. The economic base, Marx argued, was ultimately the determining one. The superstructure was a product of it, secondary and derivative. Nonetheless, he would seem to have granted this superstructure some relative independence. He conceded a reciprocal relationship of action and reaction between it and its socio-economic base.

This theoretical notion seems to have had little effect on the actual development of culture in the Communist states. It is, perhaps, the weakest part of the whole Marxist analysis. We suggest that it will not stand up to logical examination because it is not a description but a metaphor.

Metaphors can be illuminating until one tries to draw logical conclusions from them. In this respect, they are like parables.

If the whole intellectual superstructure is to be regarded literally as a mere reflection of productive socio-economic forces and *ultimately determined by them*, then it is difficult to see how they can have any reciprocal effect. The notion 'ultimately' seems to be an escape hatch. After all, it is consciousness in action— specifically class-consciousness—that brings about changes in the productive forces themselves.

This consciousness, Marx insists, is not an abstract thing but the consciousness of actual men in their class solidarity. This is always formed by the historical, cultural situation, expressed in the superstructure. *Since this is so*, it must be equally true that the superstructure ultimately determines changes in the forces of production. Of course, Marx exempted consciousness from the superstructure. Logically, then, this would mean that such consciousness has no historical form, either political, legal, religious or cultural. It would be some kind of generic and formless common sense.

But in fact, Marx argues to the contrary!

He wrote in the preface to A Contribution to the Critique of Political Economy:

> With the change of the economic foundation the entire immense superstructure is more or less rapidly transformed. In considering such transformations a distinction should always be made between the material transformation of the economic conditions of production, which can be determined with the precision of natural science, and the legal political, religious, aesthetic or philosophic—in short, ideological *forms* in which men become conscious of this conflict and *fight it out* (our italics).

The action—reaction between base and superstructure would, if It could take place, be dialectical.[64] If the superstructure merely reflects

---

[64] The cultural function of the human intellect is to escape the matter-of-factness of the merely given—of what's actually there, so to speak. For Marx's master, Hegel, the intellect provides, by way of negating the purely given, a pure alternative—the antithesis. The given, or actually existing thing, can no longer continue unchanged in the face of this negation, nor can the pure antithesis be realised. It is blocked by the actuality of the given. The new reality is a synthesis of both. This is never a compromise, in Marxian theory—or, indeed, in fact A compromise is, essentially an *alternative* to either: a synthesis is an *embodiment* of both. This more properly Hegelian than Marxist view seems to us a valuable and true insight if critically used. However, we are convinced that this very abstract and 'logical' conception of Hegel's, inverted by Marx to become the law of material process, is too 'pure' and intellectualised to deal

its base, it cannot determine it; if it *can* determine it, it, it cannot merely be determined by it. *Your* image in a mirror can affect your actions because *you* are an effective agent—not because it is.

In our view it would have been better to concentrate on Marx's theory of the cultural function of the dialectic than on the metaphor of the superstructure and substructure—or socio-economic base.

Marx believed that Communism, through the dictatorship of the proletariat, would create a New Man. This would result in the withering away of the State, and the achievement of a classless society—a cultural change of unimaginable dimensions. He was far too realistic a political philosopher to have devoted much time to speculations on what kind of culture, art or literature would spring from so cataclysmic a change in the nature of man and society.

---

adequately with reality. It is a thing of the philosopher's study. Communists retain it like an article of the Creed. We have seen that *in practice,* their 'synthesis' of individualism (the basis of the Elitist view of culture) and the managed 'mass' (the basis of the technologist's view of culture) achieves, in fact, only a practical compromise in the Communist States! In the end they all use the classical view of 'high' culture.

Our own view, for what it is worth, is that *the* element in a true dialectic is that man is spirit by everything that he is and corporeal by everything that he is. 'Thought' and 'extended matter' are high abstractions deriving from Descartes' attempts to reconcile the Renaissance sciences with the 'traditional' concepts of mind. We think that the flesh itself is conscious because, in man, body itself is spiritual—animated—and does not have consciousness attached to it There is no 'gap' to be bridged. Culturally, we live in an *interworld* of animated bodies, open to one another in their consciousness, closed off from one in their objectivised corporeality. Man is partially translucent and partially opaque.

This dialectic is dialogue, largely in a darkness intermittently flashed with lights—the tongues of fire.

We do not apologise for this incursion into anthropological philosophy. Until communicators have an adequate philosophy of the meaning of man, they will remain at the mercy of those whose notion of what man can be made *to do,* suffices to exploit and diminish him. The shabbiest politicians or business men can hire technologist or ad-men, soldiers or secret police to *use* humans—why bother to understand them?

Lenin had no such reticence. For him, art was propaganda, as was literature and the whole culture of the spirit. He was, he said 'sorry that I never had and never will have any time for art'.[65]

Again:

> Everything that is more or less sound in old art is to be safe-guarded. Art—I do not mean museum pieces, but effective art such as the theatre, literature and music—is to be influenced, but not crudely, to complete its evolution as quickly as possible to meet the new requirements. New trends are to be treated with discrimination. They must not be allowed to seize the field by mere aggression, but are to be given an opportunity to win prominence by real artistic merits.[66]

This carefully measured open-mindedness to the possibility of new art forms and literature was not to survive Lenin's death. Stalin and his successors have had no doubt that the dictatorship of the proletariat requires a frankly pedagogic socialist realism. If Communism has a philosophy of art and culture within it, it has not yet burgeoned.[67] This is in tune with the scepticism of Lenin's élitist and essentially Victorian background. The proletariat as such, he was convinced, were incapable of raising the level of their class consciousness higher than that of the

---

[65] *Recollections of Lenin,* A. V. Lunacharsky, 1933.

[66] Op. cit.

[67] This is not to say that there has not been a large and fascinating body of speculation on the nature of proletarian art among Communists, East and West. There has been. Much of it has been fresh and penetrating but as varied and personal as Western 'bourgeois' criticism. It can claim no special insight into the nature of culture that is recognisably socialist in any exclusive sense.

level of their Trade Union awareness. Consequently, Marxism of the Leninist line has always seen the Party as a cultural élite, exercising the dictatorship of the proletariat *on* the proletariat as much as on their behalf. In this sense, and in the absence of any adequate theoretical and critical foundation, the Marxist-Leninist 'line' is indistinguishable from the élitism of Dr. Leavis. What a *dénouement*!

\* \* \*

Each of the three theoretical attitudes to the communication of culture to the 'masses' has one fundamental element in common: each owes its existence to the technological organisation of society for the production of goods.

The view of the spiritual élite is a reaction to and a withdrawal from the technological base of society as hostile to spiritual values.

The Positivist view is frank acceptance of the technological base as the ultimate value *in fact*. It recognises other 'values' as ideals, the absorption of which into the socio-economic base requires technical management, through play techniques as precise and refined as any other element in the machinery of its life.

The Marxist attitude is that the technologically based socioeconomic structure of production relationships is the only reality, in an *unqualified* sense. It admits the existence and the importance of other values which it describes as superstructural. They reflect, more or less passively, the forces of production and even, in some undefined way, heighten and accelerate their change and development.

To sum up our view of these three theories:

The first theory is that culture is a flight from reality; it can affect reality only by admonition, exhortation and example. The second is an acceptance of the actual and a preservation against the corrosive effects of the possible or ideal as potentially destructive. The third is an absorption, on ultimate analysis, of the ideal into the socio-economic base, not in order to conserve that base, but in order to destroy it and replace it.

As far as the 'mass' media go and the 'mass' of men who are mediated by them, the first view abandons them as irredeemable. The second view regards them as improvable within limits. The third view regards them as replaceable by a new race of cultural Titans. All three, in our view, tend to the destruction of what is human. Of course, they are held in confused and overlapping mixtures and degrees of depth.

It is noteworthy that in some form each of them appeals, either in principle or in practice, to the need for an élite in order that the great 'mass' of men may be moved from their spiritual inertia. It is notable too that the new 'mass' media are generally conceived by each of these élite groups as powerful and even sinister in their influence upon the 'mass' to the degree to which they are manipulated by a broadcasting élite other than themselves.

The so-called power struggles from within the media, newspapers, journals, radio and television, are widely, and indeed in a sense, truly, conceived as a struggle between élites.

The basis of élitism is a claim to some special and necessary knowledge or skill. This may, as Marx proposes, merely disguise a class interest in its monopoly of the forces of production but on the level of the media themselves it is expressed in terms of a right to an ultimate control over the means of transmission by virtue of some special insight.

In radio and television, the Government claims an ultimate responsibility and right of decision. This claim is founded on the pervasive character and 'power' of the medium—even where it is not a State monopoly. In this view it is 'too dangerous' to be left, in the last analysis, in the hands of any one body other than those who have charge of the common good. As Mr. Anthony Wedgewood Benn, British Minister of Technology said last year: 'Broadcasting is too important to be left to the broadcasters'.

The body which usually claims this right, of course, is the Government; in fact, the Party that happens to be the Government.

In the Communist system, this is openly acknowledged. The Party is the élite which expresses the consciousness of the proletariat in its 'emancipating' mission.

In our techno-mercantile society, the élite, who effectively control the media as a *means* of communication, are the technocrats. They conceive it as their duty to the public to see that it is used efficiently, economically and without disturbing the stability of the common consciousness beyond what it can bear. Like I. A. Richards, it fears that if the media should present to the 'masses' any experience so intense, so new and so corrosive of the existing factual state of society—economic, social or ideological break-up would be inevitable. We raise the question: is this not *precisely* the function of the media?

The view of the proponents of an élite of 'high' culture is that ultimate control of *the means* of communicating education, information and entertainment should be in the hands of those who express the most 'intense and refined consciousness of the race'. They see the media as essentially educative of a 'mass' always in need of direction and example so that it may act with decency and decorum. They see this 'mass' as incapable of sharing in the essence and actuality of their culture at first hand. In this view, the function of the media is to provide a surrogate for it— edifying, sterilised and accessible through "simplification".

The programme-makers, centred round the Producers, struggle for control without a theory beyond the conviction that radio and television are *communication* media; they are communicators quintessentially. In the meantime, the struggle is undecided. Perhaps the reason why it is undecided, even in the Communist East (witness the role of the actual broadcasters in the Czech crisis) is the necessary ambiguity of the media themselves, and the consequent ambivalence inherent in their actual use.[68]

It is assumed, it seems to us, by all but the professional programme-makers, that radio and television are simply media—a technical *means* by which a minority can transmit, in one-way traffic, its formative ethos. As we have already hinted elsewhere in this book, this is certainly a use to which radio, television and the press may be put. We have described it as the closed-circuit use of the "mass' media; its primary function being to reach what Mr. George Waters calls 'a maximised audience'[69].

We raise as a point for discussion whether this is in fact *the* characteristic use of radio or television. Although it is certainly a use, both good and necessary, it corresponds analogously to the paternalist use of authority.[70] Its function is frankly pedagogic. Its method is openly technological. This is to use television as a national megaphone.

* * *

The notion of form and content has begged the question of communications for a quarter of a century. It is a curious mixture of metaphors. Psychologically, it depends on an image of the "mass' media and the use made of them as analogous to a container and its contents. Television is thought of as in some way 'containing' what it transmits as if this were something separate and distinct. The other part of the metaphor that

---

68  See 'A Cautionary Tale', p. 69 ff.

69  *The Allocation of Resources in the Production of Television Programmes* (unpublished), George T. Waters, 1967.

70  See chapter on Authority.

makes up this curious mixture derives from the old Greek theory of form and matter. Its modern usage is a parody. In the old theory, form was precisely that which was inseparable from its matter. It saturated it. Together they made up an indivisible essence.

If we continue to talk about programme-content without realising that we are using this mixed and meaningless language, it is not merely that we will miss the point but we shall be blocked from ever seeing it.

Our suggestion here depends on a distinction in the use of television that has been further obscured by the often misunderstood and, we believe, mistaken view of Marshall McLuhan that the medium is the message. The medium is not the message in our view; but neither is the message the 'content' of a container or a funnel.

Is it not at least possible that, as communication, television has an altogether different character and utility—that it is formally a 'speech' employed by the community to talk to itself and to enlarge itself by exploiting the range which the medium provides? If this view has any foundation then television (contrary to McLuhan), far from being 'the message', is the *material* of an art form of community-communications. The form,[71] therefore, would be the community consciousness of sharing in a common experience, not of the 'content', *but of one another*.

How can we apply these theoretical considerations to radio and television? What kind of programmes do these theories demand?

Every élite is a society—a group of individual members of a community brought together for a common rational purpose.[72] The principle

---

71 The old Greek notion of Aristotle is peculiarly useful in trying to analyse this new kind of communications. The form was not the container of the matter. It was the actuality of the matter. The matter was the potency of the form—at once the principle of its individuation and of its ability to change. Without its matter nothing was actual. Without its form nothing had any specific character. Matter and form were merely intellectually *distinguishable*—never actually separable.

72 See chapter on Technology.

of their unity is the objective work to be done. They remain individuals of like mind.

In television terms, they will *all* want a programme that will *transmit*—'tell attractively', the 'mass'— to the public, the value and utility of their common work. They will wish to have it 'properly' discussed; they will want it 'appealingly' illustrated. At most, they will agree to sugaring the pill by having it agreeably fictionalised or presented in an 'worthwhile' documentary. News and comment should be 'suitably' presented and edifying.

**GOOD NEWS IS NO NEWS: CHILDERS**

> The Minister for Health, Mr. Childers, yesterday criticised what he described as distortion in the world news media. We never read about the good work being done in countries throughout the world, only the violence, he told 100 delegates from 40 countries at a seminar on vocational rehabilitation in Galway.
>
> —Evening Press, 9th September 1969.

\* \* \*

We have suggested that the community experience is the form and the medium is the matter. Nothing perhaps divides the three attitudes we've been studying more sharply and irreconcilably than their assumptions about the nature of community. Dr. Leavis sees the cultured élite as a community of minds facing an organisation of mankind that can aspire to nothing more coherent and vital than a 'civilisation'. This civilisation *is* the organised mass, integrated by the need for communication to satisfy its material and psychological needs. The 'mass' is at best indifferent, at worst hostile to spiritual values. It corrupts language, blunts sensibilities, coarsens human intercourse.

The Positivist technological view sees the 'mass' as a material to be selectively and technically 'worked up' to the point of organisation where an increasingly large number of its members can live the full life, as consumers not only of material goods but of 'ideal' values. For this philosophy, there is no community. The 'mass' remains a societal organisation of individuals. The 'mass' media are a playground in which increasingly large numbers can be prepared psychologically and sociologically for the full intensity of the life of imaginative 'idealism'.

But where do these 'ideal values' come from; where are they to be found; what generates them? Certainly not the community; there is none. The Positivist turns, inevitably, to those who have and hold them—the cultured minority. But their acceptance of this minority's ideal values is not simple: of course, some Mozart must be transmitted. Some 'serious' discussion must take place. Religious programmes have a 'proper' role but not a pervasive one. So have Irish programmes. And Art must be honoured in its purity—for those who understand it. But the facts have to be faced because only the facts are real. The 'mass' is not ready for this intensity of experience.

> This is not to say that minority groups have no rights. They can and must be given a service. But the operation of television is too costly and too complex to be run for the benefit of a handful of people. If a service does not justify itself in terms of the mass audience then it cannot be justified. (Mr. T. P. Hardiman, Director-General RTE, The Irish Times, 30th October 1968.)

So a screening and diluting process must be provided. Political discussion must be 'balanced', explained, civilised and generalised so that it may be universally acceptable. Of course, the technologist agrees with the educated minority, but he has the general good to consider. What the public 'wants' is, by and large, a true indicator of what it can take. The technological élite has no 'ideals' of its own. It dispenses those of the cultured élite, judiciously. This dilution in what they would call a medium of imaginative illusion is a preparatory life-game. The rate of intensification of this play-experience is of paramount importance if social rupture is to be avoided. Marx's criticism of this bourgeois ideology is fundamentally sound: it is an individualism, irretrievably and irredeemably closed to true communication and true community. People can only be manipulated and managed, like a group of objects. The technological élite has evolved the precise means of most effectively manipulating them, for the greatest good of the greatest manageable number.

The greatest manageable number of people, for instance, can be served either by the 'pop' programme on radio or television or by the wholesome family series, accepting and reflecting a complacent society. Trends follow one another like the Whiting and the Snail as the technocrat thoughtfully and responsibly provides a universally palatable pablum.

The beat group is a case in point, in programmes for young people. Here, the protest writings of a number of young American 'beat' poets, Ginsberg, Kerouac, Ferlinghetti, in the middle and late fifties, have been totally absorbed. Their negation of the current societal values in the US was shocking and intense; they denied, not merely the technological uniformity and individualism of urban life, but the illusory nostalgia of the priests of 'high' culture. The irony is that their protest, now organised by big business, has been 'phased-in' and marketed in a sweetened, manageable and sterilised form, to the 'mass' public. Here another irony and divisiveness occurs: the 'younger' generation is thus allowed a certain area of protest and illusion of withdrawal from their community.

This is carefully exploited by what sociologists call *externo-conditioning*. The adolescent by education and the institutions in which he lives is first *interno-conditioned* to regard himself exhaustively as an individual in the sense of being an isolated atom, *incommunicado*. He is lonely in the crowd. He is misunderstood. He is *seeking* a community. The real protest of Ginsberg and the others would be impossible to him in the mass; it is too sophisticated, too esoteric, too resolute. But it can be idealised. The very isolation of the adolescent as Other among Others is manipulated by advertising, by radio, by television, by Golden Discs, by best-seller prizes to persuade each that the Others are buying this record, this book, singing this song, wearing these clothes, sharing the same, sad, vague, erotic loneliness. The isolated individual can 'belong' to a group by sharing its uniform tastes, using its tenth-hand imitations of the real thing.[73]

---

[73] The intellectual structure provided to the world-wide phenomenon of student revolt differentiates it from this kind of pop protest The Inter nationalists in Ireland, the *young tigers' of the Fine Gael Party, the new young Socialists of the Labour Party, the Students for Democratic Action in University College, Dublin, the People's Democracy in Queen's University, Belfast—each has a structured intellectual backbone similar in function, if not in kind, to the influence of Marcuse's thought on the American campus'. revolts and the German students' protests. The Maoist and other radical movements in the French universities, the now largely defunct Provo movement in Holland which was one of the earliest of these phenomena of protest and provocation, were also ideologically equipped. Significantly, they reach our screens only in 'News', 'Public Affairs' and 'responsible' discussions. When Fr. Austin Flannery introduced elements of real protest into a religious programme in 1968: Sinn Féin, I.R.A., Communist, Housing Action Committee activists, he was accused of using the publicly-owned media subversively. He was harried by RTE. In Dáil Éiireann he was described by Mr. C. J. Haughey as a 'so-called cleric'.

The original toughness of the protest is lost and the paradox of a uniformity of dissent that produces millions of replicas of one prototype, whose existence is justified on the grounds that he is 'different', is never adverted to. This is not the imitation that has always been attendant on good art. It is an imitation of life. Brendan McGann touches upon this in his article 'Leonardo and the Leviathan'.[74] This is not popular culture, it is merely popular conditioning. It cultivates nothing, but it manufactures the 'mass'—a hideously commercial product—and identifies it with The People.

Probably the most enervating and, in the long run, socially flaccid television programming of this kind is the 'family-viewing' type. Made to computer-calculated specifications with suitable sociological and psychological input ingredients, tempo-ed by attention-research metronomes, beautifully edited and crisply cut audio-visual clichés, they are glossily packaged imitation life-kits.

The dimension of true tragedy is replaced by pathos. Humour becomes wit, brittle and edgy but basically comfortable. The unmanageable incongruities of the really human are replaced by the contrast played for laughs or tension. Every wrinkle is ironed out, every end tied up. There are no gods to spring from the machine. The whole smooth acceptance of the status quo as fundamentally likeable and healthy, deprives the viewer of any real experience. The action of life lived on this level takes place on a huge carpet; its 'problems' are briefly faced and swept beneath it, 'solved'.

Some of the material is very good indeed. Where it is so, it fulfils the profoundly human need for a distraction which is really a re-creation. Some of it is very bad. This is not the worst. A *night's diet* of it, as Shelah Richards once said, leaves one with the feeling of irritable and

---

74   See Appendix I.

leaden discomfort of having eaten a box of chocolate sweets. One has enjoyed each one and one is very sick indeed.

Most of it is very meaningless and displaces the meaningful in the programme mix on a terrifying scale of priorities. Fred Friendly resigned as Head of CBS News in 1966 because of such displacement. He wrote after his resignation:

> In America, television can make so much money doing its worst, it cannot afford to do its best. The 1966 Vietnam hearings in the Senate Foreign Relations Committee could not be broadcast because a fifth rerun of an ancient 'I Love Lucy' broadcast could return more revenue. The fact that no one at CBS management doubted the importance of the hearings (even Lucy later agreed the hearings should have been on) could not overcome the fiscal criteria that killed the hearings. When I sat in my office watching the bank of monitors with our pickup of the Senate hearings being broadcast over a competitor's air, while 'Lucy' cavorted on ours, I was tempted to order up a superimposed slide that would read, 'Due to circumstances beyond our control, the broadcast originally intended for this time will not be seen'[75].

A similar process of dilution is observable in the treatment of folk art and culture.

The ballad of rebellion or deprivation, the sea shanty, the work song, the morris or flamenco dance, proliferate in their imitations, each

---

75    *Only Connect*, Four Studies in Communications, 1968.

copy a thinner and vaguer image of its real folk origin. The expression of a community's tacit consciousness of itself breaks up in the face of assumed 'mass' needs which are, in effect, the wants of the élite group, but diluted. In a country like Ireland where there is still a living tradition of folk art in instrumental playing, singing and dancing, the survival of its community-making function is threatened, not merely externally but internally.

The protectionist attitude of Irish culture groups, particularly the Comhaltas Ceoltóirí Éireann, is understandable. The rich historical sediment of Irish folk activities is under threat, like the dwindling rural community itself. If the Fleadhanna of Ireland and the Eisteddfod of Wales show that the threat can be met, the views of official language and musical bodies in Ireland have tended to a respectability and 'professionalism' that has more in common with the purveyors of 'popular' culture than with the community life in which they had their origin.

The school of 'thought' that has convinced itself that Irish will become socially acceptable when it is seen to be spoken casually and sung elegantly by gentlemen in tuxedos and ladies in dinner dresses is symptomatic of the rootlessness of the new bourgeois Gaelic culture. It is equally sad to see it identified with an 'earthiness' that veils a defiant anti-bourgeois loutishness. They are both pessimisms and they are both snobberies. The majority of people concerned with the development of Irish culture now recognise this to be so. What they may not recognise is that the 'black tie' school is *administratively* dominant.

A traditional programme like *Bring Down the Lamp* was criticised because it took place in a kitchen; because socks hung over the fire; because porter passed around; because men danced in their braces; because there were too many 'old' people taking part; because the 'image' was not nice—in a word, because the necessary sterility was not achieved; the purity of tradition was not preserved; the performers were not 'professional' enough. What these people require is the suppression of reality. What they lack is a savour of what is really Irish.

The international treatment of 'folk' all over the world has tended to two corruptions, one by debasement and the other by rarification. The problem for the conscientious broadcaster is to decide whether there is any change possible in folk culture at all. Is it true, as one Scandinavian said to us at the Golden Harp Festival last year, that to be a folk form *means* to be dead? Or is the only kind of change open to folk culture the provision of traditional themes and motifs for art composers and choreographers— like Bela Bartók in Hungary or Sen Ó Riada in Ireland.

The tendency to corruption by rarification has been raised to the level of a fine art in the USSR and in East bloc countries. In Russia the great State Folk companies are no longer the activity of a folk community but of professionals—the cultural arm of an élitist Party apparatus bent on giving the 'mass' not what it does but what it should see done. It is the same manipulated 'mass', nonetheless, as is created by the commercial pop enterprises in the West. The life of the folk community, like any other community, is tacit and unreflective.

Is any urban community capable of folk expression that is not a kind of museum piece of nostalgia?

The effect of 'preserving' a folk culture under threat of extinction by technological urbanisation could be clearly seen in the programmes submitted on traditional folk culture to RTE's annual Festival *The Golden Harp*. This consisted in 'raising' the folk activity, the dancer, song or story, to the level of professional perfection and style proper to the fine arts. The effect was often beautiful but, in some curious way, effete and even absurd.

We have in mind, in particular, a village story, traditionally acted out by the villagers in a Hungarian province, produced on film by what were quite evidently superb actors, singers and directors—but set in the village. It had all the phoney and bizarre air of an open-air performance of 'A Midsummer Night's Dream' by the Old Vic on the lawns of Trinity College. It ought to have worked but, in fact, it was a travesty.

Official Russian art and culture are fossilised. Witness the increased preoccupation with technique and interpretation, and a lack of creative development, in the Bolshoi Ballet and in the Moscow Art Theatre; sure signs of an art form turning in on itself.

On visits to Russia to research and make a film in 1967, Lelia Doolan and Bob Quinn noted the inertia and passivity of official organs and personnel and the nervous wariness of cultural bureaucracy. Scenes filmed of workers on a building site and of workers drinking at a pavement beer-stall in Moscow, were found to be cut out of the film when we returned with it to Dublin.

A day's filming of a young scientist wandering through Odessa which included scenes of sunbathers and swimmers at the beach, was conveniently 'lost'. The standards of modesty and puritanism officially prescribed in Communist states are of no mean order.

Many of the young people, expressive and frank during private interview, dried up in front of the Russian film team which included the official bureau's representative—the Party's man, we were told. In spite of the cultural manipulation, we sensed a bourgeois atmosphere as oppressive as our own. The spontaneous, the popular and the experimental were confined to underground life, now led by many young people and artists whose open activities, were they sanctioned, would, presumably, disrupt the system. In the Intourist bars, the no-man's-land of Russian hotels, we were permitted to dance to the latest Western 'pop' songs and pay for drink with Western currency. The wholesomeness of Russia's culture could withstand such small doses of Western decadence! Their own 'official' pop music had the flavour of old-fashioned German *Schmaltz*.

From such work as we have seen, Russian television is massively didactic, propagandist and dull. It was all distinctly edifying.

The best programmes we saw were in fact films. They were often imaginative and always beautifully photographed but, like Eisenstein's framing, the composition was always on strictly Renaissance-classical lines.

Most of all what one wants to say about Russian television is that it is closed-circuit television; doctrinaire, superior-to-inferior, self-improving, essentially patronising, unperceptive and humourless.

Each of these post-Industrial Revolution attitudes sees the life of the spirit, literature, philosophy, pure science and the fine arts, religion and myth as actually constituting culture—at least in this moment of history and in the past. Marxism alone would claim that, in some millennial future, this notion would be transcended. Its actual culture in the intellectual sense, except in science, is as bourgeois as that of Berlin or San Francisco or Belfast. It is perhaps a little more old-fashioned than the culture of Dublin and more widely diffused that that of Madrid.

\* \* \*

What we wish to propose, not as something new, but as a consideration for programme-makers and the public, is that this restricted notion of culture is a provincialism of the mind and that it is irrelevant to the tasks of the broadcaster. We have said that it is a 'precious' reaction to the ugliness and brutality of the new technology.

On this there are two things to be said at once: the first is that this technology is no longer *necessarily* ugly and brutal. It has unparalleled means to provide us with an environment of grace and beauty, if it could find the vision, hold it steadily in focus and summon the will to realise it. Sporadically, and in isolated areas, it has already often done so.

The second consideration is this; there is no longer any need to carry the minority view of literary culture on our backs like the Old Man of The Sea.

We need not react defensively to our technological environment. Already, we may pick up once more the notion of culture which antedated the Industrial Revolution.

Culture is every activity of the human person, living in community, that enlarges, enriches and deepens the common human experience of that community and its members. Community is as much an urban as it is a rural reality.

The gossip of family life is culture. The cooking habits of a region are an important part of its culture. The way of washing clothes is culture. Politics, local variations in the rules of a card game, are culture. Accents and tricks of speech, hopscotch on the pavement, the planting of potatoes in a 'lazy bed', are culture. Participation in local government, pub jokes and determined adherence to local religious practices, are culture. The habit of Sunday morning gossip in the chapel yard, people's games and occasions of fun, the forms of their social intercourse and, pervading all, a people's language, are culture. But Bach, Byron and Berkeley are culture too. As culture, the method of planting potatoes has no lesser claim on the name of culture than the Great Toccata and Fugue of Johannes Sebastian Bach.

Is this to say that all these things are of equal value? The question is not a simple one. In time of war or national emergency it is more valuable to have potatoes than Bach. Even in times of peace it is more necessary to be fed than to be intellectually stimulated. This doesn't mean that a square meal is intrinsically more important than Yeats's 'Resurrection'.

In short, there are levels of cultural activity that reveal the community to itself and the world to the community and its members to one another in a way so essential for its continual health that without them the common life lived in these other forms would grow obese or wither, would corrupt and lose direction, would eventually become sterile, lose vitality, and finally disintegrate. These are a nation's language, literature, art and philosophy. There is a principle of hierarchical importance here. That philosophy is more important in this sense than a football match does not prove that a philosopher is a nobler or more valuable person than a footballer. After all, we would wish that our statesmen should be the wisest and most virtuous of men but we would not wish them to have any special privileges in society—other than those necessary to the execution of their office. In short, a hierarchy of cultural disciplines is not an argument for a hierarchy of élites. St. Paul claimed his right to live by the gospel, but he did not. He lived by his trade of tent-maker.

\* \* \*

A people grown socially and politically adult will regard the idea of an élite as an abomination. What we would consider the most important thing to be said about culture in this sense—from Bach to bacon-curing—is that they should all be open to anyone who chooses to have access to them. The most effective blockages to this accessibility are the complementary notions of an élite and a 'mass'. They are the most vulgar products of arrogance— intellectual snobbery.

Raymond Williams has argued that there are no 'masses'. In a seminar given to RTE's Light Entertainment Department he said: 'Giving the "masses" what they want is giving nothing to nobody, because there is no such thing as "the mass"'. Again: 'if you have a fixed idea about the "masses" you cannot really take them into account, because they are not there'.

While we agree with the whole ethical protest behind this view, we suggest that sociologically, the notion of 'the masses' in both of the liberal rationalisations that we have discussed, and in Marxist theory, is as real as the notion of an élite. Abstractions are powerful sociological realities and do really describe sociological facts. We have tried to show how externo-conditioning processes by commercial interests have *made* a 'mass'. We have seen, from Mr. Hardiman, how dependent upon this artificial and contrived reality the actual management of the 'mass' media is.

The 'mass' in our view (like the élite) is not so much unreal as an immoral grouping of human beings for purposes of manipulation, like the middle-class or the working-class. Nobody would deny the social reality of the class structure merely on the grounds that it was undesirable or immoral. Williams' great insight, from the point of view of the broadcaster and the educator, is the clarity with which he has seen that the 'mass' is always other people—irrespective of class.

The notion thrives on what Seán Ó Faoláin calls 'fake-myth'—in[76] this case that popular culture is working-class culture, made by working-class people *for* working-class people. In fact, *in the main*, it is made by middle-class people *for* a "mass' that includes everyone that can be squeezed into it With the help of radio, television, film, discs and pop literature, the ghastly sociological fact is that, increasingly, everyone, or almost everyone, is squeezed into it.

The "mass' in this sense is a passive collectivity of individual atoms, as manipulable into behaviour patterns as steel filings around a magnet

Audiences are not "masses' if what we are broadcasting is culture in the sense that we have proposed. They are "families' of culture interests with overlapping memberships. Consequently, then, except for great

---

[76] The Irish, Seán Ó Faoláin

public events which would command the interest of every member of a community, *all* programmes are minority programmes.

This effectively circumscribes the area of the broadcasters' special problems of programme mix, *if he regards radio and television as cultural media in everything they do.*

If the description of culture which we have advanced in this book is valid, the whole notion of broadcasting as culture transcends the problem of Light Entertainment versus Heavy Entertainment They all have an equal claim on the name of culture.

What has been thought of as "high' culture, in the sense of those mental disciplines that reveal the nature of men and society with a singular significance and intensity, should be accessible to all those who want access to them.

The means of access to them, education, must be universally available before they will be universally demanded on radio and television. That it is not available is damnable.

Consequently, programmes of this kind can claim no special place other than to be available in sufficient quality, quantity and intelligibility to lead the viewer to use them as an illumination of his actual experience.

What we want to propose is that this function of television is a *special* function of what we have called its dosed-circuit use. It is not the use of television as an art form in itself but as a funnel.

The specifically characteristic use of television, we would contend, is an art form which not merely illuminates experience but provides it; creates it. This is the use of the medium to allow the community to experience itself and other communities. This will mean that *all* television in a true sense will be entertainment. What people do for entertainment is never heavy. In this sense, News, Public Affairs and Sport are properly entertainment.

The word entertainment is something people simply will not examine. Its identification with "light' entertainment is a pity. Without entertainment, no form of instruction is possible. What is probably meant, commonly, is the kind of distinction made by Professor Donceel, that there are two kinds of attention: spontaneous and voluntary. Spontaneous attention arises when the work and our motive for doing it coincide. This corresponds to our view of television as an art form. Voluntary attention has to be *brought about* because the work to be done is undertaken for a motive ulterior to itself. This is closed-circuit television. Where attention and the work coincide, the result is always entertainment. Where the coincidence is brought about voluntarily or by an act of the will, this is always didactic.

Drama is entertainment *because* it is dramatic. If some television "drama' as now transmitted is found to be heavy and unacceptable, may this not well be due to the fact that it has no place in the television art form as such? It was made for another medium—theatre or film. It can, however, have a place in the closed-circuit, educative, one-way transmission use of the medium.

Equally, is it not possible that much light entertainment in the sense of the synthetically popular, deliberately contrived and diluted, for example the quiz or *I Dream of Jeannie*, made for an equally synthetically contrived and diluted "mass' audience, is a use of television as a funnel; a closed-circuit propaganda medium? It is an extension of television's own proper activity perverted—at once a kind of advertising and a magnet for advertising, like the Sunday Colour supplements of the "serious' weekly newspapers.

One thing seems clearly evident from experience: that if we accept the description of culture as the whole way that people *actually* live their lives, then the technological effect of television is to give it the curiously dramatic quality that has been described as immediacy. It is not a passive mirror of that raw life-quality.

It is a dramatic transmutation of it, surely, where it comes off; so that the News itself is drama, and drama is an intensified life experience.

*The Riordans*, with all its faults, its didacticisms, its essentially up-lifting and optimistic tone, the lack of development in the characters, is more truly dramatic in television terms than The Playboy of the Western World or Hamlet. It is fictionalised reality. Like *Cathy Come Home*, with all *its* faults, the very drama arises from its involvement with the 'feel' of the life people lead, its contextual relevance and its ability to command identification for these reasons. Its reality is not a real-life reality but a dramatised one. This is the use of television as an art form; it makes a continuity by providing the dramatised material to make one essence with the form provided by audiences' life-experience.

* * *

We have quoted Mr. Hardiman's view. His predecessor, Mr. Kevin McCourt, put forward a more perceptive one in the Autumn 1967 issue of Administration[77]

> ... the public is not a homogeneous mass, it is a complex of interlocking and overlapping interests, predilections

---

77  Journal of the Institute of Public Administration of Ireland, XV, 3
Sir Hugh Green, formerly Director-General of the BBC, seems to share the same view. Speaking about commercial television and the BBC he said: 'Individual people do not only make up majorities. They also form part of innumerable minorities- and perhaps this is truer of this country than of any other in the world. People are gardeners, or enjoy cricket, of breed whippets, or like listening to seventh-century music, or are amateur archaeologists, or collect deceptive stories, or want to learn a foreign language. its seems to me that if the ideas put forward by Sir Robert Fraser in his speech were accepted as valid these minorities would have a poor deal because they would be consistently outvoted.'

and prejudices. It is incorrect to portray the world of broadcasting as one 'in which the messages of the medium fall on just and unjust alike, as does the rain'.

The 'fake-myth' that Ireland is a homogeneous community can hardly be sustained either culturally, ethnically, socially or politically.

\* \* \*

The ordinary plurality of audience interests is not merely more complicated in our case than in more homogeneous societies, it stands in constant danger of being at once exacerbated and veiled, by the existence of two States in the same island. We in the Republic have become conditioned to think of Irish cultural problems ambivalently: reflectively we think of Northern Ireland as being part of our cultural community and, at the same time, we tend to discount its existence in thinking and talking about 'Ireland'.

The culture originating in the Anglo-Irish 'ascendancy' group is, in fact, the most pervasive element in our community, not merely in its language, but in its manner, *mores*, class-conscious outlook; in its evaluations of art, politics, civics and economic thought. Yet it and its culture are regarded as 'alien' not merely by those Irish language and culture movements who are most passionately opposed to its hegemony but, in many aspects, by those 'native' Irish who share its 'foreign' values and know no others—the vast majority of our people. At the same time, the official policy of the Republic is to promote the cultural values of an aboriginal stock that is an ethnic majority but a cultural minority; that the minority culture is, by right, the principle of the whole nation's spiritual homogeneity—potentially.

RTE does not officially transmit in Northern Ireland. It has, however, extensive audiences there. Its transmissions and omissions have had profound effect there and its coverage of Northern events has had a profound effect on attitudes in the Republic, as recent developments have shown. Nonetheless, RTE's policy shares the ambivalence of the national community's.

A similar ambivalence of situation, leading to an ambiguity of thought, is evident in the attitude of Roman Catholics. It, too, derives from the fact that these claim that our national community is coincident with the population of the whole island. On this basis, Ireland is not a Roman Catholic nation. It merely has a Roman Catholic majority with one quarter of its population in religious dissent. Yet, we claim that Ireland is a Catholic nation— and think of ourselves as such.

The ordinary tensions that are a world phenomenon, created by the rural-urban industrialised sectors are, in our case, extraordinarily difficult. Our rate of urbanisation is very much faster than our rate of industrialisation and, in bulk, it is relatively recent. The social reference-frame of our urban population is still largely rural as are its thoughts, habits and feelings. Enough has been said to indicate that the argument for a broadcasting policy to meet the cultural needs of a pluralist society of this complexity, composed of many communities and of two cultures, must be very carefully articulated indeed. Whatever else may be said by way of solution, this much at least is evident: that a broadcasting service that justifies 'itself in terms of the mass audience' will do precisely what Raymond Williams said—'it will give nothing to nobody'.

More positively, the greatest possible practical regionalisation of radio and television, the greatest possible diversification of audience cultivation in the national service will be essential. The whole situation, however, takes on a dimension of urgency and even immediacy, with the immanence of routine satellite broadcasting. The obvious and unarguable desirability on cultural grounds of having two living languages among our people is threatened and indeed made unreal by the fact that the international culture that would be beamed upon us from satellite stations would be largely English in language, thin in real values, commercial in character and therefore necessarily orientated to a 'mass' audience numbered in hundreds of millions.

The difficulties inherent in our attitude to the competitive element provided by the British networks will be multiplied to the point of inundation. If we regard our problem as one of matching it rather than of providing an alternative of local immediacy and diversified community expressiveness; if we continue in our attitude to radio and television as actively transmitting and passively receiving media, then the game is already lost. If we could see them as the cultural activities of our own community in the sense for which we have argued, then *our task* has already begun. This is what we meant by the cultural crisis of which we spoke during our resignation controversy. The pluralism that we have just described is a principle of diversification. Far from constituting an obstruction in this positive task of using the media actively and expressively, it may be the very source of our salvation.

We have declared that in this debate our sympathies lie with the notion of technological culture. It is not merely that we accept as good the utilities of technological organisations, techniques and facilities. What we really mean is that the very character of this technology, if it could be rid of its Positivist philosophy and its dependence on an élitist notion of culture, would provide us with a means of promoting cultural diversification of incomparable power and appeal.

Further, having liberated Western man from a kind of slavery which subjected his body and his labour to the interests of another, technology in the hands of an élitist culture transferred him to a kind of slavery where his mind was subjected to the interests of another, and, increasingly, his body delivered from the necessity of labour at all.

Automation is the ultimate product of technology; its logical outcome is the delivery of man from the 'brute' forces of nature. Automation is already with us. In the almost immediate future, it will be a privilege to be allowed to work.

This *fact* presents man with cultural problems of a character and dimension that reduces the leap from food-gathering to agriculture, made ten thousand years ago, to insignificance. The whole of human life in the future, if it survives this era of 'neutral' science, will be an activity of culture for every last man and woman, or it will be nothing at all. We are now in some danger that it will be nothing at all.

We have argued that the technologists, armed with a cultural instrument, convinced that it has no cultural significance, have passed it into the hands of what Packard[78] and Bottomore[79] have designated the pyramid of élites, and a nostalgic, classical literary minority. Whereas, in fact, technology as a culture form is an enlargement of the area of cultural freedom.

The 19th century romantic notion of the garret artist as the intractable individualist is unthinkable in this era. Regrettably, it has been carried into the world of electronic equipment and teamwork that increasingly characterises radio, television and journalism.

What was the Romantic artist but a one-man élite? The artist in radio and television will never be a technologist, nor ought he be. But the technics provided by the technologist, including their vital and characteristic cultural effects, must be used with the same sensitivity to their value and beauty as Cézanne did his brushes, the chemistry of his pigments and the development of the optical science of his day.

---

78   *The Pyramid Climbers,* Vance Packard; cf. also *The Condition of Man,* Lewis Mumford, on the Keynesian notion of 'pyramid-building'.

79   Elites and Society, T.B. Bottomore

The differences will be: first, that Cézanne could do this and remain remote from the structures of the industrial society which supported him while he repudiated it in its intentions; the radio and television artist can never do this again. Cézanne provided the form; nature and man provided the material. In the great new media, we have suggested, the artist will provide the material and the community will provide the form. In the second place, radio and television are not quite like the tools and pigments of Cézanne. These were but an extension of him. The means at the disposal of the electronic artist are not tools. They are techniques productive of their own effects and are products of the community's co-operative genius. The television artist—the programme-maker—must be saturated in the ideology and skills of these.

Should technology continue in its neutral role, as a mere means, everything will be delivered. Nothing will be done. Nothing will be made. An effortless world of brute fact, what Marcuse has called a 'euphoria of the senses', will be available to everyone and the spirit will be dead.

Television particularly, by the very character of its technology —that is, by the coarseness of its image, by the domesticity of its setting, by the 'lateral' character of the inter-communication it promotes—not between the studio and the viewer but between viewer and viewer—by the immediacy given it in the 'crash' nature of its preparatory techniques, lives not in the world of reflective art, not in the carefully articulated world of literary imagination, not in the world of abstract concepts, but in the life-world of tacit pre-cognitive consciousness. Life immediacy is technologically possible to men through this wonderful medium to a degree and extent and in kind that we not merely owe *to* technology as an instrument, but is accessible to us *in* technology as the ultimate interworld which brings into dialogue man with man, and man with nature humanised—community.

## CHAPTER 4: THE MEDIUM IS THE MATTER

Nothing prevents the active realisation of this as a programme for reform like the perennial human reaction to the logic of any new proposition: 'After all, this is what we're doing already'. To be just, the truth is always complicated by the fact that to some extent, however fragmented and twisted the work may be, this *is* what television is doing already—breaking through the crust of prejudice, presupposition and outmoded convictions. This partial and haphazard success might be released into a flood by an adequate conception of the nature of the work to be done.

For the spirit of man is the spirit of refusal. There are no forms of culture or entertainment, or indeed instruction, that intelligence, as such, 'naturally' demands to satisfy its impulses. It is splendidly indifferent to all their solicitations and is free to refuse them. There is, therefore, no foundation for the belief that the 'mass' has cultural needs distinct from the minority's, unless they have been implanted. However horrible in some of its aspects, culture is always the implanted, the residue of the achieved, and never final. The achieved, the mere fact in its sedimentary facticity must be transcended. Intelligence and the forms of intelligence— culture—are the surplus human energies that refuse to be absorbed by the merely achieved. Intelligence transcends the given, the datum. It uses the sediment of history in man's dialectic with nature to propose and seek alternatives, possibilities, contradictions—even 'impossibilities'. To change is to live; to be perfect is to have changed often. This is a philosophy of risk.

In the past, this soaring transcendence of intellect was earth-bound, even in the titanism of the Industrial Revolution; slow in movement, limited in accomplishment. That it has made progress the existence of technology itself is evidence. It has done this not by complacency in the contemplation of facts, not by the euphoria of abundance of supply but through refusal to accept anything as sufficient; by protest, by negation, by risk, improvisation, daring and experiment, by irony, ridicule, satire and laughter it has changed the earth. This is the subject matter, this is the form and this is the task of communications as culture: to change man.

# 5

## DROCH-BHOLADH SA TIGH AGAINN
## RTE AGUS AN GHAEILGE

*By*
*Eoghan Harris*

CHAPTER 5: DROCH-BHOLADH SA TIGH AGAINN

*I don't know Irish meself but me Father thinks its gorgeous.*
—CANDIDATE IN GENERAL ELECTION 1965

*That kind of thing could endanger the country. It is not a matter of the language. You could have superior ability, even if you were an illiterate, and you do not need a knowledge of Irish in a soldier's profession. One can read in history from time to time that the most superior person might be a Yank in one war, a Frenchman in the next war, and there was an African who was very tough, but a very capable soldier, and once there was an actual savage. I am pointing out the danger of going too far in this business of making a knowledge of the Irish language a condition of promotion.*
—DÁIL DEBATES

De réir daonáireamh na bliana 1961 tá 716,420 duine sa tír a bhfuil Gaeilge acu. De réir an Roinn Poist agus Telegrafa tá 444,000 gléas telefíse ceadúnaithe sa tír. Dá réir sin tá níos mó daoine sa tír a thuigeann Gaeilge ná mar atá de ghléasanna telefíse. Tugann an daonáireamh céanna le fios go bhfuil 80,000 duine sa tír arbh í an Ghaeilge a ngnáth-theanga. Go fiú má ghlacann duine go bhfuil an figiúr sin áibhéileach is féidir a bheith rí-chinnte go bhfuil, ar a laghad, 60,000 in Éirinn arbh í an Ghaeilge a ngnáth-theanga. Dá dtarlódh sé go raibh gléasanna telefíse scaipthe go cothrom ar fud na tíre d'fhéadfaí glacadh leis go mbeadh cainteoir Gaeilge i measc gach seachtar féachnóirí. Ach le figiúir a fhágáil as an áireamh, is féidir talamh slán a dhéanamh de go bhfuil Gaeilge mar ghnáth-theanga ag cuid mhaith de lucht féachana na telefíse agus go bhfuil tuiscint ar Ghaeilge ag 30% den chuid eile—agus sí an Ghaeilge teanga oifigrúil an stáit

Ag tagairt de stáid na Gaeilge i RTÉ deireann alt 17 den Acht um Údarás Craolacháin, 1960, 'Ag comhlíonadh a dhualgas don Údaras, coimeádfaidh sé *i gcuimhne* i gcónaí na haidhmeanna náisiúnta atá ann an Ghaeilge a aisiriú agus an tsaíocht náisiúnta a chaomhnú agus a fhorbairt agus déanfaidh sé dícheall ag cabhrú leis na haidhmeanna sin a chur i gcrich' (linne an treise).

Sé cuspóir an ailt seo a thaispeáint cé mar coinníodh na haidhmeanna sin i gcuimhne.

I nuachtáin laethúla an 4ú Nollaig 1963 fógraíodh go raibh Eagarthóir Cláracha Gaeilge le ceapadh i RTÉ. Sé bhí ag teastáil, de réir an fhógra, duine go mbeadh 'ardchaighdeán oideachais, sár-eolas ar an nGaeilge agus tuiscint domhain (*sic*) ar ár gcuspóirí náisiúnta'. Is é a bheadh le déanamh ag an duine sár-cháilithe seo ná 'polasaí an Údaráis i leith úsáid na Gaeilge i gcláracha telefíse a chur i bhfeidhm'. Is annamh a tharla cáiliochtaí chomh fuaimintúil de dhíth chun dualgas chomh follamh a chur i bhfeidhm, mar ón lá sin go dtí an lá atá inniu ann ní eol d'aon eagarthóir, léiritheoir ná stiúrthóir i RTÉ céard é polasaí an Údaráis i leith úsáid na Gaeilge i gcláracha telefíse. Leis an fhírinne a dhéanamh is 'i gcuimhne' go dearfa a choinnigh an tÚdarás a bpolasaí. Dá bhrí sin, chun teacht ar pé polasaí Gaeilge atá ann ní mór dul chuig dhá fhoinse eile.

An chéad fhoinse, billeog dhá leathanach a chuir an Stiúrthóir-Ghinearálta Kevin McCourt amach i mí Eanáir 1966 faoin teideal 'Statement of the RTE Authority for the guidance of its staff in regard to the use of the Irish language in broadcasting'.

Sa bhilleog seo bhí sé pointí ar fad. Sa chéad dá phointe cuirtear síos ar an nGaeilge a chaomhnú trí na cur os comhair an phobail 'in a sympathetic, positive and imaginative way'. Sa tríú pointe deirtear nach cóir go mbeadh aon díospoireacht i dtaobh ath-bheochan na Gaeilge 'unbalanced' agus i dtaobh léitheoireacht nuachta dúradh gur chóir go mbeadh 'enunciation, grammar and diction' ar an gcaighdeán céanna agus atá riachtanach i mBéarla. Sa cheathrú pointe tugadh le fios go leanfaí leis an bpolasaí faoina mbeadh éagsúlacht ábhair sa nuacht Ghaeilge. Go 'ngríosódh' léiritheoirí an pobal chun Gaeilge a labhairt agus go leathnófaí úsáid na Gaeilge i measc páistí agus lucht leanúna spóirt. Ansin tagaimid chuig an t-aon ráiteas dearfa dá bhfuil le fáil sa bhilleog: 'that at least one programme of special interest to adult viewers be broadcast weekly on television'. Deirtear ansin go leathnófar polasaí an dátheangachais. I bpointe a cúig, aithníonn an tÚdarás go bhfuil sé 'feasable and desirable' níos mó Gaeilge a úsáid i gcláracha spóirt ach amháin 'in such a way as not to interfere with general communication'. Agus sa phointe deiridh aithníonn an tÚdarás go bhfuil dhátheangachas 'desirable' ach go mbeadh daoine gan Gaeilge 'secure in their employment'.

Léadh an paimfléad seo go poiblí do fhoireann léiritheoireachta RTÉ in Eanáir na bliana 1966 agus níorbh iontaí leo a fhaid ná a éigcinnteacht. Ina measc siúd a raibh spéis acu sa nGaeilge ba é an t-éadóchas an tréith ba láidre a dúisíodh agus iad siúd a bhí fuarbhrúite thuigeadar nach raibh ann ach dallamullóg. I measc lucht ceannais sa staisiún tugadh an 'diffusion policy' air; i measc an lucht oibre baisteadh an 'confusion policy' air. In ár ndiaidh anseo scrúdóimid cé mar a d'oibrigh an 'diffusion policy' seo, i gcláracha radio agus telefíse le roinnt blianta anuas.

## RADIO

De réir UNESCO[1] tugadh 14% d'am craolta Radio Éireann do Ghaeilge in 1959. Tugaimid anseo figiúir ó shuirbhé príomháideach a rinne Proinsias Ó Mianáin.[2] Níor bhréagnaigh RTÉ na figiúir seo.

1966: 10.2%

1967: 9.1%

1968 (Ean.-Samh.): 8.2%

I litir eile[3] deir an scríbhneoir céanna gur ísligh an céatadán Gaeilge 1 % le linn na seachtaine dar thús 2 Samhain 1968—cé go raibh sé ag cur clár teagaisc, *Buntús Cainte* san áireamh. Má tá níos mó ná 'diffusion' ag teastáil níl ach ceithre cláracha do dhaoine fásta i gceist; *Cúrsaí Reatha, Ós na Ceithre hArda, Meascra agus Fadhbanna Gaeilge*. Léiríonn na figiúir seo cén polasaí Gaeilge atá sa Radio ag RTÉ; an Ghaeilge a laghdú ó bhliain go bliain.

Cé tá ciontach, má 's ea? Dúirt an Paipéar Bán ar Athbheochan na Gaeilge (1965) go raibh 'cóiriú, eagraíocht agus riachtanais na seirbhíse fuaimchraolta á scrudú ag coiste inmheánach de chuid Radio Éireann. Gaeilgeoir a bhí ina rúnaí ar an gcoiste seo ach is léir gurbh í an Ghaeilge an chloch dheireanach ar a phaidrín. Ba é príomh-thoradh na hoibre a rinne an coiste ná fad a chur leis na huaireanta craolta is breis airgid a fháil ó lucht fógraíochta, nó, le na chur i bhfocal amháin, radio RTÉ a thabhairt níos gaire do mhúnla staisiun YBX. Is léar go bhfuil coibhneas éigin idir an laghdú a tháinig ar mhéid na Gaeilge a craoltar ar radio RTÉ agus an titim atá tagtha i gcaighdéan na gcláracha Béarla, rud ar thagair príomh-léirmheastóirí radio na tíre do ó thús na bliana seo anuas

An gnáth-fhreagra a thugann lucht bainistíochta ar an gcineál seo léinnheasa ná a rá go bhfuil an seirbhís radio saor anois ó 'chreapall' na státsheirbhíse agus go bhfuil ag éirí go geal le cláracha faoin 'saoirse' a thagann le beannacht lucht rachmais. Cé tá buartha anois i dtaobh na gcláracha ceoil a thiomsaigh Séamus Ennis agus Seán Mac Réamoinn i 'ré dorcha' an stáisiúin ? Cé leis ar cuimhin an réabhlóid intleachtúil a ghin na Thomas Davis Lectures, faoi choimirce Francis Mac Manus?

Agus ag trácht ar choimirce, céard faoi na scríbhneoirí Éireannacha a fuair obair ón stáisiún, nuair nach raibh sé chomh faiseanta bheith i do scríbhneoir Éireannach agus atá anois; leithéidí Frank O'Connor, Liam Ó Flatharta, Brendan Behan agus Austin Clarke (a ruaigeadh faoin sceideal nua).

Agus nuair a tráchtar ar shaoirse cainte cé na cláracha radio atá á gcraoladh anois a mhúscail an chonspóid Dála a mhúsclaíodh drámaí Radio Éireann nuair bhí an stáisiún faoi 'chreapall' na státsheirbhíse? Duine ar bith a dteastaíonn uaidh an t-athrú chun donais atá tarlaithe a thabhairt faoi deara, níl le déanamh aige ach éisteacht leis na glórtha Luxembourg-Mheiriceánacha, na slaoda fógraí (go fiú i lár na nuachta), an fhógraíocht a déantar in agallamha agus gan amhras an fear a deireann leat, sa chéad teanga oifigúil, go bhfuil sé 'chun a naoi'. Sa tsean-reacht ba é cuspóir lucht craolta an tír seo a léiriú; an cuspóir anois, de réir dealramh, an tír a nochtadh. Faoi stiúir Chumann na nInnealltóirí lucht rachmais atá i réim; faoi stiúir poiblí an pobal a bhí i réim.

## TELEFÍS

Le blianta beaga anuas is ar an telefís go háirithe atá ár seasamh ó thaobh cúrsaí cultúrtha agus oideachais. Ó thús bhí ceangal dlúth idir an séirbhis telefíse agus fógraíocht agus is anseo is léire an dearg-fhimínteacht a bhaineann le polasaí an 'diffusion'. De réir sceideal an Fhomhair 1968-69 feictear go bhfuil 8.67% den am craolta faoi Ghaeilge! Chun gach tráithnín a cur san áireamh tá cláracha ar nós *Triopall Treapallagus* agus *Bring Down the Lamp*— cláracha ina mbeadh beagán éigin Gaeilge—san áireamh sa bhfigiúr seo. Chomh maith leis sin cuireadh san áireamh cláracha seirbhíse ar nós an Nuacht agus cláracha teagaisc ar nós *Buntús Cainte* agus *Labhair Gaeilge Linn*.

Má fágtar na cláracha seo as an áireamh faightear amach nach bhfuil act *trí chlár Gaeilge* i gceist ar fad, *Féach, Amuigh Faoin Spéir* agus *Ceist agam Ort*. Sé tá á fháil ag an 27 % den phobal a thuigeann Gaeilge na 2.6% den am craolta! Agus táid ann adéar-fadh nach cóir *Céist Agam Ort* a áireamh i mease cláracha do dhaoine fásta agus tá *Amuigh Faoin Spéir* dhátheangach.

Ach ní léiríonn na figiúir seo féin an fhírinne iomlán. Ní mór iad a chur i gcomhthéacs an bhrú tráchtála a rialaíonn déanamh cláracha telefíse. Ar an gcéad dul síos, an Ghaeilge atá luaite againn, tá a fhurmhór le fáil i gcláracha seirbhíse agus i gcláracha oideachais. Chomh maith leis sin, taobh amuigh den Nuacht agus *Ceist Agam Ort*, níl aon chlár Gaeilge ar an aer tar éis 8.00 p.m. Is maith le lucht bainistíochta a rá, mar leithscéal dóibh féin, gurb é is cúis leis seo ná 'the general level of understanding' ach sí an chúis dairíre, faoi mar thaispeánann na rátaí fógraíochta, gur ó 8.00 p.m. amach a thosaíonn daoine ag breathnú dáiríre ar an telefís. Ní díol suime le lucht fógraíochta a chlos go bhfuil tuiscint ar Ghaeilge ag 30% den phobal. Sé a bhfreagra, 'labhair linn nuair a shroicheann sé 50%'. Fhad is atá siadsan i gceannas mairfidh an scéal amhlaidh. Tá léiriú ar neart lucht fógraíochta le fáil i sceideal an Fhomhair 1969-70. Tá an clár nuachta *Féach* imithe trín bhfáinne draíochta, á chraoladh ar 8.00 p.m., ach níor thárla seo gan agóid laidir ó fhoireann an chláir fré chéile.

Bhí polasaí seo an 'diffusion' le cur i bhfeidhm go háirithe i gcláracha páistí agus i gcláracha spóirt. De bhrí go gcraoltar fur-mhór na Gaeilge roimh 8.00 p.m. gach seans go bhféachtar i ndiaidh don na bpáistí. Ach is i gcláracha spóirt go speisialta a d'fhéadfadh polasaí den tsort seo oibriú go maith. At tagairt do chúrsaí spóirt dúirt an Paipéar Bán go 'spreagfar úsaid na Gaeilge chómh fada agus is cuí i gcraoladh na n-imeachta go léir den tsórt sin'.

Dá bhrí sin bheadh duine ag súil go n-úsáidfí an Ghaeilge le linn cluichí ceannais na hÉireann ach arís ceard a tharlaíonn: Gaeilge sa chluiche mionúir agus gan Gaeilge ar bith seachas corrabairt leamh, leanbaí sa chluiche sinsearach.

Ach ní amháin go ndéanann polasaí seo an 'diffusion' dochar do sheasamh na Gaeilge féin, cuireann sé isteach ar obair na léiri-theoirí sa stáisiún. Ní nach ionadh bíonn léiritheoirí bródúil as a gcuid oibre agus tuigeann siad go bhfuil baint idir am craolta a gcláracha agus a dtábhacht. De bharr an leathcheal atá déanta le fada anois ar chláracha Gaeilge is beag fonn atá ar fiú na stiúrthóirí sa stáisiún a bhfuil Gaeilge líofa acu aon bhaint a bheith acu leo. An té a théann i bhfeighil clár Gaeilge tuigeann sé go mbeidh sé taobh le droch-am craolta agus nach mbeidh na háiseanna ná an t-airgead aige a bheadh aige ina mhacsamhail de chlár i mBéarla— tá *Féach* taobh le leath an airgid a bheadh ag a leithéid de chlár Béarla. Ina cheann sin tuigeann sé nach bhfuil aon pholasaí cinnte ann chun cláracha Gaeilgea dhéanamh seachas a bheith ag iarraidh Gaeilge a scaipeadh trí chláracha eile. Dúirt an Coimisiún um

Athbheochan na Gaeilge 'gur cóir don fhoireann a bhíonn i mbun cláir a cheapadh tuilleadh éagsúlachta a chur ar fáil in ábhar na gClár Gaeilge agus bheith san áirdeall i gcánaí chun teacht ar dhaoine a mbeadh éirim ar leith iontu le haghaidh na gclár sin'. Mar fhreagra ar seo dúirt an Rialtas (235) 'Tá seo á dhéanamh'.

Tá fhios ag gach léiritheoir i RTÉ nach bhfuil tada dá short dá dhéanamh, nach bhfuil seans éagsúlacht ar bith a fháil i gcláracha Gaeilge faoin bpolasaí atá á fheidhmiú faoi lúthair. Má tá 'éirim ar leith' i léiritheoir faoi láthair is fada ar siúl ó chláracha Gaeilge a threoródh a éirim é. Sé tá i ndán don léiritheoir atá ag iarraidh an Ghaeilge a chur chun cinn ná réamhrá gairid do chlár bailéadaí, abairtí fánacha le linn cluiche (go háirithe nuair nach mbíonn aon imirt ar siúl) agus aithris ar scléipeanna den chineál is measa ó ITV. Sa telefís, ach oiread leis an saol taobh amuigh de, tá dlúth-bhaint in aigne daoine idir Ghaeilge agus dearóile, easba dul chun cinn agus bochtaine de gach sort. Agus ach oiread leis an saol taobh amuigh is ionann na cúiseanna—tá siad ar fáil sa Pháipear Bán i bhfocail an Rialtais nuair deireann siad, 'go bhfuil an méid Gaeilge is féidir á úsáid ar an tseirbhís radio agus ar an tseirbhís telefíse ag braith freisin ar na cúrsaí eile a bhaineann le craoladh náisiúnta. Áiritear orthu sin taobh an airgeadais de ....Tuigeann gach éinne go bhfuil 'taobh an airgeadais de' agus mianta lucht fógraiochta ag rialadh cláracha Gaeilge. Chonacamar ón scrudú a rinneamar ar chláracha radio gur léar go bhfuil baint idir laghdú i méid na Gaeilge a craoltar agus isliú caighdéain sna cláracha eile. Nior tugadh míniú níos fearr ar an scéal seo ná an míniú a thug Coiste Seasta Chonradh na Gaeilge i ráiteas speisialta, Meitheamh 1969: 'Feictear dúinn go bhfuil Údarás RTÉ curtha sa bhfaopach toisc go bhfuil dualgas orthu freastal ar mhuintir na hÉireann agus ar leas Déithe na fógraiochta. Ar ndó, níl seo indéanta!'

## BEALACH EILE

Má tá aon cheo i ndán do chláracha Gaeilge tá gá dhá rud a dhéanamh láithreach. An chéad rud ná na hAchta um Údarás Craolacháin d'athrú chun go mbeadh oibhogáid dleathach méid na Gaeilge a mhéadú de réir ráta cinnte ó bhliain go bliain. I láthair na huaire níl d'oibliogáid ach é choinneáil i gcuimhne agus chonacamar cé mar rinneadh amhlaidh!

Roimhe sin féin ba cheart deireadh a chur le fógralocht ar RTÉ agus an stáisiún a chur faoi stiúir poiblí. Dá ndéanfaí an dá rud seo d'fhéadfadh RTÉ greim a fháil arís ar an oibliogáid atá orthu agus teagasc a thabhairt i dtaobh na Gaeilge. Más teagasc amháin atá i gceist tig linn tuiscint éigin a fháil ar an scóp a bheadh acu ach na rudaí seo leanas a thabhairt faoi deara. Ó 1881 anuas tá méadú tagtha ar líon na ndaoine a bhfuil Gaeilge acu—tugtar a chreidiúint seo do Chonradh na Gaeilge. Idir 1947 agus 1961 tháinig méadú 21.7 % ar líon na ndaoine a bhfuil Gaeilge acu. Gan aon amhras sé an córas oideachais ba chúis leis an méadú—in ainneoin go raibh meánoideachas teoranta do líon réasúnta beag den phobal. Le teacht meánoideachais saor agus lena chois, méadú ar líon na ndaoine a théann chuig an ollscoil, is cinnte go dtiocfaidh méadú mór ar líon na nGaeilgeoirí sa tír sna deich mbliana atá romhainn. Ní abródh duine ar bith atá ar a chéill gur chóir oideachas a fhágáil faoi phátrúnacht lucht fograíochta! Dá mbeadh RTÉ faoi stiúir poiblí bheadh sé ábalta leanacht de chúrsaí oideachais—bheadh sé in ann cur le obair na scoileanna in ionad a bheith ag cúlú agus ag trasnú obair atá déanta. Bheadh a leithéid de stáisiún in ann polasaí don Ghaeilge a aimsiú. Níor mhór don pholasaí seo deighleáil le dhá ghné den obair. Ar an gcéad dul sios, is féidir Gaeilgeoirí a aicmiú i dhá roinn. Iad siúd a thuigeann agus nach labhrann agus iad siúd a bhaineann leas laethúil as—muintir na Gaeltachta.

## RTÉ AGUS AN GHAELTACHT

Duine ar bith a thuigeann cúrsaí teanga tuigeann sé go gcaithfidh muintir na Gaeltachta gach seirbhís atá ar fáil don chuid eile de phobal na tíre a bheith acu—agus ní hí an tseirbhís radio agus telefíse an tseirbhís is lú tábhacht.

Gan aon mhór-chaitheamh airgid d'fhéadfadh RTÉ seirbhís do chur ar fáil do mhuintir na Gaeltachta anois láithreach. Ní airgead a bhéadh i gceist ach tréithe atá ag furmhór léiritheoirí in RTÉ— éirim agus samhlaíocht.

Sé bheadh ag teastáil, foirgnimh simplí ar nós iad siúd a bhíodh ag an Airm i rith an chogaidh a thógáil i nGaeltachta Chiarraí, na Gaillimhe, Mhuigheo, agus Dhún na nGall. Mholfaimís Dún Chaoin, Carna, Ros Dumhach agus Ros Guill mar shuíomh. Níl le déanamh ansin ach Aonad no Aonaid Ghluaiste (O.B. Units), chomh maith le foireann scannán agus dream léiritheoirí, a chur ar fáil do na grúpaí áitiúla seo. Ar ndóigh, tá sé le tuiscint ó thús gur faoi stiúr agus faoi cheannas áitiúil a bheadh an t-iomlán i ngach áit acu. An cuspóir a bheadh acu, tá sé an-simplí: cláracha (idir caidrimh agus teagaisc) a chur ar fáil do mhuintir na Gaeltachta, de réir mar a thograíonn siad féin.

I dtosach na scéime seo ní cóir go mbeadh sé ar an fhoireann léiriúcháin seirbhís iomlán a chur ar fáil. Bheadh sé níos fearr sampla na Danmhairge a ghlacadh agus cupla uair sa tseachtain a chur ar fáil—ach iad bheith go maith. Sé an rud is mó tábhacht ná bealach faoi leith do muintir na Gaeltachta—Bealach na Gaeltachta—bheith ag RTÉ agus na cláracha a bheith ceangailte go ciallmhar le craoladh an ghnáth-Bhealach, mar shampla:

| An Mháirt | | An Aoine | |
|---|---|---|---|
| Gaeltacht | RTE | Gaeltacht | RTE |
| 8.15 | | Cúrsaí Reatha | Cúrsaí Reatha |
| 8.45 Nuacht | Nuacht | Nuacht | Nuacht |
| 9.00 Clár Caidrimh | — | Clár Ceoil agus Caidrimh (uair a chloig) | — |
| 9.30 Clár Teagaisc | — | | Clár Ceoil agus Caidrimh |

Is léir ón sceideal seo go mbaineann an Mháirt le fadhbanna agus cúspoirí mhuintir na Gaeltachta amháin. Dé hAoine bheadh an sceideal ag plé le cúrsaí reatha agus cúirsaí caidrimh—agus bheadh uair is cúig neomat déag de sin ar fáil ag an gnáthbhealach, ó 1.75 uair i niomlán.

Níl amhras ar bith ach go dtabharfadh na huaireanta úd an-spreagadh do na Gaeltachta ach taobh amuigh de sin bheadh buntáistí faoi leith

## CHAPTER 5: DROCH-BHOLADH SA TIGH AGAINN

ag gabháil, ní amháin do lucht léiriúcháin RTÉ, ach do shaol cultúrtha an náisiúin.

Ar an gcéad dul síos thabharfadh an córas nua caoi do léiritheoirí bheith ag triall modhanna nua ar chláracha 'beo' telefíse do dhéanamh—agus bheadh smaointe nua ag fás on gcóras féin. Toisc nach mbeadh aon mhaith bheith ag braith ar sceideal foirmiúil ó Bhaile Átha Cliath, is ar na léiritheoirí agus muintir na háite a bheadh na cláracha ag braith. Is léir go mba ionaid chultúrtha na hionaid nua sar i bhfad. Cuir i gcás, dá mbeadh a fhios ag muintir Ros Guill go mbeadh foireann RTÉ ag freastal go rialta ar an ionaid áitiúil is gairid go mbeadh ceóltoirí, filí, lucht drámaíochta agus eagraíochtaí éagsúla ag lorg am craolta. Ba mhaith an mhaise ansin an riaradh aitiúil.

Creidimid go bhfásfadh stiúradh daonlathach den tsort seo go nádúrtha sa Gaeltacht. Creidimid chomh maith nárb fhada go mbeadh muintir na hÉireann i gcoitinne ag cur ceist orthu féin, 'cén fáth nach bhfuil a leithéid againn sa tseirbhís náisiúinta' ? Creidimid go bhfuil slánú RTÉ fite-fuaite le slánú na Gaeilge ar RTÉ agus go bhfuil slánú na Gaeilge ag braith ar mhuintir na Gaeltachta.

# 6

## TWO NOTIONS OF AUTHORITY
## POWER AND SERVICE

## CHAPTER 6: TWO NOTIONS OF AUTHORITY

*'Off with their heads'*, said the Queen.
—LEWIS CARROLL

*'Do not lord it over them, as the Gentiles do.'*
—JESUS CHRIST

*The real political problem* of our contemporary world is that of the meaning of authority. During our long negotiations with the Director-General it gradually became evident that he and his management-echelon were convinced that, since we had constantly opposed his notion of authority, we must necessarily have an anti-authoritarian bias or even an 'artistic tendency to anarchy'. *What we had in fact was a deep need of authority.* There has never been any real authority. Our need was for this authority above us to be rationally exercised and, where necessary to our work, to be delegated to us. Our real experience was the constant weight of unintelligible power-structures. When this became clear, Jack Dowling in collaboration with Lelia Doolan wrote a fairly long memorandum to the Director-General on 'Two Notions of Authority', with a view to showing him that the Producers were not anti-authoritarian anarchists. They had, in fact, as clear and effective a notion of authority as he, but comprehensive enough, we suggest, to transcend his and include it. What follows is based on that memorandum.

There is one notion of authority which we might call 'authority as power' and this, we believe, is what dominates the mind of the Director-General. There is another notion, of 'authority as service', which we think ought to prevail.

Power, in human affairs, is the ability to coerce. Authority includes a right to obedience, but this should be seen as an intelligent persuasion of subordinates rather than an 'authoritarian organisation', as

Mr. Hardiman put it repeatedly. Power appears clearly in despotism, authority in familial affection. Thus, parents use their authority, out of love, in order gradually to free their children from dependence on the family structure, which supports their immaturity. Authority, in this sense, withdraws as it succeeds in its subtle work. In broadcasting this, of course, is necessary during training. The object of this use of authority is to develop the broadcaster's powers of independent judgment and responsibility.

The proper instrument of power is the will and its criterion of success is, simply, compliance. The proper instrument of authority is persuasive intelligence and its criterion of success is intelligent assent to the evidence.

It is a cynical commonplace that we lean nothing from history, yet it is plain that power alone as an instrument of social order has produced systems of human petrifacts. The resentments that remain unseduced or unintimidated are harmlessly relieved by recurring outbursts of petulant rebellion. These need not result in an overthrow of the system of power. They can be isolated by ridicule, written off as neurotic or paranoiac. Ultimately, if necessary, they can be reduced to silence by unemployment, incomprehension or, in the extreme case, by the police. Fortunately, this is not yet the case in Ireland. In justice, we owe it to our late superiors to say that none of these sanctions, except incomprehension, was ever employed in RTE. We have almost always been treated with the greatest gentleness and courtesy.

The opposite of all this is government by debate, by dialogue, by generous and candid information exchanged among moral and social equals, by the provision of alternatives for intelligent choice and human use, *by participation in decisions* and mutual solicitation of initiatives and by intellectual persuasion. These are the formative factors in the making of a disenchanted, fully adult world.

'The creation of the world, that is to say the world of *civilised* order, is the victory of persuasion over force'.[80]

RTE is a technologically organised and managed cultural enterprise. Unfortunately, our modern technological culture tends to reject the notion of moral authority. It has substituted for it the concept of legal power. This derives from the notion of law as originating in the *will* of the governor. For the jurists of the middle ages the idea that law resides merely in the will of the governor was the very principle of moral anarchy; in this sense, we still speak to-day of arbitrary power. However, partly because of its mechanical simplicity, this idea has had a successful if inglorious history. It is so easily understood and so *apparently* reasonable and realistic.

The countervailing notion of law is that of an ordinance of reason. It is sad that this notion seems so difficult and so remote from the 'realistic' view of contemporary Ireland. We are so long accustomed to being treated as cultural minors that it is hard to get people to believe that another concept of authority might actually work. We have been conditioned by a poisoned philosophical tradition, unawares.

Still, there is a general consciousness that something is really wrong about the exercise of authority in our world. Perhaps we can hope to communicate something of what we mean to readers who are already at least vaguely disturbed.

The trouble is that even if we agree that authority, properly understood, is a moral and persuasive force, we must, if we are to avoid confusion, make a further distinction. There is one kind of moral authority which is aimed at guiding others to the goal of their life and work; we can call this *authoritarian paternalism*. There is another

---

80   1. Adventures of Ideas, A. N. Whitehead. Cambridge Press; First Edition edition (1933)

kind of moral authority which is available to others as a service - contribution to a common work. This work is always something to be done corporately by morally adult and intelligent equals who are only 'hierarchically'[81] unequal. This is co-operative democracy. It is equally or, perhaps, more strictly authoritarian than the first kind of authority. The first is weighted with power; the second is enlightened by civic friendship.

'Paternalism' is not necessarily a dirty word. It always involves the substitution of the will of the superior for the intelligence of the subordinate, because of some impediment to the use of intelligence by the subordinate. But this is not always a bad thing. It is vital in this debate, which involves Trade-Unionists, teenagers and farmers, student-power movements, politically enfranchised peoples, teachers, civil servants and workers in the 'mass' media, that this point should be made quite clear. Paternalism is often a duty and therefore a moral good.

It is a grave obligation on the part of the superior to provide paternal moral authority where the circumstances require it. These seem to be of two kinds: (1) circumstances of intellectual and moral *defect* in the dependent person, and (2) circumstances of *immaturity* in the subordinate person. In these closely circumscribed situations, the substitution of the mature judgment of one man for another's lack of it is a proper and necessary work. It creates, also, a moral obligation to obedience.

Let us first take an extreme example in order to isolate the essence of paternalist authority. The mentally ill must be guided in this paternalistic

---

81  By 'hierarchically unequal' we mean that there is a real subalternation of function that does not deny but fosters the essential value of *personal* equality and that this personal equality is relevant and *engaged in the structures, initiatives and decisions* of the hierarchy. The notions of authority elaborated in and about Vatican Council II and its consequences for the theory of Church government did not abolish hierarchical status; it vitalised it. The Church, with many convulsions and set-backs, is far ahead of civil society in this area of thought.

fashion. A consensus of lunatics is an unstable guide to common action or personal decision. But their personal and common good remains inviolable. The mature man in authority may not rule them in order to do his own will but rather to substitute his will for their defective insight into their own good. This is dangerous and delicate work. Society watches anxiously over the competence and evidence of 'good-will' of the authorities who exercise it. This kind of paternalism has no part to play in a sophisticated organisation like RTE. The methods of recruiting staff and the requirements of the work preclude the employment of such. The average standard of intelligence in RTE we believe to be quite extraordinarily high.

It is equally necessary that the expert, in any field having immediate human effects, ought to be obeyed in the very line of his expertise. A man may not put aside the advice of his doctor and substitute his own judgment in a matter affecting his health or that of his family. The layman will always be as a child in relation to his doctor. This is to say that he is dependent upon the doctor's special *authority*. The patient is not dependent upon being able to see the technical foundations of his doctor's skill. It is, perhaps, more difficult in our tradition to see that we are equally dependent on the special authority of the engineer or the carpenter. The ethically important thing, however, is this: substitutional authority of this kind, however paternally exercised, is always an acknowledgment of an unavoidable failure to set up an adequate relationship. It must always aim at removing the need for this substitution, otherwise it is an inhuman cynicism. It would constitute a destructive dependence in a 'mysteriously' sacred area of personal life—an area which is defined by independence. Such an induced dependence is not merely evil; it is literally monstrous.

Another, and at least equally important, substitution of authority is needed where the subordinate has no inherent or intrinsic defect but does suffer the consequences of his proper human condition. The child is not a defective man; to treat him as if he were is immoral. His immaturity demands the service of paternal authority *in order to mature*. This is to say that the function of this kind of authority is to abolish itself. If it should continue after maturity it is tyranny. If it should fail to be available during immaturity it is an injustice.

Neither of these two concepts of substitutional or paternalist authority is of the *essence* of authority. They are merely contrived devices; in the first case it fills in the fissures in a broken humanity. In the second, authority is used to support, with the delicacy of civic friendship, the insufficiency of those who, in order to be fully human, must grow and be cultured by the society which, having given them life, has the duty to nurture it. The aim of this latter exercise of authority, even though it be paternalist and substitutional, is the creation of a superabundance of the goodness of the common work. This will spill over to the enrichment of the individual member. It will enlarge his humanity and introduce new dimensions of vision and action into the working-out of his adult autonomy. It is one of the most beautiful of the fruits of social life. Its aim is to create a society of true adults. An organisation like RTE, devoted to the common good, cannot give this increase to our people if it cannot give it to itself. In all this Mr. Hardiman has more to learn from his subordinates than to give them. Paternalism, then, has its uses. Our contention is that it does not exhaust the meaning of authority; indeed, that it is not authority in its essential and proper sense. We must, then, return to our notion of *authority as service*.

To begin with a nominal definition:

> True authority in its essence is a **fallible** principle of intelligent decision in matters not determinable by objective evidence. Its normal means is a tacit

consensus. It is exercised as a service contributed by the superior to the primary agents of production in the common work.

In this use of authority, even if the superior has greater power than his subordinate, and a lesser degree of insight and wisdom, it is still intelligence which is the determining factor in decision. The superior's intellectual contribution to the common work derives from his awareness of the value of the intellectual consensus and from an intelligent and unfeigned recognition of the human 'mystery' of his subordinate's inviolability of judgment, even where he disagrees with it.

Broadly speaking, authority of any kind is necessary because, in man's judgments about particular practical affairs, there is no possible principle of infallibility. Leaving aside for the moment the problems of the role of a perverse will in these matters, that is to say, assuming that everyone is well-disposed to do what is good and right, authority in its most proper sense would still be necessary.

The basis of the need for authority in the full and free sense is the fallibility of human judgments in all matters where the evidence *for what ought to be done in particular cases* is never objectively clear. Consequently, the intellect cannot be forced by the evidence. It requires some means, additional to the evidence, to determine the decision. This is the principle of authority; it is not a claim to infallible truth or insight. It is a claim, however, to an infallible moral *rectitude*. By this we mean that even if it should turn out to be objectively wrong it is absolutely right, morally.

An example may be helpful: if I judge that I should now lead this blind man across the road and as I do so he is struck by a car driven by a drunken driver, my moral judgment was infallibly right, notwithstanding its consequences. It is only an apparent paradox to say that while it may be objectively wrong in its practical effects, the principle of authoritative decision is infallibly right in its *moral function*.

The practical judgment differs radically from the speculative judgment. The speculative judgment bears, not on what ought to be done in particular circumstances, but rather on the objective evidence to which, it claims, all unbiased intellects may be expected to assent. That the square on the hypotenuse of any triangle is equal to the sum of the squares on the other two sides, is coercive, in its objective evidence, to all unbiased intellects working within the limits of Euclidean geometry. Practical judgments are *never* of this kind. There is no evidence which will coerce the unbiased intellect in this way.

There are, of course, purely speculative judgments *about* practical matters but these are few, general and simple. They are the principles of ethics. For example: 'The good ought to be done and evil avoided'. These allow reason a great and useful role. They are necessary in guiding us through the welter of particular matters which clamour and solicit the human will in trying to decide what is right and good in singular and unrepeatable circumstances. But they do not and cannot coerce the intelligence to judge with certainty. It cannot be absolutely certain of what it ought to judge as appropriate here and now. Who is to say, and on what absolute evidence, what is good in these particular circumstances? If a man judges how he should act, then (having taken into account everything that *can* be taken into account), he must judge in full knowledge that he may be objectively wrong. But here and now he can do no other; *and he ought and must do it.* He acts, not out of any claim to an objective infallibility but out of that moral authority to act in situations of partial obscurity, which men call conscience. *This is a principle of absolute rectitude.* If its practical outcome is good, the act is evidently virtuous. If its outcome is evil, the act is equally virtuous.[82]

In matters of great moment such a man's condition may be pathetic or even tragic, but it is morally impeccable. This is so because he has acted infallibly in the line of moral obligation. This centre of *moral* infallibility is the core of man's humanity and it is inviolable. To invade it by an 'authority' that is a mere claim to legal power is an inhuman arrogance. To entrust a man with its exercise and then invade his exercise of it, unsolicited, is an outrage.

This has been the basis of our disagreements within Irish television. It was only when our superiors in RTE saw clearly that this was what we were claiming that they were moved to 'short-circuit' our efforts and quickly supply an alternative. Their alternative was to provide an organisation of 'vertical' power-structures suitable to the administration of a private-enterprise factory. The real nature of this organisation is revealed in the Director-General's 'apologia' issued after our resignations.[83] He asserted that the organisation was 'programme-orientated' and, *at the same time*, that all the divisions were of equal importance! Fatuousness is only the defence of the absurd. Our superiors never really saw the philosophical foundations of our position. We hope that it is not arrogant to say so; but the alternative is too uncharitable to be plausible.

\* \* \*

---

82   Conscience is formed by and acts out of the virtue of daring and not from caution or from calculation. The name of this principle of daring is prudence. What an irony it is that this word prudence has come to mean almost its diametrically opposite vice, pusillanimity!

83   Published in the national daily newspapers on 31st May 1969 and circulated to RTÉ staff; see Appendix III

None of this is an argument against authority; in fact, it is an argument for it. We have suggested that the true notion of authority that is valid, simply speaking, is the concept of authority as a service. It is evident from what we have said in the preceding paragraphs that this service is necessary. Mature and reasonable men and women of good will, sincerely attempting to orientate their practical judgments in the line of their professional work, may have genuine grounds for doubt whenever the evidence is not objectively coercive. It seldom is, except in the simplest cases. By coercive we mean demanding assent without even the possibility of things being otherwise.

It is morally certain to men of good will, for example, that an attack on the personal honour of an individual on a television programme is ethically inadmissible. It is equally evident that the duty to reveal the truth of a conspiracy to defraud or deceive the public, in which the public authorities are negligent or even quiescent, creates an obligation to reveal it. Television or radio programmes are not Courts of Law, nor are they police instruments. Like newspapers, however (or indeed like private citizens), they have rights and duties to inform the commonwealth. The situation must be revealed, but it may destroy the reputation of a man who, not yet having been judged in law, has the right to a presumption of innocence. What is the television Producer to do? No coercive moral criterion can be applied to his judgment.

Is he therefore to say that he has no duty? Only a cynically facile theory would say so. An adult's duty is to act out of that very freedom which the non-objectivity of the evidence creates in him. This is why he is in need of authority and not mere power; he must be equipped with a moral right to make decisions that may be wrong, not simply an actual power to make objectively correct decisions. Such a useless power could not be exercised. This is a difficult doctrine because it runs counter to the whole drift of the post-renaissance moral culture, in which we are saturated.

We say that the adult man must decide. He must weigh his duty to the common good; this *includes* his duty to take into account the integrity of another's personal honour. It may be the Producer's duty to put this man's reputation at risk by establishing a *prima facie* case against him; it may not. There is no coercive evidence. There is only a free judgment made out of the virtue of prudence. The very exercise of this virtue involves the obligation to take counsel where the nature and consequences of the situation can be made less obscure by expert knowledge. A superior does not necessarily have this expertise; a lawyer or confessor may. Neither one has the responsibility. The superior in the *supportive nature* of his authority may have the ultimate accountability. The responsibility remains with the Producer as the adult agent of decision, until the burden of his conscience requires relief. The right to decide cannot be removed from him without injustice, since if he is not adult he should not have been entrusted with his task. If he is adult, his act of judgment is inalienably his own and only he can justly alienate it. If the weight of conscience is too much he must go to his superiors for authoritative relief. If he is grossly and repeatedly wrong when he does act out of his own judgment, he ought to be removed as being prudentially immature or deficient in judgment.

Men and women are not ethical abstractions or moral diagrams. Neither are they isolated individuals on the model of the liberal ethic. They act within, on behalf of, and with the support of the group of their peers.[84] Further, the burden of a prudential decision of the kind we have been discussing may be personally insupportable, not through

---

84   The peer group, in our philosophy of authority, will be all those contributing to the work to be done, including the 'hierarchically' structured line of those with accountability, but not exclusively.

failure of personal nerve, nor through limitation of insight. It may be insupportable because the personal decision, having been truly and responsibly made, may bear upon the corporate common good of the society and need to be sustained by its authority and power. No man needs support when he is objectively right, but when he is not. Authority and power are vested, in proportionate degrees, in *the whole* hierarchy of an institution's structures of authority. Ultimately, they are vested in the highest executive authority *as to accountability.* In a fully adult society, an individual television or radio Producer may (indeed often must) seek that supportive authority as a *necessary service.*

This seeking will not then be an act of moral infantilism but of moral maturity. The giving of it by the superior will not depend on his agreement with it but upon the authority with which he supports his subordinate's right to make it.

This is a hard saying and who can hear it?

We have been speaking of the superior's role as a moral service to his adult subordinate in a job which, by its very specification, bestows a right and duty of executive decision. The Broadcasting Authority has the legal right under the Act to appoint officers and servants. Television and radio Producers are senior officers, not merely servants of this Authority. Their function is, in its last analysis, a decision-making one. It is never, in its essence, a mere servant-role. This has been at the heart of our disagreement with the Director-General and his immediate executive staff. They could not or would not see this.

In our view, much of the student unrest, industrial 'wild cat' strikes, farmers' obstructive petulance and non-co-operation, adolescent truculence, housing action committee and civil rights movements' street politics and revolts, State bodies' discontents, all have similar origins. More seriously, the gradual corrosion of popular confidence in civil government within the democracies have the same inchoate set of common causes. The problem is as old as the Greeks: what is the ultimate metaphysical basis of the right of one fallible man to impose his will upon other responsible adults in a common task? To say in an era of almost universal moral adulthood that it rests on the democratic *origin* of his appointment will no longer hold as being sufficient. If its *very mode of operation* cannot be democratised and humanised, politically and socially man's faith in democratic order will break down. Despair in the workability of civil order will replace that political optimism of Western man that has sustained our culture in its slow growth from Athens, through Jerusalem, to the United Nations. Our Western crisis of authority is only the crisis of our almost universal culture. Our experience in RTE is exactly the same, but worked out in its local sharpness of focus and immediacy of human contact. Each side could feel the hurt and bewilderment of the other. We each face the other, not in malice, thank God, but in uncomprehending dismay.

* * *

It is not a foregone conclusion that a growing subtlety of intelligence will win through to a social structure of greater and more sensitive insights. Failure of the human experiment in corporate growth is attendant upon every crisis. Crisis and not a nineteenth century evolutionary development is the characteristic of human history.

We have treated of the substitutional authority of paternalism both in the sense of substituting the will of the superior for the immaturity of the subordinate and in the sense of making up for the inabilities of the mentally or morally defective to work out their own good. We have treated of authority as a 'service' to the morally adult in a common work. We should like to conclude this complex chapter by developing an important corollary to this latter mode. This is the notion of delegation of authority by means of the notion of subsidiarity. This was first developed by Leo XIII in the late 19th century, but has remained largely dormant until our time.

It may be formulated as the general principle:

> Whatever function in the body-politic *can* be carried out by a subsidiary group or individual *ought* to be discharged by it. The common life will then be enriched, and participation deepened, by growing responsibility and involvement.

This has obvious consequences for the ideas we hold on the problems of the delegation of power and responsibility. Like authority itself (but unlike mere power) delegation is a proportionate concept. This is to say that it posits a structure of proportional responsibility. It is not a levelling equality, meagrely shared out. It is *truly* hierarchical in that it produces organically related and economically necessary structures of decision-making. These are initiative-evoking centres of energy, vested in people with special insights of intelligence and imagination.

The degrees of responsibility delegated to these structures will be effective and creative in exact proportion as the superior divests *himself* of these responsibilities and, in turn, accepts accountability for them to his own superiors. This concept of delegation is a far cry from delegation of the superior's own power as a mechanic of 'load-shedding'. The essence of this new kind of administrative maturity is a growth in moral intensity and clarity of insight. Organically related social structures are an orchestration of centres of creativity. Their *raison d'etre* is not merely intelligence as such; it is the *diversification of intelligence*. Liberty and responsibility contribute this diversity to the common good as its freshest flower and most vital hope.

## CHAPTER 6: TWO NOTIONS OF AUTHORITY

If delegation is a compromise with purely quantitative demands on limited energy and time; that is to say, if work is delegated simply because its sheer quantity and complexity cannot be borne by one man, the *limitation* of authority will tend to be regarded as being equally important with the practice of it. In industrial history the desire for job satisfaction, the need of prestige, the realisation of individual ambition, resulted in delegation by internal power-struggles, the outcome of which had a purely utilitarian value. The 'victor' (whether superior or subordinate) was inflated, not enriched. The organisation, of course, gained by this forced diversification. Its flexibility increased in its management structures but the souls of the worker-echelons were further and further alienated from the common purpose by the 'disciplines' and by the taylorisation[85] of their contributions to it. The workers 'defence' organisations grew in power and, also, increased their bureaucratic efficiency. The Trade Unions engaged in the power-struggle to the point of open class-war. This presented these power-structures, capital and labour, with a stark choice: mutual assimilation or mutual destruction. Both 'Western' capitalism and 'Eastern' socialism now tend to technological assimilation.

The strong subordinate manager tended in the past to fight for his limited autonomy; the weak manager with an instinct for survival held his place and improved it in strict proportion to his success in predicting and anticipating the will of his superior and in 'keeping his files straight'.

Now in more sophisticated times, technical training in 'management sciences' as internalised conditioning factors, has replaced the older idea of extrinsic legal limitation on the exercise of subordinate

---

85  A system of rationalising work introduced by an efficiency expert of that name: Fredrick Winslow Taylor- known to his contemporaries as 'Speedy' Taylor because he was the father of time-and-motion study.

power. Both of these devices suffer the same defect: they are inhuman and impoverishing concepts of delegation. What they delegate is not authority but power. They do this only on a quantitative basis and upon a purely utilitarian motivation.

In our own time, the *notion* (but not yet the *structures*) of the delegation of authority, as a means of enrichment and personal growth, is emerging to meet the demands for a humanisation of work. In this view of delegation, the superior shares his authority in order to increase it; not out of fear of losing it, by being quantitatively unable to exercise it. The real bestowal of moral authority on subordinates is a recognition of the social and cultural maturity of men and women serving one another in a common task. Within the structures created by this philosophy, delegation to subsidiary groups and persons will be sought by the superior in all its plenitude. It will not have limits 'built in' but new roles of responsibility and creativity filled out. It's ideal is a complete autonomy of action, proportionate to his function, for the mature subordinate.

This concept of authority, as against the 'vertical' concept of power, will entail a confident acceptance by the superior of responsibility for his subordinate's independent and often dissident judgments. Its means will be a system of candid consultation in non-coercive mutual aid. The authority ultimately vested in the chief executive will be available to his subordinates in order to support and develop their independence of judgment and to relieve, in extraordinary cases, the burden of personal conscience.[86]

---

86 The relationship of the broadcaster to the common good, like that of the soldier, the policeman or the politician, is direct and immediate. The discipline of the policeman or the soldier may not be used to require him to injure the common good. This is not the greatest good of the greatest number; it is not the good that is identical with that of each member of the community *de facto*. It is the good life that is brought into

This is the view of authority which we have claimed for our colleagues in the Programmes Division of Irish television. This is the view which we have urged in negotiation, in daily action and in writing. This is the view which Mr. Hardiman and his administrators have steadily blocked, frustrated and obscured.

The result, in our view, is that the national broadcasting service, in its internal affairs, is now in a torpor. If it is not moved it will ossify, become a technological 'neutrality' and will fall, in its use, to the highest bidders, political or commercial. Its cultural functions will cease. The loss will not be internal merely. Radio and television were intended by the Irish community to help it grow. Authority in our sense, we believe, can promote this growth; power will stultify it.

---

existence as a unique *common work* by the fact of the community's living together in a common culture.

# 7

## THE SWEET RACKET
## ADVERTISING AND THE 'MASS'

*It's a sweet racket if ya can keep the boys in line.*
—AL CAPONE

*The mountain sheep are sweeter
But the valley sheep are fatter;
We therefore deemed it meeter
To carry off the latter.*
—THOMAS LOVE PEACOCK

*The productive power of our industry threatens to make our culture subordinate to our economy. More goods and services may lead to a tremendous pressure upon the consumer to adopt more and more luxurious living standards for the sake of keeping the economy healthy.*
—REINHOLD NIEBUHR

*Gee, just thinka what God coulda done if only He had the dough.*
—SCHNOZZLE DURANTE

Who wants advertising? The answer is clear. The advertisers and their agents want it. What have they to say for it? They are, perhaps, badly served in their quotable spokesmen. What they have written, so far as we have been able to gain access to it, seems to us even more astonishing and alarming than what they do. In his now famous *The Strategy of Desire*,[87] Ernest Dichter, President of the Institute for Motivational Research wrote:

---

[87] The Strategy of Desire, Ernest Dichter, Martino Fine Books 2012

> We are now confronted with the problem of permitting the average American to feel moral even when he is flirting, even when he is spending, even when he is not saving, even when he is taking two vacations a year and buying a second or third car.

What kind of 'average' is this American? There are no less than 27 million Americans living below the poverty line.

* * *

Again:

> One of the basic problems of this prosperity, then, is to give people the sanction and justification to enjoy it and to demonstrate that the hedonistic approach to his life is a moral, not an immoral, one. This permission given to the consumer to enjoy his life freely, the demonstration that he is right in surrounding himself with products that enrich his life and give him pleasure, must be one of the central themes of every advertising display and sales promotion plan.

The theological implications are equally clear to Mr. Dichter.

> There is no irony or at least no cheap sarcasm intended by our putting it like this. If the Christian ethic is to survive into the age of technology, it must soberly appraise the implications of the endless acceleration of consumption of goods that advertising postulates as necessary to keep the wheels of technology going. It

'necessitates abandoning the concept that man is born and made to suffer and to live by the sweat of his brow. The concept of original sin and the humility of man is a dangerous one. It may be a prerequisite for maintaining his dependency on father-like figures in the religious and political sense. But if we believe in the final goal of human maturity, it will have to give way to a new insight, the insight that man is only at the beginning of his potentialities, that the more he becomes independently (*sic*) free of superstition and crutches of all kinds, the more he will indeed be fulfilling his final destiny of being in the image of God'.

The Irish reader may feel that this is so incredible that we might well be suspected of making it up. At best it is, perhaps, not representative of the real views of Irish advertisers. One hopes that it is not. Yet the logic of the theory of the consumer-technology leads ineluctably to this extraordinary view, not only of human maturity as self-indulgence without 'superstitious' restraint, but to a 'god' as The Great Consumer and man as his image. Undoubtedly Irish advertisers would sincerely feel that Mr. Dichter was going too far. They, like most decent men, would draw the line long before this. What we would like to know is: where do they draw it to-day? Where would they draw it tomorrow? Even if they could tell us, we must still ask them the really vital question: By virtue of *what principle* would they draw it at all?

Mr. Kevin McCourt has expressed views on this.

We believe that once the notion of consumption-stimulation is admitted being necessary to the growth, in Mr. McCourt's sense[88], of the technologically organised economy, there is no *built-in* principle of limitation. Only a pragmatic judgment can be made: a period of 'controlled inflation' is followed by a credit squeeze. Each phase calls forth fresh advertising efforts: the inflationary period demands advertising in order to further stimulate the economy; the deflationary period requires advertising in order to overcome the effects of the credit squeeze. No arbitrary limitation on the volume or nature of advertising is possible because the system of production demands a limitless consumption and waste.

For example, the editor of the American business journal, *Sales Management*, wrote in 1960:

> If we Americans are to buy and consume everything that automated manufacture, sock-o selling, and all-out-advertising can thrust upon us, each of our mounting millions must have extra ears and eyes and other senses—as well as extra income. Indeed, the only sure way to meet all the demands may be to create a brand new breed of super customers.

---

[88] Mr. Kevin C. McCourt (es-Director-General of RTE) in an address to Advertising Press Club, 7th November 1968, pointed out that 'whatever was to be achieved for Ireland and its people could no longer be secured by prayer alone. The high protective policies of the 30's, 40's and 50's, if they were the means whereby industry attained growth, were also the cause of our being a production-oriented rather than a market-oriented society'

He added: 'Advertising is part of the cost of selling. Total advertising expenditure in the Republic now exceeds £8 millions.' We would add that in a reasonable human society, its economic efforts *should* be orientated to the production of necessary goods and not to a 'marketing system' characterised, on Mr. McCourt's own suggestion by a waste by dissipation of £1.6 millions per year (*The Irish Times*, 8th November 1668). £8 millions would provide piped water and sewage to 200,000 Irish homes and farms.

## CHAPTER 7: THE SWEET RACKET

They have done so. Consumption, of course, included making up, using and replacing war-material, human lives, space and missile research. It has worked, and the 'super customer' is with us.

2,000 millions of his fellow humans live in destitution, but they have done it! They are on the moon and there are more cars than families in the U.S. Also, the American way of life is now for export.

Vance Packard, quoting this journal, comments:

> Consumption must rise, and keep rising. Some marketing experts have been announcing that the average citizen will have to step up his buying by nearly fifty per cent in the next dozen years, or the economy will sicken.

Some of us think that a system of values that allows 17 per cent, of the world's population to consume 40 per cent of its primary products is already sick. We feel it reasonable to assume that to double this consumption will make it sicker. Of course, we are aware that the Irish consumer or advertiser is still a far cry from this level of behaviour. But the signs of new attitudes are gently evident.[89] What does concern us are the two facts: (1) that our economy is dependent on the British and

---

89   The Irish Times, 18th July 1969:
Mr. P. Finn, director of Five Star Supermarkets Ltd., returned yesterday
from the United States after a three-week fact-finding visit during which he examined the most advanced supermarket and shopping centre operations with a view to incorporating these in future super-markets which Five Star plans to open.
Not surprisingly Mr. Finn's Managing Director appeared in Cork and delivered the following gem to the Press: *(Cork Examiner,* 18th July, 1969):
Mr. Michael Williams, managing director of Five Star, the retail division of the Williams group of Tullamore, with whom I visited the site commented: 'we feel it is an ideal location within the centre of a new housing complex. It is probable that this idea of driving to a shopping centre and shopping within the services provided will take a little time to grow on the consumer in Cork. Therefore, we will have to make a greater effort in advertising and promotion within the area, at least at the beginning until the consumer becomes accustomed to this form of shopping'.

that (2) a U.S. economy that must increase its consumption by nearly 50 per cent to remain viable will use its productive and financial might to include both the British and our own people in this gormandising of world resources. The aim will be, not to increase the quality of life, but the range and level of profitable investment. The logic of technological production for profit is already with us. What, do we really believe, can hold its inevitable dialectical development in check? Who is going to cry 'stop' and why? What, in the human spirit, can possibly survive this orgy of consumption-amid-want?

* * *

We in Ireland are still largely a primary producing country, attempting to convert to an industrial economy, mainly on a profit-motive basis. Our small-farm social structure has been condemned to death. Industrialisation will require us, increasingly, to stimulate demand. To accumulate the necessary capital, we must save. These are contradictory aims. The contradiction, apparently, impresses nobody.

Was Denis Johnston right: does the Irish mind really inhabit 'cloud-cuckoo-land'?

Even if this contradictory policy were possible of implementation, it would have to survive our entry into the EEC. If this happens, and even if graduated checks on economic inundation from Europe were successful, it is surely likely that our semi-State broadcasting services will be used extensively to advertise European goods, to the detriment of our own. Industrial competition from mammoth EEC Corporations will be met, according to this mercantile theory, not merely by native efficiency but by hard, advertised selling-campaigns.

---

What the 'consumer' may fail to realise is that a phrase like 'until the consumer becomes accustomed' is a euphemism for 'until the consumer becomes *conditioned by advertising*'. This is a far cry from the notion of advertising as information.

Are the ethics of this dilemma to be dismissed as irrelevant because their consideration would lead us to unprofitable conclusions? Is it now self-evident that we must sensibly have the best of the worst of all worlds?

We do not say that these are insuperable difficulties. We do say that if we do not begin to think seriously about them and their cultural consequences, they may well remove from our people any real reason or desire for a separate identity. Perhaps we Irish no longer think this a serious price to pay for a smaller but richer population? It is difficult for us to believe that the Irish people would think so in its present mood, if they fully realised the facts. Radio and television should be concerned that every possible means is used to give them a realisation of the truth. Our experience is that advertising (and programming set up in an advertising frame-work) will not do this. Advertisers are not concerned with truth but with profit.

What are the cultural consequences?

What does radio and television advertising achieve and what does it not achieve?

First, 'mass'-media advertising does *not* have the effect of an information announcement. This kind of function is a valuable social service and it is still largely the purpose of newspaper 'classified* advertising. It is not common on radio or television because they are too expensive for the dissemination of 'one off' pieces of information. By 'one off' we mean a single insertion.

Second, persuasion is a process of intellectual and emotional illumination by evidence. Radio and television advertising is not persuasion in any but a Pickwickian sense. Real persuasion might well be a public service. One has seen, for example, a useful campaign for road-safety or public health being conducted in this way. In our view, however, certain limitations on the use of the media even for these laudable purposes are necessary.

Third, repetition used to the point where the intellect is blunted in its critical powers, and the will is pulverised through exhaustion, is evil even if the purpose is the promotion of the public good.

Fourth, coercive modern persuasion techniques are based on two factors:

a. Repetition, endless and emotion-evoking, in principle.
b. The removal of those accustomed intellectual and emotional contextual supports and values which constitute our identity.

Totalitarian 'brainwashing' and 'third degree' methods are, we understand, based on these. Of course, the advertising method is much more refined. It takes careful account of existing cultural prejudices. It has, however, one enormous advantage over political 'brainwashing': it does not have to concern itself with any serious ideological message. It is not bothered about being *believed*; it only seeks to be *effective*. Nobody is seriously asked to believe that a washing-powder can make his shirt 'whiter than white'.

The advertising designers are concerned with the conditioned reflex responses that will be made at the point of sale. Intellectual convictions about the claims of the product are irrelevant. The whole conceptual process is virtually side-stepped; the emotions of envy, guilt, fear and sexuality are associated with the brand image. These are sufficient to activate a purchase-response. This is sub-human in a grave sense.

It is not, however, the most serious result of advertising methods. The debasement of language itself as a means of intellectual communication has the effect of creating a new attitude to knowledge. Wisdom becomes 'instant information' packaged in adjectivally used 'nounclots', e.g. health-radiant, farm-fresh, whole-meal loaf. This use of language gradually destroys the propositional form of human discourse. It does not really propose anything to the intellect. It merely conditions the emotions. These determine the will —intellect rusts. The whole dimension of depth, of the necessarily tentative, the chastening modesty of unavoidable ignorance, the element of mystery, are all drained out of our language, our responses and our intellects. They are replaced by the immediately intelligible, universally acceptable and instantly available image. Human thought and even wisdom are no longer regarded as being difficult to acquire: they are assumed to be as 'instant' as a cup of patent coffee.

The fact that true human knowledge *is* difficult, partial and shot through with doubt, criticism and reservation, slips into the background. Thinking within these delicate areas becomes the prerogative of scientifically trained elites. The majority of ordinary decent people are left a prey to their desires and concupiscences.

The repetition of the inanities of advertisements would not, we suggest, be sufficient to launch them successfully into the conditioned reflex-arc. The surrounding context of people's convictions and emotions must be adjusted to receive them. This is done most powerfully on television where entertainment and information can convey a pattern of living and belief with sly effectiveness. True, this must not be done with such violence as to set up a consciousness of the dissonance between the image-world of programmes and the real world of life.

It is the real world that is increasingly capable of adjustment to close the gap. 'Wants', not needs, are created both by the advertising and by its programme context. Technology is benevolently available to deliver the goods.

Those who are too dispirited or too unambitious to be affected are regarded (and come to regard themselves) as misfits and drop-outs. A vast uniformity of demand, with a highly diversified system of supply, disguises the enormous dreariness of this consumer paradise. The 'weak' and the nauseated are left in their self-contempt. Nothing can be done for them. They can do nothing for themselves.

* * *

Is it only the moralist, the philosopher and the political crank who are concerned to introduce some critical element into the consideration of this consumer utopia? Surely not. The professional broadcaster is deeply concerned and alarmed, but most of our business contemporaries in Ireland seem to think that these are exaggerated predictions about a far distant future. For some reason that they have not yet been able to disclose, they seem convinced that these cassandra-like prophecies could not possibly apply to us. In any case, they seem to say, let's face it; these are the facts of contemporary life. The adult and mature man must learn to face them and live with them. The Irish people, we were recently told, wish to have a modern industrial standard of living; they cannot also enjoy a traditional Irish way of life. This may be true. It is surely permissible to ask whether the abandonment of the traditional must necessarily entail an acceptance of precisely the kind and degree of horror which we will face when 'satellite' international programming is constantly with us. Will this be advertising-free? Will we think it worth while to try providing an antidote or will we just join in a situation that is hopeless?

Do the Irish people really know the true nature of the choice that is being made for them? We doubt it. The plea that we must lose the integrity of our minds because we cannot afford the expense of saving them, is seldom expressly made. It is, however, generally assumed. It is also simply not true. We resigned from work we were dedicated to, in order to give witness to this simple obligation: that one of our professional colleagues had charged us all with corrupting the public mind; the charge deserved sincere investigation.

\* \* \*

Advertising pressure on programmes is something like submarine warfare. The aggressor is almost continually submerged, only infrequently does a depth charge such as that provided by *Home Truths* force him to surface. But, although submerged, advertisers can see clearly—their periscope, so to speak, is the TAM system.

The word TAM has now entered into common usage. As Mr. Dillon-Malone remarks[90] 'most people know that TAM stands for Television Audience Measurement'. It would, we submit, be more accurately described as Television Advertising Measurement. The matter can easily be resolved by asking what TAM is and what it is for. According to the same source TAM-rating is a 'purely quantitative measure of the numbers of people viewing'. Leaving aside the sheer aesthetic pleasure of numbers in the abstract, it seems reasonable to ask: who would want such a measurement? We find that three kinds of institution not only want these magic numbers but are even willing to pay for them; the clients, according to Mr. Dillon-Malone, are Radio Telefís Eireann itself, the advertising agencies, and the major advertisers. Simple arithmetic shows that two out of the three clients are selling. RTE sells programme time. The agencies sell skill. The advertisers buy time and skill. It is in another sense that they sell their goods. The implication of TAM publicity is, however, that RTE has a *programme* need for the number of 'thousands viewing' and that this dovetails with the advertisers' needs of 'cost per thousand viewers'.

---

90   The Language of TAM Ratings, Patrick Dillon-Malone, Director of Irish TAM Ltd.

According to TAM publicity the reports are used by RTE for a 'variety of purposes'. This is usually followed by instancing three such various purposes, presumably in the order of their importance.

Firstly, TAM is supposed to have the function of 'assessing the reach and relative popularity of different programmes'. Since the popularity function[91] is adequately discharged by the Audience Research Service of RTE, a cost-saving device presents itself. The suspicion that the first purpose is merely window-dressing is confirmed by the other two aims which are seen as 'proving the message-giving power of the medium to potential advertisers and determining the rates at which it is fair and reasonable to charge advertisers for going on the air at particular times of the day and of the week'.[92] In other words, since RTE does its own audience-reaction research, it must appear that TAM has no function but to tell advertisers what space to buy and to tell RTE how much it should charge. But this is evidently not so. It has the vital function of telling RTE what kind of programmes it must transmit and at what times—if it wants to stay in business. Its 'programme' function fails to move even Mr. Dillon-Malone to enthusiasm. 'TAM-ratings' he tells us, 'do not tell the whole story about television programme performance'. Mr. Fred Littman, head of Audience Research in RTE, puts the matter more succinctly:[93] 'Advertisers want to know how many listeners or viewers they are reaching. Hence, when selling time, a prime need is to have an agreed system for measuring the size of audience for the periods spot advertisements or sponsored programmes can be broadcast'.

---

91   We are not, of course, suggesting that there is no function for 'Audience Research' to assess numbers viewing; there is. The actual origin and role of TAM is our consideration here.

92   Dillon-Malone, *op. cit*

93   'Audience Research in Irish Broadcasting', Fred Littman, EBU Review, May 1968

The TAM system in fact, as its history shows, has from the beginning been a creature of commercial television. It grew up in Britain following the Television Act of 1954, which created a commercial television network. TAM's own brochure[94] admits that it was not created by the programme companies: 'right from the start of ITV, the *advertising* industry decided to create an industry service' (our italics). This 'industry service' was set up as a wholly owned subsidiary of a firm called United Broadcast Audience Research Limited. It is jointly owned by the Attwood Group and the A. C. Nielsen Company—two huge market research organisations. In 1961 TAM moved to Ireland to meet the needs of the Institute of Advertising Practitioners.

RTE, having signed a contract with Irish TAM, began to receive its reports in April 1962.

This, then, is the commercial basis of a system which began to regulate programming schedules. There is no need to spell out the endless ramifications of the TAM's system's effect on programming. Suffice it to say that programmers know that the cultural needs of the people must at certain times of the night give way to the logic of the ratings. The most sinister aspect is that the reasons for programme-scheduling decisions are unacknowledged; confronted by the real needs of the nation and the financial needs of the station, the programmers seek safety in numbers.

Mr. Littman writes:

> ... the cost of all forms of audience research is of the order of £60,000, more than half of this arising from the need for TAM's continuous measurement of television

---

94  *Made to Measure;* a Description of TAM, its Operation and its Service.

audiences to satisfy the advertisers who provide about half [1968] of RTE's total income.[95]

The notion whereby an instrument of selling gradually assumes the status of a programme-determinant leads inevitably to other misunderstandings; 'the ratings', as Mr. Dillon-Malone points out 'provide the television station and its advertising clients with *a common currency, a common language. As with any currency everything depends upon the trust and confidence of those who employ it*' (our italics).

As with any language, indeed! George Orwell must be laughing through his harp-strings.

Any pretence that these ratings do not affect the programme-makers' work is ridiculous, although Management continues to deceive itself that this is untrue. It supports its own self-deception by occasional acts of defiance. This bravery is a source of some amusement to the Producers who, like all professionals, know what makes their organisation tick.

Religious programmes have, for nearly five years, been trying to get more suitable viewing times. As one distinguished member of the Bishops' Interim Committee said to us, holding religious services at tea-time on a Sunday evening is not merely unedifying, it is downright embarrassing. Attempts to get Art programmes a regular 'slot' near the main News bulletin, two years ago, never came nearer than 11 p.m. Perhaps the most notorious of these scheduling struggles has been to get the only adult Public Affairs programme in Irish an adult audience. *Féach* (referred to in the chapter on Irish policy in RTE) has been a subject of dispute between Mr. Liam Ó Murchú and the Controller's office during the whole of last year's schedules and continues to be.

---

95   Mr. Hardiman's memorandum, 30th May 1969, shows this proportion to be 60 per cent.

Agricultural programmes, which could be regarded as vital in this country, were denied an extension of their programme time in the projected schedules for 1969/70, on the same basis.

In the planning and reviewing of schedules, Lelia Doolan had much experience of the immediate influence of TAM-ratings on the structure of the programme 'mix'. The Editorial Board, and the Heads of Department Group, of both of which she was a member, had a primary function in the planning of the schedule. It was her continual experience that proposals made on a purely programme basis were measured against 'audience-size' criteria (TAMs). At peak periods[96] they were sadly, and reluctantly, adjusted in the interest of securing popular—'mass'—audiences.

The fact is that programme people had come to a realisation of the limitations that would be imposed upon their ideas. Soon they ceased to have them. The consequence was, they lost the ever-present sense that they were being restricted at all. It is this kind of tacit acceptance of restrictions without the need for *anyone* to actually advert to them that made the system tolerable. So conditioned by this horizon of unuttered restriction have programme people, at all levels, become that we have heard some of our ex-colleagues hotly deny that they even existed. In fact, Jack Dowling was told that advertisers had not influenced the suppression of *Home Truths*! Both programme control and the Producers played the rules of the game. TAM was a cheerful umpire.

* * *

The meeting of our Trade Union branch which met to consider our resignations from RTE is in curiously sharp focus in our memories

---

[96] See Appendix II.

for many reasons. Not least, we remember it for one brief reference to advertising.

One of our colleagues asked, in evident sincerity and good faith, if our antipathy to advertising was not of very recent origin. The inference seemed plain: that our concern over Bob Quinn's 'attack' on the ad-men's influence on the station's cultural policy was not the *real* cause of our actions.

Of course, we did not believe it to be the only cause of the station's ills. Bob Quinn's case-history is one of working-class reaction to RTE's cultural pre-suppositions and assumptions. Lelia Doolan's and Jack Dowling's were certainly later than his and from a more complacent middle-class base. Jack Dowling's began in London in 1955 when he took up a business career on retiring from the Irish Army. Lelia Doolan's began after the Advertisers' Advisory Council had successfully muzzled RTE's family advisory programme, *Home Truths*, in 1966/67, with the concurrence of the Controller of Programmes.

\* \* \*

As early as February of 1967 Jack Dowling put a proposal in principle to the Controller of TV, Mr. Michael Garvey, for a study: a State monopoly of receiving-set manufacture, distribution and maintenance would, he thought, permit the station to finance itself without advertising.

The basis of this proposal for study was an attempt to reconcile two different sets of sentiment on the problems of financing monopoly broadcasting. Briefly, these were (1) fear of pressure and interference from advertisers and (2) fear of Government and Civil Service restriction.

One of these sentiments is centred on the fact that 60 per cent of the station's income is derived from advertising. Actual experience shows that business interests will always push their competitive advantage when possible. They will combine to their corporate advantage when necessary. The light entertainment programme *Noble Call*, for example, had to be taken off the air, without even notifying the Producer, because representatives of the liquor interests were actually found in the studio trying to entice floor staff to include their branded products in camera-shot. This effort was clumsy and it failed.

Jack Dowling's proposal was for a State control of the present radio and television manufacturing companies' activities, the hire of all receiving apparatus and its maintenance. This would mean that the Department of Posts and Telegraphs or the RTE Authority would directly manufacture radio and television equipment or licence its manufacture for a fee. The whole distribution of receiving sets would become the right of the Authority on a weekly or monthly hire basis only.[97] Their installation and maintenance would yield an income from the operating profit of this distribution monopoly, plus the present annual licence fees. To get the maximum return on this scheme it ought to be prepared in time for the introduction of colour television in 1972. The estimated yields at, say, ten shillings per week for television sets and, say, 2/6d. for radio sets could be considered on a model:

Assume a set count of:

| | |
|---|---|
| Estimated number of black and white television sets 500,000 at 10/- per week rental (weekly yield) | £250,000 |
| Estimated number of colour television sets 50,000 at 25/- per week rental (weekly yield) | £62,500 |
| Estimated number of radio sets 750,000 at 2/6d. per week rental (weekly yield) | £93,750 |
| **Total:** | £406,250 |

---

97   This is the system upon which Irish telephones are hired to subscribers. We are not allowed to buy our telephones. Why would we buy our colour television sets?

This would realise a total weekly yield of £406,250 or, annually, £21,125,000. A trading profit of 15 per cent, in this sum would replace the revenue from advertising with an income of £3,168,750. The licence fee by 1972 could certainly be reasonably set at £6 for combined radio/television and £2 for radio alone[98]. This would yield, having deducted collection charges of £300,000 an income of £3.5 millions and thus a total net income for broadcasting expenses and reserves of £6.5 millions.

This could be expected to grow with the expansion of colour television to a plateau of, say, 600,000 television and 800,000 radio sets. People could be expected to convert to colour television very much more readily if they could hire, rather than purchase it at £250 per set.

The problem of capital acquisition of existing hire and rental companies, in view of conversion to colour television, will present an unrepeatable opportunity between 1970 and 1975. The Authority could begin phasing-in this scheme for colour only. By 1975 monochrome could be included, residually. The rental companies need not be bought out until their returns make it uneconomic for them to continue in operation. They will, by then, have had a very nice innings. With sufficient warning, no injustice need be done.

Another method of financing broadcasting, of course, is to raise the licence fee to its economic level. This would, unfairly, have the effect of taxing those least able to afford it. By 1972 this might well be £10 per television set. Such a course, in our view, would be deplorable.

---

98   As we go to press we learn that the RTE Authority has made application to the Department of Posts and Telegraphs for an increase in the television licence fee. *The Irish Press* (10 September 1969) learned unofficially that the increase would be 'in terms of a 25s. increase from £5 to £6-5-0'. RTE's Annual Report (1969) and £2 (radio).

The poor and the dependent would bear the burden.[99] Further, this fee would only hold the quality of the service at its present level.

Direct total subsidy from central funds is certainly possible. Many people think it highly desirable on ethical grounds, but it seems to us that official sentiment would be strongly opposed to such a course at present. However, for what it is worth, we would wish to go on record as favouring this 'public service' method of financing an instrument of the national culture. We think the mixed licence and advertising method is the worst possible expedient.

It has been said by some of our younger Producers that nobody could possibly work in a commercial radio or television station without being oppressed by the pressure of advertising. They are quite wrong. To many older men and women, the advent and continuance of advertising was a liberating experience! In fact, it is possible to trace an interesting sociological contour-line around those in the broadcasting services who advance this view of advertising as 'keeping the station out of the hands of the Civil Service', and discover, within the contour-line, a preponderance of ex-radio personnel from Henry Street. This is understandable.

Prior to the introduction of extensive advertising sponsorship for programmes in Radio Eireann, the dependence of professional broadcasters on the administrators of the Department of Posts and Telegraphs was, apparently, a chastening experience indeed. Once the station's financial dependence on the money-bags of the advertisers began to be felt, the restrictions of budget control by central government servants was seen as 'the dead hand'. The relative informality of advertising agency procedures had all the charm of the 'Ode to Freedom'.

---

99   It would, of course, be possible to institute a system of differential charges or compensations but, in our view, this always risks some form of means test.

The attendant fear that government subsidy or total government financing of broadcasting would facilitate government interference with the station's work, derives from the working of the old Wireless Telegraphy Act, we imagine. This was the law under which Radio Éireann operated. There was then no authority with independent powers such as the Broadcasting Act now provides. The programme-makers were servants of the Minister. There is no more reason to fear government interference on foot of a subsidy than there is to fear it on foot of a licence fee. A truly independent and vigorous Authority should be as well able to stand up to a Minister or Civil Servant, if the Act and the Courts protected them in either case.[100] Fear of Government is directly a psychological emotion, and only indirectly financial. Historically, it is understandable that broadcasters operating as servants of the Minister would welcome release from his tutelage. Evidently those who first tasted the heady wine of commercial 'freedom' have pleasant memories of it.

Retribution has only begun to be felt. Those who first welcomed it are now in positions of power and high responsibility. One wonders if they recognise the sound of a new note of alarm.

Of course, it should also be borne in mind that two other factors were freely operating in 1960 which have, perhaps, now become at least self-conscious. The political parties (all three) were then in the high noon of the liberal ethic. Only a few people in Ireland had any real misgivings about the possibility of a morally viable free-enterprise system. Advertising was not then the scientific conditioning factor in our daily lives that it has since become. The horizon of national poverty in the late forties and fifties made generous spending on 'luxuries' like radio and television unthinkable. The national scene has radically changed.

---

100  See chapter on Broadcasting Acts 1960-66.

A yearly growth rate of 4.5 percent was then unforeseeable. A buoyancy in the economy represented by a net increase of yield of £10 millions was unimaginable. Our national leaders still think of broadcasting as a luxury and of its financing in terms suitable to 1959-60.

Of course, any real transition to 'public service' or advertising-free methods of financing the broadcasting services cannot changeover cataclysmically. A model such as we suggested for study would have to provide for an interim 'phasing-in' of the new method and 'phasing-out' of the old.

The reader should be clear that we were concerned only to have proposals studied. We were not urging any specific solution. We did not have one. Our aim was to try to jolt our people out of the assumption that a commercial radio and television service, based on three unexamined propositions, is part of the natural law. These propositions were:

1. That the present Act is sacrosanct.
2. That advertising is the only method of financing the service that can reconcile solvency and freedom of broadcasting.
3. That the national aims can be promoted within a commercial service without Government subsidies.

It is desirable, in this spirit of enquiry, to examine another model of financing which involves an important, but disputable, value judgment: that broadcasting in Ireland is essential in order to meet the challenge of 'international' culture and retain our own identity. This will become increasingly difficult when satellite television is used on a world scale. Our present level of expenditure will be altogether insufficient for television, *even if we remain satisfied with its present quality.*

Again, what follows is only a study-proposal:

The revenue earned by RTE from advertising runs at over £2.5 millions a year out of a total income of £5.5 millions. The buoyancy of Government revenue currently runs at over £30 millions a year. The proportion of this swallowed up by rising costs varies widely from year to year; in some years it may be around £10 millions, in others around £20 millions. On average, the increase in Government revenue per year in real terms (after allowing for rising costs) is probably well in excess of £10 millions. It is part of the business of Government to decide how this increased revenue is to be spent. One of the options open to the Government is to bring about a phased reduction in RTE advertising to half its present level, replacing the revenue lost by a subsidy. To do this would cost about £1 million, which could be met from the buoyancy of revenue over a period of, say, four years without any great difficulty at all.[101]

Yet this does not go far enough. What is desirable is less advertising and a better service, which means spending more. Let us therefore pose a more daring question. Would it be within the national resources, at least as a transition expedient, to halve the amount of advertising on RTE and at the same time double its total income, to over £10 millions?[102] Apart from advertising, RTE's major sources of income would be licence fees and Government subsidy. Any very large increase in licence fees is open to the serious objection that it is a form of regressive taxation, which affects the poor much more severely than the rich. As we have said we certainly would not support it.

---

101  A flat 1 percent Gross National Product as a subsidy; such a subsidy would eliminate year to year interference by bureaucrats. Something similar has been done for CIE to the tune of £2 millions a year, theoretically for a limited period.

102  1969 money values are used throughout this discussion.

CHAPTER 7: THE SWEET RACKET

A doubling of RTE revenue could best be brought about by direct subsidy. Let us consider a simplified model of RTE income, in which licence fees and reduced advertising bring in £4 millions and direct subsidy from general taxation furnishes £6 millions to make a total of £10 millions. Is this in the realm of the possible? As a medium-term objective the answer is clearly in the affirmative. A Government decision to give RTE this kind of income pattern by 1975 and to move gradually towards it, is quite feasible.

It would involve a decision to devote £1 million a year of the revenue buoyancy to the purpose, which certainly could be done. By 1975 the current budget will be around £600 millions so a subsidy of £6 millions to RTE would represent about 1 per cent, of the total spending on current account. The proposition, summed up in generalised terms, would be that by 1975 RTE's revenue from licence fees and advertising would be 40 per cent, of the total and the remaining 60 per cent, direct subsidy, representing roughly 1 per cent, of the current budget. The formula could be maintained in the years after 1975, which would give RTE a steady increase in income, in line with the growth of national income and Government revenue.

To follow this kind of policy is within the national resources, but a decision to follow it involves a value judgment that the money would be well spent. Given a vigorous Authority, interested in culture rather than politics, and a committed Directorate, this is possible. A technical Directorate would only waste more money. However, among the considerations which support this value judgment *per se* are the following: the quality of the national radio and television service is an important part of the national standard of living, even though it cannot be set down in economic statistics of national well-being. Spending on the service could give a very good return. The difference between the cost of a mediocre service and an excellent one, expressed as a figure per head of the population per year, is most likely to be between £2 and £3. Taking into account the size of national income per head, projecting its rate of growth into the coming decade, and recognising the declining urgency of further increases in material standards of living, except among small farmers, it appears quite sensible to spend the money required to have an excellent broadcasting service.

To give one illustration of growing national wealth: between 1967 and 1968 personal expenditure on consumer goods and services is estimated to have risen from £772 to £849 millions, an increase of £77 millions[103]. Those who would wish to hold that the country cannot afford to increase its spending on the broadcasting service by £1 million a year clearly have the onus of proof upon themselves.

The N.I.E.C. has stated in its Report on Full Employment that the volume of resources devoted to persuading people to spend, compared with the volume devoted to persuading them to save, is clearly out of line with the Government's long term economic objectives. While the public are constantly being exhorted to save, there seems to have been very little effort to follow up this N.I.E.C. comment by studying seriously the pressures brought to bear on people to make them spend rather than save.[104] From the point of view of increasing economic growth through a higher rate of savings and investment there is a case for reducing the volume of advertising on RTE.

The idea of reducing advertising to half its present level is put forward as an interim compromise between the present position and a non-advertising BBC-style service. Half the present level would be

---

103   N.I.E.C. Review of 1968 and Outlook for 1969, p. 29

104   Cf. Central Bank Report 1968/69, p. 17, on consumer spending. The criticism of this report on consumer spending have never been so devastating on the dangers of inflation. They foresee, in the next few months, an increase in consumer spending which will run the nation into real trouble.

tolerable to listeners and viewers, would give the advertisers a reasonable opportunity to present their wares, while reducing the objectionable aspects of intensive campaigns waged by established industrial giants fighting out their commercial battles in the homes of the nation. It would also very probably give the programme-planners more flexibility in judging the content and timing of programmes.

At the risk of repetition, the financial limits within which RTE operates were decided at the beginning of this decade. What may have been economic necessity then is certainly no longer so now, and the quite arbitrary limits on RTE's finances clearly need re-appraisal, as they are contrary to the overall national interest.

Of course, a mere reduction in the quantity of advertising would not suffice, in our view. The real damage is done by the practical impossibility of ignoring the advertisements during a programme. The 'unavoidability' of the advertisements in a night's programming plus their association with the programme-matter are the main causes of disquiet. One cannot realistically be expected to 'turn down the ads' continually. One just suffers being bombarded by them. The advertising breaks are certainly aesthetically offensive. This is not their worst feature. The fact that they are associated with programmes in the transmission time-schedule means that the most expensive advertising seeks peak viewing time.[105] This, together with the fear of a switch-over to BBC or ITV stations means that programmes of the widest possible appeal will be scheduled to combat the competition. This, unfortunately, is usually (but not invariably) the 'slick, canned ready-made' from abroad or a not-so-slick imitation from home sources.

If the economic argument for reduction of the quantity of advertising were to include a complete *dissociation of advertisements from*

---

105  Cf. Appendix II

*individual programmes,* much would be gained. If the total volume were to fall by half and if that were to be transmitted in, say, two 'blocks' of scheduled time each night (say after the news) they would have no immediate influence on the scheduling of programmes. This system is followed in some Continental stations; for example, in Switzerland, Italy and the Netherlands. Even as a permanent system it would have enormous advantages over the present one. As an interim system of bridging the period of transition to 'advertising-free' broadcasting it has much to recommend it.

* * *

The really essential question remains unanswered: who, apart from the advertising interests, *wants* advertising? If people don't want it why should they be asked to endure it? The economic arguments of 1959-60 do not now obtain. The viewer pays for the advertising anyway. The advertisers' contention, that by increasing demand for mass consumption they promote mass production and thus reduce prices, is very naive indeed. Even the most unsophisticated customer is now aware of the countervailing price-rings, and the virtual monopolies by interlocking holdings who keep prices up. They know, too that Governments 'rack-tax' to keep mass consumption down. These taxes are absorbed into prices and further inflate them. The whole process is a spiral of inflated consumption and inflated wages, absorbed in the main by inflated prices. Advertising is the stimulant of production. The evidence that it does not reduce prices is that they continue to rise with its volume and intensity. It raises profits.[106]

---

106 Increased production brought about by increased demand, stimulated by advertising has a commercial purpose, not an altruistic one. Advertising agents are hired by manufacturers and distributors because it is profitable to hire them.

The economy is now buoyant; the dangers of inflation are consequently more pressing than the alleged unpopularity of large-scale State subsidy. National savings are the main weapon against inflation in a buoyant economy. This savings campaign is being scientifically defeated and frustrated by using the national broadcasting service to urge spending upon those whom we are simultaneously urging to save in the national interest. As late as 22nd July 1969 in Dáil Eireann, Mr. Charles Haughey, Minister for Finance, commented on a section of the Finance Bill (1969) by saying that he thought it reasonable to raise money by increased taxation on luxury items like motor cars, yachts, refrigerators, caravans and television sets. This, he thought, would have the desirable social and economic effect of 'damping down' consumer spending.

Mr. Haughey cannot be unaware that his colleague the Minister for Posts and Telegraphs was busy, through the State broadcasting services, at the opposite task of promoting spending in these very areas of consumption, through advertising. This seems to us odd to the point of eccentricity.

In 1969/70 the economic as well as the cultural argument would seem to favour 'advertisement free' radio and television.

# 8

## THE (DIS)ORGANISATION...MAN
## THE STRUCTURES OF RTE

## CHAPTER 8: THE (DIS)ORGANISATION...MAN

*'If seven maids with seven mops swept it for half a year,*
*Do you suppose', the Walrus said,*
*'That they could get it clear?'*
*'I doubt it', said the Carpenter,*
*And shed a bitter tear.*
—LEWIS CARROLL

*Fire in each eye, and papers in each hand.*
*They rave, recite, and madden round the land.*
—ALEXANDER POPE

*Agent: 'There's more in this, sir, than meets the eye, I'll warrant*
*Captain Boycott: 'Whose eye? Nothing meets my eye; nothing whatever.'*

R*adio Telefís Éireann is* made up of a corporate governing body called the Authority, the Director-General and other 'officers and servants', numbering about 1,500 persons.

The Authority provides two national broadcasting services: radio and television.

Television is organised to make and transmit 22 hours of 'home-originated' programmes per week; it buys in about the same amount of foreign material. Radio provides an average of about 100 hours of broadcasting each week.

Few viewers or listeners realise the enormous work-load which this puts on the staff. No small country in Europe provides anything like this output for a comparable population. If the station's work were to be assessed in terms of quantity alone, this could be judged a very remarkable feat indeed. We often forget how small a nation we are. Our 2.9 million people judge our work as if we had resources of money, technical skill and talent similar to Great Britain's or even the Netherlands'. We do not have them and we ought to stop thinking of our services as being comparable to theirs.

RTE is organised into seven divisions. Three of these are programming; four are servicing divisions, originally designed to keep the programme units running. The three programming divisions are Radio Programmes, Television Programmes and News Programmes.

*The Radio Programmes Division* is operated under a Controller, who is responsible to the Director-General.

*The Television Programmes Division* has its own Controller, with similar responsibilities.

*The News Division* works under a Head of News who acts as Editor-in-Chief for both radio and television. He, too, works directly to the chief executive. Responsibility for the Authority's publication, *The RTE Guide*, and for the library, is thought by some to pertain to Mr. McGuinness. The Deputy Director-General is, we understand, 'officially' responsible.

*The Engineering Division* is a servicing-complex. It provides five central engineering services to the organisation as a whole.

In addition, there are two groups which provide direct engineering and technical facilities to the programming divisions. These two technical groups are the Television Production Facilities Group and the Radio Production Facilities Group, each with its Group Head. The Radio Facilities group is directly responsible to the Director of Engineering. The Television Group is thought to be directly responsible to the Controller of Television, by programmes personnel; it is treated as an independent service-unit by the Head of News. It is asserted to be *de facto* responsible to the Director of Engineering by engineers. The documentation on this confused relationship baffles analysis.

A circular from the Controller's office, with an internal office diagram, shows that the Controller and his programme staff regard the Production Facilities Group as being in the Programmes Division. This would probably be asserted, on challenge, to be the 'official' establishment.

The Head of News does not, apparently, share this 'official' view. For example, inter-office memoranda originating from Programmes Division are written on the green memo-sheets which the Programmes Division uses. These are normally used by the Production Facilities Group also. When, however, they write to Mr. J. McGuinness (Head of News) or members of his staff, they must use ordinary *white* paper! The fact is that the Facilities Group was designed to provide the Programmes Division with its own facilities. It serviced, as a 'bonus', the News Division, which was then merely a bulletin-issuing department. Since the 7 *Days* team became incorporated into the News Division and political commentaries a feature of its work, that Division became a larger programming unit. It now has to struggle for its share of facilities. It has to argue for its place in priority-schedules. It obviously cannot be independent if it has to depend on the Programmes Division's facilities. It insists, in practice, on treating the Facilities Group as a service independent of the Television Programmes Division.

The 'family-tree' charts, held by the various Departments and Divisions, and purporting to indicate the line of managerial responsibilities, have dotted lines to show informal liaison and continuous lines for formal responsibility. Of course, these must be read in conjunction with the official correspondence. This, in fact, conflicts.[107] This, however, worries few. Organisational paradox is the oxygen they breathe.

*The Personnel Division* is responsible for the recruitment of staff and training, for labour relations and for personnel administration and working conditions. This Division is headed by Mr. Oliver Maloney. He is also Secretary to the Authority.

*The Sales Division* is responsible for the sale of radio and television advertising time in the Republic and at its London office. Its Controller is Mr. Robert Gahan.

*The Financial Control Division* handles disbursements for purchasing, wages and contracts. Mr. Vincent Finn is its Financial Controller. It also collects and accounts for monies due and provides financial advice and recommendations to the Director-General and the Authority.

Mr. John Irvine, the Deputy Director-General, has responsibility for certain specialist advisory groups and services.

The purpose of this large and complex organisation of manpower and materials is to make programmes. The present Director-General, Mr. T. P. Hardiman, has said, in his 16 page memorandum issued on the occasion of our resignations, that the actual structures of organisation are 'programme-orientated'. He meant, presumably, that they are simply instrumental means to permit the programming divisions to do the Authority's essential work. If this has any real meaning in ordinary language and thought, it is, surely, that the work of the supporting services is subordinated to that of the programme production divisions. It is not without significance that he goes on to re-assure the technical personnel that no one division is more important than any other. It is permissible to ask: why not? That all are necessary is not evidence that they are equally important. If the whole organisation is

---

107 See "A Cautionary Tale", p. 109

'programme-orientated', then the programmes divisions must, surely, take precedence.

The fact is that there is considerable tension in RTE and its programme divisions. Since Mr. Hardiman became Director-General this has become more pointed in fact and more confused. He is an engineer. His path to his present office was through these technical structures. His training and the cast of his mind is technological. There is, naturally, a sharing of unuttered sentiment with his professional colleagues, and a common way of assessing and formulating problems and policy. This relationship does not exist with programme people. What psychologists call the personality profiles of the creative and the administrative types of character are very dissimilar. Their attitudes to organisation are distinctively different. A great deal of the difficulty in the broadcasting services derives from this psychological and sociological fact.

Few among the general public realise how complex and technical the production of radio or television programmes is. The range of electronic and other equipment is quite amazing to the uninitiated. In the making of a television programme the Director may require two, three or four electronic cameras. These will give him an equivalent number of pictures from which to choose. Television cameras are manned by highly trained camera-crews. These, like the sound-men, have the nerve-wracking and physically strenuous job of pushing heavy instruments around the studio floor under the voice control of the Director, whom they cannot see and who cannot see them. They are artists. They know roughly what the Director wants on his three or four monitor-screens and speakers. The camera-men get the pictures, "compose' them and offer them to the Director. He is in constant voice-control of all the camera-men simultaneously. He will require corrections to their pictures, or alternatives. In addition, there will be many sources of sound accompanying the pictures. The actors or other performers will be serviced with microphones, sound booms, 'fish-pole' microphones; tape-recorded sound, gramophone discs, 'live' sound-effects or even sound from outside the studio may also be used. An often intricate and artistic lighting-rig is constantly subject to change by the lighting-director and his crew as the show proceeds. The programme Director is in touch with the sound-supervisor and the lighting-director by radio-intercommunication.

A skilled vision-mixer executes the Director's choice of picture from those 'on offer'. A floor-manager co-ordinates all the movements, speech and actions of the performers and crews on the studio floor. The Director is in constant two-way dialogue with him, also. At the same time, the tele-cine room may be providing additional visual and audio material from film or tape or scanners or slides, or all of these. The 'outside' sources are also controlled by the Director on radio-intercommunications and by a system of cues. The Director's Production Assistant is constantly reviewing the split-second timing-schedule for all of these and keeping her Director informed of their relationships. She must also call out the warning cues to all participants from her copy of the script. The artistic designer, who has created the settings, sits with the Director. He constantly studies the actual images for transmission and advises the Director on the way the multiple sources are being fully resolved into an artistic unity on the receivers' screens.

In Irish television, mainly for reasons of economy, the television Director is also the Producer of the programme. In this latter role, he must be able to conceive the programme idea and prepare estimates of cost. He must know who is most suitable from those available to perform; must write the script or have it written, make a floor-plan for its execution; make a camera-movement and 'shot' script, convey his requirements to the specialists in the design, graphic and film departments, control his budget, negotiate agreements, order materials and stage properties, review the law, watch the station's policy, and make such a unity of all of these that it can be realised in the studio. He must also make travel and subsistence arrangements and co-ordinate the work of all contributors, participants and technicians. He must consult with the Planning and Control engineers on the most economic use of studios and technical facilities and try to provide that quality of leadership which will keep everybody working and, as far as possible, happy. This requires unusual qualities of mind and body.

The Producer-Director in television is at once an artist and a manager. He will not (and ought not) be a technical expert in all these fields. But he must have a detailed working knowledge of all. By temperament, then, he will tend to be sensitive, intelligent, educated, introverted, ego-centred without being egotistical, free of that 'group-dependence' which characterises the 'organisation-man', the administrator or the modern engineer. He will tend to work best in ad-hoc groups of enthusiasts and to be at his worst in rigid 'in-group' structures. His mentality tends to be orientated to the work to be done rather than dominated by procedures and precedents. He has an almost inexhaustible capacity for 'getting around' or ignoring forms of organisation and method that confine his imagination, ingenuity and liberty to the well-tested and the dependable. The bureaucrat thrives on these and leans heavily on the shared predictabilities of his 'in-group'.

Almost identical considerations apply in the cases of soundmen, lighting-men, camera-men, film editors, designers, photographers, graphic-artists, vision-mixers, wardrobe and make-up artists. These are organised administratively under engineers. They are artists by training and temperament. They are all programme-makers and creatives.

The creative programme-maker needs an organisation that is structured to his peculiar work and temperament; the professional administrator needs organisation of quite a different kind that will protect his job-security anxieties. Yet these different types must live and work together harmoniously. How is this possible or is it possible at all? The honest answer, we think, is that nobody really knows. Television is still a young medium. It was invented and its techniques were moulded by technologists. The organisations which did develop tended to transplant the conditions of film production into the new medium but without the film tradition's informality. Its aesthetic standards were also transferred. Engineers tend, on the whole, to make motor-cars look like 'horseless carriages' and television images look as smooth and 'resolved' as film images.

Because nobody really knows how to organise the requirements of the types of work and people who make television into a unity, the great need, we have argued, is for experiment and then for training and re-training. Improvisation is not experiment. Many methods of organisation have been improvised in the eight years of RTE's life. They have all failed. Most have been simply useless: two have been dangerous.

There was a comfortable kind of obviousness about RTE's first programme organisation. This was deployed in Departments, each with a Head directly responsible to the Programme Controller. There were Departments of Drama, Sport, Public Affairs, Children's and Women's Programmes.

The great virtue of this kind of organisation was that it provided maximum control with the minimum number of people reporting administratively to the Controller. Its great defect was that administrative control is the least important element in programme production. The values of imaginative initiative are vital. They never survive any administrative control that is not immediately decision-making. The secondary disadvantage is that Heads of Department who have imaginative subordinates can only *interfere*. If they do not interfere, they tend to have no work to do and thus make mischief.

The programme initiative lies inevitably with the Producer-Director, if the programmes are to have any character. He, of course, is not self-sufficient. He needs immediate access to the real source of policy *decision*. In most healthy television or radio stations this source of decision is the Controller. Intermediate programme managers have only the power to make mediations, not decisions. They, therefore, tend to be side-stepped, evaded and eventually ignored. It *seems* that the Departmental system is not so much a bad system as a useless one. The title 'Head of Department' tends to be an accolade, not a real function in programme-making. If the Heads are Producers, there is a waste of their talents in using them as administrators. If they are not, their administrative work is a waste of time since their Producer subordinates will regard their views as ill-informed. Perhaps if they had *real* control over budgets and *real* powers of decision, the Heads of Department system might work. We simply do not know. We do know that, in fact, they never have worked in Ireland except in cases where very strong personalities were available.

In any case, this system was replaced in 1963 by assembling Producers under Group Editors, with the exceptions of Sport, Drama and Children's programmes. This was to some small extent a formal recognition that the real programme initiative was properly vested in the Producers.

This effort to provide an organisation for programmes was called the 'vertical group' system. It was ingenious and imaginative. It was also an attempt to relate the work of production to the needs of television as a public service. It was devised by the Swedish Controller, Gunnar Rugheimer. Its programmes (and their makers) were grouped with Executive Producers, who did not cease to be active, professionally. Each Group was assigned responsibility for certain transmission days. The hope was that each day's broadcasting would have a distinctive range of interests, appealing to characteristic *audiences* in the viewing population. This meant that persons whose main interest was in, say, Public Affairs could have a night almost to themselves, so to speak. The undesirable habit of passive 'mass' viewing of everything transmitted would cease.

This method failed at length for lack of sufficiently sophisticated and experienced group-leadership. Further, the Producers were themselves inadequately trained and far too heavily overworked to sustain so selective an output. Moreover, the Editors tended to become the old Heads of Department under another title. Their role was short-lived. It did not so much die as fade away. It left the Groups under the administrative supervision of Executive Producers.

The scheme now included a working-leader, the Executive Producer, who had no *exclusive* access to the Controller. Any Producer could see the Controller when necessary. His work was constantly reviewed and commented upon by the Group executive and the Controller. The scheme's main defects were that it came too soon in the life of the station. It was devised and implemented by a powerful Controller whose personality took inadequate account of the defects of training and experience in his subordinates. His being a 'foreigner' compounded the difficulties. His clarity and energy of mind were not qualities that recommended him to people who, in the Irish tradition, regarded vagueness as a valuable instrument of survival in an ambiguous world. Once more the Producers killed the system by ignoring it as irrelevant. They just got on with the job.

When the present Controller of Television, Mr. Michael Garvey, took office in the Winter of 1966, he transferred one of the Executive Producers to Drama as a manager, returned another to production duties and promoted a third to an administrative post on his own control-staff.

Drama, Children's and Schools' programmes, Presentation and Sport were Departments, each with a Head that had survived all vicissitudes. Television Features, Religious programmes (now a large part of our output of home originated work), Irish programmes and Light Entertainment, were headless and group-less. *Newsbeat* had an editor who had no directorial experience but was a fine journalist and broadcaster; light entertainment programmes were organisationally unidentifiable. There were also 'Special Projects' handled by a Senior Producer, Jim Plunkett Kelly. Agricultural programmes had a brilliant performing Head who had had no television experience but was an acknowledged expert in his field.

In order to bring this residual patch-work of all the previous organisations into some kind of relationship to himself and, at the same time, avoid having to deal personally with forty Producers, Mr. Garvey created an Editorial Board. This was his immediate planning group.

Its membership consisted of two Editors, each 'responsible' for about a third of the programme output; The Assistant Controller continued to have his former responsibilities. In addition, he was given what Mr. Garvey described as 'special responsibility' for Public Affairs programmes and Sport. The Editorial Board also included the Head of (imported) Film, the Head of Television Production Facilities and, in some undefined role, the Head of Planning. Excepting the Assistant Controller, these officers had executive titles but no executive power over Producers. The Editors' role was to 'stimulate, facilitate and advise' the Heads of those Departments and those projects and programmes that had only an editor (with a small 'e'), or a Senior Producer or a Producer-Director.

The Head of Presentation was responsible to the Head of Planning, but refused to obey him. Similarly, the Head of Children's and Schools' programmes refused to work to her Editor. The Editors had the further duty of communicating production 'sentiments' upward to Management and downward to the Producers. This was not a very clear organisational situation for a £5 million a year public utility.

A new organisational factor had been introduced about a year previous to the foundation of this Editorial Committee. The Production Facilities Group had been made directly responsible to the Controller of Programmes (Television). It was led by Mr. T. P. Hardiman as Assistant Controller (Facilities). Mr. Jack White had remained as Assistant Controller (Production). When Mr. Garvey's Editorial Group was formed, Mr. Hardiman was promoted Director of Engineering. His successor, Mr. George Waters, did not have the status of Assistant Controller. He was simply Head of Production Facilities. Mr. Garvey had, under his own immediate control and disposition, therefore, all the necessary technical advice and services he needed to implement his policy. But he had no workable programme-producers' organisation.

*  *  *

The quite extraordinary state of programme-makers' disorganisation described above created a sense of insecurity and disquiet among Producers. They were corporately in disarray. The engineers and technicians were highly organised, not as a satellite service but *within* the Programmes Division, upon which they now secured a grip of chilling firmness.

Our new Controller was a highly cultivated, gentle and administratively inexperienced man. His technical adviser was an experienced engineer and manager. When this strange structure took its first severe strain, during the crisis over the transfer of *7 Days* to the News Division, the middle management of engineering and technical staffs of the Programmes Division suddenly realised that they were 'line-management', not production staff; they felt that they could not join in any Trade

## CHAPTER 8: THE (DIS)ORGANISATION...MAN

Union action. They would, therefore, be available to Management to carry on the station's transmissions during a strike. Not unnaturally, they seemed to us like a team of potential 'blacklegs'. Yet they, too, were programmes personnel. This did little to create confidence in the minds of a production staff whose members faced a bitter struggle for what they believed to be the future of free television programming.

The hitherto informal relationship of liaison between the Programmes Facilities Group and the Director of Engineering now took on a more formal character, but officially it remained, like a foreign body, within Mr. Garvey's command. In what was otherwise an administrative porridge, this technical element was a frame-work of administrative efficiency which owed its loyalty to programmes but its viable existence to the Engineering Division and its clear-minded and far-seeing Director.

On Mr. McCourt's retirement in March 1967, Mr. Hardiman became Director-General and was succeeded as Director of Engineering by Mr. George Waters, the Head of Production Facilities, an old colleague. The station, in its radio and television activities was now completely in the firm and competent hands of engineering administrators. They knew little about creative programming, but they did not realise this.

Meanwhile the affairs of the Television Programmes Division had effectively passed into the hands of the Trade Unions' House Committees. No attempt to re-organise the production groups was made, notwithstanding Mr. Garvey's promise after the *7 Days* agreement that this would be done. In fact, never once from that time until just before the next crisis in September 1968 did Mr. Garvey hold a conference with all his Producers.

The Controller's Editorial Committee was in what can only be described as a chronic state of internal contradiction. Some of its members thought that, at least *de facto*, they had executive authority over the Producers and some (including, on challenge, the Programme Controller) that they had not.

One of them, Liam Ó Murchú, after the *7 Days* settlement, complained in writing to his superior that his job was being made impossible and that the Controller was not dealing with the difficulties. He had been given, he felt, responsibility without authority or power. So had Mr. Denis O'Grady, the Head of Planning, since his Head of Presentation would not obey him. Mr. Ó Murchú's group included Miss Maev Conway of Schools' and Children's programmes. She had continued to ignore him as her programming Editor. Mr. Jim Plunkett Kelly refused to acknowledge his appointment. Father Romuald Dodd, Religious Adviser, editorially ignored him also, as having no part to play in his field of religious policy. Nonetheless, he was well-liked!

Features Producers, appealing to the terms of their job specification supplied by the Controller of Programmes, refused to allow Mr. Ó Murchú to intervene in their production decisions. Finally, in exasperation, he decided to force the issue and ordered one of the Producers, Seán Ó Mórdha, to make a production arrangement contrary to the policy of his programme.

Ó Mórdha refused and appealed the matter to a Trade Union meeting. This meeting instructed a delegation to interview the Controller of Programmes to determine if Mr. Ó Murchú's organisational role held executive power. The Controller ruled that it did not. The Editorial system virtually collapsed. The Programmes Division was once again in organisational chaos.

The Programme Controller now had no producer-organisation that anyone could regard as workable by central programme

Management. The Engineering management personnel, most of those in Cumann na n-Innealltóirí and some of those outside it, were in full control of all the means of production and, by order of a Newsletter

(9th August 1967) from the Director-General of that time, they were reporting to the Director of Engineering, Mr. Waters. They were still nominally under Mr. Garvey, as far as we can make sense of it.

This situation was, now, so incredible that the General Secretary of the Trade Union, Irish Actors' Equity, Mr. Dermot Doolon, let it be known that his Executive were not prepared to intervene any further in what was, in effect, a managerial collapse. He informed the Chairman of the House Committee (RTE television branch) of this policy, for his guidance. He undertook, also, to bring it to Management's attention. There then immediately followed a further policy-crisis. Mr. Hardiman ordered yet another programme to be transferred to the News Division from under Michael Garvey's Divisional control and Jack White's editorial supervision, and the matter got lost.

Evidently, confidence in the Programme Division's organisation and management was gone, among the upper Directorate of RTE.

The self-respect and morale of the programme Producers could not tolerate this. They decided, if necessary, to inform the Director-General that, if this order was not rescinded, they would call in their Unions. He rescinded the order. The Producers proposed consultation. He then suggested that the Producers should elect a consultative group of six to work out, with him and his staff, a new organisation which would 'engage the Producers of programmes at the earliest possible stage in planning'.

The result of this series of consultations was a unilateral imposition of the old Departmental system on the Programmes Division.

The Producers withdrew from the consultative group and an Equity Trade Union meeting sent a resolution of protest to the Director-General. They notified him that, as a result of his highhanded treatment of their representatives, any further discussions would take place only through their Trade Unions.

After eight years of organisation and re-organisation, RTE was back where it started, with a Departmental system led by Programme Heads. The Producers once more got on with the job.

# 9

## ACTS TO GRIND
## THE BROADCASTING AUTHORITY ACTS, 1960-77

# CHAPTER 9: ACTS TO GRIND

*'I'll be judge, I'll be jury', said cunning old Fury;*
*'I'll try the whole cause, and condemn you to death'.*
—LEWIS CARROLL

*Mr. Hilliard : This television service will not be run by Beelzebub but by nine responsible people.*
—DÁIL DEBATES

*While there have been lots of changes in the Prague studios, some of the producers who were there in Pelikan's day are still around. If you ask them why they've stayed on despite the ever-increasing restrictions, they'll tell you: 'If we didn't do the work, someone else—less qualified, more politically motivated—would do the job. And it would be worse for everyone'. When you suggest that this is the argument the Nazis used for following Hitler, they shrug their shoulders and walk away.*
—PAUL FOX, THE LISTENER

## ACTS TO GRIND

On the 31st March 1971, most of the present members of the Authority are due to retire. The legislation on broadcasting may then be due for official review and possible amendment. It is time we and the new Minister, Mr. Patrick Lawlor, began to think about the lessons of the Authority's first ten years.

The Broadcasting Authority Act, 1960, established an Authority with both the power and duty to provide 'a national television and broadcasting service'.

The legislation under which radio and television are broadcast in the Irish Republic enables the Government to appoint the personnel of the Authority for such terms not exceeding five years as the Government thinks fit. The remuneration paid to such members is fixed by the Government. Their expenses are paid by the Authority. This Authority, consisting of seven to nine members, has the right to appoint a Director-General, with the approval of the Government. He is the Authority's chief executive officer. The Act empowers them to appoint such other officers and servants as they think fit. Only the Director-General's post is established by the Act. All other offices are created at the discretion of the Authority. All members of the Authority are in the precarious position of holding their posts at the complete whim of the Government, who may remove them at any time without the necessity of giving reasons for such removal (Sec. 6).

All public broadcasting rights in the Republic allowed under the Act are vested in the Authority alone; it may exercise its functions through its officers and servants.

No member of the Authority may be a member of either House of the Oireachtas, nor a nominated candidate for election. Six of the nine had been members or at least active workers for the Fianna Fáil Party when we resigned. The other three had no party affiliations or public commitments as far as we know. These were:

## FIANNA FÁIL SUPPORTERS:
The Chairman. Dr. C. S. Andrews
Mr. James Fanning
Mr. Ruairi Brugha
Mrs. Sean T. O'Kelly
Mr. Michael Noonan
Mr. Michael O'Callaghan

## UNAFFILIATED:
Professor Theo. Moody, T.C.D.
Mr. Fintan Kennedy, I.T.G.W.U.
Mr. Donall Ó Moráin[108]

The functions of the Authority under this Act, apart from the purchase and use of property and other administrative matters, are to establish and maintain a national television and sound broadcasting service. It has the power to make, purchase, hire and relay programmes of an educational, informative or entertaining character. It is not obliged under this Act to do any one of these in any specific way, except that it is obliged to 'bear constantly in mind the national aims of restoring the Irish language and preserving and developing the national culture'.

The Act covers the transmission of sound and television programmes but not the reception of these, except that receiving-sets may legally be held only under a licence from the Minister for Posts and Telegraphs. Consequently, British or other off-shore radio and television agencies can transmit programmes for reception in the Republic without any of the disabilities of the Act and with some of its benefits.

This competition has a profound effect on our programme-making and transmission policy. If the Authority should decide under the Act (as it consistently has done) to transmit information, news or features which are controversial in nature or are currently the subject of public debate, it is required to be impartial and objective and refrain from expressing its own views. Nonetheless, it may transmit political party

---

108   Since June there have been some changes. Mr. Michael Noonan resigned to seek election to Dáil Éireann as a Fianna Fáil candidate, as did Mr. Ruairí Brugha. Mr. Fintan Kennedy went forward as a candidate for election to the Senate. This left three vacancies, two of which have been filled; Mr. Stephen Barrett, ex-Fine Gael T.D., and Mr. Liam Hyland of Fianna Fáil.

broadcasts. The subsection under which party political broadcasting is permitted [Sec. 18 (2)] is a qualification or exemption from the impartiality obligation [Sec. 18 (1)]. Presumably, therefore, there is no need to fulfil the impartiality clause in these broadcasts, except a moral one! While there are no specific penalties for failure to comply with the law, the Government's right to remove members of the Authority from office at will must be a very powerful factor in the Authority's decisions.

The periods fixed for any broadcasting of programmes must be approved by the Minister for Posts and Telegraphs. The Authority may broadcast advertisements, except on religion, politics or industrial disputes. There is a common impression, even among professional broadcasters, that the Authority is obliged by the Act to transmit advertising. This is untrue. What it is obliged to do is secure its own revenue. This must be sufficient to meet current and capital expenditure, without charge to the national Exchequer. The power to transmit advertising is purely an enabling power—not a mandatory function. The Act reserves to the Minister the approval of the time-scheduling of advertisements and the daily amount that shall be permitted, should the Authority use this power to transmit advertisements. It does.

The Minister may, after consulting with the Authority but without its consent, appoint advisers to it, either as individual experts or by membership of advisory committees. Although the Authority and Director-General must have regard to such advice, neither is bound by it.

The Act requires that it is the Minister who will be responsible for the collection of licence fees, which are paid over to the Authority, less a service charge. In addition, during its first 5 years the Authority might be paid by the Minister a sum not exceeding £500,000 p.a.

A most important power reserved to the Minister is to direct the Authority in writing to refrain from broadcasting any class of programme-material or particular programme item. In similar fashion, he

CHAPTER 9: ACTS TO GRIND

may direct the Authority, under the Act, to broadcast any announcements by or on behalf of any Minister of State in connection with his ministerial functions. This has been done once in the history of the station, when the Minister for Finance wished to address the Nation on the economic situation after the maintenance strike in 1969[109].

We should like to discuss, briefly, some of these provisions of the Broadcasting Authority Acts 1960-1966, in so far as they have impinged on our attention as professional broadcasters. These views, of course, have no legal value nor are they intended to have any: they bear only on such professional matters as might properly engage the public mind if the Act were to be reviewed for amendment or replacement.

As Mr. Arthur Noonan, the political correspondent of the *Irish Independent,* pointed out during the controversy on our resignations, there is a serious duty on broadcasters to keep the Government and Dail Éireann advised on the workability of its enabling legislation. It is a first principle of social philosophy, if not of law, that legislation that is not respectable will not and cannot be respected. To continue to keep such legislation on the Statute Book is to invite public contempt, not only of the legislation, but of the Legislature.

The most fundamental consideration arising from the Act is that RTE enjoys a monopoly of both radio and television broadcasting within the State. Only the Authority has the right of public broadcasting. But for producers of programmes this is, in practice, an illusory monopoly from the start. Any cultural advantages to the community which a true monopoly might secure are undermined by the fact that

---

109   We have since been authoritatively informed that the Minister's letter requesting air-time was informal and that the Government has never in fact invoked this right under the Act. Mr. Hardiman claims to have insisted on the Minister's requiring the service in writing. He did, but the Government hold that this did not invoke the Ministerial Statutory Powers- therefore it has never been used. What nice games we play!

BBC, and a number of ITV stations, can be received by large numbers of our people in the Republic.

In theory the BBC, in Great Britain and Northern Ireland, is independent of those 'audience ratings' like TAM which dominate what are quaintly called the 'independent' television companies. In fact, no organisation given a national task could reasonably be expected to see its audiences melt away, particularly if they should go to another 'competing' agency! Audiences are too easily seduced to be held, in competitive circumstances, by 'quality' programmes alone. So the BBC follow the TAMs as anxiously as the 'independent' stations do. So do we.

This so-called 'monopoly' was clearly in the minds of the Legislature, the Government and the informed public before the Bill was drafted in 1960. The majority report, for example, which was. submitted to the Government by the Television Commission in 1959 expressly states that a worthwhile programming project for an Irish television service—

> would seem to demand a certain minimum number of hours of broadcasting per week. To some extent, the minimum number of hours required for an Irish television service has to be considered in the light of the number of hours per week occupied by the BBC programmes and the probable length of the imminent ITV programmes.

So, indeed, it has proved to be. The station does not have any effective monopoly of Irish television or radio audiences, nor can it hope to have one. It would be less mystifying if people would stop talking about it as if it had. With the station dependent on advertising for 60 per cent, of its revenue, it must chase TAMs to meet its statutory obligations under sections 24(a) and (b) to 'pay its way'. Otherwise, the advertisers won't buy time.

However this is not the only way in which the sole right to transmit affects the programming authorities in RTE. Contrary to facile cynicism, the fact is that the Irish radio and television Producer is a highly conscientious and dedicated public official, intensely concerned with the effects on the public mind and taste of a real balance in programming. Often, the fact that a programme is transmitted at all means that the same subject-matter cannot reasonably be touched on again for a considerable time. The standing temptation, therefore, is to overload controversial programmes with every possible point of view in order to attain this balance of fair play. As entertainment (and information and education must be entertaining if they are to be useful) the programmes are often a mess.

When one brings together the consequences of the real transmission monopoly with the unreal audience monopoly, one discovers that the national broadcasting services have the worst of both worlds. The facts of competition drive the programme-planner to structure his transmission of good material to match the viewing on offer by the British programmes. A good Western at peak viewing hour on ITV must be matched by a good Western, if viewers (and advertising revenue) are not to be lost. Our competitors, vastly richer than we, set the style and pace. Of course, this would remain true to a considerable extent if there were no advertising, but one important and powerful set of incentives would have been removed. The pressure to 'match' competing programmes would come from the Producers of programmes and not from the top. Further, if there were no monopoly of transmission; if, for example, programming-control by regional Authorities were permitted under law, the temptation to 'match' would be further reduced since local immediacy is, we suggest, the most powerful antidote to undesirable kinds of competition, that we have. RTE's present audience rating is able to stand up to this enormously powerful competition only because of the pull of local Irish flavour. The 'national aims' mentioned in the Act can best be served, it seems to us, by diversification of interest and control, as far as this is practicable.

The method of appointment to the Authority provided under the Act affects the television programme-makers mainly in the creation of an atmosphere of suspicion and distrust. Again and again, in the past three years, we have heard the question asked by senior executives: 'Do you think that we are playing 'footsie' with politicians?' The answer can only be: 'We just don't know, but the *prima facie* evidence is appallingly uniform'. The fact is that in eight years of practical broadcasting on television no really embarrassing programme on public affairs has ever been transmitted. This is not only surprising; it is, humanly speaking, quite shocking. It is no part of the duty of a national broadcasting service habitually to embarrass the Government; but if it is to be impartial it must occasionally do so. One would think that in eight years at least one public row of critical importance might have been healthily expected about an actual transmission. Such 'rows' as have occurred have had a kind of ritual air of mutual outraged innocence on both sides. One has only to compare them with the realities of the Czech, French, or British tensions between broadcasters and their Governments, to see the superficial nature of ours.

The Cork housing scandal programme was never transmitted on the plea that the case was sub judice on the day of transmission. It was not. The Mountpleasant Square land-development programme was never transmitted. The Special Branch programme was never transmitted. There were many others.

Actual interference, outside those provisions of the Act which require the Minister to forbid transmission in writing, has been construed as the exercise of any citizen's right to protest. Why shouldn't a Minister have this right? This is a specious argument. The Minister is not 'any citizen'. He is the most powerful citizen in the country as far as the life of RTE is concerned. His power is not confined to the station's dependence on him in his daily departmental functions. That he has the power to silence the station's voice altogether is not sinister, if it can be shown objectively that the public good demanded such an action and that the grounds for such an action are publicly stated and can be assessed by the public. That he should have the power to subvert it through appointments and selective prohibition is very dangerous indeed.

The Government appoints the Authority; the Minister must consent to the appointment of the Director-General chosen by the Authority. Neither is above suspicion. In fact, each is constantly suspected. The appointments to senior executive posts in RTE are made by the Government's nominees. The majority of these nominees are known to be supporters of the Minister's party. Is it a mere 'peasant cynicism' to think that this has no purpose? Those who make the law seldom have to break it. This is not cynicism; it is a sound democratic scepticism, which is the basis of political health in any society. The self-censorship of senior officials, in a poor, small country which is notorious for its preoccupation with job-security, is constantly rationalised as being a 'sober prudence'. Any programme-maker in the Public Affairs sectors of RTE who does not share this career-security syndrome knows clearly that the fear of criticism from a Fianna Fáil Authority is the real but disguised motive behind every timorous decision. A primary function of the Authority and the Director-General in programming should be to keep Government and commercial interests off the Producers' backs. They do not do this. Even if they did, nobody would believe it; the system of appointment has too obviously a purpose. The fact that the members of the Authority themselves are removable at will by the Government nullifies any hope of independent policy making, or an anti-Government stand where the public good demands it.

This kind of suspicion is inevitable and, in view of events, one can say with moral certainty that it is well founded. Anyway, it will continue as long as the present system of appointments under the Act continues.

The law's most troublesome provision is what is called 'the impartiality' section. It led Senator (now Deputy) Garret FitzGerald to introduce a Bill in the Senate for its amendment, among other things. The provision, in any Act of Parliament, for the enforcement of moral rectitude is notoriously difficult—in fact, impossible. During the debate in the Senate on this Bill, Senator Eoin Ryan substantially criticised Senator FitzGerald's proposal for a Judge to sit on what, in effect, would have been a Court of Impartiality. Senator Ryan's objection was based, in his experience as a lawyer, on the fact that in practice this is precisely what Judges as such cannot do. Impartiality in an actual programme is mainly a question of fact, not of law. In the practice of law, Judges hand over consideration of the factual elements of a case to a jury. In developed democracies, the ordinary citizen, not the specialist, is the safe judge of what is fair and reasonable in relation to facts.

What we would wish most to say on this section is that it is really unworkable. This is not to say that impartiality is unworkable but that a legal enforcement and assessment of it is impossible. This is simply because no power can impose virtue by legislation. Impartiality is part of the virtue of justice and not part of the *apparatus* of law. In the last analysis a programme will only achieve impartiality within the general concept of the station's output and within the programme series of which it is a part, where that is the case. When it does achieve impartiality, this will come from a sense of fair play and the good judgment of Producer and participants, or not at all. No programme was ever ultimately influenced in the making by an awareness of the terms of legislation. The latter merely conditions and prescribes the general attitude. The only people we have ever heard quote the impartiality obligation in this context were the timorous element in senior Management. What is wrong here is not the law but modern Irish attitudes to it.

It is understandable that the Government would wish to have some objective norms embodied in the Act. The Parliamentary draughtsmen had more sense than to try to do an impossible thing. They simply enjoined on the Authority what moral decency would dictate in any case—that they be impartial. The only protection the Government can have against bad professional standards of broadcasting is the protection that the community has against bad government. If the impartiality of Government is not evident to the people, the people can change it. If the impartiality of the Authority is seriously defective, it can be removed. If a Producer seriously offends he can be removed by the Authority. In any of these cases ordinary human prudence is the criterion—not an abstract provision of law. Imagine a Bill being introduced into the Dail expressly purporting to provide for the impartiality of the Minister for Justice, his Department's administration and the Courts' fairness!

However, it must be sadly said that in our experience the main trouble about the impartiality section comes not from the Minister but from the Management. RTE Management has no adequate notion of its own obligations, the Producers' duties or the limitations of human prudence, except a quantitative 'balance'. Its eight years dialogue with the Producers has led Management to express publicly that it realises the limitations on a mathematical concept of programme balance. Nonetheless, in its daily exercise, all this is forgotten and the quantitative notion goes into action like a conditioned reflex at the first whiff of 'danger'. The vice of RTE Management is that of all bureaucracies: it cannot really protect its administrative 'tail' if imaginative and intelligent people are given freedom of action. Intellectual daring is not an administrative virtue. It is a broadcaster's central nervous system. Prudence is the virtue of daring, not of caution; it is, in fact, the golden mean between precipitancy and caution.

Of course, the situation was not improved when the Taoiseach (1966), Mr. Lemass, claimed that RTE is an instrument of public policy, meaning Government policy. The difficulty is compounded when the Authority's Chairman is of the same view.[110] However, it would be ungenerous to make too much of such an evidently Freudian slip as Mr. Lemass's. That Minister's wishes were father to many thoughts which, one hopes, never found really adequate expression.

The financial character of RTE is determined by section 24 of the Act. This is, perhaps, a more serious cause for concern than any other provision in the Act. Though daily less troublesome than the impartiality section, its influence runs through all the station's work. To see the point one must consider this in its actual working relationships to sections 17 and 20. Section 24 is enforceable in law. It says that the Authority must provide a revenue sufficient:

a. to meet all sums properly chargeable to current account, and—
b. to make suitable provision with respect to capital expenditure.

In order to do this the Act provides powers to the Minister and the Authority to use the radio and television licence fees and (section 20) to broadcast advertisements for money.

At the same time Section 17 requires that:

---

[110] Cf. *State-Sponsored Bodies,* Garret FitzGerald, p. 53.

> In performing its functions, the Authority shall bear constantly in mind the national aims of restoring the Irish language and preserving and developing the national culture and shall endeavour to promote the attainment of these aims.

Our experience and, we believe, that of the general body of our colleagues and the public, is that these provisions for financing broadcasting on the one hand, and promoting the national culture on the other, are incompatible in practice. It was foreseen that this would be so and it is so. In this chapter we are merely concerned to point out what we believe to be a well-recognised anomaly: that the cultural aims of the nation, including the restoration of its old language, depend upon building up and promoting a structure of values towards which advertising, and the TAM-rating race consequential thereon, and the 'sub-culture' which it promotes, are inimical.

Section 31 provides two controls on the service's rights to broadcast under the Act: the Minister may 'direct the Authority in writing to refrain from broadcasting any particular matter or matters of any particular class', and similarly, he may require it to broadcast any departmental announcement by a Minister of State by or on behalf of the Minister.

These may appear reasonable provisions in a democratic country. Every State, and even the most primitive community, jealously guards the right of any person or group to address all its members collectively. This right of free speech is not denied by creating safe-guards for its exercise and against abuses. Radio and television have provided a power of immediacy and emotive impact that no responsible Government can ignore. Also, it is a national monopoly under Irish law. It well may be that most Governments, like most people, over-estimate or misunderstand the effects of these media on the public mind. Professional broadcasters enjoy no particular privilege in this matter; they are as likely to be wrong as anybody else. They are, perhaps, more constantly aware of the difficulties and pit-falls. The effects of the 'mass' media on people's attitudes is a matter for empirical investigation by psychologists and social scientists. Their findings are sparse and tentative so far.

Having said these necessary things, one might reasonably ask whether an 'omnibus' power of prohibition on broadcasting 'any particular matter or matters of a particular class' is a wise and prudent power to give to a Minister of State in this vital area of public information. Ministers of State in democratic countries, no less than totalitarian ones, are party officials. Public policy is party policy, although under constitutional and customary limitations. It would be cynical to reject this method as essentially biased and partisan. It is the very essence of democratic effectiveness. But it has its dangers, particularly for an authority like RTE that has a transmission monopoly. A public policy must be carried through, certainly. It should be carried through, in times of internal peace, publicly and under conditions permitting of adult criticism. At best there is an unfortunate 'logic' in the growth of State power that creates an irritable paternalism in public officials, including Party members who are public officials. At worst there is a natural opportunism which will seek to secure silence on anything that may prove to party disadvantage. Democratic theory does not depend on having a Minister whose personal integrity is above suspicion. Legal safe-guards are necessary because weak and evil men are common and because even good men are commonly tempted. This is one of the main reasons for having law and democracy at all. It seems unreasonable, therefore, to hand over to a Minister such complete and absolute power over media which have a duty to stand in judgment on the Minister's impartiality and integrity. No political philosopher in the democratic tradition would advocate that the people should hand such powers to a Minister over the Press.

Of course, it is true that RTE enjoys a State monopoly of broadcasting while newspapers do not. This certainly puts a heavy responsibility on the national broadcasting services. These have no real domestic competitors to offer a platform to those whose views might be unacceptable to RTE. True: but how does the Minister's power to *prohibit* any item protect such people? It cannot. It is surely not suggested that the freedom traditionally thought essential to the Press, does not apply to radio and television at all? The events in Czechoslovakia and France during 1968 demonstrated beyond doubt that the peoples' liberties depend on a constant flow of information and comment in which they can have confidence. This confidence cannot long survive under the present kind of law. We venture to think that it has survived at all only because of the vigilance of the Irish newspapers, the professional recalcitrance of radio and television journalists and the readiness of opposition politicians to criticise the Minister and his Authority. The question is: is this fair and ultimately sufficient? The mere threat of invoking the Act may be enough to bring a mainly party Authority into line.

There is no really legitimate reason for Government interference in suppressing news or comment in peace time. The claim made by the Minister that the Government, being ultimately responsible for RTE, must have the right to suppress its work is not self-evidently sound. Nothing that has ever been said on this provision, that we have read, constitutes a reasoned case. The Government, of course, feels a need for this security and, therefore, must have it! This is bad law and, in the long run, bad government, we think. That it is bad broadcasting we know only too well.

The law on obscenity as it stands is sufficient protection against overt corruption of morals. It is doubtful if this was ever the purpose of Section 31. The stopping of such enterprises as the Vietnam news reporting expedition or the Biafra project, in order to avoid the Government's foreign policy's being critically appraised by the public, is obviously the kind of thing for which this section was really intended to provide. This is very dangerous and, in its exercise, downright bad for the nation as well as the broadcasting service. In the first instance, the Minister did not make his requirement in writing, as the Act demands for transmission. The Director-General acted on a verbal intimation. This caused our professional journalists instant alarm. They realised that, under a Government appointed Authority and an 'approved' Director-General, it was possible for the Government to suppress a disinterested search for news *without the public knowing it*. In the case of the recall of the *7 Days* team from its mission to Biafra we all suddenly realised the fact that there was no need any more for Ministerial interference. The powers given under the Act and the predictable attitudes of the Authority were sufficient to procure a halt to news-gathering by *anticipation* of Government interference. Self-censorship in the circumstances was more than possible, it was evident. Under the system of party appointments it could always be suspected. It almost always was and is suspected; often wrongly, no doubt, but always reasonably.

This strikes deep into the professional broadcaster's confidence in his superiors. Timidity is a contagious disease. Quickly the broadcaster, anxious to get on with his job, will also begin to anticipate criticism by his own immediate superior. Caution becomes the price of internal peace. It may ultimately destroy public confidence in the news and in the impartiality and integrity of news comment.

If the Act is to be reviewed, as we think reasonable, these considerations should be taken into account. What can we suggest?

First, appointment to the Authority should not be left to the Government. Why should this important matter not be in the hands of a committee of both Houses of the Oireachtas in consultation with the Government?

Second, it could *then* be argued that the power given to the Government to remove members of the Authority at will should be repealed and instead that the members of the Authority should have statutory protection against the abuse of such power by the Government. A useful parallel from Bord na Móna ought to be considered: Under the Turf Development Act, 1948, the members of Bord na Mona are appointed by the Government. The period of appointment is the same as in RTE, for a period not exceeding five years as the Government shall fix. The members are eligible for re-appointment. The powers of the Government to remove a member of Bord na Mona from the Board are much more limited than in the case of RTE:

> If at any time it appears to the Government that the removal from office of all or any of the members of the Board is necessary in the interests of the effective and economical performance of the functions of the Board the Government may remove from office all or so many of the members of the Board as the Government considers necessary in the interests aforesaid [Turf Act, Section 10 (1)].

> The Government may also remove from Office any member of the Board who becomes incapable through ill-health from performing his duties or who has been

> absent from meetings of the Board for six consecutive months without good reason [Section 10 (2)].
>
> Whenever the Government removes from office under this Section any member of the Board, the Government shall lay before each house of the Oireachtas a statement in writing of the fact of the removal from office of such member and of the reasons for such removal [Section 10 (3)].

It is evident that much greater protection is given by these provisions than by the Broadcasting Authority Act. Where the Government have to state reasons for a removal of a member of the Board and lay it before the Oireachtas it brings the whole issue into the public forum for open discussion and the parliamentary opposition can then bring in a motion to have the matter debated and the facts can be aired publicly. This is a useful and sufficient deterrent against the abuse of Government power and in the RTE case would protect members of the Board from victimisation at the hands of the Government where they wished to act contrary to Government wishes on any particular issue.

It is submitted that no self-respecting member of so important an Authority as RTE should accept less than such terms if he is to be protected from unwarranted Government interference in his functions.

Third, the appointment by the Authority of a Director-General, if the Authority were above suspicion, ought not require Ministerial approval. The only reason for it would be Ministerial fear of independence in the exercise of this office. This is intolerable.

Fourth, the national culture and values are being constantly undermined by repetitive advertising, the only aims of which are to increase consumption and spending. We have said that very little is known with certainty about the effects of these media but we do know that repetition4is the essence of the effect of broadcasting on behaviour. No culture (or indeed policy of thrift) could possibly survive this endless campaign of psychological conditioning without injury. There are two possibilities. The power to transmit advertising, given under the Act, might be simply withdrawn. Alternatively, the kind, volume, and timing of advertising might be radically altered; it ought, in our view, be dissociated from the programmes. It could be transmitted in advertising 'blocks' of time, as in some stations like the Dutch, Swiss and Italian.[111]

Fifth, while impartiality should certainly be enjoined, its terms should be admonitory. It would be enormously helpful if the Minister would expressly disclaim numerical notions of 'balance'. Management might be encouraged. The Act could allow for a Committee of the Oireachtas or a Press and Communications Council to hold sittings of enquiry into allegations of partiality of a grave and protracted nature, on request by the Minister or by the leaders of the Opposition.

As we have pointed out above, the attitudes of politicians on the very real problems of impartiality has been very much more liberal than those of Management. We suspect that this is not because politicians are better people than managers; rather, politicians face effective opposition to dictatorial or repressive attitudes, while managers do not.

---

[111] 'Advertising is in a separate class. It is dependent to a large extent on repetition. It provides the images and the sound supporting the images on a regular basis. Its effectiveness lies in the repetition of the same message again and again.' - T.P. Hardiman, Irish Press Interview (Part 2), 2nd April 1969

Alas, the prestige, power and courage of managers are more fragile things than those of statesmen.

Sixth, we suggest that the terms of Section 31 (a) should be circumscribed to cover 'times of war and declared national emergency'. Section 31 (b) can, of course, be abused by a Minister but, if the Director-General should be empowered by the Act to grant the Government the facility of addressing the nation *only* in receipt of a demand in writing, the admittedly ugly suspicion of seeking Party advantage in publicity would be avoided. The possibility of abuse of this power by an unscrupulous Minister is reduced by the fact that it cannot be done secretly. The power of the Minister to direct the Authority in writing to refrain from broadcasting any particular matter or matters of any particular class, contained in Section 31 (1) of the Act should be exercisable only in times of national emergency as defined in Article 28 (3) (3) of the Constitution, and should come into force not by virtue of the Broadcasting Authority Act, 1960, or any amendment of same, but only by virtue of an Act of Parliament passed to deal with a national emergency pursuant to Article 28 (3) (3) of the Constitution. To give RTE a sole monopoly of broadcasting news and comment on current events on radio and television, and then to give the Minister sole and unchallengeable authority to censor such news or features as he wishes, is tantamount to giving the Minister absolute powers of censorship which are completely incompatible with the fundamental rights relating to freedom of expression guaranteed by the Constitution.

Finally, it might be argued, indeed it has been argued, that the freedom of action and judgment which we think essential for a national broadcasting service is being (insolently and cynically) denied to the Minister of State who is responsible to the Oireachtas for it. Why, if professional men ought to be trusted in their duties, should a Minister of State not be trusted to carry out his, fairly and without niggling legislation?

This is a fair question. Let us try to give a fair, if unpopular answer to it. It is not a pleasant subject for politicians. It is an important one for freedom-loving citizens.

The whole tradition of constitutional government since the Greeks is that the gravest alienation of rights a people can make to any of its members is the power to rule over them. It must be guarded, as we have seen, not merely on the assumption that rulers may be corrupt men but that *this power itself is a corrupting thing*, even when men are virtuous. Jealousy of its exercise, therefore, is the characteristic of freedom in democracies. Governments have the quite terrible powers of raising and maintaining armed forces and police, the power of waging war, of suppressing rebellion or civil commotion, of levying taxes and duties. All of these are enormous concessions to give mortal men. If exercised by the upright, without anxiously devised restraints, they would corrupt angels. The very notion of constitutional democratic rule is to circumvent this corruption of the good, not merely to prevent the election of the evil. To be real about it, subordinate powers can, of course, be seriously abused. But ordinary remedies are ordinarily sufficient to control them. In addition (an important addition) the curious moral restraints exercised upon a man by public criticism of his actions by his professional peers is a feature of civilised life. It does not suffice for Government powers. These operate in democratic societies against the pressures of political opposition. The weakness of this is that, in real democracies, oppositions are potential governments. They can be corrupted into quiescence in petty tyrannies by this golden promise.

# 10

## WHAT CAN WE DO?:
## PROPOSALS FOR UNMASKING THE 'MASS'

# CHAPTER 10: WHAT CAN WE DO?:

*Practical men, who believe themselves to be quite exempt from intellectual influences, are usually the slaves of some defunct economist... but soon or late, it is ideas not vested interests, which are dangerous for good or evil.*
—JOHN MAYNARD KEYNES

*My countrymen are not Athenians; they are persuaded only by irrelevancies.*
—CARDINAL POLE

## WHAT CAN WE DO?

'Never resign', say the practical men. 'Never knock down if you can't build up'. We believe this to be literally nonsense. We do not believe that 'you can't beat the system'. In fact, our argument is that one must try to beat the system and go on trying. That is why we resigned and that is why we wrote this book.

We hope that the reader will have noticed that we have argued for experiment, investigation and enquiry, not for dogmatic conclusions. The need is for the recognition of problems.

In attempting to summarise these problems here, our selection is necessarily personal.

\* \* \*

A recognition of the true character of broadcasting technology should be institutionally reflected in structures of organisation which will give creative programme-makers an authoritative voice in programme initiation, development and execution.

We believe that the most misleading habit of mind is one which sees all problems in terms of the quality of personnel involved in their solution. 'It all comes down to people, in the end'. It does, in a sense. But this is not sufficient. Because we have argued against rigid organisational structures and have sympathised with our colleagues in their detestation of them, it has been assumed that we are against organisation as such. In fact, we have tried to put forward the view that proper forms of organisation can enlarge and deepen the work to be done and release the creative energy of those who do it. Flexible institutions, therefore, as much as (if not more than) the quality of personnel, must be suited to temperaments and tasks of their nature diverse.

For example, we have proposed an experimental unit for routine programmes; *ad hoc* assemblies of talent for special projects and systematic investigation and experiment for Drama, Light Entertainment, etc., using control groups to measure results. This experimental unit could operate on selected programmes of a repetitive kind and have its work compared for quality and quantity against that of a conventionally organised production-unit. The success of all this implies a study of the needs of audiences, their attitudes and patterns of participation. The internal structures must be brought into relationship with the public needs, institutionally.

* * *

In addition to these studies and experiments, RTE requires 'a stomach for failure'. This will call for an act of faith in the integrity and insight of programme-makers of all grades. It will need the active but sub-alternate[112] participation of technicians, technologists and technocrats. It will ask of these men that they realise the limitations of their competence and that the dynamic modem world of thought cannot (and

---

112  A system in which roles of dominance change with the special requirements of each task and situation.

ought not) have the orderly neatness and 'realism' of a Dutch Interior. Thought is the area of risk that defines our humanity. Its real enemy is not force but caution.

\* \* \*

The need for strong, clear-minded programme control by professionally and nationally committed Producers, headed by a leadership of unchallengeable intellectual and moral stature, in both radio and television, is paramount.

\* \* \*

We need, too, a philosophy of broadcasting that will animate native structures, institutions and the working relationships between men and women of real mettle. The doctrinaire pragmatism which has been the daily instrument of the immediate past and which is so much part of our general Irish malaise since the Rising, is now a tattered thing. The effort of thought will be great; its continued neglect will be disastrous. It should, we feel, be built into a system of training, re-training, self-criticism and open debate among programme-makers and all their supportive colleagues. This should be extended, where possible, to include the public, and other broadcasting organisations. International 'Festivals' have become increasingly discredited as a form of meaningful professional exchange of ideas.

\* \* \*

Such thought will be fruitful in action only if a philosophy of delegated authority is articulated, interiorised and acted upon with, again, 'a stomach for failure'. This implies the abandonment not only of power-concepts but of power-structures. That the difficulties are enormous, we know. The Broadcasting Act as presently framed implies that the power-concept is natural and normal. The religious, moral and cultural traditions of our people all hold some elements of this notion of power. As a people, we both admire and fear it. But our traditions also hold valuable elements of responsibility, dedication and democratic independence, which must be allowed to develop institutionally. We think that we have indicated at least the principles of such a view of authority.

* * *

Radio Telefís Éireann must face up to the contradictions inherent in the notions of promoting a national culture and remaining dependent financially on advertising. It is a curiosity of our Irish situation that everybody really knows this but nobody in authority is moved, either by conscience or public pressure, to do anything about it. The facts are known and, presumably, understood. The opinions have been canvassed and largely agreed: advertisements on radio and television are ugly and pernicious in their effects and intentions. Apart from the Government, probably reluctantly, and the commercial interests, enthusiastically, nobody wants them on their screens. Yet there they are, night after night, determining the quality and placing of programmes and doing their anti-human and degrading work. It is simply not true that they are a necessary evil. They are a necessity only to the lazy-minded and the profit-makers. We have suggested their being phased out altogether. We plead, at least, for their displacement from their direct relationship to programmes in the transmission schedule. In the interim, if vested interests and public indifference are immovable, then surely we might expect an iron control over their placing, by the Authority and the Minister.

We have suggested alternative means of financing the service.

* * *

## CHAPTER 10: WHAT CAN WE DO?:

The whole notion of 'culture' which we have inherited from the 19th century, it seems to us, is now under challenge. 'High' culture and 'popular' culture are the creations of 'high' society. They are a literary snobbery at worst and a mindless bigotry at best. It is, as we have tried to show, based on a false and easily identifiable analogical argument. This is the notion that people must be given what they want or at least what their 'betters' think they need. The truth is that human needs in the bodily sense have specifiable objects which satisfy them. Hunger can be appeased by bread or potatoes; its objective satisfaction is known to be food. The spirit of man has no determinate and generic object which will satisfy it in this sense. It bloweth where it listeth. It seeks the eternal. It never rests in the choices it makes and no man can say what choices *should* satisfy it. That there is one culture for the 'high' and another for the 'popular' taste is an insensitive myth. What is true of the human spirit and what differentiates it from the bodiless Spirit, is that it can be seduced. The easy, the vulgar, the facile, the meretricious and the false, if repeatedly and sweetly offered—without intelligible alternative—will become not only the diet of the human spirit but the stimulants of its appetite. That a national television service should subscribe to such a view of its people's 'needs' is a scandal.

The quantity and quality of imported film material demands examination in its cultural effects. While this must and ought remain a feature of our output, the bulk of it need not come from the United States and Britain. We need a far wider cultural exchange than this. We have bought some of this kind of material in the past. The cost will be considerably higher. It is assumed that we require the instant availability of the English language: Poles, Scandinavians, Swiss, and other Continentals do not. We are told that the Irish people do not *want* subtitles. Of course they don't. We have conditioned our people to 'instant' enjoyment of television as a medium that requires no effort.

Having created the want, we must, of course, satisfy it; else the British networks will capture a large element of our audiences. Clearly, then, this proposal can have meaning only if we can secure superb material. Again, this is a matter of what we can really afford[113] as against what we *think* we can afford. This also holds true for programme material exchanged, and for co-productions.

\* \* \*

We have pointed out that in a world about to enter into satellite communications on an almost unimaginable scale, intensity and duration, a thin and 'universally intelligible culture' is a terrible danger. It may level out and destroy all our local values and idiosyncrasies. We hold that the only defence against this international uniformity of spirit is regional diversity—the greatest possible measure of decentralisation and diversification of control and initiative.

All other things being equal, we know from audience reaction indices and TAM-ratings that Irish viewers prefer Irish material, programme for programme. The task is to increase the amount and quality of this native work. By regionalisation, we would increase its intensity and spread the load. Besides this general need, in view of increasing cultural internationalism, the unique and now beleaguered Gaeltachts need to have their dying culture revitalised. This is always a matter of living dialogue—not being talked *at*. It can best be done by communicating its special values with their compatriots', and among themselves. At the moment they are being served by the remote and largely formal attempts of RTE to implement its obligations under the Act. We have put forward proposals in the chapter on Irish culture to this end. We propose, therefore, the creation of as many regional radio and mobile

---

113   See chapter on Advertising.

television units, under local control, as there is a demand for and for which there are resources.

*Their* enemy will not be uniformity, but amateurism—the Celtic thing. Initially, the quality may well be extremely tatty. But this must be risked. Anyway, this is vitally important only when one thinks of television or radio as 'show business' or miniature cinema. It is a matter of secondary importance if we regard radio and television as being primarily and essentially communications between members of a culture-community. The smallest possible communities must have the means of communicating and arguing with themselves and one another. Above all they must have *real* decentralisation of financial and administrative authority and independence in policy-making. The availability of professionally trained personnel will be a major problem. They can be trained and provided, if we want them.

Because this will be expensive, we must forestall the objection that it will be wasteful. The only things in Ireland that we waste without shame are people. We have already sent a million of our youth abroad in a generation; it was too expensive and wasteful of our resources to keep them at home. We now face a future in which it will not be necessary to export them in order to waste them. If we do not move ourselves, we may see our children grow fat bodily, but spiritually wither, at home.

\* \* \*

Since the foundation of television in Ireland was based on the assumption that we needed to preserve our cultural identity from the influences of the British networks, it was inferred that we should match their transmissions hour for hour, or as nearly as possible. From this assumption we slipped into the further assumption that we had to match their programmes, kind for kind, style for style, film for film.

Since the British were doing much the same thing vis-a-vis the Americans, the whole process defeated the original assumption. By employing this competitive matching, our very attempt to preserve our national identity absorbed that identity into an imitation of international culture.

\* \* \*

Do we *need* to transmit as many hours per week as we do? Serious consideration should be given to shorter broadcasting hours from a central station by a lessening of its bulk-production. There is also much value in having 'repeats*' as a regular evening feature of the schedule; say, on one night a week. Again, we merely plead for an active realisation of a problem.

\* \* \*

The legal root of our 'mass' communications system is the Broadcasting Acts of 1960-1966. These are not of Sinai; they came from Dublin. We have examined them as far as our experience and limited competence permitted. We have put forward seven proposals for their amendment in the previous chapter.

These might be considered with the necessary adjustments to provide for regional broadcasting.

\* \* \*

We have made specific recommendations on the method of appointing the Authority. It seems to us that their vocational composition is also a matter of vital concern. Since 1961 the persons appointed have been, uniformly, Establishment figures. Academics, business men, representatives of cultural institutions, do not normally provide the kind of youthful, enquiring zest and the capacity for new insights that are necessary in the communications field. We propose that a large part of the Authority's membership should be drawn from the fields of arts, letters, philosophy and science. Intellectual and artistic distinction rather than representative dependability seem to be the qualities required. Nice people are a waste of time on such a Board as the Broadcasting Authority.

* * *

This is the end of our professional participation in these matters.

Vale!

# APPENDIX I
## LEONARDO AND THE LEVIATHAN

*by*
*Brendan McGann*

This Appendix has been omitted due to rights issues.

# APPENDIX II
## ADVERTISING DATA

# (A)

# ADVERTISING CLASSIFICATION OF TRANSMISSION TIMES FOR PROGRAMMES

Peak viewing times are from (approximately) 7 to 10 p.m. each night. There are occasional exceptions for great national occasions. These are 'prime' time, and are mainly filled with entertainment designed for 'mass' audiences, for advertising revenue purposes.

| A. Time | 7.00 to 10 pm | Sunday |
| --- | --- | --- |
| | 6.45 to 10 pm | Monday to Friday |
| | 7.00 to 11 pm | Saturday |
| B. Time | 10 to 10.30 pm | Sunday to Friday |
| C. Time | 6.15 to 6.45 pm | Monday to Friday |
| | 6.15 to 7.00 pm | Saturday |
| D. 1. Time | Before 6.15 pm | Monday to Saturday |
| | Before 7.00 pm | Sunday |
| D. 2. Time | 10.30 to 11.15 pm | Sunday to Friday |
| | 11.00 to 11.30 pm | Saturday |

# (B)

# THE ALLOCATION OF RESOURCES IN THE PRODUCTION OF TELEVISION PROGRAMMES

*A dissertation presented for the Autumn 1967 Master of Business Administration Degree Examination (extract)*
by George T. Waters

A statement of the general objectives of a National Broadcasting Service is as follows:

(a) From the Broadcasters' point of view:
1. Maximise audience.
2. Maximise quality of programmes.
3. Entertain.
4. Inform.
5. Educate.

(b) From the Audience point of view:
6. Obtain maximum satisfaction.
7. Minimum cost.

In the particular case of Radio Telefís Éireann, the following objectives can be added to (a):[114]
8. To maintain financial viability.
9. To be impartial and objective in the presentation of programmes.

---

114 'Statement of Objectives—RTE'. Consensus of opinion among participants in RTE Management Course run in conjunction with the Irish Management Institute 1965.

Examination of this set of objectives show that numbers 1, 7 and 8 are inter-related because of the financial structure of the system. RTE's revenue is obtained from licence fees and advertising. Both of these sources of income depend on audience size. Thus 1 is considered to be an objective representative of the other two.

Objectives 2 and 6 are likewise related as it is reasonable to assume that maximisation of audience satisfaction is consistent with maximisation of programme quality. Thus, a second objective to be met can be considered to be objective 6.

Objectives 3, 4, 5 and 9 may be considered as constraints and can be included as such in the Resource Allocation Model. The problem may thus be formulated as follows:

> The maximisation of audience size and audience satisfaction while at the same time observing the constraints imposed by the requirement to produce a programme mix reflecting entertainment, information and education with impartiality and objectiveness in presentation.

A measure of Programme Effectiveness might then be defined as a function of:
1. Audience satisfaction.
2. Audience size.

[We forbear from commenting on this beyond reassuring the incredulous of its authenticity]

# APPENDIX III
## DOCUMENTS

# PEARSE KELLY'S NOTICE OF RESIGNATION AS HEAD OF NEWS

NOTICE TO STAFF OF NEWS DIVISION

11th November 1968.

I have today handed my resignation as Head of News to the Director-General and it has been accepted.

While I am making no statement as to how this has come about, other than that it was inevitable, I do say that it is with every genuine regret I leave the News Division[115].

We all worked together with enthusiasm and something of a pioneering spirit to create a news operation in which we could take pride.

I believe we succeeded to a considerable degree, in spite of the many obstacles and frustrations which have confronted us from time to time. I have memories of enterprise and achievement which I shall recall with a great deal of pleasure, and also of something else which I value greatly— comradeship.

I wish the staff of the News Division the greatest success in the future in striving to create and maintain the highest standards of journalism, of which I know you to be capable.

It may be tough going, but you can do it.

Good luck.
Pearse Kelly

\* \* \*

---

115  We have now been informed that Mr. Kelly was asked by Mr. McCourt with the concurrence of Dr. C. S. Andrews, to resign. No reasons were given, except their desire for 'a change'.

# LETTER ON 'HOME TRUTHS' POLICY

Programme Controller,
Radio Telefís Éireann,

1st January, 1967

Dear Michael,

You asked me to give you a short 'brief' on the *Home Truths* policy. Here is what I have been able to assemble in the past few days:

It is essentially an *advisory* programme.
It advises the lower income groups on:
   a. Their rights in law and equity: 'This is Your Right'.
   b. Their health: 'Your Very Good Health'.
   c. Their diet: 'Domestic Science'.
   d. Their cooking: 'Cooking by Jimmy Flahive'.
   e. Their home recreations: Olga Deane's occasional pieces and John Fanning's 'Down to Earth'.
   f. Their incomes and budgets: 'Bills, Budgets and Bother' by Tomás Roseingrave.
   g. Consumer and customer advice to the Housewife: 'How Much?' by Mary Murphy.

These are the 'set pieces'. They do not, never have, and were never intended, 'to report on the facts merely'. They have certainly never been understood by the newspapers, the critics, the criticised or the viewers to be anything but a working-class programme, for working-class households and families. It is partisan in-so-far as this majority section of our people are under-privileged and imposed on by Business, Government, Administration and (I regret to say) by the mass-media.

The 'philosophy' of the programme is naively based *directly* on these documents:
1. The Guide to the Social Services.
2. The Summary of the Health Services.
3. Mater et Magistra.

We are working through these booklets systematically.

This was the scheme discussed with your predecessor and encouraged by him.

*Home Truths* has, I think, gained the confidence of a large body of working-class viewers because:
a. It is 'committed' to them in the simple sense of recognising that they are being exploited; exposing and opposing it.
b. It is not afraid to risk litigation in naming people and products.
c. It is not afraid to risk Government disapproval in criticising the daily administration of 'enabling' legislation.
d. It is not afraid to offend advertising interests by giving the lie to misleading notions about products and their effects, e.g. Smoking (three times), Dental Caries (twice), Sweets (over-eating), Canned Foods, etc., etc.

It has survived thus far because it has depended on social scientists for its facts and has worked them to exhaustion. To suppose that this programme has an 'objective' (in the sense of an 'impartial' and uncommitted) reporting purpose is an afterthought of such transparent ingenuity as to be just funny! If it *were* to become its policy, most viewers, I feel, would quickly see the joke but not the humour.

Yours sincerely,
Jack Dowling

\* \* \*

# LETTER TO TAOISEACH ON THE OCCASION OF THE CANCELLATION OF RTE COVERAGE OF VIETNAM WAR

18th April 1967

'The undersigned employees of Radio Telefís Éireann protest in the strongest terms at the action of the Government in relation to RTE's proposed coverage of Vietnam.

'We urgently request the Taoiseach and the Government to reconsider the machinery by which the cancellation of this project was effected.

'We consider that such action strikes dangerously at responsible broadcasting and at the dissemination of objective news.

'We fully endorse the request of the National Union of Journalists for discussion with you.'

Copies were sent to the Chairman of the RTE Authority, the Director-General, the Controller of Programmes (television), the Controller of Programmes (radio) and the Head of News.

The following signatures were attached:

Rita Archer, Michael Bogdanov, William R. Bell, Michael Cutliffe, Minnie Byrne, Marguerite Broderick, Eugene Bellington, J. O. Butler, Brian Cleeve, Marianne Crowley, Pan Collins, Ian P. Corr, T. R. Crowley, Tim Costello, John Cummins, Joan Caffrey, Frances Cassidy, Tom Cleary, Joan Collins, M. Campion, J. Condron, Noeline Coffey, D. Cunningham, John Loughlan, Fergal Costello, Paul Davis, Lelia Doolan, J. V. Doyle, Jack Dowling, Ted Dolan, C. Duignan, Dan Donohue, Brendan

Duggan, Vincent Deignen, Nessa Dowley, R. Davis, Brian Eustace, Jim Fitzgerald, Christopher FitzSimon, Donall Farmer, Ria Farren, Deirdre Friel, Mike Fenton, Brian Farrell, Rita Foran, Don Farrell, Patrick Gallagher, Aileen Geoghegan, B. Grogan, Terry Gough, Margaret Gleeson, Godfrey Graham, Eoghan Harris, Stuart Hetherington, Patrick M. Hayes, Maureen Hurley, Dick Hill, Dana Hearne, Patricia Hughes, Jim Jones, Patrick Kearney, Justin Keating, M. Kelly, Oonagh Kavanagh, K. Kilroy, Louis Lentin, Anne Logue, Lona Moran, Sean Mac Réamoinn, Gerry Murray, Mary Murphy, Muiris Mac Conghail, Anne Makower, B. Mac Lochlainn, Michael Murray, Liam Moore, John McColgan, P. McBreen, Brian McCartney, Seamus McDonnell, Valerie McGowan, Peter McEvoy, Max Mulvihill, D. Mulhall, E. Massey, P. V. Manning, Philip Mullaly, Ted Nealon, Brendan Neilen, Joyce Neylin, Padraig Ó Siochrú, Aindreas Ó Gallchóir, John O'Donoghue, Denis O'Grady, Sean Ó Mordha, Gerry O'Donovan, T. O'Connor, M. J. Olohan, Colm O'Byrne, Mairead Nx Ndill, Oliver O'Farrel, Colette O'Rourke, Liam O'Flanagan, Michael Purcell, Shelah Richards, Gráinne Ni Ruairc, Charles Scott, Michael Slevin, Vincent Scally, Liam Smith, J. Noel Sparks, Ann Sheehy, Seamus Smith, Tom Walsh, Derek Walsh, Adrian Vale, Janet Wynne, Bill St. Leger, Seán Kelleher, W. A. Ryan, Jack Merriman, Nora Lenihan, David Thornley, Rosemary Fenlon, Michael Morris, Simon R. Weafer, John Bowman.

Members of the National Union of Journalists employed by RTE were not asked to sign the letter, as they had already made their representations through the Irish Secretary and Council of the union. The Council asked for a meeting with the Taoiseach.

* * *

*From:* Director-General
*To:* Each member of the staff

1st May, 1967

In view of the recent widespread publicity given to the cancellation of the proposal to send a News team to Vietnam, I think it necessary to bring the following to the notice of all members of the staff.

The Vietnam project was conceived and planned within the organisation as desirable in the interests of news and informative programming. The concept was an enterprising one and reflected a commendable desire within the organisation to concern itself with the major events and happenings in the present-day world. The decision to abandon the project was taken by the Authority after very careful consideration of the new circumstances brought to its notice. This decision was made by the Authority alone and there was no question of any infringement of the Authority's independence in programme matters being involved.

The decisions of the Authority on broadcasting matters are binding on the staff of RTE, and the fact that certain members of the staff should have issued a public letter to the Taoiseach protesting in their capacity as employees of RTE at what was described in the letter as the action of the Government in relation to the Vietnam project is to be deplored. I must go on record to each member of the organisation that public criticism by members of the staff of a matter involving the governing body of the broadcasting service is inadmissible.

The framework of the organisation has been shaped so as to provide as much communication as possible upwards and downwards in an organisation of this size and complexity. There is adequate machinery for representations by the staff, primarily through the Divisional Heads, and in the more serious issues, direct on request to me. I think I do not have to assure you that responsible representations will always receive consideration, but I do insist on the observance by members of the staff of these proper organisational channels to the exclusion of others.

Kevin C. McCourt,
Director General.

\* \* \*

## BOB QUINN'S LETTER

Clare Island,
Wednesday, 14th May 1969.

Dear Friends and Colleagues,

Over the past couple of years, it will have become apparent to the more perceptive among you that RTE (hence forth to be known as the Factory) has been developing along certain regrettable but inevitable lines.

These tendencies towards a large, impersonal technocracy have been justified on the grounds of efficiency, the same grounds on which the wholesale exploitation of the resources of this country by our speculative leaders is based. In this sense, the Factory is fulfilling one of its functions, i.e. the reflecting of the country as a whole. This of course is ignoring one of its other, equally important functions, the educational one. It is also ignoring the fact that one has not only the duty of reporting fairly what is happening, but if the situation is serious enough, of intervening personally, not as an organisation man, but as a man.

The Factory, as we are all aware, has grown into a large organisation. Organisations are not run by people. They are run by the systems which people invent to avoid the business of thinking. Eventually the people become functionaries of the systems, in some cases, happy functionaries, in most cases, vaguely dissatisfied employees. The liberal conservative would describe the latter category as an expression of the Human Condition. This is not only rubbish, but dangerous rubbish. The human condition is defined by man; the degrees of its comfort or discomfort are the direct responsibility of man.

What can one person do?

When confronted by a monolith which proposes to eat you, even in the nicest possible manner, you must do something. The worst thing to do is to allow the monolith to define the terms of the battle. Ignore its pleas for logic, because it uses logic to obscure the truth; ignore its calls for reasonableness, the assumptions and premises of which are entirely questionable; query its sacred cows, its gods and its liturgies, its systems, its impeccable phrases imported from the respectable corruption of business management. Ignore above all its offers of a comfortable place in the technocratic womb; its bribes of security, status and free burial service.

Having ignored all of these expressions you will find yourself out of a job. And you can't afford this because you have a mortgage, an overdraft, a hire-purchase agreement and a realisation that you were never free. So you will not follow the advice in the preceding paragraph. That is when the organisation laughs.

What all this amounts to is that you can do absolutely nothing. You are completely trapped. You must now enter a period of despair, in which you will fulfil your functions in a perfect mechanical, unthinking, organisational manner. And this is all that is required by the system of organisation in which you work. And that is why the organisation decays and becomes a bloated and swelling corpse, feeding the increasing number of parasites but incapable of directing itself because there is no life, no human spirit to quicken it.

This I suggest is the situation in which the Factory finds itself. This despite the efforts of bright young men in advertising agencies to string gaudy beads round the neck of the corpse, the vile body, in an effort to persuade the people of this country that their property is still working on their behalf. It is not. It is simply a vehicle for the frustrated fantasies of ad-men, the megalomania of insane technocrats and the sanctification of the acts of a conservative government. If one looks closely at those lines, one will see evidence of the greatest sell-out ever perpetrated on a nation—by the nation itself, through its sons.

And what do I propose to do about it? Mine is a personal philosophy of responsible irresponsibility. It attempts to counter the organisation's pseudo-philosophy of irresponsible responsibility. If you follow me. I propose to get a boat and sail off, Charlie-Bubbles-like, into the setting sun. All contributions will be tolerated, and appreciated if they're in the form of moral support.

Yours sincerely,
Bob Quinn
[A short biography was appended]

\* \* \*

Mr. Jim Plunkett Kelly,

Programme Head,
Features Department, TV.

23rd May, '69.

Dear Jim,

Since I understand that it is not legally possible to resign a contract unilaterally I must ask you to have me released from my present obligations to serve RTE as a Producer-Director immediately.

My reasons are: in general, that the radio and television services are in such a state of morale that they cannot carry out their functions in the life of the nation, either culturally or technically. In particular, it seems to me that the progressive dominance of programming by technicians and administrators in radio has been disastrous; sheer quantity dominates everything and everyone. The level of programming in television entertainment and public affairs comment is steadily falling.

Specifically, I am of the view that these public services, through a failure to delegate programming authority, have become the personal empire of the Director-General in a sense never intended by the Broadcasting Act. Real control of programmes, nominally vested in the Controllers of radio and television (and proportionately to their production staffs) is exercised by the Director-General alone in its real integrity. The only true delegation of his statutory powers is to a carefully chosen 'policy committee' of Administrators and Chief Journalists. The facade of Programme control in radio and television has now the single substantial function of cutting off the actual programme-makers from the sources of real decision.

Our two services lack organisation and structures orientated to their essentially cultural functions. Our two Programme Controllers have failed to provide the necessary leadership and professional inspiration. Intellectual and imaginative daring, the desire to try new forms and procedures are all progressively neglected or even actively suppressed. Our Directorate seems to me to be without serious moral conviction or independence of judgment. The clarity of purpose, standards of professional broadcasting conduct, candour with staff and the public all seem to be lacking. I regard this as culpable and deliberate policy.

Management has substituted for these qualities a nervous self-censorship which it expects its subordinates to have the 'common-sense' to anticipate in their programme-making. My superiors seem to me to have no real interpretation of RTE's role of impartiality other than a shrewd and cynical anticipation of external pressures and censures.

I think that a close examination of the programme schedules will reveal that considerations of advertisers' requirements and not the national cultural and entertainment needs, determine its structure. The hegemony of technologists and administrators has introduced a caution suitable to the Civil Service rather than a spirit of adventurous experimentation in ideas.

A Programme production staff, initially inadequately trained, is not only overworked and neglected in professional continuation-training, but increasingly blamed for lack of ideas and technical finesse. The climate of RTE does not stimulate ideas. It is repressive, pragmatic and contemptuous of individuality, eccentricity or novelty. It encourages only conformity and seems to treat intellectual dissent as a curious species of mental instability.

Vertical managerial edict is increasingly substituted for growing capacity for subordinate initiatives. Administrative convenience more and more takes precedence to programme quality as the criterion in disposing of our meagre resources in budgets and facilities.

Finally, the emerging impression that the present Management thinks that it is evolving an adequate philosophy of national broadcasting from the intellectual resources and experience of a handful of Engineers, Managers and Journalists fills me with alarm.

My hope is that the Director-General (and his radio and television Controllers) will allow themselves to see what is so plain to everybody else, including the public, that the present situation of RTE simply cannot be allowed to continue or we shall have everyone of talent outside and only a dull but administratively efficient mediocrity within. This is already well on the way to being our situation.

Yours sincerely,
Jack Dowling

\* \* \*

## JUST GROWING PAINS

(*Evening Press*, Tuesday, 27th May, 1969)

In the spirit of RTE's statement of yesterday's *Evening Press* (now repeated in part in this morning's *Irish Times*) in which RTE welcomes dissent, I attach these comments:

*Despite what the angry young men (and women) employed as producers by Radio Éireann are saying about the station and its internal workings, a spokesman for RTE said today they were 'pleased' with this attitude.*

Presumably, therefore, the older members of senior management and staff are excluded from the area of welcome dissent. Bob Quinn is 34, Jack Dowling is 51. Are these the young men with whom RTE is pleased? How infantile must you be before your dissent is welcome?

*Advertising considerations do not control programmes here.*

Leaving aside the question of whether advertising pressures should or should not control programmes, the above statement is patently false. I instance a few specific examples and leave space below for you to add examples from your own experience:

The *Home Truths* affair; the threats of civil action from advertisers, the Advertisers Advisory Council's pressure, which subsequently suppressed and ultimately led to the dropping of the programme when its real force was spent.

Dramas, and half-hour short story series where stories were contracted into a 26-minute slot and had to bear an interval in the middle as well. This requirement controlled the adapters and the producers.

*Noble Call*, in which the interference of advertisers led to the dropping of the programme.

The daily fact that shots taken by producers in Drama programmes, Current Affairs programmes, Outside Broadcasts, must take cognisance of the controls of advertising.

A memo circulated some years ago by the Assistant Controller of Programmes in which he advised that the producer does not have to be a detective but must take a reasonable care in excluding advertising from shots. This is a control.

*However, one must keep in mind always that more than half of our income comes from advertising ...*

Surely this qualifies the previous statement.

If one must keep it in mind, it is a control. The two statements contradict each other.

*But I would like to repeat once more that advertising considerations do not control our programmes.*

Another contradiction.

If there is no problem, why is it necessary to repeat the assurance. Both statements (no control, but keep it in mind) are supposed to be kept simultaneously in consideration. This can't be done logically on paper, so how can a Producer be expected to cope with it as a daily reality? It turns him into a contortionist.

*Our producers are part of this controversy...*

If they are, why were Bob Quinn and Jack Dowling allowed to withdraw? They took management at its word. They are no longer part of the controversy, because they engaged in it.

*... and we believe this is a good thing.*

If it was that good, why was no attempt made to contain and absorb fruitfully the two most controversial statements made—those of Bob Quinn and Jack Dowling.

They are now outside the station and excluded from the 'good thing'. Somebody is fooling somebody, in hope.

Nobody is fooling anybody, in fact.

*... but one should remember that we are 7 years old ...*

Tir na nÓg.

*One could regard the attitude of our producers as a kind of growing pains.*

It's painful for Jack Dowling alright, now that he and his family are being supported by their friends.

*He said new divisional (sic—department?) heads had been appointed ... These people were being built up ...*

Built Up.

The heads who are now being built up are:

Chloe Gibson, after 15 years service in the BBC as producer and four years as Head of Drama in RTE.

Maev Conway, after years of experience in Radio and responsibility in television as Head of Children's programmes for some years.

James Plunkett Kelly, after 17 years in radio and as a senior producer in television since its inception.

Michael O'Hehir, after long years' experience as Head of Sport in radio and in the same capacity in television since the beginning.

Denis O'Grady, after experience in television in England and as Producer, Executive Producer and Head of Planning in RTE.

Padraig Ó Raghallaigh, after years of experience as a senior programme man and administrator in radio and similar experience in television, including the post of Assistant Controller of Programmes.

Bill Harpur. after years' experience of film and experience as Head of Film in television for the past 7 years.

Liam Ó Murchú, after experience of holding senior administrative posts in television since its early years and as Editor in charge of Irish, Social and Educational Programmes.

Joe Murray, after training and experience in Agriculture and experience of working in the Agricultural Department in a senior position.

Alpho O'Reilly, after long years' experience in his field both in theatre and television in Ireland and overseas, as well as 7 years' experience of running the Design Department in television as its Head.

Kevin O'Connell, after years' experience in radio and television, both in senior operational and management positions.

Lelia Doolan, after experience as performer and Producer in the Station, since 1961, and as Editor of Drama and General Features.

The combined cultural and administrative abilities of this group, all of whom have had several years' experience in positions of responsibility, is now to be 'built up'.

By whom?

*... and were being trained to look after their own divisions* (departments?)

By whom are these people being trained?

What is the competence of the trainers that exceeds the competence of the people they are training?

*They were also being given more authority each day...*

Each day?

The fact is that on appointment they were *given* and not *promised* authority. This authority was not conditional, at the time of appointment, that at some future time these heads might *become* sufficiently built up and trained to exercise it. They were chosen, as was stated at the time, because their qualities and experience made them fit for appointment.

The job specifications for conditions of service of these Heads is now invalidated, while still under negotiation, by this unilateral statement on the part of RTE. The public, and members of staff in the building at large and in their own areas in particular, can now see that the Heads do not have the authority delegated to them which they believe they have a right to exercise. Producers in our departments can now rightly ask us whether we have today been given a sufficient ration of authority to justify their obeying us. They have as evidence the public statement by an RTE spokesman. We have a word, and a piece of paper, which is now worthless.

These remarks of mine may seem needlessly pointed. It is a pity, moderate opinion would say, to be so brutal and extreme. The reason I do it is because I believe we suffer from a more extreme and violent brutality, one that is hidden from us; hypocrisy, lack of candour, lack of trust and trivialising prevarication, which masquerade as honourable and 'considerate' human behaviour. We have been given promises; they are empty. I for one can no longer believe in what senior Management says. It might be possible to believe in what it does. I think we need a sign. Show us one.

In the spirit of healthy disputation in which I and, from yesterday's statement, it appears, RTE top Management believe, I would expect the same scrutiny and open disagreement with what I say here to be the function of us all. It is my opinion that out of this debate we shall grow, not shrink.

Lelia Doolan,
Wednesday, 28th May 1969.
Head of Light Entertainment.

29th May, 1969

Miss Lelia Doolan,
Head of Light Entertainment.

Dear Miss Doolan,

I have considered with the Assistant Controller of Programmes the criticisms of the organisation which you made publicly at the meeting in the canteen on Monday last and which were consequently reported in the newspapers. I have also considered the contents of the document entitled 'Just Growing Pains', which you circulated yesterday to various members of the staff.

I my view (and I know the Assistant Controller of Programmes has already expressed a similar view to you) your conduct at the public meeting on Monday last was incompatible with your responsibilities as a Programme Head. It is a matter of deep concern to me that the views you expressed should have been based on information which you should have known to be incomplete and misleading. Your attitude to your senior colleagues, as evidence in the document 'Just Growing Pains', and in your public statements has been detrimental to the best interests of RTE.

I have given serious thought to relieving you of your duties and terminating your contract with the organisation on the ground of misconduct. But I am reluctant to lose those abilities which we all recognise and value.

As a Programme Head you have ample opportunity of expressing your views on all aspects of organisation and policy within the Programme Heads Committee. But your position also entails a confidential responsibility towards the Controller of Programmes and RTE as a whole. Breach of this confidence must make it impossible for a proper working relationship to be maintained with your superiors and with your colleagues.

RTE can only retain you in your present executive post if you cease to carry out what amounts to a public campaign of dissent from the form of organisation that exists and from the structure within which responsibility in RTE is exercised. Any further breach by you of the standard of behaviour expected from persons in posts of responsibility such as you hold will leave me with no option but to review immediately your present contract which, as you know, expires at the end of August, 1969.

Yours sincerely,

T. P. Hardiman,
Director-General.

\* \* \*

Dear Mr. Hardiman,

I have your letter of warning; it seems to me nothing less than an ultimatum.

I wish to summarise as briefly as possible the causes for my recent actions: I believe the substance of Bob Quinn's and Jack Dowling's alarm to have been well-founded. I believe the station is continuing to produce programmes that are dangerously and increasingly trivial, emasculated and contrary to the national cultural spirit.

I believe your policy of management to be responsible for this deplorable state of affairs and I now have evidence from you that you are immovable in it.

As I have told you often in the last 18 months, we have a body of Producers who are cultured and responsible men and women. We have a corps of committed and sincere production crews and staff. It seems to me that you cannot bring yourself to trust them as I do.

My own colleagues among the Heads of Department are dedicated and honourable people, but they hold only the shadow of the power which you have nominally delegated to them.

I had hoped that the kind of dissent that Bob Quinn, Jack Dowling and I wished to voice could be fruitfully contained within the organisation. This kind of internal dissent is, I think, more and more a need of our maturing national conscience. As I am now clearly seen by you to be the one voice which cannot be heard in dissent, I wish hereby to tender my resignation.

Yours sincerely,
Lelia Doolan

\* \* \*

29th May, 1969

Miss L. Doolan,
Head of Light Entertainment,
TV Programmes Division,
RTE,
Donnybrook,
Dublin 4.

I have your letter of resignation of 29th May which I accept with regret.

I believe RTE to be tolerant in regard to the expression of dissent by members of staff. I am sorry that you cannot see your way to accept in full the requirements essential to the function of Programme Head.

Yours sincerely,

T. P. Hardiman,
Director-General.

\* \* \*

# CIRCULAR FROM DIRECTOR-GENERAL ON THE OCCASION OF OUR RESIGNATIONS

In recent days, several general criticisms have been made against RTE. These include charges about a bureaucratic structure, censorship of programmes, advertising and financial pressures, denial of free speech and disregard of national interests.

The following notes have been prepared to assist in an understanding of RTE's position and attitude. The notes relate to the following headings:

1. The general framework and structure of the broadcasting service;
2. The interpretation of RTE's statutory obligation of impartiality;
3. The role and function of advertising in the broadcasting service;
4. 'Censorship', advertising and other pressures.
5. The relationship of facilities and finance to programmes;
6. The problems of a national broadcasting service in a changing society.

T. P. Hardiman,
Director-General.
30th May, 1969.

## SECTION 1: GENERAL FRAMEWORK AND STRUCTURE OF THE BROADCASTING SERVICE

It has been charged that RTE is a bureaucratic institution, in which there is not a proper devolution of authority to programme producers and other creative personnel.

The basic function of RTE is to make programmes and its organisation is designed to this end. There are seven Divisions, each with a large measure of autonomy, working to the Director-General. There are three programming Divisions—Radio Programmes, Television Programmes and News and four non-programming Divisions—Engineering, Personnel, Financial Control and Advertisement Sales.

Because broadcasting is about programmes, the form of organisation is and must be programme orientated. The four non-programming Divisions are essential to the programme-making process: Engineering provides technical facilities in radio and television; Personnel provides staff; Sales and Financial Control provide money. There is no class distinction involved in this relationship. It does not mean that any one Division is less important than any other. Without any one of these services, the programme-making process would cease and, contrariwise, without programming, the non-programming Divisions would have no reason to exist.

RTE is organised primarily on a functional basis. Day-to-day operations are not organised from some centralised unit which is the source of all power and authority. Responsibility and authority are exercised by the seven Divisional Heads in the first place and then by the various functional levels in their Divisions. In the programming Divisions particularly, the number of grades intervening between the Divisional Head and those essentially involved in the business of programme-making is purposely kept very small to facilitate the maximum possible delegation of responsibility.

Two of the factors associated with bureaucratic forms of organisation are (a) centralised control of the authority to spend money and (b) a network of constraining rules and regulations. In RTE, authority to spend money within budgetary limits agreed at the beginning of each financial year is delegated to more than 150 cost centres, including many basic operational levels. In the matter of rules and regulations, these are few in number for an organisation employing more than 1,500 people and spending about £5.5 million per year, and where they exist, they are interpreted in a liberal manner.

Ultimate responsibility for the broadcasting service rests with the RTE Authority. The Authority has corporate responsibility for meeting the duties prescribed in the broadcasting Authority Act. The Authority works through a chief executive, the Director-General, whose responsibility it is, in concert with the whole of the staff of RTE, to carry policy into practice in broadcasting terms.

The Director-General co-ordinates the activities of the seven Divisions in RTE. Although each Division is largely responsible for the conduct of its own affairs, matters arise daily in each Division which require consultation at a senior level with one or more other Divisions. This is particularly the case as between the three programming Divisions where a high degree of co-ordination is necessary. This co-ordination is exercised by the Director-General through the Programme Policy Committee which meets twice weekly (Tuesdays and Fridays) under his Chairmanship. The main area of interest of this Committee is programming and this is reflected in its membership which is made up of the Deputy Director-General, six (Controller of Programmes, Radio, Assistant Controller of Programmes, Radio, Head of News, Deputy Head of News, Controller of Programmes, TV and Assistant Controller of Programmes, TV) representatives from the programming Divisions and two (Director of Engineering and Director of Personnel and Secretary) representatives from the non-programming Divisions. (Advertisement Sales Controller is not a member). This is mainly a deliberative committee dealing with policy and important medium and short term issues. Views and comments are sought of those attending mainly on programming matters of current importance in the organisation: broad policy guidelines on certain issues are developed from time to time: and, generally Divisional Heads in the programming areas have readily available to them in the Committee a wide spectrum of views and information from other parts of the organisation to assist them in making decisions relating to matters affecting their own Divisions.

In addition to the Programme Policy Committee, a Committee of the seven Divisional Heads meets about once a month, normally soon after Authority meetings, to receive a report from the Director-General (who acts as Chairman of the Committee) on the most recent Authority meeting and to deal with broad issues of an administrative nature.

To sum up, the basic organisational framework is, therefore, a really simple one—the RTE Authority, dealing with policy and recommendations from the Director-General who co-ordinates the work of the seven Divisional Heads, who exercise their responsibilities through their senior executive staff. As part of this framework, there are the two Committees referred to earlier—the Programme Policy Committee—a forum in which major, medium and short-term policy matters are debated—and the Divisional Committee which concerns itself more with longer-term organisational problems.

# SECTION 2: THE INTERPRETATION OF RTE'S STATUTORY OBLIGATION AS TO IMPARTIALITY

Section 18(i) of the Broadcasting Authority Act, 1960, places a duty on the Authority 'to secure that, when it broadcasts any information, news or feature which relates to matters of public controversy or is the subject of current public debate, the information, news or feature is presented objectively and impartially and without any expression of the Authority's own views'.

We have never analysed this section in a totally legalistic sense by way of case studies nor attempted to define how it should be observed through a range of hypothetical situations. The words 'objectively' and 'impartially' have always been taken at their face value as meaning that the important facts or arguments of a situation should be presented uncoloured by any expression of opinion which might be seen to be an RTE opinion and that the presentation should be fair and unprejudiced.

The number of channels and frequencies available for broadcasting is limited in any country and the State reserves to itself the allocation of the right to use this scarce public asset. Maybe one day it will be possible to have an unlimited number of broadcasting channels: in that event, democracy might best be served by having editorial commitment in a multiplicity of broadcasting outlets in the tradition of the press. For the immediate future, it seems as if there can be only one broadcasting authority in this country. There are manifestly many points of view to be reflected and a broadcasting service such as ours, in being impartial and in accepting the restriction on its freedom to editorialise, must invite in as many champions for as many causes as it can but not enter the ring itself.

No broadcasting service can or should be impartial in all matters: it is not impartial about crime or racial prejudice or religious intolerance. The essential point is that it is statutorily barred from itself adopting an editorial policy or expressing editorial opinion on current affairs. Over a period of time it is committed to maintaining a balance between the various conflicting points of view.

It is reasonable to think of the concept of balance as something more than a measurement of the arguments for and against. It should be a deliberate attempt to go beyond the presentation of two rehearsed sides in each question in pursuit of a comprehensive understanding of a problem which will be as near the truth as possible.

## SECTION 3: THE ROLE AND FUNCTION OF ADVERTISING IN THE BROADCASTING SERVICE

The sale of commercial time in order to attract advertisement revenue by RTE is not an end in itself. It is an element in the means of financing broadcasting and is a vital part of the resources which have been applied to bring broadcasting in Ireland to its present state of development. Even with a substantially higher licence fee but without advertising, RTE would have £2 million less income per annum and would not have achieved anything like its present stage of progress.

Advertising has been a part of Irish broadcasting since 1932 when Radio Éireann began carrying sponsored programmes on a regular basis.

In recent times there has been a substantial swing towards the acceptance of advertising in European broadcasting services as a supplementary means of broadcasting finance.

When the Radio Telefís Éireann Authority was established in 1960, it was envisaged by the Oireachtas that advertisement revenue would be necessary to help to pay for the planned television service. Section 24 of the 1960 Act requires the Authority to pay its way. This has only been possible with the support of substantial advertisement revenue.

In the past seven years the contribution to revenue from television advertisement sales exceeded £12 million and for the past two years it has provided 60 per cent, of the total income. The original plans for the television service were on a much more modest scale than our operation today and were based on a considerably lower percentage of home originated programmes than the 54 per cent, now achieved. The rapid development of staff and resources involved has been possible only because advertising provided the money for these developments. Equally, the buoyancy of income has enabled the development of the radio service to be undertaken and the construction of the new radio centre to be started.

Having this source of income apart from licence fees has not only provided the money for growth, but has helped towards a financial independence without which it would be more difficult to maintain programme, autonomy.

In RTE the programmes come first and the Sales Division may not and does not interfere in programme matters. In and around programmes time is available for advertisements of the 'spot' variety. There is complete separation of programmes and advertising and the booking of time in programmes gives no rights whatever to the advertiser in relation to the content or presentation of a programme. However, RTE must take care not to favour the interests of one advertiser against another, e.g. by identifying individual products in programmes. Where a programme may impinge on commercial matters, the Sales Division must be given reasonable warning so that it can protect advertisers' interests, e.g. by moving commercials which might appear ridiculous in the context of the programme.

There is close co-operation between the Programme and Sales Divisions in the scheduling of commercial breaks. Home originated programmes of up to 30 minutes duration are not usually broken, and especial care is taken to avoid breaking programmes where continuity of argument or artistic unity may be affected. On the occasions when special programme considerations obtain, breaks are re-scheduled or cancelled with a loss of revenue.

RTE is concerned that claims in advertisements are valid and that the standards of presentation are acceptable. It was the first advertising medium in this country to issue a Code of Standards and now subscribes to an advertising industry code which is supported by advertisers, advertising agents and all major media.

# SECTION 4: 'CENSORSHIP', ADVERTISING AND OTHER PRESSURES

As already indicated, the structure of the broadcasting organisation is designed to give maximum prominence to the programme-making Divisions and to delegate the greatest possible amount of decision-taking to programme staff. But the chief executive in broadcasting has also the function of editor-in-chief and as such, is properly concerned in the process of decision-taking in important programme matters which involve policy, statutory obligations, or the balance of responsibility in the organisation. The Authority's responsibility is not one-sided and the Director-General as the interpreter of Authority policy must have regard to wider considerations than may always be apparent to those intimately involved in the programme-making process.

The quality of the programmes in any broadcasting service, however, depends on the character and professionalism of its staff. As indicative of a general attitude, the senior staff in RTE concerned with making editorial judgments approach the problems of programme matter on a 'why not' rather than a 'why' basis.

Charges have been made of unwarranted 'censorship' of the *Late Late Show* items. An analysis of the examples does not support the case that an arbitrary or autocratic process of rejection operates. For example, the cases cited include a reference to an item on the Referendum which was not included in a particular Late Late Show. But it was previously agreed that the important constitutional issues of the Referendum should only be dealt with in serious public affairs programmes and not in a *Late Late Show* context.

It should be appreciated, too, that the final decisions in such matters are not made by the Director-General. In the last analysis they are decisions of the Programme Controller or Assistant Programme Controller reached after discussion by all concerned. A *Late Late Show* may be judged successful by having a good controversy or 'set-to' but this must always be tempered by broader considerations.

Examples have also been quoted of advertising, etc., pressures in connection with the former *Home Truths* programme, but the allegations do not represent the real position. For instance, RTE is unaware that there were anything like eleven threats of civil action from advertisers.

It knows of a few cases where actions were threatened but these threats were not from advertisers. It is also alleged that a reference to smoking being harmful to health was rejected. This is simply untrue. Publicity has been given consistently to the development of research on cancer and smoking, and a special programme was mounted on the U.S. Surgeon-General's report on this subject. The Authority itself of its own volition has recently decided to phase-out cigarette advertising at a loss of revenue of some £300,000 per annum.

*Home Truths* was originally conceived as an information programme primarily for housewives, etc. It was accepted that, as far as valid research was available, it could make analyses of products and services and provide objective judgments of comparative values. RTE recognised that it must show the same fairness towards commercial interests as to any other interest in the community. After the withdrawal of the first producer in January, 1967, the policy of the programme was unchanged and it continued to be a vehicle of important public consumer information.

Suggestions to the effect that the content of the *Home Truths* programme was subject to censorship by the Sales Division are untrue. There was advance advice to the Sales Division on the content of the Home Truths programme to avoid the placing of inappropriate advertising in adjoining slots. The responsibility always lay with the Programme Division to make the final judgment about the content of the *Home Truths* programme.

Frequent pressures arise in the broadcasting environment. Representations, views, suggestions, etc., are part of the whole stock-in-trade of broadcasting and at times strong influences are brought to bear on

RTE in pursuit of particular interests. RTE must consider arguments that are fairly made but it must not, and does not, yield to pressures which would minimise the truth, exclude important facts or devalue integrity. It is here that the impartiality obligation comes fully into play and the public expect high standards of strength and judgment from RTE staff in this difficult field.

## SECTION 5: THE RELATIONSHIP OF FACILITIES AND FINANCE TO PROGRAMMES

Charges have been made that too much emphasis is given to technical non-programming requirements of broadcasting to the detriment of programme-makers.

A look at the division of expenditure in RTE is sufficient to appreciate that this is not so. In the present financial year total expenditure will amount to nearly £5.5 million. Of this, £3 million will go to the three output Divisions to meet salaries and wages and programme production costs. Over £1.25 million will be spent on engineering services including substantial expenditure directly related to programme production and the operation and maintenance of the broadcast transmission system. The remaining £1.25 million goes to meeting superannuation, interests and depreciation charges and the cost of the other service Divisions.

From an initial value of approximately £2 million the value of plant and equipment has now reached the figure of over £4 million. This is a reflection of the increasing sophistication and complexity of our programming. In November there was a considerable increase in radio programmes and the total output in radio programmes is now almost twice what it was a few years ago.

In previous years it has been possible to finance our capital requirements from our revenue: in this financial year, however, because of the sudden escalation of costs over the past two years or so, it will not be possible to provide any money from revenue for capital development. This poses new problems as, if the organisation is to keep abreast of its counterparts in European broadcasting, development of facilities and techniques is essential.

An understanding of these relationships is important to an appreciation of the problems of programme financing.

## SECTION 6: THE PROBLEMS OF A NATIONAL BROADCASTING SERVICE IN A CHANGING SOCIETY

Concern has also been expressed about the existence of free speech in RTE. This is certainly a matter of deep concern to us all, since no worthwhile broadcasting service can exist in an atmosphere of undue restriction or suppression of ideas.

In considering this problem in RTE, it is important to ask if there is not among us, as in society as a whole, a general undercurrent of protest and dissatisfaction. Our own problems may, therefore, be as much a manifestation of a general movement as a product of our internal circumstances.

In RTE we have a higher concentration than in most other sectors of Irish society of people who are intellectually talented, interested in and committed to the improvement of the society in which they live and anxiously seeking outlets through which they can contribute to this process. What they do and how they do it is necessarily affected by our understanding of the role of broadcasting in our society.

As matters stand, broadcasting must be seen as a public service, and it cannot, therefore, be legitimate that individuals in RTE should seek to use it arbitrarily. The people who work in the broadcasting service must accept the legislative concepts which surround it and the corporate function of those entrusted with it, viz. the Authority.

This is not to say that broadcasting must simply reflect the status quo. It inevitably has a leadership function to perform and determining this role and how it should be performed in individual instances is the difficult area of policy decisions.

RTE must continue to develop a policy framework and a broad strategy inside which programme-makers can freely operate. If the existing structures for this purpose are deficient within the organisation, it behoves all of us to strive to improve them.

* * *

# JOINT STATEMENT BY JACK DOWLING AND LELIA DOOLAN

What Conradh na Gaeilge describe as the Anglo-Americanisation of the Irish mind by the mass-media is of course at the root of our concern.

We should like to make two points in elucidation of our agreement with them; first, our programme schedules are determined by advertising requirements: for example, *Féach*, a serious Public Affairs programme in Irish, is transmitted at tea time on Sundays; serious religious programmes and discussions are scheduled outside the peak viewing period; programmes on fine arts are relegated to the late evening transmissions. None of these attracts advertising revenue because they are for 'minority' audiences.

Second: Anglo-Americanisation is built into the structure of RTE itself; in the selection and training of its directorate and administrators whose techniques are based on the American and British managerial systems and whose evaluation of structures are drawn from the national policy of largely foreign industrialisation and consequent urbanisation. The values that can find expression are limited by these institutional structures.

This has created within the television station a rejection of the urban versus rural antagonisms which have fragmented our traditional community. We are only too conscious of the neglect of rural needs. The fact that our home-originated material is imitative of Anglo-American 'canned' programming is only an effect of these two causes. We would submit that this process is not inevitable.

Because we regard television as an important cultural medium and because we are professional programme makers in this cultural field our disagreements with Management tend to be expressed in terms of structures, daily decisions and psychological conflicts between creative and administrative personnel of diverse cultural backgrounds.

Technocrats are trained to isolate all those elements of a problem that are measurable and manageable. Artists tend to find expression for all those things that are not measurable and not manageable. This is a world-wide phenomenon: to quote Mr. Hardiman:

> In considering this problem in RTE it is important to ask if there is not among us, as in society as a whole, a general current of protest and dissatisfaction. Our own problems may, therefore, be as much a manifestation of a general movement as a product of our internal circumstances.

We altogether agree. The 'internal circumstances' are, frankly, conflicts between technologically trained minds who devise our structures and control their use, and creatively formed minds who try to make programmes. The former control resources; the latter are controlled by them.

It might be useful to balance Mr. Hardiman's assessment with that of the philosopher, Bernard Lonergan, who sees society itself as a system of communications; he writes that to require ideas to be examined, evaluated and approved by bureaucrats is the same thing as to declare that all new ideas are taboo:

> The principle of progress is liberty, for the ideas occur to the man on the spot, their only satisfactory expression is their implementation, their only adequate correction is the emergence of further insights; on the other hand, one might as well declare openly that all new ideas are taboo, as require that they be examined, evaluated, and approved by some hierarchy of officials and

bureaucrats; for members of this hierarchy possess authority and power in inverse ratio to their familiarity with the concrete situations in which the new ideas emerge; they never know whether or not the new idea will work; much less can they divine how it might be corrected or developed; and since the one thing they dread is making a mistake they devote their energies to paper work and postpone decisions. (Fr. Bernard Lonergan, S.J., Insight, Longmans, 1957. Pp. 234-5.)

In a statement running into seventeen foolscap pages, Mr. Hardiman places himself on trial before our six general accusations:

1. That the structure of the broadcasting service is inappropriate to its cultural function.
2. That he has no adequate interpretation of RTE's statutory obligation of impartiality.
3. That the role and function of advertising in the service is corrupting.
4. That there is self-censorship in anticipation of advertising and other pressures.
5. That there is friction arising from the relationship of facilities and financing to programmes.
6. That he has shown no concrete awareness of the station's responsibilities in a changing society.

Not surprisingly, he has found himself not guilty on any charge.

We cannot ask you to consider a detailed reply to all of his extraordinarily lengthy judgments upon himself. We propose to do this in a book which will review his management of the station since his accession. However, at this point, we should like to answer one or two pieces of his apologia.

1. If the complex organisation which he outlines in Section One is 'programme orientated' why are so many of our programmes so bad? Why is so much good talent draining from the station and why have we lost 15 per cent of our viewers—a majority of these (30 per cent approximately) in the formative young adult age group?

2. If the statutory obligation to impartiality is as liberally interpreted as stated in his document why did Mr. Hardiman find it necessary to tell a meeting of twelve senior Producers that any public or current affairs programme requiring a continuing editorial supervision would be transferred to the Head of News, Mr. J. P. McGuinness. Why did he inform Lelia Doolan regarding a *Late Late Show* item, that the station regarded itself as being in an election situation one fortnight prior to the issue of the writ of election?

Further, why did he find it necessary to change or excise public affairs items from the *Late Late Show*, viz. an item to discuss the biography of Éamon De Valera; change in title of a programme from 'That RTE has Failed the Public Trust' to 'That Irish Eyes are Shut'; ban a discussion on the Referendum a week after the results had been declared; change a discussion of the Criminal Justice Bill from the proposed panel to a 'safe' panel of lawyers; insist that politicians should not be permitted to appear on the *Late Late Show*; ban an item on corporal punishment because persons had threatened civil action against a newspaper. Ban an item on the rating system and then restore it under pressure from the Producer and Programme Heads on condition that no politicians took part.

'For example, the cases cited', Mr. Hardiman remarks, 'include a reference to an item on the Referendum which was not included in a particular *Late Late Show* but it was previously agreed that the important constitutional issues of the Referendum should only be dealt with in serious public affairs programmes and not in a Late Late Show- context.' Lelia Doolan was administratively responsible for this show and Gay Byrne was its Producer. Not only was it never agreed with them but they were ignorant of any such agreement at any level. With whom then was the agreement made? With the Government? With the Whips? Or with some higher echelon of the bureaucracy? In fact this programme was prepared for the Saturday *after* the Referendum results were in. The insistence that the *Late Late Show* because it is 'popular' and an unsuitable place to air serious issues is a literary snobbery that deprives ordinary people of hearing non-technical discussion of public affairs; it implies that only well-educated minorities have this right.

Lastly, Mr. Hardiman claims that these decisions were not his but, 'in the last analysis, those of the Programme Controller'. Lelia Doolan as ex-Head of this Department can say that this is simply and bluntly untrue. A policy document for the show was provided by her with the full knowledge of the Controller of Programmes. This policy has now been overruled by the Director-General who claimed to be ignorant of its existence.

Further on his document; the *Home Truths* issues are 'old hat'. Managements denial of pressures is fatuous. These are the facts: Before Christmas 1966 the Controller of Programmes sent for Jack Dowling to express concern about the policy he was following and accused him of exceeding his brief. This brief had been submitted to the Controller's predecessor and approved by him. It included among six other items the following: 'to discover and investigate malpractices in administration of commercial practices which might have direct bearing on the foregoing (advisory services) and to right them as far as fair comment and publicity permit'.

Jack Dowling was asked to amend this policy and refused to do so.

Mr. Hardiman professes to be unaware that there were anything like eleven threats of civil action from advertisers. He is quite right. Presumably he is referring to Jack Dowling's speech at the Teach-In in the canteen. Jack Dowling did not say that advertisers had threatened legal action, he did say that there had been eleven threats of civil action that were bluffs. These were: by a manager of a canning factory; by a meat wholesaler and retailer; by a fruit and vegetable merchant; by a solicitor; by a builder; two threats from fish merchants; two from butchers; a threat of an order of restraint from the High Court from the manager of a co-operative.

None of these was brought to the attention of the Controller of Programmes but were treated by the Producer, Jack Dowling, for what they were, bluffs.

If these issues are only of historical interest why then has no similar programme been initiated?

Mr. Hardiman again remarks: 'In RTE the programmes come first and the Sales Division may not and do not interfere in programme matters'.

Mr. Dowling was ordered by the Controller of Programmes to get a graphic artist to change the name of a brand of toothpaste to a fictitious brand name—he refused. An item on Mr. Charles Haughey was ordered to be removed from *Home Truths*. Mr. Dowling refused. It was taken out of the tape without his knowledge by means of a razor cut.

Further; the Controller of Sales objected to four items at a meeting with the Controller of Programmes, Assistant Controller of Programmes and the senior Producer of his group. At this meeting a letter from the Advertisers Advisory Council was read which complained about the policy of the programme. One of these was a health item about smoking which the Sales Controller said would seriously embarrass his advertisers. After a debate of nearly three hours the Programme Controller ruled that the three commercial items should be dropped but that the smoking item would remain since it had come from the office of the Minister for Health.

Further: Mr. Hardiman's document makes no reference to the disappearance of three programmes which had been completed prior to the transfer of *7 Days* to the Head of News; these were, an item on property sales at Mountpleasant Square; housing conditions as seen by Father Sweetman, s.j., and Special Branch activity in student circles. As none of these three matters of public concern are yet resolved it cannot be argued that they could not have been transmitted for reasons of topicality.

Finally, nothing in Mr. Hardiman's long document other than an appeal for all round improvement leads us to believe that he is aware of the gravity of the situation. Our action was taken in the hope that he would be brought to an awareness of it.

As we said during the Teach-In it would be ridiculous to place the blame on any one person. We certainly have no desire to place it all on Mr. Hardiman. We believe him to be subject to many constraints: structures which make him remote from the needs of his staff; his own technological background; colleagues who surround him with commercial and other demands; a Broadcasting Act that is at once commercial and educational in the most profoundly contradictory senses.

Our action was reluctant and repugnant to us. But our hearts and hopes are with the people within the station who must carry on the daily struggle for better television for the Irish nation.

Jack Dowling, Lelia Doolan.
2nd June, 1969.

# INDEX

# 7

7 Days xvii, xx, 96, 98, 102, 103, 104, 107, 114, 130, 137, 138, 140, 141, 143, 144, 145, 146, 147, 148, 149, 151, 152, 155, 157, 158, 159, 160, 161, 163, 164, 166, 167, 173, 175, 181, 188, 192, 194, 195, 196, 202, 213, 216, 222, 223, 224, 225, 226, 227, 236, 260, 279, 413, 422, 423, 424, 444, 507

# A

Abbey Theatre 22
Administration 85, 195
advertisers 385, 393, 394, 397, 398, 407, 435
Advertisers 279, 383, 389, 398
advisory committee 17, 23, 432
Advisory Committee 7
Aiken, Frank 126, 127, 148
Ailliliu 265
Amuigh Faoin Spéir 358
Andrews, Dr. C. S. 95, 115, 116, 142, 149, 153, 430
Andrews, Eamonn xiii, 4, 17, 18, 19, 20, 22, 36, 45, 69, 71, 94, 95, 142
Annual Report (RE) 38, 41
Annual Report (RTE) 400
Aquinas, Thomas xviii, 195
Aran Islands 10, 308
Arigna strike 225
Aristotle 327
ARISTOTLE 41
Arts Council 14
Athlone 25
Attorney General 120
Attwood Group 395
audience research 395
Audience Research 76, 188, 189, 224, 227, 247, 394, 395
Authority 127, 227
Authority, The (RE, RTE) viii, 4, 12, 13, 16, 17, 18, 19, 20, 21, 22, 23, 24, 25, 29, 30, 35, 36, 37, 38, 40, 44, 47, 56, 57, 60, 68, 69, 70, 76, 79, 90, 91, 92, 94, 95, 96, 100, 101, 111, 113, 115, 122, 125, 127, 128, 138, 139, 140, 141, 148, 149, 150, 151, 152, 153, 156, 157, 158, 161, 162, 166, 169, 170, 181, 194, 209, 215, 257, 258, 288, 354, 399, 400, 402, 411, 428

# B

Bach, J. S 338
Baird, James Logie 6
Ballad Session 92
Ballymun 224
Barrett, Stephen 431

Barry, Michael  4, 28, 30, 35, 40
Barry, Tony  xiv, 73
Battle of Waterloo  307
BBC  18, 28, 29, 30, 43, 60, 62, 114, 115, 220, 406, 407, 434
Beethoven, Ludwig von  313
Behan, Brendan  357
Beirt Eile  32
Belfast  106, 250, 252, 253
Belton, Patrick  60
Benn, Anthony Wedgewood  325
Berkeley, G  338
Biafra  147, 444
Birthistle, Joan  xiv
Blaney  116
Blaney, Neil  9, 10
Blythe, Ernest  22, 68
Bogside  226, 255
Boland, Kevin  145, 147
Bord na Mona  445
Bottomore, T.B.  347
Brennan, Charles J.  8, 22, 68
Brennan, Joseph  68, 69, 113, 116
Bring Down the Lamp  191, 227, 334, 357
Broadcasting Act  81, 114, 174, 214, 257, 402, 453, 476, 507
Broadcasting Estimate  16
Broadsheet  32
Brogeen  227
Browne, Bishop Michael  60
Browne, Noel  19, 149
Browne, Vincent  xiv, 247
Brugha, Cathal  68
Brugha, Ruairi  68, 430, 431
B Specials  254
Buntus Cainte  188
Byrne, Gay  62, 82, 83, 84, 89, 179, 180, 195, 201, 216, 505

# C

Cabinet  70
Cabinet, The  113, 253
Canada  41, 272, 273, 274
Carberry, Sean  252
Carr, Bunny  158
Carroll, Joe  226
Carty, Michael  112
Catholic Herald  143

Cathy Come Home 343
CBC 41
CBS 114, 333
Ceist Agam Ort 358
Cézanne 347
Changing Face of Ireland, The 62
Chief Whip 112
Childers, Erskine 116, 163, 227, 328
Children's Programmes 160, 201, 203, 259, 419, 424, 481
Chubb, Basil 144
Church in Crisis-By what Authority 196
Cine Club 92
Civil Rights Association 226, 248
Civil Service 398, 401, 477
Clarke, Austin 357
Cleeve, Brian 74, 103, 108, 144, 162, 191, 214, 215, 222, 470
Clonfert, Bishop of 82
Club Ceili 265
Colleges and Institutes of Technology 244
Colley, George xx, 192
Collins, Pan 157, 164, 165, 470
Comhairle Radio Éireann 8, 22
Comhaltas Ceoltóiri Éireann 60
Comhlacht Comhairleach, An 213
Commission on the Revival of the Irish Language 359
conciliation tribunal 162
Conciliation Tribunal 162, 165
Congo 125
Conradh na Gaeilge xiv, 501
Constitution of Ireland 97
consultative group 198, 199
Consultative Group 198, 204, 205, 207, 209
Controller, Assistant 124, 133, 140, 147, 178, 180, 181, 189, 191, 195, 197, 202, 215, 216, 230, 231, 233, 421, 422, 479, 481, 484, 490, 506
Controller (radio) 176
Controller (television) 97, 99, 101, 113, 117, 118, 120, 121, 122, 123, 131, 132, 133, 135, 137, 145, 147, 153, 155, 156, 163, 164, 167, 175, 176
Conway, Maev 50, 78, 96, 199, 221, 229, 424, 481
Cooper, Ivan 226
Cork 16, 25, 59, 106, 119, 122, 436
Correspondence One 251
Costello, Fergal 235
Course of Irish History, The 75
Cover Story 61
Cremin, Monsignor 192
Criminal Justice Bill 180, 504

Cronin, Adrian  240
Cronkite, Walter  114
Crosbie, George  18, 23, 68
Cruise O'Brien, Conor  170
Cumann na nInnealltóirí  241, 244
Cusack, Edith  50, 53
Czechoslovakia  443

# D

Dáil Éireann  8, 60, 112, 114, 160, 161, 163, 431
Daily Mirror  318
Davidson, Alan  248
Day, Rev. Fergus  54
Deasy, Rickard  106, 111
debates  82
Debates  19
de Gaulle, Charles  256
Department of Agriculture  66, 107, 111
Department of Education  57, 221, 277
Department of Fisheries  104
Department of Health  54, 121
Derry  26, 226, 248, 249, 252, 255
Derrynane  256
Descartes  321
De Valera, Éamon  4, 26, 61, 97, 178
Devlin, Bernadette  26, 226
Dichter  383
Dichter, Ernest  383, 384, 385
Dillon, James  313
Dillon-Malone  xiv, 393, 394, 396
Director-General  xx, 4, 18, 23, 24, 28, 30, 31, 39, 40, 60, 63, 76, 91, 97, 113, 120, 121, 125, 127, 128, 133, 136, 138, 139, 140, 141, 142, 146, 147, 148, 149, 151, 152, 153, 155, 157, 159, 160, 161, 164, 165, 166, 171, 175, 177, 178, 181, 183, 189, 191, 193, 194, 195, 196, 197, 198, 199, 200, 201, 202, 203, 204, 206, 207, 209, 210, 214, 216, 217, 218, 224, 229, 230, 231, 232, 233, 234, 235, 236, 240, 241, 243, 247, 254, 256, 258, 283, 329, 343, 365, 373, 376, 386, 411, 412, 414, 415, 423, 425, 430, 432, 437, 444, 446, 448, 467, 470, 472, 476, 478, 485, 487, 488, 489, 490, 491, 496, 505
Director of Personnel  153, 157, 176, 197, 198, 205, 206, 209, 243, 490
Discovery  92, 266
Dodd, Fr. Romuald  53, 73, 157, 164, 193, 195, 267, 287, 424
Donnellan, Fr. Luke  6
Donohue, Oliver  237
Doolan, Dermot  xiii, 153, 162, 165
Doolan, Lelia  xvii, xix, xxii, 103, 135, 146, 151, 152, 153, 157, 164, 179, 181, 183, 187, 189, 194, 199, 208, 279, 470

    aftermath of resignation 235, 258
    and analysis of Management contradictions 233
    and clashes with TP Hardiman 504
    and demand she stay silent 234
    and filming in Russia 336
    and Memorandum on Authority 365
    and resignation of Jack Dowling 230
    Appointment as Head of Light Entertainment 211
    experience of impact of TAM ratings 397
    Joint statement with Jack Dowling 501
    resignation from RTE 234
    Resignation letter 508
    resistance of interference with Late Late Show 216
Dowling, Jack xvii, xxi, 161, 162, 191, 192, 195, 197, 201, 202, 203, 205, 214, 229, 236, 246, 279, 397, 470, 478, 480. *See* Plunkett Kelly, Jim
    aftermath of resignation 235
    and Memorandum on Authority 365
    approach to legal advice 119
    approach to producing Home Truths 105
    being told of the moral case for advertising 122
    data processing experience 200
    development of Home Truths 104
    Director-General's hesitation to face 194
    dissent of 202
    funding model suggestions by 398, 399
    Joint statement with Lelia Doolan. *See* Doolan, Lelia
    letter on Home Truths 469
    management response to resignation 237
    meeting with Michael Garvey. *See* Garvey, Michael; *See* Garvey, Michael
    personality of xvii, xviii, xxi, 197, 207, 398
    Pressure to abandon consumer protection 120
    resignation from Home Truths 122
    resignation letter of 478
    resignation of 230, 231, 232, 233
    resistance to pressure to pander to advertisers 121
    scriptwriting by. *See* Quinn, Bob; *See* Quinn, Bob
    suggestions for organisational change 189, 199, 245
Dublin 4, 8, 11, 24, 25, 35, 41, 43, 45, 59, 77, 79, 102, 108, 143, 145, 217, 226, 250, 271, 336, 458
Dublin Corporation 145
Dublin Diocesan Press Office 83
Duffy, Hugh 46
Dunne, Sean 161

# E

Eadie, James 163

Editorial Group  135, 137, 139, 151, 164, 181, 182, 183, 184, 186, 187, 198, 422
Editor(s)  50, 53, 54, 66, 92, 135, 139, 168, 180, 182, 184
Egan, Sean  149
Electra factory  143
engineers  187, 219, 279
Engineers  xviii, 220, 241
   Director of Engineering  46, 133, 136, 170, 176, 219, 243, 412, 413, 422, 423, 425, 490
   Engineering Section  29
   Planning and Control  417
England  151, 309
Equity, Irish Actors'  238
European Economic Community (EEC)  221, 388
Eurovision  47, 61
Evening Herald  44, 148
Evening Press  328, 478
Exchange  191

# F

Fahy, Joe  163
Famine  277
Fanning, James  22, 23, 430
Farmer, Dónall  xiv, 201
Farrell, Brian  103, 108, 222, 223, 471
Féach  143, 212, 213, 214, 226, 227, 246, 257, 258, 259, 260, 358, 359, 396, 501
Feeney, John  84
Fianna Fáil  7, 16, 17, 35, 67, 68, 97, 99, 100, 112, 113, 116, 144, 181, 430, 431, 437
Financial Controller  63, 414
Fine Gael  18, 60, 67, 97, 98, 247, 331, 431
Finn, Vincent  63, 414
Fisher, Desmond  143
FitzGerald, Garret  153, 438, 440
Fitzgerald, Jim  471
FitzGerald, Jim  50, 54, 73, 78
Flahive, Jimmy  103, 468
Flanagan, Oliver J  21, 84
Fleadhanna  334
Forde, Fr. Francis OMI  267
Forty Years of Irish Broadcasting  xiv, 3, 5, 38
Friendly, Fred  333

# G

G.A.A.  32
Gaelic League, The  78, 95
Gael-Linn  17

Chairman of  60, 68
Gaeltacht  361, 362, 363
Gahan, Robert  119, 414
Gallagher, Matt  143
Gallagher, Patrick  143, 145, 146, 157, 164, 214, 222, 223, 224, 471
Galway  xiv, 27, 60, 83, 106, 328
　　Bishop of  84
　　Cathedral  83
Gannon, Noelette  105, 106
Garda
　　Special Branch  144, 145, 146, 147, 148, 149, 150, 436, 507
Garda Patrol  190, 200
Garvey, Michael  xvii, 54, 78, 101, 102, 117, 118, 120, 131, 133, 141, 145, 146, 151, 152, 153, 154, 156, 165, 167, 172, 206, 208, 253, 398, 420, 425
General Election  8, 67, 216
Gibson, Chloe  xix, 54, 220, 232, 480
Gogarty, Frank  226
Golden Harp Festival  335
Goldie, Grace Wyndham  115
Gorham, Maurice  xiii, 5, 8, 9
Goulding, Cathal  226
Government  161, 163, 169
Government (Irish)  7, 8, 9, 12, 14, 15, 16, 17, 20, 21, 36, 47, 57, 58, 62, 69, 114, 127, 128, 138, 144, 148, 150, 152, 153, 181, 226, 227, 253, 324, 325, 404, 405, 406, 430, 432, 433, 437, 438, 439, 440, 445, 446, 448, 470
Government (Nigerian)  148
Gray, Ken  67, 140
Grealy, Des  142
Great Britain  xiii, 308, 412, 434
Greene, Hugh Carleton  181
Gulf Oil  192, 223, 224

# H

Hall, Frank  62, 71, 225
Halloran, Professor James  29
Hardiman, Thomas P  43, 63, 133, 135, 136, 165, 169, 170, 175, 176, 181, 189, 195, 196, 197, 198, 201, 204, 207, 209, 230, 232, 235, 243, 244, 329, 340, 343, 366, 370, 396, 422, 433, 447, 485, 488, 504, 507
Harpur, Bill  188
Harris, Eoghan  xiii, xxi, 103, 104, 109, 137, 144, 145, 146, 148, 151, 152, 153, 157, 164, 191, 193, 194, 195, 196, 212, 213, 214, 222, 231, 234, 235, 237, 238, 240, 246, 257, 258, 259, 352, 471
Harty, Dr. Michael  193
Haughey, Charles J  67, 97, 98, 109, 110, 111, 112, 116, 331, 409, 506
Headlines and Deadlines  103

Head of News   43, 44, 110, 115, 116, 143, 149, 152, 155, 156, 160, 163, 166, 167, 176, 193, 195, 224, 254, 255, 275, 412, 413, 467, 470, 490, 504, 507
Head of Planning   421, 424, 481
Head of Presentation   43, 421, 424
Head of Religious Programmes   247
Hegel, G.W.F.   320
Henry Street   7, 25, 401
Hierarchy, The   192, 193, 368
Hill, Dick   103, 104, 109, 137, 145, 146, 189, 195, 222, 223, 471
Hillery, Dr. Patrick   56, 57, 225
Hilliard, Michael   4, 16, 17, 19, 21, 58, 429
Home for Tea   53, 92, 98
Home Truths   xvii, 98, 103, 104, 105, 106, 118, 120, 121, 122, 123, 128, 135, 276, 393, 397, 468, 469, 479, 496, 497, 505, 506
Horgan, John   193, 225
Horizon   267
Houses of the Oireachtas   445
Housing Action Committee   149, 331
Housing and Unemployed Action Committees   226
Humanae Vitae   192
Hume, John   226
Huntley, Chet   114
Hurler on the Ditch   82, 98
Hyland, Liam   431

# I

I Love Lucy   333
India   293, 309, 310
Industrial Revolution   308, 309, 310, 311, 312, 314, 316, 318, 337, 338, 349
Institute of Research and Standards   104
I.R.A.   226, 331
Ireland   366, 367, 388, 392, 395, 403, 419, 457, 481, 493
Irish Actors' Equity   xiii, 59, 78, 95, 123, 206, 425
Irish Club, London   4
Irish Congress of Trade Unions   22
Irish Countrywomen's Association   276
Irish Housewives' Association   104, 105
Irish Independent   7, 9, 157, 260, 433
Irish language   209, 212, 236, 259, 261, 288, 344, 353, 354, 431, 441
Irish Management Institute   85, 86, 89, 208, 284, 464
Irish Press   26, 116, 175, 176, 226, 248, 251, 260, 297, 400, 447
Irish Times   9, 26, 54, 58, 61, 79, 82, 110, 140, 141, 225, 252, 329, 386, 387, 478
Irish Transport and General Workers' Union   22
Irvine, John   46
ITV   261, 360, 395, 407, 434, 435

Ivor Kenny 225

# J

Jackpot 92
Jacobs' Awards 59
Jennings, Patrick 54, 221
John Irvine 146, 414
Johnston, Denis 388
Johnston, Michael 50, 53, 106, 240

# K

Kearney, Pat 50, 53
Keating, Bil 211
Keating, Justin xiii, 66, 221, 224, 471
Kelly, Fr. Jack, S.J. xiii, 235
Kelly, James Plunkett 50, 53, 59, 78, 162, 195, 197, 201, 212, 214, 481
Kelly, Pearse 43, 44, 46, 60, 115, 142, 467
Kennedy, Fintan 22, 23, 161, 288, 431
Kenny, Invor 89
Keyes, Michael 8
Kippure 27

# L

Labhair Gaeilge Linn 54, 61, 91, 188, 357
Labour Court 162
Labour Party 237, 331
Laing, R.D. 280
Larkin, Jim 265
Larkin, Jim, Jnr 162, 165, 240
Late Late Show, The 32, 92, 98, 179, 227
    abuse of Galway's Bishop and Cathedral on 83
    audience reaction to 32
    Bishop and the Nighty, affair of 82
    Catalogue of Director-General's interference with 504
    censorship of 210
    consequences of not staying in its place 179
    consequences of studio on interviewees 265
    creation of a community's self awareness 89
    cultural importance of 85
    DG continual political interference in 195
    Director-General blocking invitations to the authors for 247
    Director-General's acknowledgement of censorship of 496

    Director-General's denial of censorship of  496
    Director-General's justification for censorship of  496
    Frank Hall the presenter of  62
    Gay Byrne's fight to include politics on  216
    Oliver J Flanagan's denouncement of  84
    prevented from discussing legacy of DeValera  178
Lawlor, Patrick  429
Leavis, Dr. F.R.  313, 317, 323, 328
Leland, Mary  104, 106, 122
Lemass, Sean  4
    Assertion that RTE was not independent of Government  114
    Demand for favourable programming  62
    Retirement  116
Lenihan, Brian  149, 192
Lenin, V.I.  322
Lennon, Bishop Patrick  193
Lentin, Louis  78, 471
Leonard, Hugh  78
Leo XIII  378
l'Estrange, Deputy G.  160
Let's Draw  32, 227
Levin, Dick  220
Like Now  191, 211, 227
Linnane, Joe  61
Liston, T.K.  162, 166
Little, Paddy  7
Littman, Fred  xiv, 77, 394, 395
Longford, Earl of  10
Lunacharsky, A.V  322
Lynch, Jack  116
    First Cabinet  116
Lynch, Patrick  xv, 8

# M

Mac Conghail, Muiris  103, 137, 145, 147, 148, 149, 150, 151, 152, 157, 158, 222, 471
Mac Con Midhe, Pádraic  8
Macra na Feirme  68
Mac Réamoinn, Sean  xiv, 240, 356, 471
Maloney, Oliver  100, 197, 202, 205, 206, 209, 221, 241, 243, 245, 414
Management Appreciation Conference  85
Many Hands Make Life Work  271
Marcuse, Herbert  331, 348
Marian College Hall  30
Mart and Market  190
Marxism  318

Art as a form of class consciousness 319
criticism of bourgeois norms and forms of media 330
élitism of the Leninist variety 323
lack of a theory of art in Marx 319
role of art in 318
Marxist 208, 293
Marx, Karl 320, 321, 324
Master Butchers' Association 106
McAteer, Eddie 225
McCann, Eamonn 226
McCourt, Kevin 39, 40, 41, 42, 43, 45, 56, 57, 60, 62, 63, 71, 76, 79, 84, 85, 95, 96, 101, 110, 111, 115, 125, 128, 142, 149, 150, 151, 152, 154, 155, 158, 161, 163, 164, 165, 169, 343, 354, 385, 386, 423, 467, 473
McCrow, Bill 50
McCullough, Joe 145
McDowell, Vincent 226
McEvoy, Peter 235, 471
McGahern, John 83
McGann, Brendan xiii, 332, 460
McGilligan, Patrick 19
McGrath, Raymond 18, 23
McGrath, Tom 53, 240
McGuinness, James 115, 116, 125, 142, 150, 152, 161, 165, 224, 254, 255, 256, 412, 413, 504
McHugh, Roger 9
McKenna, Siobhán xiv
McLuhan, Marshall 327
McManus, E.B. 18, 23, 60, 71
McNeill, Hugh 157
McQuaid, Dr. John Charles 4
McQuillan, Jack 60
Melody Fair 61, 92
Michael Keyes 8
Midland Tribune 22
Minister for Education 56
Minister for External Affairs 126, 127, 148
Minister for Finance 22, 409, 433
Minister for Health 104, 328, 507
Minister for Justice 67, 149, 439
Minister for Local Government 145
Minority Report (Broadcasting Commission) 11, 15, 16
Missing, Believed Dead 270
Monaghan, Michael 214
Monaghan, T.J. 8
Montreux Festival 211
Montrose 18, 23, 25, 32, 66, 110, 160
Moody, T.W. 8

Mooney, Ria  59
Morris, Michael  29
Mountpleasant Square  436, 507
Mozart, W.A.  313
Mullaghanish  28
Mullen, Michael  145
Mullen, Verona  32
Mumford, Lewis  347
Murphy, Mary  103, 105, 106, 121, 122, 124, 468, 471
Murphy, Senator D.F.  162
Murray, Bill  63
Murray, Georgia  144
Murray, Gerry  124, 195, 471
Murray, Joe  66
Murray, Michael  471
Music in View  61

# N

Napoleon  307
National Union of Journalists  44, 110, 242, 470, 471
Naughton, John  297
NBC  114
Nealon, Ted  103, 162, 222, 223, 471
Neff, Sid  105
Newsbeat  61, 71, 91, 92, 98, 103, 140, 190, 227, 421
News Conference  254
News Division  27, 29, 43, 44, 45, 46, 64, 115, 125, 126, 142, 143, 155, 156, 157, 161, 164, 166, 167, 173, 188, 190, 201, 204, 222, 226, 241, 256, 412, 413, 422, 425, 467
N.F.A.  106, 110, 111, 114
Ní Cheannain, Áine  68
Nicholas, Mother Mary  269
N.I.E.C.  406
Nielsen Company  395
Nigeria  126
Noble Call  399
Noonan, Arthur  157, 260, 433
Noonan, Michael  68, 430, 431
Nora Connolly  97
Northern Ireland  252, 254, 344
Nowlan, Prof Kevin  145
Nuacht  91, 143, 357, 358, 362

# O

O'Brien, Dermot  4

O'Brien, George  20
Ó Broin, Leon  xiii, 8, 9, 11
O'Callaghan, Kate  xiv
O'Callaghan, Michael  430
O'Connell, Daniel
    de Gaulle visit to his house  256
O'Connor, Frank  30, 357
O'Dea, Jimmy  4, 59, 61
O'Dea, Liam  153
O'Dea, Tom  176, 283
O'Donoghue, John  32, 68, 103, 108, 162, 225, 471
Ó Faoláin, Seán  340
Ó Faracháin, Roibeard  46
O'Farrell, Myles  254
O'Farrell, Rory  144
O'Flanagan, Liam  471
Ó Flatharta, Liam  357
Ó Gallchóir, Aindreas  xvii, xxi, 78, 96, 154, 162, 192, 195, 199, 201, 214, 215, 279, 471
O'Grady, Denis  50, 53, 106, 120, 124, 248, 424, 471, 481
Ó hAnnracháin, Fachtna  162
O'Hara, Aidan  xiii
O'Hara, Mary  4
O'Hehir  481
O'Hehir, Michael  52, 159
Ó hEithir Breandán  212, 213, 257, 258, 259, 260
Ó hEithir, Breandán  xiv
O'Herlihy, Fr. Jerome  227, 246, 247, 248, 249, 251, 252, 253, 254
O'Higgins, Tom  97
O'Kelly, Mrs Sean T  68, 430
O'Malley, Donogh  221
Ó Maoláin, Thomas, Senator  20
Ó Móráin  68
Ó Móráin, Donáll  60, 71, 258
Ó Mórdha, Sean  195, 196, 424
Ó Murchú, Liam  54, 135, 182, 183, 187, 195, 198, 212, 213, 220, 231, 257, 258, 259, 396, 424, 481
On the Land  61
Open House  62, 265
O'Quigley, Senator J.B.  21
Ó Raghallaigh, Padraig  43
Ó Raghallaigh, Pádraig  46, 78, 481
O'Reilly, Alpho  186, 191, 481
O'Reilly, P. P.  32
O'Reilly, P.P.  50, 53
Ó Riada, Seán  265, 335
Ormonde, Seán  10

Outlook 200, 227
Outside Broadcast 43, 50, 63
outside broadcast unit 172
Outside Broadcast Unit 77, 190
Outside Broadcast Unit(s) 43

# P

Packard, Vance 347, 387
Parker, Phil 43, 46
Pick of the Pops 92
Planning and Control 63, 186
Plato 318
Playboy of the Western World, The 343
Policy Committee, The 177, 210, 214, 215, 216, 224, 233, 240, 490, 491
Posts and Telegraphs
    Department of 11, 57, 399, 400, 401
    Estimates of 138
    Minister for 7, 8, 16, 17, 57, 68, 113, 116, 127, 148, 163, 409, 431, 432
Potter, Maureen 4
Presidential Election 97, 178
Producer-Director 32, 50, 81, 93, 101, 104, 129, 162, 168, 177, 183, 184, 185, 194, 238, 242, 265, 417, 419, 421, 476
Producers xv, xix, xx, 4, 29, 33, 34, 52, 53, 64, 65, 76, 77, 78, 79, 80, 91, 93, 117, 118, 123, 124, 131, 132, 133, 138, 139, 141, 181, 197, 207, 211, 212, 220, 231, 235, 236, 237, 242, 246, 285, 325, 376, 397, 419, 421, 424, 435, 453
    delagated authority to 201
    lack of Irish speakers among 212
    Letter to, seeking support for commercials 124
    meeting with the Director-General 194, 196
    Meeting with the Director-General 196
    personality of 71, 150, 177, 365, 486
    powers under the 7 Days Agreement 167
    relationship with production crew 94
    relationship with the Editorial Group 135
    representation of 238
    representatives group 201
    sent to religious programmes for their sins 267
    suspension of 158
    working conditions 185, 191, 420, 422, 425
Production Assistants xv, 29, 50, 65, 72, 81, 135, 136, 156, 158, 162, 167, 183, 186, 238
Production Facilities 93, 136, 173, 413, 422
    Ambiguity in reporting lines for 136
    Assistant Controller 63
    Department of 94
    Head of 86, 135, 198, 421, 422

Radio 412
Television 412
Production Facilities, Group 63
Programmes Division xii, 29, 33, 43, 46, 63, 65, 93, 114, 117, 123, 130, 137, 142, 143, 153, 154, 156, 157, 161, 164, 168, 181, 182, 183, 188, 189, 195, 196, 197, 199, 200, 201, 204, 210, 219, 236, 241, 381, 412, 413, 422, 423, 424, 425, 487

# Q

Question Time 163
Quinlan, Senator Patrick 22
Quinn, Bob 262
   and filming in Russia 336
   letter of 284, 473
   rejection of RTE's middle-class culture 398
   walkout 229
Quinn, Evelyn 177

# R

Radio Luxembourg 9, 15, 307
Raymond Williams x
   on the mass media 217, 339, 345
Reaction Index, Audience 247
Real Charlotte, The 102
Referendum (on PR)
   programme on 180
   restriction of coverage of 505
Religious Adviser 267, 424
R.E.L.O 61
Report of the Television Production Committee 190
Report on Full Employment (NIEC) 406
Richards, I.A. 313
Richards, Shelah 332, 471
Right of Reply 227
Riordans, The xx, 61, 66, 73, 77, 98, 103, 191, 227, 343
Rising, The, 1916 78
Roberts, Charlie 4
Rooney, Celestine 157, 164
Roseingrave, Tomás 103, 105, 106, 107, 468
Roth, Edward 4, 24
Rothschild, Baron 307
RTE Club 164
RTE Guide 412
Rubenstein, Helena 122

Rugheimer, Gunnar  xix, 40, 41, 42, 43, 44, 45, 46, 47, 51, 52, 56, 60, 71, 78, 79, 95, 96, 97, 98, 99, 100, 101, 102, 112, 113, 115, 117, 118, 119, 130, 132, 133, 141, 142, 199, 240, 419
Russia  293, 335
   research trip to  336
   television of  337
Ryan, Senator Eoin  438

## S

School Around the Corner  92
Scott, Michael  23, 133
Sheridan, Monica  49
Sheridan, Niall  26
Showband Show  61
Skeffington, Senator Owen Sheehy  21
Skinner, Bill  195
Slevin, Michael  73, 153, 162, 195, 196, 242, 471
Spain, Eric  xiv, 65, 77, 219, 245
Specials  192, 193
Spectrum  92
Sunday Independent, The  24, 161
Sunday Times, The  11, 226
Sweetman, Father Michael  149, 507
Sweetman, Gerard  247
Sweetman, Rosita  xiv
Swift, Dean  231, 238

## T

TAM Ratings  76, 393, 394, 395, 397, 434, 456
Taylor, Fredrick Winslow  379
Teen Talk  61, 92
Telefís Feirme  67, 75, 98
Telefís Scoile  56, 98, 221, 227, 277
Television Commission  10, 14, 16, 18, 434
Television, Radio and Film Guild  129
The Island  271
The Politicians  100, 103, 137, 160, 161
The Professors  61
Thornley, David  103
Trade Union Group, RTE  78
Trevaskis, Brian; abuse of Bishop, Cathedral of Galway on Late Late Show  83
Trinity College Dublin  22
Turf Development Act, 1948  445

## U

United Nations 126, 377
Universal Education Act (1870) 310
University College Cork 238
USSR 293, 308, 335

## V

Vatican Council II 368
Vietnam xx, 125, 126, 139, 147, 250, 333, 444, 470, 472

## W

Wall, Mervyn 14
Walsh, Odran 14, 130, 157, 164, 165
Walsh, Ronnie 32
Wanderly Wagon 190
Waters, George 46, 86, 135, 136, 219, 326, 422, 423
Waugh, Evelyn 10
Wednesday Special 213, 214
Whiddy Island 192
Whips' Agreement 100
Whitehead, A.N. 367
White, Jack 43, 44, 46, 52, 60, 99, 112, 115, 119, 122, 133, 141, 142, 144, 145, 146, 147, 148, 151, 152, 156, 163, 168, 172, 187, 191, 193, 194, 197, 210, 216, 220, 233, 422, 425
Why Don't They Shoot People? 270
Wilkinson, P.P. 18
Wireless Dealers Association 8
Wireless Telegraphy Act 6, 402
Woolf, Virginia 88
Word in Action 267
Workers' Union of Ireland 80, 191, 215, 235, 238, 243

## Y

Yeats, W.B. 55, 238, 338

## LAST WORD

Far and few, far and few,
Are the lands where the Jumblies live;
Their heads are green, and their hands are blue,
And they went to sea in a sieve.

Printed in Great Britain
by Amazon